All good
wishes for
Xmas 1924

F J W.

D1283245

157.

A.18 B58

DON ROBERTO

"DON ROBERTO" BY JACOB EPSTEIN

DON ROBERTO

BEING THE ACCOUNT OF
THE LIFE AND WORKS

OF

R. B. CUNNINGHAME GRAHAM
1852—1936

BY

A. F. TSCHIFFELY

WILLIAM HEINEMANN LTD
LONDON :: TORONTO

FIRST PUBLISHED 1937

PRINTED IN GREAT BRITAIN
AT THE WINDMILL PRESS, KINGSWOOD, SURREY

To the Memory of
DON ROBERTO

Our trails have met,
   May they meet again

"Figure and character go with us to the grave."
— SPANISH SAYING.

CONTENTS

CONTENTS

x

CONTENTS

xi

ILLUSTRATIONS

ILLUSTRATIONS

LINE ILLUSTRATIONS IN THE TEXT

INTRODUCTORY NOTE

AFTER a number of years, during which the tide of life carried me to some strange places in far-away lands, I found myself back in England, early in the year 1932. Somewhere among my belongings in a trunk was a manuscript I had written, and as American publishers had rejected it, I intended to try my luck in London. However, like their cousins—and brothers in the modern craft—two English publishers also refused, with thanks, to accept what I had written, their opinion being that my material lacked style, and was, in every respect, unfit for publication; or, in other words, that my story would never be a "money-maker."

Disillusioned, and with a sadly depleted purse, I was making preparations to return to South America, when a telegram arrived, containing an invitation to lunch in a Spanish restaurant in London. Reading the name of the sender, who signed himself: "R. B. Cunninghame Graham," I could hardly believe my eyes, for although, in the past, I had read several books which, presumably, were written by the sender of the telegram—about whom I had heard many strange tales—I had always felt that he was a kind of myth; a man who had never existed in the flesh.

Next day, when I entered the restaurant, a gentleman—who was sitting at a table with a lady—rose and came towards me, stretching out a powerful hand. As I looked at the romantic figure with its flowing mane of white hair, thin aquiline nose, pointed moustaches and beard, it suggested one of Velázquez's cavaliers come to life; but I knew that this could be no one else but my host.

What the conversation was about during the delightful

meal which followed formal introductions, would make too long a story to relate now. Before we parted, according to my host's request, I no longer called him: "Mister Cunninghame Graham," but just: "Don Roberto." From that day on, I frequently met my new friend, for we had a great deal in common, and within a short time, thanks to his recommendation, my badly fingered and soiled manuscript was turned into a book. In reviewing it, critics were so kind to me that I immediately found many readers, and as a result of this, and due to the insistence of my friend, I settled down to writing in London.

Time passed, and my friendship with Don Roberto grew. Once, when I asked him why he did not write his autobiography, he told me that I would find the answer in the preface to his next book that was about to come out. Not long after, when he sent me an autographed copy of his *Writ in Sand*, I read:

"It is a natural desire in the majority of men to keep a secret garden in their souls, a something that they do not care to talk about, still less to set down, for the other members of the herd to trample on. This is most manifest in those who write their own biographies, confessions, memoirs, or by whatsoever title publishers palm on them, just as a card-sharper palms a card upon a mug. Possibly, St. Augustine and Jean-Jacques Rousseau imagined that they had unpacked their budget so completely that nothing remained to tell when they had set down their misdeeds, that, after all, in their cases, were never very black, to feed their vanity. . . . Most likely, in writing about other people's characters, I have done nothing but reveal my own, without my knowledge. If so, a *fico* for the revelation. . . ."

Having made a mental note of this answer to my question, I began to think over some of the autobiographies I have read; and, the more I reflected, the more I was struck by the truth of what my friend had written.

One day, as I was sitting in the book-lined study in Don Roberto's house which overlooks the River Clyde, just below Dumbarton, he told me that for years his friends had asked him to write his biography, but that, because he felt that his life could not possibly be of interest to anyone, he preferred not to do it. "After all," he added, "practically everything I have written is really autobiographical."

For some time I tried to convince my friend that he owed the world the story of his life, written by himself, but although I argued, and tried every means of persuasion, all my efforts were of no avail; not even my plea for those who, due to circumstances over which they have no control, are obliged to stay at home, and to whom such a book would give pleasure.

Two or three nights later, when we again sat together in his study, talking about books, politicians, prize-fighters and many other subjects, but chiefly about horses and trails we had ridden over, there was—as is often the case on such occasions—a momentary pause in our conversation. I was watching sparks whirl up the chimney, and listened to the crackling of the burning logs and the rain beating against the windows when, suddenly, my host startled me by saying: "I have been thinking over what you said about my biography." For a few moments I looked at the speaker in silence, wondering what he was about to say. Presently he continued: "There is only one man I'd like to write the story of my life."

After another short pause, I asked: "Yes?——Who's that?"

"You," was the answer; and before I had recovered from the shock, my friend rose from his seat and stretched out his hand, and with an inimitable smile added: "Will you do it for me?"

Mechanically my hand stole towards his, and thus the contract was signed and sealed. This happened over three years ago—three long years, I sometimes feel, and then again as if it had been but yesterday. When I started on what I realised would be a long and difficult task, I felt as a weakling might on being asked to climb an unconquered mountain peak, clad only in a bathing suit.

In one of the books written by Don Roberto, I came across a passage in which he says that his horses, being unshod, left no traces in the sands. However, remembering that once he had told me that most of his short stories were really auto-biographical, I read and re-read everything he had written during forty years, and in this way, with his assistance, I managed to re-construct his life. Two years passed, and though my manuscript was getting bulky, it was still full of holes I made great efforts to fill in, but the more I searched and wrote, the more I realised that I could not cope with the task I had undertaken. Then my friend left for South America where he suddenly died.

His unexpected death was a bitter blow to me, and for some time I was quite unable to think clearly and, therefore, had to put my work aside. Finally, when I sadly returned to it, and read through what I had written, I came to the conclusion that it was worthless, and that the best thing to do was to start the whole "Life" afresh. Whilst I was destroying the big pile of paper, I suddenly remembered that, shortly before Don Roberto departed on his last journey he had advised me to weave some of his own writings into my manuscript, and I recalled him telling me that in doing so I would get my backgrounds right. Accordingly, I started my long story afresh, and when the skeleton of his life was more or less complete, masses of old documents and letters came into my hands, and thanks to this great stroke of luck I found the missing links I had been looking for, especially in letters he had written to his mother ever since he was a boy.

It has been said that in setting down biographies of friends, the writers are faced with the conflict between truth and affection. If this is true in some cases, I firmly and emphatically state that everything I have written (or, rather, pieced together), is not merely based on fact, but that it has happened exactly as related, and this without an attempt on my part to dramatise any incident or to embellish it with floral language. Unlike some—rather more daring than convincing—modern biographers, I have not placed the subject of this book on the Freudian dissecting table. This I leave to readers who may choose to do so, or to future writers of "Don Roberto As I See Him," "Don Roberto, The Man And His Private Life," or any similar title self-styled "psychologists" hang on to their wares.

The best psychological analysis of Don Roberto was written by himself. More than once he admitted having contradicted himself, in writing and speech; but then it must be remembered that only men who lack the fatiguing gift of being able to think for themselves, can truthfully say that they have never contradicted themselves, or changed their opinions. Unfortunately these happy mortals constitute the vast majority in this world of ours, a world in which imagination and independent thought are sins equal to witchcraft, rare gifts which expose one to the chance of the stake, for, like eccentricity or unconventionality, they place one outside the corral in which the unthinking masses happily ruminate.

In writing as I have done, I have not attempted to produce what is called a "biography." In a sense, Don Roberto wrote his own "Life"; and to reconstruct it, I had to find the scattered material and then with patience to join together the—in many cases, minute—pieces, not unlike in the making of a mosaic. If I have succeeded, this knowledge will be an ample reward for the three years I have worked to produce this volume.

Finally, I wish to express my deep gratitude to all those who have assisted me with information and advice, and I must apologise for being unable to state the origin of certain passages I have reproduced, for a few age-stained newspaper cuttings I have found among old documents, give no clue as to where they were printed. Here and there I have woven into my story long passages written by Don Roberto himself, but, in order to make easy reading, I have not made use of quotation marks, which is entirely in accordance with my late friend's wishes.

No doubt, in addition to bad English and faulty grammar, I have erred from the narrow and perilous literary path at other—to me invisible—twists and bends. Unfortunately, however, inability has made it impossible for me to conceal such errors under a dazzling cloak of adjectives and adverbs which are often most helpful in hiding literary sins.

With this, taking the blanket off my horse, and trotting him before you *en nature*, I humbly doff my hat and await your judgment, trusting, oh generous critic and reader, that if imperfections and blemishes are discovered, they will be forgiven.

A. F. TSCHIFFELY.

CHAPTER I

A HUNTING ACCIDENT IN IRELAND—THE BIRTH OF
DON ROBERTO—GLIMPSES OF FAMILY HISTORY

DURING the rebellion, in 1845, some of the officers of the Scots Greys, stationed in Ireland at the time, were invited to a hunt near Ballinasloe.

The hounds were in full cry, and the field riding hell for leather, clearing ditches and fences, when, in an open space, a riderless grey was seen, galloping madly. After the runaway had been caught, a rider came staggering towards him, breeches and clothes soiled, with blood flowing from a nasty wound in his head.

Having explained that, in falling, the horse had accidentally kicked him, the horseman was about to remount when he collapsed. Fortunately a carriage was near, and soon the victim of this hunting accident was driven towards the house of a friend.

That night, when the merry sportsmen gathered, Major William Bontine, a young officer in the Scots Greys, was among the party, joking about his fall and making light of the wound he had sustained, little dreaming that a tiny splinter of his fractured skull would influence the whole life of his yet unborn son and heir, whose career was to be as exciting as that of the most glamorous hero of any cloak-and-sword romance in fiction; a son who was to be built by Nature for his part in life, as no producer of stage or film drama ever cast a character.

Five years after this accident, early in 1851, when aged

I

twenty-eight, Major Bontine—who was wealthy and owned three big estates in Scotland—married Anne Elizabeth Fleeming, the third daughter of Admiral the Hon. Charles Elphinstone Fleeming. The bride, who was twenty-three years old, was a girl of rare beauty, of the Spanish type, with dark, soft eyes and olive complexion.

Off and on, during the first year of their married life, the Major suffered from severe headaches which, according to the doctors, were caused by the old fracture in his skull which had healed imperfectly.

On the 24th of May, 1852, a son was born to the Bontines: Robert.* The proud father wrote the following note to his mother:

"May 24th.

"MY DEAR MUM,—

"Thank God it is well over. A young gentleman appeared at one o'clock this morning (Monday). Poor Missy is doing very well, but has had a dreadfully severe trial. I had to give her cloroform (chloroform), for nearly an hour. The Doctor says that she is very well and quite out of danger, but for some time the case appeared very serious. She has suffered a great deal, poor child. Give my love to Katon.

"Yours affectionately,

"WM. BONTINE."

In the following short family history I shall try to show that this baby boy was a strange synthesis of two races which very rarely mix. This infant, Robert, with the blood of *hidalgos* and of Scottish kings flowing in his veins, was to become a miraculous mixture of the two, and, perhaps owing to this, was destined to live in the romanticism of a Byron and in the idealism of a Don Quixote.

* The birth was registered in the District of St. Luke, Chelsea, on the 22nd of June, 1852, and the place of birth is given as 5, Cadogan Place, London.

2

MAJOR WILLIAM BONTINE (SCOTS GREYS)

THE HON. ANNE ELIZABETH FLEEMING

Major Bontine, whose name appears under various spellings all through Scottish history from the 13th century, dropped his real name, Cunninghame Graham,* owing to a curious custom of this family under the provisions of an old entail, according to which the eldest son had to bear the surname and arms of Bontine during the lifetime of his father, after whose death he used the name of Cunninghame Graham only.

CUNNINGHAME GRAHAM OF ARDOCH AND INCHTALLA

This entail dates back to the year 1770, when Robert Graham of Gartmore inherited the "Ardoch" estate in Dumbartonshire, from his cousin, William Bontine. The mother of this Robert Graham of Gartmore was a daughter of the twelfth Earl of Glencairn. When the last Earl of Glencairn died in 1796, the proprietor (or laird) of Gartmore succeeded to part of the Glencairn estates and assumed the name of Cunninghame, in addition to Graham.

*Names ending in "ham" or "hame" are few in Scotland. The first part of Cunningham (or Cunninghame) is Gaelic, and stands for "king", and the second part was probably added after the Saxon invasion in the eighth and ninth centuries. The syllable "ham" (or "hame"), stands for "homestead", "abode", or "seat." Thus the name Cunninghame means "King's abode, homestead or seat." The differences in ending ("ham" or "hame"), were made to distinguish descent from one particular family or another. The meaning of the name *Graham* explains itself.

3

Thus it came about that, owing to this peculiar clause in the settlement of succession of the Ardoch estate, Robert Bontine Cunninghame Graham, the subject of this biography, had to call himself *Bontine* until his father, the officer in the Scots Greys, died, in the year 1883.

For the sake of clarity I shall hereafter refer to Robert Bontine Cunninghame Graham as "Roberto," and later as "Don Roberto," as he liked to be called by his intimate friends.

There are many strange stories in the history of the British peerage, but probably the strangest among them is associated with the house of Montrose. The task of sorting out all the ramifications of the Graham family in the peerage of Scotland is so complicated that I prefer not to attempt it, for the chances are that were I foolhardy enough to do so, I would get hopelessly lost among these intricate ancestral trails, and in the end would lead the trusting reader into a jungle, out of which I would not be able to find a way.

Antiquarians, such as Andrew Lang, always called Don Roberto "The Uncrowned King," for according to them, as the rightful Earl of Menteith (in view of the illegitimacy of the Stuart line), he could claim the crown of Scotland by descent from Robert II. As we shall see, Don Roberto himself took only a very passive interest in titles, but it used to be the boast—and a very rightful one, according to certain eminent authorities on such matters—of his ancestors, that their blood was bluer than the King's. Their name is closely interwoven with the most stirring scenes in the history of Scotland; both in glory and in shame it figures in the topmost place.

The whole earldom of Menteith was continually involved in broils with Highland neighbours. Norman barons visited the district periodically, as when Sir Edward Hastings was ordered into Scotland by Edward I in 1298. He went to assist in the conquest of Scotland, and promptly married the heiress of Menteith, Lady Isabella de Comyn. The ninth Earl of Menteith, who seems to have been a man of great courage and good sense, was taken prisoner at Durham in 1346, and executed by Edward III. "Sir John The Grahame of the Bright Sword" fell at Falkirk, slain in defence of Sir William Wallace, the national hero of Scotland. A tombstone in the churchyard of Falkirk, which has been several times renewed since it was first placed there, bears the inscription that "Sir John Grahame, equally remarkable for wisdom and courage, and the faithful friend of Wallace, being slain in battle by the English, lies buried in this place." Sir John of the Bright Sword was Wallace's intimate companion and counsellor, and his death was the sorest blow inflicted on Scotland before the betrayal which surrendered Wallace to the English conqueror.

The misfortunes which from the beginning of their history had always pursued the holders of the title of Menteith, so thickened in the reign of Charles I that they eventually overwhelmed the earls entirely; or, as Don Roberto wrote about them: "Many a bill for a suit of armour from Milan, or an overdue account from Toledo for swords, must have disturbed the slumbers of the Earls of Menteith from the days of David of Stratherne downwards. Still they were a cheerful as well as an unfortunate race, not apparently humorists, but of a sanguine temperament. . . ."

Dazzling as is the lustre which surrounds the name of Sir John of the Bright Sword, it is not greater than the shame which covers that of another Grahame, who in 1437 made himself famous (or infamous), throughout Europe by the murder of King James I. And yet it is doubtful whether, according to the ethics of the time, Sir Robert Grahame was not as heroic a patriot as his ancestor in the thirteenth century who fought and died under the banner of Wallace. The story of Grahame's rebellion became famous owing to the heroism of Catherine Douglas, whose exploit in thrusting her arm through the bolts in place of the bar which should have arrested the advance of the assassins, has been immortalised in Rossetti's *King's Tragedy*.

Sir Robert Grahame had been imprisoned on some pretext which offended his sense of justice and promoted the revengeful design which he subsequently carried out with complete success. "Assassin" is an ugly word, and it should hardly be applied to the straightforward conduct of Sir Robert, who, before he began operations, withdrew to the Highlands, formally renounced all allegiance to the King, and declared his intention of putting the sovereign to death with his own hand. It was at Perth, in February 1437, that Sir Robert Grahame surprised the Royal Court, hunted the King into a sewer, and slew him in his foul retreat. "Thou never hadst mercy upon those of thine own blood," exclaimed Grahame as he thrust his sword through the King's body, "therefore thou shalt have no mercy here, and as for a confessor, thou shalt have none but this sword."

On this terrible tragedy the tables were soon turned, for Sir Robert Grahame was captured, flung into prison, and tortured to death with all the malignant ingenuity of torturers who might have given the Spanish inquisitors a lesson in the art of prolonging human existence in order to protract agony. But Sir Robert was as unflinching when being torn to death by the pincers of the torturer as he had shown himself ruthless in meting out vengeance to his enemy. He kept a high heart and a dauntless tongue to the very last, wholly refusing to admit that he had done any wrong. He had renounced his allegiance to the King, he had declared war, he had carried out his campaign, and he insisted with pride that his memory would be honoured as that of one who had rid the world of a cruel tyrant.

Sir Walter Scott remarks that his confidence was misplaced

and that his memory, instead of being revered, was execrated
in a popular rhyme which ran:

> "Robert Grahame
> That slew our king,
> God give him shame!"

As a curious instance of the way in which the branches of
genealogical trees are often intertwined, it may be interesting
to mention that the Catherine Douglas of the heroic attempt
to bar the door with her slender arm, was an ancestress on
the maternal side of the Grahame family, and that Don
Roberto was directly descended from the heroine of the
King's Tragedy.

The Earls of Menteith were comparatively uninteresting
persons up to the birth of William, the seventh earl—that is
to say, those of the name of Graham. This earl, in claiming
to be the rightful heir to the Earldom of Stratherne, thereby
put his blood in degree equal to that of Charles I. (The unlucky
boast about the blueness of his blood induced the ruin of the
family.) The King stripped him of all his dignities and
confined him to a castle in the North, and, depriving him of
his titles of Menteith and Stratherne,* forced on him a
pantomimic title of Earl of Airth.

In the time of William, the seventh Earl of Menteith, the
house of Menteith fell into complete decadence. His grandson
William, the eighth Earl, endured great poverty. In 1661 he
succeeded to the title. In London he tried in vain to recover
the money owing to his family by the Crown. In 1663 he
married his sister Elizabeth to Sir William Graham of
Gartmore. She died, and Sir William married again, but his
second wife left him.

---

* In 1870, Major Bontine claimed the Earldom of Menteith. The Committee of Privileges of the House of Lords heard the evidence, but as they
came to no decision the dignities are still dormant.

7

Before his own death, in 1694, he wished to leave the earldom to the Marquis of Montrose, but the King objected. Therefore, when he died, after a life of poverty and misfortunes, his personal estate went to his nephew, Sir John Graham of Gartmore. Thus expired the earldom of Menteith, one of the most illustrious titles in Scotland.

A lower depth of misery had to be touched by one who called himself Earl of Menteith. In 1744, when the peers of Scotland sat at an election, and according to custom the name of Menteith was called, a thin, cadaverous-looking youth informed the assembly that he was the Earl of Menteith by right of birth and of descent, and was at present studying medicine in Edinburgh. From that moment until his death, although warned by the House of Lords to desist, he never dropped his claim. For a year or two he regularly attended all elections of a Scottish peer, but at last he seemed to have become disgusted, and used to retire from Edinburgh before the day of the election. Gradually he sank into obscurity, and little by little into mendicancy, and at last sustained himself by begging from house to house, under the title of "Beggar Earl." In 1747, he published a pamphlet entitled: "The Fatal Consequences of Discord, or a Political Address to the Noble and Rich Families of Great Britain." Finally, neighbours near Bonhill, in Dumbartonshire, came upon the body of the Beggar Earl by the roadside.

"So, like a cadger's pony," wrote Don Roberto, "passed away one who without doubt had in his veins the blood of a king of Scotland, and whose ancestors had been the proudest in the land."

The next Grahame who appears prominently in the annals of Scotland is Sir William Graham, who held Gartmore for the Commonwealth, and who seems to have been—during the Protectorate—a tried and trusty officer of Oliver Cromwell's. The Protectorate passed; the rabble rout of unclean satyrs to whom England was given over under the Restoration came and went; and again we find the Grahams of Gartmore playing a conspicuous part in the history of their native land.

As previously stated, one of Don Roberto's ancestors succeeded to the lands of the Cunninghames, Earls of Glencairn, another distinguished family. Thus the whole property extended to well over 10,000 acres, and was situated partly in Perthshire, Stirlingshire, Dumbartonshire and Renfrewshire, in the most beautiful region of Scotland, part of which has been immortalised by Scott in *The Lady of the Lake*. The Earl of Glencairn was the friend and supporter of Knox and of Robert Burns the poet, who, in a letter to Mr. Peter Hill, a bookseller in Edinburgh, makes a reference to one of the Grahams. "Does Mr. Graham of Gartmore ever enter your shop now?" the poet wrote. "He is the noblest instance of great talents, great fortune, and great worth that ever I saw in conjunction. . . ." (Chambers's *Burns*, Vol. III, page 117.)

Gartmore stood as the frontier fortress of the Scottish Lowlands. Within cannon-shot of its battlements rose the stern and rugged mountains in which the lawless clans preserved an almost complete independence. The frontier of Graham's country marched with the frontier of Rob Roy's Highlands, and Rob himself was once a prisoner in the dungeon of Graham's castle, for the Grahams had no sympathy with the thieving of picturesque caterans who raided the Lowlands at their own will and pleasure. When they caught them, they hanged them, for the Grahams of Gartmore had the right of pit and gallows. To this day three stones in the avenue still mark the old tree upon the branches of which Don Roberto's ancestors used to hang the bandits of the hills.

Fox, Burns and Sir Walter Scott often stayed as honoured guests at Gartmore, and it was there that Scott wrote the greater part of *Rob Roy*.

The deeds of the "Gallant Grahams" who have played distinguished parts in the history of their country, are recorded in two large volumes called *The Red Book of Menteith*.

As stated before, Roberto's mother, the Hon. Anne Elizabeth Fleeming, married Major William Bontine in the year 1851, being then twenty-three years of age. She was the third daughter of Admiral the Hon. Charles Elphinstone Fleeming, and a sister of the fourteenth Lord Elphinstone. Her mother was a Spanish lady, Doña Catalina Paulina Alessandro de Jiménez,* who, as we shall see, met the Admiral in Spain, and later gave birth to Roberto's mother off the coast of Venezuela, on the 10th of February, 1828, the year in which the Duke of Wellington formed his first administration, when Charles X still occupied the throne of France, and during which Scott published his *Tales of a Grandfather*.

The earliest recollections of Roberto's mother, as a child, were the sounds of demonstrations in favour of the Reform Bill. In her youth she visited Italy with her mother and sisters, and she retained a recollection of Pope Gregory XVI, of whose Church her mother was a member, though her brother and sisters were brought up as Protestants. She was on intimate terms with her cousin, Baroness Keith, who married the Comte de Flahaut, Aide-de-Camp to Napoleon Bonaparte and subsequently French Ambassador in London. She saw much of Louis Napoleon, and was one of the last survivors to remember the personages who played the principal parts in the strange world drama of the *coup d'état* in 1848.

Don Roberto's maternal grandfather, Admiral Elphinstone Fleeming, was born in a ten-gun brig in 1773, and therefore

---

* The Alessandro family came from Italy and had settled down in Cadiz. According to Spanish custom, Doña Catalina, on marrying a Jiménez, placed her maiden name before her husband's surname, with the word "de" (of) between the two.

remembered the days when swords were in general wear. He became a midshipman when he was between eleven and twelve years of age, a post-captain at four-and-twenty, and later a general in the Spanish army. Although he was a friend of the Venezuelan liberators, Bolívar and Páez, he was a welcome guest of Ferdinand VII. He danced at the famous ball the night before the Battle of Waterloo, which he watched as a spectator, and saw the siege of Maracaibo, the last Spanish hold on the American continent.

According to records I have found, the Admiral must have been a man of genius, besides being what is often called a "lively spark." Very good-looking and attractive, he lived like a veritable human tornado. This probably accounts for the fact that, by the age of forty, his curly hair had turned perfectly white, a change which, in his case, was most becoming, accentuating his refined and distinguished features.

During his adventurous youth, whilst stationed in Spain, he eloped with a young nun, carrying her to his ship, which set out to sea as soon as the two were on board. If he thought that "Once aboard the Lugger and the Nun is mine," would hold good in his case, he had not reckoned with Fate, for during the second night of his "honeymoon" cruise, his ship was attacked by a Salee rover, and on hearing the thunder of the guns, the nun died of fright. When her body was taken back to Spain to be interred, priests and people spoke about "Divine judgment," and made such a scandal that the Admiral had the corpse taken back to his ship, to be buried at sea.

A keen rider, Elphinstone Fleeming always hunted when he was ashore. During intervals of duty at Gibraltar, he brought out ten couple of hounds from his estate in Dumbartonshire, and founded the Gibraltar Hunt—known as the Calpe Hunt. Being a man of extravagant ideas, and possessing the necessary means to carry them out, he once startled the conventional and sedate Londoners by bringing over from Spain mules and muleteers, with which he drove through Hyde Park.

Back in Spain, he happened to be riding past the Cathedral in Cadiz as a lady and her beautiful daughter were coming out after mass. Before the Admiral could avoid it, his fiery Andalusian horse splashed mud over the two ladies' gowns and mantillas. Dismounting to apologise, he was so struck by the young girl's beauty that he immediately fell in love with her; and thus it came about that after a short courtship, Admiral Elphinstone Fleeming, who was forty years old at the time, married Señorita Catalina Paulina Jiménez, barely fourteen years old, the daughter of an old family of Spanish *hidalgos*. The wedding took place in the Consulate and Cathedral in Cadiz. On the way down the Cathedral steps, as it was raining, she lost a satin slipper, so the Admiral lifted her into the carriage in his arms, to the delight of the sailors of the fleet.

Shortly after the wedding, the newly-married couple arrived in London, on the day before the Derby. Finding not a horse for love or money, the Admiral hired an undertaker's team and drove to the race-course in state, to the delight of all the road, and the admiration of his youthful wife, who, coming straight from Spain, was delighted with the team of long-tailed blacks, and thought their stately steps and waving manes fit for the carriage of a prince.

In 1828, ordered to Carácas upon a semi-political mission, his flagship, the "Barham," anchored outside La Guaira, then an open roadstead, in a troubled sea.

The day they made port, the Admiral's wife gave birth to a daughter, who one day was to become Roberto's mother. As soon as Doña Catalina could sit a mule, they went to Carácas and took an ancient Spanish house near the Cathedral. The Admiral came and went at intervals for three years, now

ADMIRAL THE HON. CHARLES ELPHINSTONE FLEEMING

sailing north as far as Halifax, now visiting the Bahamas and Port Royal, but spending a good deal of his time in Venezuela with his wife and child.

Once he took into port a two-decker which would neither sail nor stay, so without consulting the Admiralty, he simply took her in and had her cut down to a frigate. On being called upon by the Admiralty to pay for his experiment, he retorted by writing for his pay, which, since he had entered as a midshipman, he had never drawn—and so the matter was settled.

In the West Indies, in those days, diplomacy seems to have been as much part of an admiral's duty as manœuvring a fleet; and as telegraphs had not been invented and communications were difficult, an admiral on board his flagship was a little potentate, for the Admiralty would worry him but little, and at rare intervals. At that time, Páez and Bolívar, the greatest Venezuelan heroes of the epic struggle for independence against Spain, having expelled the Spaniards, had come to loggerheads, and in some mysterious way Admiral Elphinstone Fleeming became adviser and general mediator between the two.

When, finally, the Admiral was recalled to England, he sailed with a veritable menagerie aboard his ship. As passengers he had "Tony" and "Caballero," two pacing ponies presented to him by Bolívar and Páez. (The ponies frequently cantered up and down Rotten Row, and finally died at Cumbernauld, in Scotland.*) There were also a tapir, parrots and peccaries, some boa-constrictors, and a small marvel of the animal creation, in Venezuela known as *chirhuiri*, which used to eat up ladies' petticoats as they sat at meals, making them subjects for the sport of fools as they rose with their raiment shorn to the knees.

* Among his treasures, Don Roberto showed me two bracelets made of some hairs of these two ponies' tails.

When the Admiral returned from Jamaica, the Scotch people feared that his wife might be *black*, or at least *coloured*, for they had heard she was a Catholic; and that, in their eyes, was the same as a heathen.

Although in years an old man, the Admiral remained active until he suddenly died when, with a feverish cold, he put out to sea from the Isle of Wight.

This brief survey of the more salient features of family history will show that it was no mere chance that led Roberto into the strange paths he trod during his long, amazing and stormy life.

CHAPTER II

A YEAR after Roberto's birth, a brother arrived on the scene, and seven years later, in 1860, his third and last brother was born.

Charles Elphinstone Fleeming Cunninghame Graham, Major Bontine's second son, shared Roberto's boyhood at Gartmore, Finlaystone and subsequently at Harrow. From Harrow Charles entered the "Britannia," and during his time in the Navy saw service in the Mediterranean, on the North American station, and on Queen Victoria's yacht, the "Osborne." He retired from the Navy as a Lieutenant, subsequently receiving the rank of Commander, and devoted the next twenty-five years of his life to the Royal National Lifeboat Institution, of which he became deputy-chief Inspector. He twice received the Royal Humane Society Medal for saving life. On the first occasion, while serving in the Royal Yacht, he dived overboard at night in Portsmouth Harbour, and saved the life of a waterman who was drowning. On the second occasion, while an inspector of lifeboats, he took a line out to a wreck. On retiring from the Lifeboat service, he became a groom-in-waiting to King Edward VII, and afterwards to King George V. He died in 1917, aged sixty-four, leaving a wife and two descendants.

The youngest son, Malise Archibald Cunninghame Graham, lived only twenty-five years. A brilliant scholar and a gifted musician, he was educated at Winchester (College), and subsequently at Oriel College, Oxford. Ordained by Bishop

Harold Gore-Browne, he became a curate at St. John's, Winchester, where he endeared himself to the parishioners of what was one of the working-class parishes of the town. Before his ordination he acted as organist to St. John's Church, and later, when a curate there, he was also director of the choir. Owing to overwork his health gave way, for he had never been strong, and the strain reacted upon his weakly frame. On doctor's orders he then spent some time on the Continent, where it was discovered that he was suffering from tuberculosis. Finding that his strength was rapidly failing, he returned to his mother's residence in London, where, on the 26th of November 1885, he died. According to records I have found, he had done a great deal of good during his short but brilliant life, and by his will he bequeathed a considerable sum of money to his Church.

Most of Roberto's early youth was spent in Scotland, on his father's estates of Gartmore, Finlaystone and Ardoch, but frequently, for long spells, he stayed with his Spanish grandmother, who, after the death of her husband, the Admiral, lived in the Isle of Wight.

Major Bontine's old injury, sustained when he fell in the hunting field and was kicked on the head by his horse, gave him trouble at ever-shortening intervals, the complaint manifesting itself in spasms of recklessness, accompanied by severe headaches and fits of violent temper.

Roberto's parents, together with his grandmother, Doña Catalina, decided that the eldest son of the family should learn the language of Cervantes and be brought up in the Spanish way; and thus it came about that Roberto gradually spent more and more of his time in the Isle of Wight with his grandmother, who—judging by many conversations which I had with him late in his life when we became friends—must have been the first to kindle the fire of adventure already smouldering in his youthful breast.

ROBERTITO, AGED 6, WITH HIS MOTHER

Doña Catalina was a highly intelligent, brilliant and altogether remarkable woman, who had not only travelled a great deal, but who took a keen interest in everything in life, and who continued to improve her active mind by diligent reading. It was she who told Roberto about Spain, South America, and many other strange lands he longed to see.

Seventy years later, when, during visits, I sat with Don Roberto in his house at Ardoch, his estate overlooking the River Clyde, he would retell some of these stories. At night, especially when it rained and gusts of wind blew through the stately trees outside, the two of us often sat near the fire in his study, chatting until the candles were nearly burnt out.

During his frequent stays in the Isle of Wight, Roberto's grandmother told him the story of the great earthquake in Carácas, when his mother, Anne Elizabeth, was not quite three years old. His grandmother, Doña Catalina, had a little negro slave girl, one year older than Anne. When the earthquake took place Anne and "Pug," the little slave girl, whom she had bought in Jamaica, were missing. After the wild panic, caused by the terrible disaster, was over, the Admiral and his wife searched for Roberto's mother and "Pug," whom they finally found, fast asleep, in the Cathedral, where they must have followed the many people who had rushed there during the panic.

As soon as "Pug" could speak, she kept saying to little Anne: "Buy my brother Robert!" This the Admiral's wife proceeded to do, and would have bought the whole family, if her husband had not stepped in.

Often, Doña Catalina told little Roberto about famous episodes in Spanish and South American history, but, naturally, what most delighted him were stories of her own and his grandfather's personal experiences. He heard how, during a banquet in Bogotá, in typical South American fashion,

17

his grandfather was hailed as: "El Nuevo Nelson," an extravagant title which greatly amused him.

A local poet was ready with a flattering song, part of which went as follows:

"Viva, viva, viva Bolivar!
Viva el nuevo Nelson,
Recibiendo de Páez esta demostración. . . ."

After the banquet, which—probably to give orators and poets time to indulge in their verbal acrobatics—had started at ten a.m., there came a bull-fight, and the flag-lieutenant, fired either by emulation or with wine, after trying in the native way, to throw a bull down by the tail, fell from his horse and remained prostrate in the middle of the ring. The bull advanced, smelt him, and turned him over with his horn. As the man lay motionless, the beast passed him by quite unconcernedly, going to the far side of the ring. The people, in their simple faith, espied a Lutheran, and shouted: "Heretic! Even the animals perceive his heresy!"

Another story Roberto never forgot was one about his grandfather, when he had gone to Malaga to visit the Governor of the town. It being Eastertide, the Governor took him to the port to free a criminal, for according to an old custom, on every Easter Day, one of the convicts who rowed in the galleys of the King was picked out by a stranger to be set free.

Turning to the Admiral, the Governor invited him to choose a man, and he, pointing at a prisoner in the long row, said: "This man I choose."

Some months later, journeying towards Madrid, the Admiral, his wife and servants, all duly armed with blunderbusses, were one day upon the road which was made unsafe by bandits. Whilst the party toiled up a rocky path, a troop of seven mounted men appeared. Terror assailed the travellers, for no doubt these seven men were the famous bandits known as "Los Siete Niños" (The Seven Children).

The chief advanced, and greeting the Admiral with his hat in his hand, said: "Admiral, these roads are dangerous. I and my followers have come to be your escort through the hills."

Don Roberto's grandfather thanked him, saying that no escort was required, but the bandits took no notice. The day wore on, and still the chief rode chatting by their side, talking of many things. When evening began to fall, and the red mud walls of a little town appeared in the distance, the chief suddenly called to his men, who wheeled their horses round and cantered back in the direction from which they had come. Riding up close to the Admiral, the chief said: "I am the man you took out of the galleys upon that Easter Day. I knew you at first sight, though you, no doubt, had long forgotten me. The road across the sierras is beset by petty thieves, mere peddling scoundrels who, had they met you, might have been troublesome. Whilst I was with you, and my men, you were safer than had the King's own guards escorted you. We are 'Los Siete Niños,' and so . . . with God." He turned his horse and galloped down the road after his fellows. The Admiral saw him no more, but Roberto's grandmother used to relate the story to the last day of her life.

In spite of all the thrilling tales she told him in the Isle of Wight, Roberto was happiest when, together with his brother Charles, he was at home in Scotland on his father's big estates where they had ponies to ride, for ever since Roberto could walk, horses were a passion with him. All the members of his family were keen riders, with the exception of his mother, who, though very fond of horses, was terrified when she had to ride one, being afraid of all but a dark chestnut, "Zarina," which, however, she rode as seldom as possible. Charles was a good horseman, but Malise, who was rather

19

delicate, was but an indifferent performer in the saddle, preferring, like his mother, music and books.

When they were in Scotland, the boys spent a great deal of their time at "Finlaystone," one of their father's estates, in Renfrewshire. The old house, perched on a rock above the Clyde, was surrounded by stately trees, and a brook with many waterfalls ran through the estate. From the house one looks down on to the river where the steamers pass, following along the fairway marked by buoys. On the opposite bank, on a rock, is Dumbarton Castle, and near the front door of Finlaystone House stands a huge yew-tree under which John Knox preached.

Roberto's special pet on this estate was a black Shetland pony which, though it was exceedingly bad-tempered, he took a delight in riding. However, since his earliest youth, "Gartmore" was his favourite home.

The vast white house, after the Georgian style of architecture, said to have been first built in 1680, and later rebuilt by William Adam, was situated, surrounded by a beautiful park, in the middle of the ten-thousand-acre estate. The sea, it is said, once covered this whole district, as far north as the rocks at the foot of Stirling Castle.

In the West, Ben Lomond, seldom without a cap, dominates the land, in winter resembling a vast white sugar-loaf; in summer a cone of yellow, amethyst or opaline lights.

In the distance, to North and West, the district of Menteith is shut in by mountains and rolling hills.

To the North-east, within cannon-shot of Gartmore, lies the Lake of Menteith,* covering an area of a little over a square mile, with its three islands which are famous in Scottish history.

Inchmahome, the largest, has been the burial-place of

* The Lake of Menteith is the only "lake" in Scotland; the others being known as "lochs."

20

ROBERTITO (AGED 8)

the Grahams of Menteith for centuries. In the roofless choir
of the thirteenth-century Augustinian priory are the graves of
many of the illustrious dead, buried beneath sculptured
stones, in some cases surmounted by recumbent figures.
Outside the ruined church, memories of the past cling to the
island. Crumbling walls reveal the confines of that domestic
part where, for some weeks after the battle of Pinkie (1547),
Mary Queen of Scots spent what probably was the most
peaceful episode of her stormy life. Even to-day, the flower-
beds can be distinguished where, legend has it, Mary walked
during that quiet time.

This oval space, known as "Queen Mary's Bower," is
about eighteen feet by twelve, and is still surrounded by a
double row of boxwood.

The ruins of the priory are screened by a number of
beautiful old trees, chiefly Spanish chestnuts, and sequoias,
and the whole island is shaded by birches, willows, hawthorn,
alder and holly. Among the grass and in the cracks of the
crumbling walls grow many wild flowers and mosses, but, as
far as flowers are concerned, the island looks its best in spring,
when masses of daffodils wave in the breezes like so many
yellow fairy bells.

The ruins of the principal castle of the old Earls of Menteith
—now dwindled to a pile of stones from which spring alders,
birches and sycamores—are still to be seen on a smaller
island, Inchtalla, situated within a stone's throw of Inchmahome, on which were the gardens and parks. On the third
and smallest island, Inchcuan (Dog Isle), were the kennels
in which were kept some of the Earl's dogs.

Gartmore was probably the most beautiful estate in
Scotland. In the spacious halls, rooms and corridors hung
pictures, painted by famous masters; and the old furniture,
tapestries, armour and many objects of art were in their
right setting in the old Georgian house with its Adam ceilings

and staircase walls panelled with oak from ships of the Spanish Armada. Outside was a wide expanse of gravel and a long avenue of beeches, underneath which stood the old gallows-stone.

The woods surrounding Gartmore estate would have been a veritable paradise for lovers of Nature, for besides the many varieties of trees, bushes and plants which grew in profusion, the wanderer would have seen stags, roe-deer, capercailzies, squirrels, etc.

No wonder Roberto and his brother liked to be at Gartmore, where they could ride afar, swim in the lake, and generally enjoy themselves to their heart's content.

At intervals, after having reached the age of eight, Roberto accompanied his grandmother when she went to Spain, where the two stayed with relations in Cadiz and Gibraltar. By this time he spoke Spanish and English equally well, and during his stays in Scotland he had acquired, to a certain extent, the speech of the region, but Gaelic he never learnt. His grandmother's family in Cadiz possessed fine horses, on which, after his lessons with a tutor were over, he often went for long rides in the salt marshes. Young Roberto had a look of the panther about him. Like his brother Charles, he used to terrify his mother by his reckless feats of agility. Frequently when she sat in her chair in front of the house, he would leap neatly over her head.

Once, together with his brother, he dragged a boat from the Lake of Menteith to the River Forth. Taking a few provisions, the two boys rowed down-river to explore the world. When they were missing, a wide search was organised, and finally the two youthful adventurers were caught by a policeman near Stirling. Naturally, when the boat was found to have disappeared, everybody thought the boys had met with an accident on the lake.

When Roberto was eleven years old he was sent to "Budbrook Park," a preparatory school in Warwickshire, run

GARTMORE, EXTERIOR AND INTERIOR

by a Doctor Bickmore. Of all the subjects he was taught, he liked classics best, but, on the whole, school-life did not agree with him. Three years later, having reached the age of fourteen, he was sent to Harrow where, for two years, together with his brother Charles, he was in the Headmaster's House (Dr. Butler).

There, however, he soon developed a dislike for classics, owing to the system of teaching; and although he excelled in the playing-field, he was, to quote his own words to me, "totally unfit for that institution, the English public school."

After two years, in 1866, he left Harrow and was sent to a private school in Brussels, where he learnt French very rapidly, probably thanks to his knowledge of Spanish. It was at this school that he had his first lessons in fencing, an art in which he later excelled and which, in after-years, was to help him out of a tight corner.

Whilst at school in Brussels, he wrote a letter, parts of which I reproduce, including spelling mistakes.

> "116, Rue Sans Souci,
> Bruxelles.
> Nov. 16th, 1868.

"MY DEAR MOTHER,—

. . . I am working very hard at Spanish. I go three times a week to the Spanish master now and I am learning to write letters in Spanish but I cannot do a thing to my name one of those long flourishes which the man insists on. I have a fencing master twice a week. There is to be a grand Te Deum to-day because it is the King's birthday and I suppose there will be an awfull scuash of people in the cathedral. . . .

> "I remain
> "your affectionate son
> "R. C. GRAHAM."

23

I had a splendid walk the other day to a place called Villers le Ville where there is an old ruined ebbley.

Having spent a year in the school in Brussels, Roberto's parents decided that he would learn more with private tutors. Accordingly, from 1867 to 1869, until he was seventeen years of age, he spent his time studying at home or in Spain, where his grandmother's family always received him with open arms.

In the meantime, his father's condition had not improved, and although doctors were consulted, the only thing they could do was to send in big bills, for Major Bontine was known to be a wealthy man, and, to say the least, a liberal spender. Anybody who went to him, with even the wildest and most fantastic business proposition, was sure to get a sympathetic hearing, and if the Major was promised a two- or three-hundred-per-cent turnover for his investments, he immediately parted with whatever sum such cunning charlatans suggested.

Roberto's mother suffered a great deal, for her husband's temper had become almost unbearable; but, being a woman of great character, she bore her cross patiently.

Major Bontine wanted Roberto to join a Horse Guards' regiment, but this idea did not appeal to him, for he was much too individualistic to put up with military routine, drill, stereotyped discipline and all the humdrum that goes with a soldier's life. Realising that, at times, his father's mental condition made him irresponsible for his actions—especially when he almost literally threw money out of the window—he took things to heart, for he realised that this could not go on indefinitely without causing the ruin of the family.

Roberto was tall for his age, strong and wiry, but sensitive and inclined to be impulsive. When his mother noticed that he occasionally became morose, she decided that something must be done. He had often expressed a wish to visit South America, a continent which had called to him ever since his grandmother told him stories about it.

As chance would have it, a friend of the family—whose name is of no consequence in this "Life," but to whom I shall refer as Mack—happened to arrive in Scotland on a short holiday. He and his elder brother had settled in the Argentine, where they managed a ranch. During the course of conversation, he said that he was trying to find a man who might be willing to go into partnership in the Mack concern in the Argentine. The opportunities of making a fortune, according to him, were marvellous; and he described everything in such glowing terms that Mrs. Bontine was struck with an idea.

When she and her husband were alone she suggested that Roberto be given the necessary capital to go into partnership with the Macks. On hearing this, the Major must have had visions of Roberto making a vast fortune, for he immediately went to speak to his son, who was reading in the library.

As Roberto listened to his father's words, he could hardly believe his ears, for what he heard sounded too good to be true: Argentine! TERRA ARGENTUM! the "Land of Silver," picturesque people, Pampas, horses, cattle, adventure, Life!

The next few weeks at Gartmore were both happy and sad—happy because Major Bontine and Roberto were enthusiastic, though not exactly for the same reasons, and sad because there was so soon to be a parting. When the news that Roberto was leaving for the wilds of South America spread among the family and friends, they began to talk, saying that it was odd to allow a mere boy to go among semi-savages, for, after all, the best circles were open to him. True, he was a strange young man, for it was rumoured that he refused to recognise class distinction, a shocking attitude he had once expressed when he said that there were only two classes, namely, the genuine and the humbugs.

CHAPTER III

ON a wet, cold and dreary day, late in November 1869, Roberto, accompanied by his parents and partner, arrived in Liverpool, where the little group boarded a four-thousand-ton ship called the *Patagonia*.

The parting, about which the subject of this biography had never spoken to me, must therefore be left to the imagination. Thoughtful Mrs. Bontine had packed a number of books in Roberto's trunk, knowing that her son would appreciate their company on so long and dreary a sea voyage; and before the vessel sailed she promised to send him a regular supply of literature.

The voyage was uneventful until—partly under sail and partly under steam—the little Spanish port, Corunna, was reached. There, like a small, pathetic army of refugees, between three and four hundred poor Galicians boarded the ship, carrying babies, pet birds in cages, bundles, blankets and mattresses. People rushed about as if the Day of Judgment were at hand, hustling, bustling, chattering, shouting and swearing until everyone was on board. Old women hugged their sons, and men stood stifling down their tears, their patched and parti-coloured clothes looking in keeping with the scene. Girls raised an almost Arab wail, and in the midst of the confusion stood a priest. The emigrants struggled round

27

him, some of the women kissing his clothes, the men grasping his hands in theirs—hard, horny and deformed by toil—and asking to be blessed. Women, with coloured flannel petticoats clattered up the gangway, and boys raised the shrill cry they use in Portugal and in Galicia when excited, which sounds like a horse neighing, and from the crowd of hot, perspiring men and women there came a smell as of wild animals, mixed with the bundles of salt fish, which almost all of them bore in their hands. Some dragged great parcels wrapped in striped blankets tied with innumerable knots, and others carried on their shoulders the little ark-shaped trunks, covered with cowskin with the hair on.

At last, when all the bundles and the trunks, the water-bottles, and the poor household treasures, which the emigrants, driven from their idyllic Old-World life by overwhelming taxation, were taking with them, to wring and salve their hearts in the New World, were put on board, hard, knotted hands reached out and grasped for the last time, friends and relatives embraced, weeping upon each other's breasts. When the gangway was pulled away from the ship, the emigrants, all stretching out their arms towards the priest who stood on the jetty with a bulky umbrella in his hand, cried: "The blessing, father; bless us once more before we go!"

Finally the ship glided out into the steady swell of the Atlantic Ocean; hands, handkerchiefs and blankets were waved as the poor emigrants saw the shores of their homeland float away from them, and finally, when the ship appeared to be alone in a universe of water and sky, men, women and children squatted down amongst their bundles, some to break into a high-pitched song, others to weep silently. How they all fitted into the crude, small vessel was a mystery, and it can easily be imagined what sufferings they had to bear as, packed together like sardines in the aft part of the ship, they were rocked and bumped until, after what must have seemed an eternity spent in a floating inferno, they reached the Promised Land: a land bare of traditions and of everything that hitherto had made their lives, a land in which they would eat their fill and lose their individuality, a land from whence they would regard their homeland with a mixed feeling of contempt and pity, after the fashion of self-educated men.

The next port of call was Lisbon from where Roberto wrote to his mother:

> "MY DEAR MAMANA,
>
> "I like Lisbon awfully and was very much amused with the boatmen, especially one who told me his name was Gibraltar Jack (Speak Inglis, Captain, goddaam, . . . yes). . . ."

On the way to the River Plate a number of the unfortunate emigrants died, and were buried at sea. Such was the fate of some of these courageous or desperate wretches. For all the others knew, or perhaps even cared, that of a number of the others was to be much less merciful, for the land which called them was wild in those days, and the savage Indians fought desperately to check the advance of the white invaders who, day by day, penetrated further into their vast domain.

After a wretched passage the coast of South America was sighted, and towards evening, some twenty days after leaving Corunna, the vessel sailed into the beautiful Bay of Rio with the red-roofed town in the shape of a horse-shoe and jagged peaks in the background.

Roberto and Mack, desirous of stretching their legs, and of having a change of food, paid some negroes to row them ashore, for in those days ships anchored out in the bay. He now found himself in an entirely new world, in a Rio which, during his lifetime, was to change into a big, modern city with even a hideous skyscraper to disfigure the glorious landscape.

D

In the late 'sixties, however, no bright politician had as yet thought of imitating North American or European cities, and Rio consisted chiefly of quaint colonial houses, sandy streets, and palm-lined avenues in which loafed negroes and mulattos, people with pure white skins being fairly rare.

As the two companions walked along, they were frequently accosted by dusky women who waited for seafaring men to hire them. At night many of these women, and mere girls, beckoned to the passers-by, sitting at the open windows of their houses, the interiors of which were lit by candles, the flickering light and the silhouettes of female forms seeming both attractive and picturesque.

Until late that night, the two young men wandered about; and the next day the ship once more proceeded on her southward journey.

After several uneventful days the ship anchored about a mile out of Monte Video, where a number of passengers were taken ashore in small, flat-bottomed sailing boats, and then the vessel slowly proceeded upon the wide muddy Rio de la Plata towards Buenos Aires, the Mecca of the Promised Land. Owing to its colour and enormous width, the Spaniards had formerly called this river the "Yellow Sea," an error which can be understood when one considers the fact that a man standing on its shores sees a horizon of water.

From Monte Video Roberto wrote to his mother:

"Hotel Oriental, Montevideo,
1870.

"There is a revolution here, and one in Entre Ríos, so we are rather uncertain as to our movements. The last time I wrote to you I was entering the harbour at Rio de Janeiro. I don't think I ever saw so magnificent a view. . . . I am afraid Entre Ríos will be in a very bad condition after Urquiza's death. They say he was about the only man who could rule the gauchos. The rebels have been driving off the cattle from the estancias, and behaving generally in a brutal way. . . ."

Finally, when in the far distance towards the south-west, Buenos Aires* was visible, its low-roofed houses looking like those of a miniature toy town at the end of a yellow carpet with a light blue background, the *Patagonia* dropped her anchor. Emigrants who had never been visible during the long voyage came up on the crowded decks to join the others who were busy packing their bundles, or looking towards the land which had called them across the sea. All that could be seen from the ship was the town, situated on a low "barranca" or long hill, and beyond it and along the shore, a dead-flat expanse of green which, in the far distance, appeared to melt into one with the blue sky.

Presently, a small fleet of whale boats came sailing towards the *Patagonia*, and when, after a great deal of shouting and fussing, the passengers and their belongings had been transferred into them, they ploughed through the water towards the shore. When the depth was not sufficient for the whale boats to proceed further, people clambered on to flat, two-wheeled carts which waited for them, and when all was ready, the drivers whipped up the horses which, snorting and splashing, pulled the crude vehicles towards *terra firma*. Even then, however, the complications of landing were not done with, for on getting off the flat-topped carts, the passengers found that a low, muddy marsh had to be traversed, and, unless they did not mind getting wet and muddy up to their knees, they were carried to the firm, dry land on the backs of negroes.

* In 1535, when the Spaniards, under Mendoza, arrived, the captain of the expedition exclaimed on landing: "Qué buenos aires!" (What good airs), and hence the name of the new-born colony, now the mighty city of Buenos Aires.

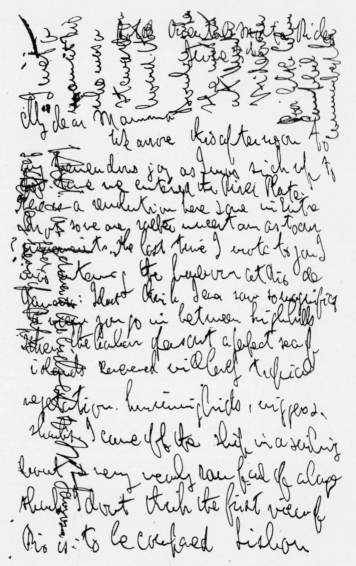

ROBERTO'S HANDWRITING WHEN AGED 17 (1870)

Here we have to leave the brave emigrants, who were soon to be absorbed in the vast, mysterious continent, either to be swallowed up by their fellows or else to become rich and unrecognisable at the end of years.

In a rickety cab, Roberto and Mack drove to a hostelry which was run by a Swiss named Claraz, a tall, black-bearded man of learning, who was a great naturalist.

"Claraz's" was the favourite meeting-place for ranchers or "camp" men, as they are called in the Argentine; for whenever such pioneers came into town they were sure to meet old friends in this hostelry, a "bachelors'" establishment where—to put it in popular terms—the sky was the limit.

Only a few streets in the town were paved with rough cobblestones, and wherever Roberto looked he saw horses, which were the only means of locomotion, so much so that even the few beggars who were to be seen, begged on horse-back, for in those days the greatest misery of a man in the Argentine was to be on foot. Indeed, murderers, thieves and other criminals were not sentenced to death, but, instead of being executed, they had to serve in the infantry for a certain number of years.

Already, during the sea voyage out, Roberto had noticed that his companion was a heavy drinker, but what he had seen on the ship was nothing compared with what he saw Mack do at Claraz's hostelry when he joined "camp" men who had come in from the "frontiers" to paint the town red. It was advisable not to sit reading late at night at Claraz's, for, as Roberto found out, one of the practical jokes of fellows coming back after an evening spent in merriment was to shoot the candles out—an annoying experience for the peaceful reader, to say the least, especially when he was aware that neither the legs nor the hands of the merry marksmen were any too steady at the time.

The south-western frontier of the Argentine was wild and dangerous, for the Pampa Indians were fierce, cruel and cunning, and their skill in horsemanship was amazing. The rare ranches in the great sea of grass were fortified with deep ditches. Some of them had a small brass cannon that was chiefly used to signal to the sparse neighbours, for its range was short, and the Indians took care not to advance too near, and separated when it was fired, so that it did but little execution on the open plain.

The life, wild, dangerous and lonely, threw off strange characters, for only men of resolution, who held life cheaply, or outcasts from society, cared to settle in a district where the government could give scant protection and a man was ruined in a night by Indians who drove off his cattle and left him destitute. Still, there were some who, neither desperate nor outcasts, resolutely took up land and settled down.

About half a century after the Spanish conquest, the gaucho came into being. Men who had committed some crime fled to the Indians for protection, and often inter-bred with Indian women, and thus the gaucho was evolved. They were quarrelsome, seldom excited, but, when aroused, ready to kill a man with great indifference. Many could jump on a bare-backed, unbroken horse, and ride him to a standstill by sheer strength.

Having spent a few days in the city, Roberto and Mack made ready to depart for Entre Ríos, a northern province which is situated, as its name ("Between Rivers") indicates, between the rivers Paraná and Uruguay. (See map, p. 85.)

Having weighed anchor outside Buenos Aires, the steamer which the two companions had boarded glided up the yellow waters of the River Plate, and later entered the River Paraná. At night the stars, though not so bright as in the northern hemisphere, seemed far more luminous, and gleamed more yellow and more phosphorescent than do their sisters of the

North. Water-hogs, startled from their sleep, plunged with a splash into the stream and swam for refuge to the reedy banks. Moths, large as humming-birds, hung round the binnacle, making the helmsman curse, while the pilot, sounding with a cane, guided the vessel up the stream. Mosquitoes seemed to be following the crude craft in clouds, tormenting the passengers who had no nets to protect them against the fierce attacks.

Hours, which seemed long as days, went past, and still the steamer, struggling with the current, pressed into the night. At times she ran her nose against the bank, or a sandbank, backed and was helped by all the crew pushing her off with poles; then shivering, swung into the stream, strove for a minute with the hurrying water, and once more glided through the light mist which descended shortly before dawn.

At last the stars waxed paler and the air more chilly, and men, sleeping upon the deck beneath the awning, their heads upon their saddles, with their long silver-handled knives close to their hands, stirred and drew close their ponchos in their sleep. Others sat up and lighted their black cigarettes, smoked silently and then lay down again, the white dew glistening on their blankets and their hair.

As the dawn brightened, the whistle sounded, echoing through the woods. The vessel edged into the bank, as if by instinct, and her side rubbed against a pier made of rough planks and almost level with the stream. Some sleepy soldiers, smoking cigarettes, came through the mist like spectres, and a man dressed in uniform stepped from the pier on to the deck, went down below and in a little while came up again, wiping his lips, and with an air of having done his duty to the State.

A diligence, which should have met the steamer, had not arrived, so the passengers, each with his handbag, or with his saddle, took their way through a rough path in the woods.

After half a mile, when they came out upon a plain, the diligence, drawn by six horses, came whirling towards them in a cloud of dust. Before the vehicle had stopped everybody scaled it as if it had been a fortress, and the horses were once more whipped into a fast gallop. A short league away Roberto beheld the little town of Gualeguaychú, flat-roofed and white, silent and shining in the sun.

Stuck on the plain like a chessboard on a table, and with the streets all intersecting one another into squares, the houses all flat-topped and painted white, with the towers called *miradores* (watch-towers), and the church resembling a mosque, the little town had a sort of oriental look. The sandy, unpaved streets, in which lean yellow dogs prowled after offal all the day and howled at night in chorus at the moon, smacked also of the East. There, however, the resemblance ended, and the line of posts, to almost every one of which a horse was tied, and the great stores, in front of which stood hobbled horses, was purely Argentine. There were horses everywhere; in every open space they fed, attached to ropes, in all yards they stood, or were led down to water by their owners, with a long picket rope curled like a lasso in the hand. Men dressed in loose black cashmere trousers, with high patent leather boots, the tops all worked in patterns with red or yellow thread, their ponchos fluttering in the wind, rode past on silver-mounted saddles.

Wild and barefooted boys, on bare-backed ponies, careered about the outskirts of the town in which all men went about armed, their knives and pistols sticking out below their coats. During the hot hours of the day all slept, leaving the streets deserted and the stores wide open. The sun declining put new life into the town, and in the various stores men sat and talked, criticising the horses and the women as they passed. Still later on, the evening brought the ladies of the place into the *plaza*, all dressed in Paris fashions of a year ago, to saunter up and down in groups beneath the orange trees, in which the fireflies flitted, making the heavy leaves seem all alive with light. As the ladies passed by, the men made compliments to them which they pretended not to hear, and yet were piqued if no one paid them, for, as the saying was: "even a compliment from a black man is better than indifference from a prince."

In the still air the tinkle of guitars sounded, and at the iron-grated windows on the streets men stood, flattening themselves against the bars, to talk to women.

Roberto had taken quarters in a dirty little hotel kept by a Basque. The rooms all looked down upon the patio in which the foreigners assembled, drinking and singing comic songs, or telling anecdotes. As in the hotel in Buenos Aires, it was well to shut the door and put the candle out, for the chief form of wit was shooting at the lights, and if any guest was foolish enough to sit and read, a shot was pretty sure to knock the plaster from the wall, close enough to his head to make things dangerous, especially since the marksman was generally drunk.

Within a square of the hotel was set the police station, and in a lane hard by, some huts in which half-caste Indian girls (called *Chinas:** Chinese), with several mulatas, and two or three Hungarian and German girls, become too faded for Buenos Aires, sat painted at their doors. Vice was so unattractive, set, as it was, in a mud hovel thatched with straw, that many whom the love of virtue bound but lightly, were yet virtuous from disgust. Morality was looked at in the Latin way, with the result that, on the whole, life was far cleaner than in Anglo-Saxon lands where, nature being what it is, the same things happen, but are rendered meaner by concealment.

---

* "China," a term applied to Gaucho girls of Indian blood. It is also used in other Latin-American countries; why, no one seems to know.

"Santa Ana," the "estancia" (ranch) which the brothers Mack were managing for a Dane, was situated at a distance of some leagues from the little town, Gualeguaychú.

When Roberto's companion had completed his business—invariably settled over glasses of *caña* (a native rum that was so fiery and raw that it went down the throat and into the stomach like a torchlight procession), their luggage was loaded on a wagon, and when everything was ready and a final drink had been taken, they mounted on none too tame native ponies and dashed out of the little town, raising a cloud of dust as they galloped beside the vehicle which looked as if it would fall to pieces when it bounced over uneven parts of the wide, sandy track.

Every now and again they met or passed gauchos who, in those days, wore the peculiar, trouser-like garment called *chiripá*. This ingenious and, for riding, practical garment, probably originated when gauchos roamed about far from where tailors, string, needles and cotton could be found, and it consisted merely of a long, square piece of cloth which was brought up between the legs from the small of the back, and then fastened with a long sash which was wound round the waist. In this manner a sort of very loose trouser was made, the cloth falling down in folds at the sides. Often, under the *chiripá*, were worn very wide white cotton drawers, usually ornamented with coarse lace at the bottom. This peculiar garment was very practical for riding, though not for walking; but then it must be remembered that these men rarely walked a hundred yards.

The better-class gaucho dressed in loose black merino trousers, tucked into high boots with the feet made of calf-skin and the legs of patent leather, embroidered with flowers or an eagle, worked in coloured thread. Their spurs were made of silver and had huge rowels, and were worn dangling off their heels, kept in place by silver chains clasped on the instep. Around the waist they wore red silk sashes, covered by a broad belt of leather, full of pockets and fastened by silver coins. Under the belt, the tassels and a foot or so of the sash, dangled down on the leg, and gave a note of colour on the baggy, black merino trousers.

On the way to the estancia, the travellers stopped at a "pulpería," that is, a prairie store and saloon combined in one. Usually they stood on a little rise, had white-washed walls, flat roofs, and doors that were studded with thick iron nails. Inside, hanging from pegs, were stirrups, girths, spurs, bits, bridles and horse-gear of all kinds. Upon the shelves were rolls of gaudy cotton goods and ponchos, and above the wooden bar were rows of bottles containing strong liquors. A palisade, running up almost to the roof, protected the proprietor when fights broke out, sometimes between two rival guitar-players, again, between gauchos over a stolen horse, or for any other grievance, usually magnified by alcohol.

Outside the store were tied the horses of the customers, looking about nervously when they heard the least noise, or, if they were tame, patiently waiting in the sun with half-closed eyes, heads hanging down and resting a hind-leg.

When a man entered the *pulperia* and called for a drink, he struck the counter with his whip, or with the flat of his long knife, which was carried in a silver sheath, stuck into the belt, across the small of the back. The etiquette was to invite the company, and, in all cases, to hand the glass to the man nearest to the drinker, who touched it with his lips, handing it back with a grave *"Gracias, caballero," "Gracias, amigo."*

An empty bullock-cart, straw-thatched and with a heavy pole sticking up like a mast, served as roosting place or shelter from the sun to the wild, stringy-looking chickens, or to a game-cock fastened by a string tied to one of his legs.

In the close vicinity of many stores were straw huts,

inhabited either by Indian-looking girls or women, who dealt in "love."

Here and there cattle-tracks led through woods of thorny trees, and on the rolling plains fed sheep, cattle and horses. Parrots and paroquets flew shrieking in the branches of the trees, and built their long and hanging nests from a dead bough. Humming birds fluttered round the flowers, hovering like butterflies as they sucked out the honey from their hearts. Deeper in the recesses of the thickets, water-hogs (*carpinchos*), had their lairs. A hum of insects filled the air, and tortoises, like walking stones, trailed themselves on the sandy soil. The river ran, a yellow flood, between the banks of trees. Herons and pink flamingos fished in shallow places, and on the gaunt, dead branches of the willows, vultures sat and nodded in the sun. An air of mystery and of danger brooded on the place, especially near fords to which tracks of unshod horses led, making the traveller wonder who the riders were who passed so frequently.

On the way to Mack's ranch, Roberto for the first time saw long-haired gauchos driving half-wild horses over a stretch of open plain. A cloud of dust hung over the swiftly-moving herd, and from its depths the thunder of their hooves made the plain tremble. The herdsmen, on their mustangs mad with excitement, galloped behind swinging *lazos*, or whips, and yelling like Indians.

At last the travellers sighted their goal, a low, long house with a corrugated-iron roof. Near it were several other adobe constructions which served as sheds and store-houses. A few tall weeping-willow trees afforded some shade, for "Santa Ana," the ranch, stood in the middle of an enormous stretch of open ground, on a little hill, or *loma*.

For some time past, Roberto had had apprehensions about his companion's habit of drinking, and after he had been introduced to his elder brother and the Dane—who owned the ranch—he witnessed a bout of drinking that filled him with disgust. Those were days of hard work, hard swearing and hard drinking in the New World.

The ranch was a rough and crude place, the furniture in the principal hut consisting of a table, a few *catres*, or "scissor" camp-beds, a few rickety chairs, an oil lamp or two, besides the occupants' trunks and personal belongings. The mud floor of the dining-room was littered with bits of paper, used matches and similar rubbish, and chickens, ducks and even pigs frequently invaded the habitation.

There was not much to choose between the quarters of the owner and those of the gauchos, with the exception, perhaps, that some of the latter had no beds, preferring to sleep on the hides in one of the sheds, or just on the sheep-skins of their saddles.

The arrival of Roberto, and the return of the younger Mack, was an occasion to be duly celebrated, everybody on the ranch and even some neighbours who lived many leagues away, being invited to join in the "fiesta." Towards evening the visitors began to arrive, most of them on horses, but a few women in wagons.

Whilst several sheep were being roasted over a fire in the open, the gauchos drank Brazilian rum, and when the meal was ready they feasted like cannibals, squatting round the fire. When night fell, women appeared mysteriously, and presently, to the tune of a guitar, they danced, or sang wailing songs in high falsetto voices which their ancestors had brought from Spain after inheriting them from Africa. The gauchos' dances were all slow, and danced almost without lifting their feet from the ground, and with much waving of handkerchiefs, except for a valse which they danced nearly all the time unmoved, and with a rapt expression on their faces, as if they were accomplishing an act of faith or a religious rite.

The women sat in a row, waiting for the men to invite

41

them to dance. When a man was tired of eating, he left the fire for a while, and after having danced solemnly, he usually treated his partner to a drink of gin, which they both drank out of the bottle's mouth. All this time some of the men sat near the fire drinking *maté**, or discussing horses' brands, or stood in groups, addressing compliments to the dancers upon their prowess and their charms. Beyond the dark curtain of night, the stillness of the plain was broken only by the bleating of the folded sheep, or the shrill neigh of stallions fighting for their mares.

The fun lasted throughout the night, and only when the first streaks of purple on the Eastern horizon announced the arrival of another day, did the visitors prepare to leave, for in those days unless it was unavoidable, no one travelled in the dark.

Roberto soon settled down to the new life, but he realised that the money he had invested in the purchase of new land and cattle would be lost, for his partners did but little work, spending most of their time drinking and making merry.

Finding the native dress more comfortable and practical for riding, he discarded his riding breeches, and wore the wide *bombachas* (trousers), or the *chiripá* of the gauchos.

Riding half-wild mustangs was one of his chief delights, and, being young, adventurous and daring, his ambition was to be able to sit broncos as the gauchos did.

South American ostriches, or *rheas*, abounded in the region. These graceful birds, called "Desert's Mirth" by the Quichua Indians, were often hunted on horseback.

First of all, the riders spread out in fan formation, and, cantering slowly forward, soon found in front of them a band of ostriches. Then, suddenly, the horsemen sprang into full speed, with shouts, and with their greyhounds bounding

* A kind of green South American tea, made from the leaves of the *Ilex Paraguayensis*, a kind of laurel.

42

ROBERTO, AGED 17, WEARING THE GAUCHO COSTUME DESCRIBED ON P. 38

in front of them, the outermost edges of the fan (which at the start had been a good half-mile apart), contracted, enclosing in a wedge the frightened birds. The bolas whistled through the air, the ranks were broken, and each man chased a particular group of ostriches, which fled, skimming across the high brown grass, their wings extended wide to catch the wind.

But the pursuers strained every nerve to cut them off, and now and then one fell, his legs entangled in the bolas. If by some accident he missed his mark, as he scoured past, he stooped and picked up the bolas from the ground, or, if he did not see them, threw down his scarf or poncho to mark the place; then quickly he unfastened a spare set of bolas from round his waist, or took them from beneath the sheepskin which he wore upon his saddle, and galloped onward shouting, his hat blown back and kept in place below his chin by a silk cord, forming an aureole about his head. On every side, groups of wild horsemen and of frightened birds, were disappearing on the low horizon of the plain. Towards evening the gauchos reappeared upon the waves of the prairie, their horses bathed in sweat, but all with several ostrich skins upon their saddles, from which the blood dripped slowly on to the horses' flanks. They gathered on a rise of the ground, jumped off their horses, unloosed their girths for a few minutes, and then, striking into a canter which looked like clockwork, returned homewards.

It is not necessary in the Pampas to ride well; a man must fall well, that is, on his feet. Standing once, watching the always interesting spectacle of a horse-breaker (*domador*), struggling with a violent buck-jumper, Roberto rashly remarked that the man rode well. "Yes, he sits well," was

The gauchos called wild horses *baguales*, having adopted the word from the Indian who called them *cahuales*, which is evidently a corruption from the Spanish word *caballo* (horse). No American Indian language or dialect had a word for horse, an animal which did not exist in the Americas until the Spaniards imported a great number.

the answer; "let us see how he falls." Fall he did, after one or two more plunges, and his horse on the top of him. After a struggle the bronco regained his feet; but the man never stirred again. His epitaph was: "What a pity he did not know how to fall !" "But, after all," remarked a bystander, "he must have died because he was very delicate," so incredible did it seem that a man could have been fool enough to let a horse fall on him.

Knowing very little about the country, Roberto envied the gauchos who occasionally passed near the ranch, driving horses and cattle towards Uruguay. The riders' mounts were adorned with glittering silver trappings, and in the men's wide belts, decorated with many coins, were stuck long knives in elaborately carved silver sheaths, while from their heels dangled enormous spurs made of the same metal.

When Roberto arrived in the Argentine, General López Jordán led an insurrection against the government of President Sarmiento. Occasionally rumours of revolutionary activities reached the ranch, and every now and again riders could be seen cantering past in groups, evidently on their way to a distant place where, in all probability, the revolutionary army assembled. Sometimes such travellers spent the night on the ranch, sleeping in a shed on their sheepskin saddles, but before dawn broke, they rode on again, silently and mysteriously.

Disappointed with the prospects for the future, and tired of the monotonous life on the ranch, the youthful Roberto longed to ride into the unknown. One day, when he was cantering afar, he met some cattle-drovers, and after a short conversation with them, decided to follow wherever they happened to be going. The horses and cattle they were driving were to be sold in Uruguay, and so Roberto became a cattle-drover.

All went well for two or three days, and he was just beginning to settle down to his new life and surroundings when a wild-looking cavalcade dashed out of a wood and forced him and his new companions to join the revolutionary army. Although some of the men pleaded to be allowed to go, their words were of no avail, and when they realised that argument or an attempt to escape would mean having their throats cut, they abandoned the cattle and followed their captors, laughing and joking. Roberto tried to explain that he was a foreigner, but when one of the gauchos prodded him in the ribs with a lance, he wisely said no more, and went along with his companions.

The revolutionary gauchos were wilder than the horses they rode, long-haired and with their naked feet stuffed into boots made from the skin stripped from the hind-legs of a horse. Their protruding toes gripped the tiny, ring-like stirrups like a vice, and from their heels dangled and jingled huge, rusty spurs, which clattered on the ground like fetters when they walked. Their arms were antiquated carbines, which, for convenience, they never cleaned, but bore them rusty, as befits a man not born to be the slave of anything. They loaded them up to the muzzle with anything that came to hand. Their sabres usually they turned to daggers, or if they did not, stuffed them below the girth; for their chief weapons of offence were *bolas*, which they slung to a hair's breadth, and rarely missed their aim. Most of their horses were half-wild, and more than half, unbitted; but that did not disturb their riders, who rode them with their long hide reins buttoned into a thong tied round their jaw, and with a halter always in their hands, in case they suddenly stepped into some burrowing animal's hole, or crossed their legs and fell. Thus they galloped over the sea of grass, throwing their hats upon the ground, and leaning down to pick them up again, at full speed, and as if each one of them had a dozen necks. They rolled their cigarettes and struck a light from flint and steel, at a full gallop and on horses which, if you touched them accidentally, were almost sure to buck. Their riders' hair and ponchos fluttered in the wind, and now and then they swung their whips, which hung from straps upon their wrists, in circles in the air. Occasionally they yelled "hee-hoo!" out of the joy of life, and, galloping, cursed their horses and their mothers if they stumbled, winding up their litany of oaths upon a certain woman of ill-fame who, after having borne a bastard to the Fiend, incontinently burst.

As the wild cavalcade swept past solitary huts, women in a panic dragged their children to safety, and when they had barred the crude doors they huddled together murmuring: "Ave Maria, Dios nos libre."

Towards morning, the *partido* or group of revolutionary soldiers and their new recruits arrived at headquarters where, after having been interviewed by the leader, they mixed with the other *revolucionarios* who had taken possession of a ranch.

The long-haired gauchos sat near fires made with bones, dry grass and thistle-stalks. In a kettle which, on long marches, was invariably carried under the horse, tied to the girth, water was heated, and *maté* drunk, the little gourd into which was stuck a silver or metal tube being solemnly handed round the circle. One man, kettle in hand, made it his duty to prepare this tea-like beverage, refilling the gourd when it was empty, and handing it to the next man in the circle. The men sat on their saddles, or on horses' or bullocks' skulls, and thus, assembled by the fires, waiting for the next drink of *maté*, and smoking quietly beneath the southern stars, they chatted about horses, revolutions and people they had known.

Roberto soon became fascinated by these strange-looking sons of the wilds, and as he sat, listening to their many tales, he was glad to be among these men, and he did not care what the morrow might bring.

Talking about horses, the gauchos agreed that an animal with a white hind foot is sure to be fast; that a light chestnut with a white tail and mane is to be distrusted; that a dun—

unless he has a black tail and mane and red eyes—can never be good, and that a horse of any colour with a white ring round its fetlock is very unlucky. Greys, they said, will not stand the sun; roans are slow, but tough; and piebalds usually first-rate mounts for any kind of task.

Having debated horses from all angles, the conversation changed, and all ears listened to a long-haired and bearded gaucho who told the story about the assassination of an Argentine dictator, General Urquiza, who was pompously called "El Supremo" or "Napoleon del Sur" (South), Spanish America having been extremely fertile in so-called "Napoleons." (It was said that he had owned 180,000 horses. A good horse cost a Spanish ounce, or, roughly £3 15s.)

Urquiza had ruled his men with a rod of iron, tempered with personal suavity, treating them half as children, half as savages, and they responded after the fashion of their kind, taking all leniency for weakness, and thinking power was given to a man by some wise Providence beyond their ken.

The gaucho told his listeners how Urquiza used to drive slowly through the country, accompanied by his rustic cavalry of gauchos, and how the inhabitants used to gaze towards the coach and murmur: "There goes El Supremo." Then he gave details about his death; how, one evening, when he was sitting in his plate-glass ballroom, drinking *maté* with his daughter, he heard the sound of spurs upon the courtyard tiles; how a number of gauchos, headed by a tall, one-eyed negro, broke into his room, and how the leader, drawing his long knife, shouted: "Death to all tyrants!"

Little did Roberto dream that, in years to come, he would be given almost the same cattle-brand as that formerly used by Urquiza. (Urquiza's brand consisted of this figure, with which thousands and thousands of his animals were marked: ႔ Later Roberto used a very similar brand: ⵟ)

Among the revolutionary gauchos who were seated round

the fires were two who immediately attracted Roberto's attention. One was a tall, strong and fair-haired young man, about twenty years of age. Talking to him, he found that, the son of a German father, he was born in the country, and that, although his name was Francisco Vogel, he could speak only Spanish. The witty gauchos, on learning that Vogel was the German word for "bird," had nicknamed their young companion "Pancho Pájaro" (Pancho being the short name for Francisco, and *pájaro* the Spanish for "bird.")

The other man with whom Roberto immediately made friends was a picturesque gaucho named Angel Cabrera, who entertained the company by playing a guitar with which he accompanied his songs, of which he appeared to have an inexhaustible repertoire. Cabrera was a *payador*,—that is, a rhymester who accompanied himself on a guitar. Never in all his life had he done what is called "honest" work. No cow, no horse, no sheep, still less a *china* girl, ever escaped him. Well-built, long-haired, he could ride a wild horse as if the two were one being, embodying strength, wickedness and rebellion. About his kind he used to say: "The townsman sings and is a poet, but when the gaucho sings he is a *payador*." Considering himself to be a bit of a philosopher, he constantly interrupted his songs with sayings and adages, although, as a rule, they had nothing to do with the subject of his song or conversation, as the case might be. "Waste not your graces on a deaf man." "Amongst soldiers and with prostitutes all compliments are held excused." "Who shall say it is the post that is at fault if the blind man did not observe it in his path?" "A good horse is better than the prayers of saints." "My teeth are nearer to me than my kindred." These were a few of the countless sayings he solemnly quoted to the assembly before they wrapped themselves up in their ponchos and blankets for the night.

In the morning Roberto was given a lance—a weapon he

had never handled—and then he was asked to mount a half-wild horse to show what he could do. For a few moments he hesitated, but when he saw the sly grins on many faces, he leapt on the horse, which pitched him off before he knew what was happening. Three times he mounted, and three times he was sent flying, for to make things more difficult, he was told to mount with the lance in his hand. At the fourth attempt, however, he stuck on, and rode the bucking horse to a standstill; and thus ended his initiation as a fully-fledged gaucho in the revolutionary army.

Day by day new "recruits" were brought in, and whilst *partidos* set out to round up more men, the others amused themselves, eating, sleeping and gambling.

As all the horses were kept under guard in an open piece of plain, escape was practically impossible and very dangerous, for if a man was missing, a search of the surrounding country was immediately organised, and as some of the gauchos were expert and uncanny track-readers, a man on foot had next to no chance of being able to go far before he was caught and one of his captors "played the violin," as they called cutting a throat.

Racing and cockfighting were the national sports, the former for short distance, two or three furlongs, with innumerable false starts, all of set purpose and with the object of tiring out the weaker horse before the race began.

During idle moments—of which there were many—the revolutionary soldiers arranged races, and the gambling was heavy, money, silver horse-gear, guns, rifles and silver-handled knives changing hands. Barefooted, and with silk handkerchiefs tied round their heads, the riders made pretence to urge on their horses, leaning forward on their necks and shouting wildly, but all the time holding them well in hand. All gaucho races were run barebacked, but this made no difference to the riders, who were more at their ease on a horse than they were afoot. All the starts were flying, and by mutual consent, if a man saw his horse was but an inch behind the other's, or if he noticed that his adversary's mount (for all the races were confined to two), was getting out of hand, he stopped and, getting off, walked slowly back again to the starting point. This naturally upset the temper of a violent horse, who, at the next attempt, would rear and plunge and break out sweating, and perhaps run half the course before he could be stopped. When at last they got away, each gaucho shouted: "*Vamos!*" and then they plied their whips, the horses close to one another, for if a man could bore the other rider off the course, he won the race.

But at this game all gauchos were adepts, as well as at trying to kick the opposing horse's chest, to put their feet below the other rider's heel and hurl him to the ground, all of which was reckoned fair, and part of racing.

For cockfights out in the open a primitive sort of arena was prepared by making a kind of small, circular fence of sticks over which were hung ponchos. No matter of what origin, all men were equal in the arena of the cocks. The love of blood and money levelled most of the spectators to a mere mass of animals, with bloodshot eyes, mouths open and lips drawn back upon their teeth, sweating with interest and following every wound the birds inflicted with their sharp steel spurs, all pity laid aside, and for the time savage as tigers, ready to quarrel with their brother if the red cock struck out the other's eye and he had criticised the stroke.

The remnant, those who cared not for the blood, and in whom the skill and fortitude of the trained cocks neither excited nor evoked compassion, called the odds with regularity, marking each turn in every combat; and when at last the victor dashed his spur down through the brains, and then himself fell dead beside his foe, just crowing out his victory as he fell, stretched out their hands to take the dirty, greasy dollar-bills that their bird had gained them with his life, with a low chuckle of content. Those who had no money to gamble with staked their silver spurs, knives, horse-trappings, or any other article they possessed; and some were so carried away by the gambling spirit that they played for their ponchos and blankets.

Roberto soon became a perfect gaucho, and when the crude and almost grotesque little army began to make raids, spreading terror wherever it appeared, his abundant crop of red hair had grown considerably. Cabrera and Pancho Pájaro were always near him, for by this time the three had become good friends. Wherever he went, Cabrera carried his guitar, strapped to his back in order to leave his hands free to guide the horse and to hold his long lance. Pancho had an antiquated rifle and usually no ammunition, and therefore, on the rare occasions when they came to grips with a *partido* of the enemy, he had to use his long knife which he handled with the dexterity of the true gaucho.

When passing a river, if he could avoid it, no man rode into the water first, especially if he wore silver spurs or reins, for it might chance that he received a knife-thrust in the back from a too admiring friend, or perhaps merely because the sudden lust to kill, so frequent amongst dwellers of the plains, rose in the heart of the man who followed immediately behind.

The great brown plains of Entre Ríos wore an unfamiliar air. Herds of tame mares had run half-wild. They snorted and made off, a thousand yards away, their manes and tails streaming out in the wind. The cattle had become as fierce as buffaloes, and anyone who lost his horse had to make long detours, for to approach them was as dangerous as to come near a tiger or a lion. Sheep were close-herded by armed men who, if they were forced to ascend a hill, dismounted, and creeping on all fours surveyed the country cautiously. Having made sure that all was quiet on the plain beyond, they remained as short a time as possible standing against the sky.

The sight, on the horizon, of a band of men made the few dwellers in the scattered, mud-built huts flee to the woods, driving their horses, carrying their wives and children at full speed, leaving their scanty household goods to the protection of their dogs.

People were helpless when a revolutionary army scoured the plains, living off the cattle, taking as many horses as they chose, and forcing all the men into their ranks. There was no appeal when a detachment, headed by some bloodthirsty old sergeant who had passed a life in revolution, or some young officer without experience, arrived before the lonely hut on the plains. Whenever a *partido* unexpectedly arrived at a ranch, the men often at once killed a cow or two, drove up the horses and chose the best of them, and said to the unlucky owner of the horse: "Saddle up, friend, and help to save the country from the savage *Reds*, or the *Whites*," as the case might be. No tears or prayers of either wife or children were of the least avail. If there was any disinclination on the part of the miserable man, knives would be drawn, swords tapped significantly, and he would be adjured not to lose time, and force the patriots to cut his throat. Throat-cutting appeared humorous to the gauchos of those days, whose daily lives, and the necessity of slaughtering animals almost every day (for they lived only upon meat), rendered them bloodthirsty, reckless of their own lives, and careless of the lives of others. Naturally, the man did not wish to endure so much for the sacred cause of liberty, and saddled up, grasped the lance they put into his hand, and sallied out to follow where fate should call him.

An army raised in such a fashion was but a terror to its own countrymen, living upon the country, wandering about, and taking care to avoid serious engagements or put their lives in peril. The sort of life they led suited them admirably; always on horseback, they roamed about, living on the inhabitants. The "armies" seldom met each other in the field. Upon the rare occasions when they were obliged to fight, they either galloped about wildly, after the style that Bedouins have affected since the beginning of their history, firing such carbines as they had, without effect or aim, or else charging with the sabre and the lance. Then the fighting became serious, for neither side gave quarter, despatching such prisoners as they took either by lance-thrusts, or with the knife that every gaucho soldier carried in his belt. The victim, thrown upon his face was seized by the hair, generally by some old sergeant who took a genuine pride in the performance of his job. The knife was plunged into the throat, just below the right ear, and drawn rapidly across the throat. Then the head was wrenched back, and the executioner pressed his foot on the victim's back, to make the blood flow out more rapidly. A few convulsive movements and a horrid gurgling sound, and then the body lay limp upon the ground, like a mere bag of empty rags, with the face distorted horribly. A pool of blood, that rapidly turned to a rusty red, was left upon the ground to mark the tragedy, until the rain washed it away, or the fierce sun dried it to little particles, that were carried off by the wind.

When the troop moved away, they left the body lying where it fell, for the hawks and vultures to devour the flesh, and leave the bones for the wild dogs to pick.

If there was but a single prisoner to deal with, the sergeant wiped his knife upon a tuft of grass, or on his boot, tried the edge with his thumb, and then returned the long blade into its sheath, behind his back, stuck into the belt. Sometimes he would remark, "that one was not mean of his throat."

If there were several prisoners, he passed on methodically to the next, till he had finished all the batch. His comrades stood round to see the spectacle, talking and laughing with the prisoners, till it was their turn to be killed. None of them ever showed the slightest fear, smoking a cigarette if it was offered them, and at the signal throwing it away, frequently with a jest, and stepping forward as unconcernedly, to all appearance, as if they had been just about to mount their horses.

As all the rank and file on either side were forcibly rounded up like cattle, and forced to fight, occasionally fathers and sons, or brothers, found themselves opposed to one another.

As in most revolutions in the Argentine and in Uruguay, the armies called themselves "White" or "Red," and although the gauchos had no idea why they were fighting or what their leaders wanted, besides power, every man proudly called himself "Red" or "White," as the case might be; and often gauchos attached themselves to one side or the other simply because they gave one of the two colours preference over the other.

On a moonlight night, a *partido* of "Reds" rode up to a ranch where they hoped to plunder all the cattle and sheep. Roberto, Cabrera and Pancho Pájaro were among the raiders. As it happened, this ranch belonged to Pájaro's father, who favoured the "Whites." Pancho very wisely said nothing about this to his companions, for he knew only too well what the consequences would be if he breathed a word of protest. Suddenly, from a wood, a party of "Whites" broke cover, and charged upon Roberto's column.

Pancho had no cartridges, so fought with his long knife. Guns cracked, *lazos* whistled and bolas hurtled through the air, and soon the "Whites" were routed.

Pancho, who rode a fiery horse, spurred out from the ranks, swinging the bolas and then throwing them at a fugitive's horse, which, being caught by its hind legs, soon faltered. Pancho, riding like the wind, ranged up and drove his sword through the man's back. He fell without a groan, the blood staining a fine poncho. Pancho, getting off his horse, advanced and turned the body over with his foot. As the moon fell on the dead man's face he saw that he had killed his own brother. The gauchos said that from that time he would be accursed by God. Thus it happened, for soon after Pancho's father died, and the house became deserted.

When the revolution ended, Pancho took to a roaming life, visiting the far-flung frontiers of the republic, where he traded with Indians; and eleven years later, when Roberto went pioneering in Texas, he again met Pancho, who still roamed about like a lost soul, trading, and helping buffalo-hunters.

The revolution over, Roberto—who was then barely eighteen years old—found himself in a small town. Hearing about an injustice that was committed by the authorities, he organised a meeting of protest, with the result that he, together with a number of other citizens, soon found himself locked up in a filthy jail. Fortunately, however, the Macks heard about his plight, and they, together with the British Consul, managed to have him released. Had it not been for this timely and almost miraculous intervention, Roberto's career might easily have ended there, and the world would have been the poorer for the loss of a man whose amazing life had hardly begun.

Together with the Macks, like a prodigal son, Roberto returned to the ranch, where he remained for some time. With his long hair and native horse-gear—silver head-stall with the throat-latch loose upon the throat, the bit with a silver half-moon swinging on a hinge beneath the lower jaw, the massive silver cups on either side of the animal's mouth—he was now a perfect gaucho. Like the natives, he rode on a sheep-skin saddle which was mounted with silver at each end, and from the horse's neck dangled a pair of flat, raw-hide hobbles.

In a neighbouring ranch the overseer, or *mayordomo*—an Englishman—lay dangerously ill with typhus fever. Medicine, and fresh bread, for which rare article of food in those parts the fever-stricken man longed, were only to be procured in the distant town, to reach which a large and swollen river had to be forded. Young Roberto immediately undertook this perilous service, partly swimming the horse over in the dark. He reached the little town, procured the medicine and the bread, recrossed the river in safety, and returned to the sick man's bedside, where he kept watch for many hours in his wet clothes, without a thought of the consequences to himself.

The result was that Roberto caught the fever, and lay for many days between life and death; but youth and a good constitution, aided by the nursing of rough but kindly companions, pulled him through, though he rose from the crude sick-bed the shadow of his former self.

Due to his illness, Roberto had not written to his people in England for some time. His mother, anxious for news, communicated with the British Consul in Buenos Aires and with the Macks, whose replies to her inquiries I reproduce.

> "British Consulate,
> "Buenos Aires,
> "December 11th, 1871.

"Mrs. A. E. Bontine,
   "London.

"MADAM,—

"In reply to your note of 8 July last I beg to state that having written to Dr. Wells H.M's Vice Consul at Gualeguaychú asking for information respecting Mr. R. C. Graham, the annexed extract from his letter will furnish you with some tidings. Your enclosure I also forwarded to Dr. Wells who retains it at present as he thinks Mr. Graham may appear there in a few days.

> "I am, Madam,
>> "Your obt. servant,
>> "(Signed) FRANK PARISH."

> "British Vice Consulate,
> "Gualeguaychú,
> "Oct. 26/71.

"DEAR SIR,—

"In reply to your letter making enquiries relative to Mr. R. C. Graham I have the satisfaction of communicating to you that he was in Gualeguaychú yesterday and I am informed expressed his intention of proceeding to Cordova. I ascertained he left this town this morning. I have repeatedly seen him lately, in fact I have attended him professionally for some trivial ailments of no importance whatever.

"I conclude the reason his family have received no tidings of him is owing to his having been down with Typhus fever up the Country, although at the present moment his health is excellent. . . .

> "(Signed) H. WELLS."

> "Gualeguaychú,
> "August 20th, 1871.

"MY DEAR MRS. BONTINE,

"I received your letter of 7 July a few days ago, and I am very glad to be able to tell you that the last time I saw your son, which is about a fortnight ago, he was very much better, though he has been very seriously ill. For two months my brother and I took the best care of him at the estancia de Santa Anita, and as soon as he could bear the journey we got a carriage to convey him to Dr. Forbes' house in Concepción del Uruguay where he is at present. I have advised him as soon as he is strong enough to bear the journey, which I expect he will soon be now, as after such a severe illness it would be scarcely prudent for him to knock about any more in this country I believe he intends returning home.

"I got three letters for him the other day which I have forwarded to him. The postmarks on the envelopes were Feb. 8 and March the mistake I saw was addressing them to Monte Video, which is the capital of the Banda Oriental and as there has been a revolution there for about two years or more I expect the letters had been there for some time. Revolutions in the South American Republics are of too frequent occurrence as my brother and I have found out to our cost to induce any one to invest much capital in them at all events in stock and I am afraid there is no hope of getting any compensation from the Government for losses, as the Argentine Ministro says he will pay no claim for any damage done by the rebels, and the same with regard to the National forces unless you have receipts and he also stated that he considered foreigners in some degree as rebels for carrying on business in a province which was in rebellion against the National Government. . . .

"(Signed) . . . XXX ." ("MACK.")

Unable to remain inactive long—for he had done nothing but ride about and read books which his mother regularly sent to him—Roberto held a council of war with the Macks, and they decided that his plan to use his remaining capital in buying cattle and selling them in Uruguay, was a good one.

A few days later, as luck would have it, Angel Cabrera,

Roberto's old revolutionary companion, rode up to the ranch with his guitar slung on his back. Ever since the revolution had ended he had ridden over the country, singing and entertaining people at ranches and saloons, and when he had heard that Roberto was safely back on his old ranch, he had made up his mind to drop in for a few days, or even weeks, "unless his seat got the 'pampas itch,' " as he called the desire to move on.

When he heard about Roberto's proposed cattle venture, he at once became enthusiastic and offered his services, which were immediately accepted, Cabrera being appointed *capataz*, or foreman, although no other hands had been engaged. In due time, however, the services of a number of other gauchos were procured, cattle were bought, and the herd was driven towards Pelotas in Uruguay, where *charqui* (dried meat), was made to be exported to Puerto Rico and Havana to feed slaves.

The place where the animals were slaughtered was primitive and filthy, to say the least. Wet or dry, cattle were killed in the open, in a kind of huge corral where the mud and blood were ankle-deep. The stench was almost unbearable, and in summer the flies were so thick that men tied handkerchiefs to their mouths when they worked. The intestines of the slaughtered animals were thrown over a fence where hundreds of pigs were being fattened, and what they left was devoured by *chimangos* and *caranchos*, two birds of prey very common in those regions.

Fazendeiros, as big ranchers in Southern Brazil are called, used to drive their cattle to Pelotas. The dusky bosses, most of whom were mulattos, used to ride on elaborately worked silver saddles, and they were always accompanied by slaves who followed them afoot. White women were never seen, except when walking, chaperoned by old women or slaves. During the daytime only mulattos and slave women were visible, but occasionally the white women could be heard in the houses behind the shutters.

The average troop of cattle Roberto took over to Uruguay, numbered about five hundred head. Some of the *peons* (hands), he employed were half-caste Charrua Indians, called *Tapes*. They made excellent cow-boys, but were dangerous when drunk.

Wild dogs, called *perros cimarrones*, were very common in those days, and here and there, especially in bush country, herds of wild donkeys roamed about. They were very shy and could gallop with remarkable speed.

Quitanderas, as the ambulant prostitutes were called, travelled all over the country on horseback, calling at ranches, villages and settlements. (The origin of the name *quitandera* is unknown.)

Often, when camping out, Roberto had to eat iguanas, armadillos, and other peculiar foods which the average European would shun.

After a few trips to Pelotas, he was so disgusted with the cattle business that he decided to combine money-making with adventure. Not that cattle-droving in those days was not adventurous enough to have satisfied most men, but he longed to see and do things, and to know the vast country and the people to the marrow.

Frequently he heard about Indian incursions in the southern pampas, regions which he longed to visit in spite of the savages who often raided settlements, killing, plundering, burning and driving off the brave pioneers' cattle. Hearing that, across the distant Andes, high prices were paid for horses, he bought a number of mustangs, and, assisted by Cabrera and several other gauchos, started on the long march towards Chile.

"Gualeguaychú,
"Oct. 10th.

"MY DEAR MOTHER,—

"I came here last night and saw your letter to Don Diego. I will come home with him soon, but I couldn't come until I have been to Cordoba.* Horses are very scarce there. The Indians carry off all they can lay their hands on. I have therefore bought thirty or forty at twenty dollars a piece, and hope to sell them there at about eighty or a hundred dollars each. I have also hired a man to help me take up the horses. I expect to be away a month, and will then come home as soon as I return. Poor Don Diego who has lost all his cattle, horses and everything else with the revolution has taken to drinking, and is in a state bordering on Delirium Tremens. His brother and I have been trying to get him out of town, but it is of no use. I have just come from a part of the country called Ibicuy, an old Indian camp. It is by far the most curious country; sometimes you have to go for miles crawling through thick woods, leading your horse. The woods are perfectly swarming with humming-birds (*picaflores*), and there are lots of cannibal fish, water-hogs, and all sorts of animals. I am getting much stronger again, but am still a fearful object without any hair. I had a very bad fall the other day from a wild horse which I foolishly mounted before I was strong enough. The brute fell on top of me and squashed me a good deal. . . ."

During this long journey Roberto for the first time saw the seemingly endless pampa,† the wide ocean where the waves appear to roll without advancing or receding.

* The town of Córdoba is in the Argentine. After having written this letter Roberto decided to pass through it, and on to Chile.
† "Pampa," in the Quichua language, means "space."

In the evening, when a suitable spot was found, the bell-mare was hobbled, and whilst two or three gauchos rode round the troop of horses, the others collected fuel—dry thistle-stalks, grass and bones—and lighted a fire to prepare *maté* and food.

After meals, especially at night, the long-haired and bearded Cabrera would sit on his saddle, tune his guitar, and sing gaucho songs in a high falsetto voice. Then, again, he could not resist coming out with some of his favourite native adages, emphasising his words by raising a horny finger: "The fox who comes out of his burrow in the daytime, comes out to be killed"—"Trust not a mule or a mulata wench"—"Never go to a hut where the dogs are skinny, for he who does not feed his dogs will starve his guests"—"If a woman is a harlot and gets nothing for it, she might just as well remain respectable."

Taking it in turns, some of the men rode round the herd throughout the night, straining their eyes and ears, constantly on the alert in case of an attack by Indians. The other men lay down on the sheep-skins of their saddles, rolled up in their ponchos, and slept with their heads resting on the saddles under which were tucked their long knives and rifles. As the night wore on, the blazing bones and other fuel gradually smouldered down into a glowing cake, throwing a bluish light upon the sleeping figures by the fire. Slowly all noises ceased, except the munching of the horses and an occasional whistling by one of the mounted watchers, or the shrill shriek of a night-bird. Gradually even the sound of the munching ceased, and the horses stood still, hanging their heads and resting on their hind legs, alternately.

Towards dawn, white mists crept over the plain and the dew lay like frost upon the sleepers, making them turn uneasily, and instinctively draw their ponchos over their heads, while the horses hunched their backs and stood with their heads bending to the ground.

Before the sun rose in all its glory, giving warmth and cheer, the men had drunk a few *matés*, and once more the horses were being driven along, the travellers leaving behind a wide, dark trail where they had disturbed the dew—a trail that resembled the wake of a ship, or a gigantic black snake, winding over the pampa from the eastern horizon. Gradually the atmosphere became hotter and hotter, and in the afternoon, a wise gaucho predicted that a *pampero* was coming. The air grew heavy, the sky appeared to be lowering, and presently the first forerunners of the storm—short gusts of wind that raised dust in whirls, like waterspouts—proved that the gaucho weather-prophet was right, for these were sure signs that a *pampero*, or terrific storm, was on its way from the southern plains.

Hurriedly the spare riding horses and the bell-mare were hobbled, and then the men formed a wide circle round the troop; and not a moment too soon, for suddenly the storm broke with great violence, lightning played continuously, furious rain ran along the soil like hail, and thunder seemed to be shaking the whole world. The wind swept everything before it, throwing the horses into a wild panic. Finding that they were shut in by a circle of gauchos, they finally calmed down a little, and, turning their tails into the wind, stood trembling nervously.

After about ten minutes the storm died down as suddenly as it had come, the sun once more shone in a clear blue sky, and the travellers continued their journey over the rain-sodden plain which was again practically dry when camp was pitched in the evening.

Although some of the regions they had passed through were dangerous owing to hordes of marauding Indians, who occasionally came up from the far South, Roberto and his men reached the foothills of the mighty Andes without having lost a single animal. Ahead, they could see the white peaks glittering in the azure sky, and when they had rested the horses in good pasture, they started the slow and arduous climb up rocky valleys. Natives of these regions had recommended them to be extremely careful lest they be caught by a *viento blanco* (white wind), as they call blizzards, which have claimed many victims who were foolhardy enough to travel when the weather was uncertain.

Undisturbed, but made cautious by these warnings, the travellers set out on the last and difficult lap of their long trek, and slowly drove the horses higher and higher into the rocky wilderness. *Puna*, or mountain-sickness, made progress doubly difficult and slow, for if the animals had been hurried, many would have died. During the crossing of the high, cold and wind-swept mountains, several went lame and had to be abandoned to their fate, but finally the goal was reached, and when all the horses had been sold at a considerable profit, Roberto and his companions started on their long return journey.

Some time after his return to the ranch, Roberto planned another expedition with horses, but this would have been dangerous, as will be seen from the following letter he wrote to his mother:

> "Estancia de Santa Anita,
> "Feb. 10.

"My dear Mama,—

"I have been unable to get up country at all on account of the revolution and I think the best thing I can do is to come home as I think I see my way to a good thing now. Mack and another Scotsman having had all their cattle killed, wells destroyed, and lost everything, are going about the country buying hides and wood and making immense profits by it. They have promised to

ARGENTINE, 1874—1877

Reproduced by the courtesy of the Museo Histórico Nacional, Buenos Aires.

take me into partnership which might be thought of
when I come home and can explain everything
properly. . . . I went up to a little town in the camp the
other day, a good way from here, a very old little place
called Villaguay where there was once a Jesuit Mission.
It had been a thriving place once, but, like all Spanish
American inland towns, is gradually falling into decay.
I was riding a young horse through the town when he
got frightened and began to buck. I should think the
whole population of the town came to see the fun, and
there were loud shouts of: 'El gringo se va al suelo,'* but
luckily I did not, as there were some uncommonly hard
stones to fall on. . . . For the past three months there
has not been a drop of rain, so that the camps are in a
very bad state. At this place is the only water for leagues.
It is a very curious sight to watch the wild brutes, cattle
and deer come down to drink in thousands. They come
down with clouds of dust and a noise like thunder with
the galloping on the hard ground, then they all bathe and
paw about. I caught a fine horse one evening there, a
tame horse that had got away and had been running a
long time wild. I could do nothing with him, however,
mostly because he threw himself over backwards and
refused to get up again. I was obliged to let him go as
I could not cope with him at all. . . ."

Although the revolution in the Argentine was supposed to
have ended, marauding bands of raiders still attacked and
plundered ranches, so Roberto suddenly decided to make an
overland trip to Paraguay where, he had heard, fortunes
awaited enterprising men.

The Paraguayans had fought a losing war against
Argentina, Brazil and Uruguay, and a year before Roberto

* The "gringo" is coming off.

set out to see what were the prospects in Paraguay, Francisco Solano Lopez, the ruthless dictator and tyrant of that ill-fated country, was slain whilst fleeing with his mistress, Madame Lynch.* *(See also pp. 94-95.)*

And so Roberto, mounted on his favourite horse, a light grey called "Bunny," and set out from the Argentine province of Entre Ríos, to ride North into the unknown, a distance of some two thousand miles as the crow flies.

In the North of the Argentine he passed through the territory of Misiones where, in former times, the Jesuits had founded some thirty little towns. From there he penetrated into then little-known regions, inhabited by Toba, Guayacuru, Mocobio and Lengua Indians, and territories delivered up to that fierce-growing, sub-tropical vegetation which seems to fight with man for the possession of the land. Finally he penetrated far into the *Chaco*, a name which, in the language of the Guarani Indians, signifies *Hunting Ground*.

For days he rode through the forests on the narrow trails, and sometimes, at night, he heard the jaguars snarling in the thick brushwood. Ant-eaters with their long bushy tails, and claws so formidable that even the jaguar fears them, waddled slowly across his path, and monkeys chattered in the trees. His horse snorted and took fright, as in the thick and reedy grasses by the river-sides water-hogs plunged with a loud spash into the stream, and Roberto shivered as the sloth's mournful "Ai" resounded from the tops of the tall trees. Starting at dawn, he saw the forests shrouded in white mist, and pressed his horse to his hardest walk to make a league or two before the sun should blaze down upon them. Green snakes hung from the trees, and from recesses of the forest rang the full note the bell-bird sounds, as if it called to Mass in some mysterious chapel of the woods. Parrots in flocks

---

* Lopez was killed on the 1st March, 1870. Of him, Don Roberto wrote: "His bust defiles the dark recesses of the Ternmensian woods. So far no bust of Judas mocks Gethsemane." (*Portrait of a Dictator*, 1933.)

flew screeching through the trees, macaws soared over him like a flight of parti-coloured falcons, piercing the ears with their harsh cry, and by the river-sides flitted toucans, looking like gigantic and misshapen kingfishers.

By the deep stagnant backwaters of great rivers, looking like dead logs, basked alligators that scarcely moved as the rider passed upon his way, for in those days they had but little fear of man.

The greatest difficulty on the journey was the crossing of rivers. Sometimes, where dug-out canoes were to be found, this was accomplished easily enough, holding the horse by the halter, and making him swim beside the canoe.

Before Roberto and his horse plunged into rivers, he had to make quite sure that neither he nor his animal had a cut or an open sore, for devilish little cannibal fish, known as *pirañas*—or *carribes*—attack in thousands if they smell blood.

Far in the interior, Roberto became acquainted with the Indians' method of making their dug-out canoes, and he saw them use their blow-pipes and poisoned darts that make a wound no bigger than a pin's head in a man; and yet he dies before he has the time "to call upon the name of Jesus more than thrice."

Having penetrated far into territory then unknown, claimed by Brazil, the traveller decided to turn south and to head for Asunción, the capital of Paraguay. For three days he and his horse floated down a river on a raft made by friendly Indians. The river was shut in between seemingly endless walls of vegetation, and as the crude raft slowly drifted down-stream, tropical birds flitted by, like flights of amethysts and topazes. Immediately after the sun had set, thousands of frogs croaked with harsh, metallic note, and clouds of gnats and mosquitoes made life a purgatory.

Leaving the raft, Roberto rode through forests of gigantic

hardwood trees, which were crowned with bright flowers, yellow, red and purple, hanging in clusters like bunches of grapes. These flowers are the trees' funeral wreaths, for they belong to the lianas that wind round the trunks and crush the sap out in their folds. In the vast labyrinth of the jungle, red howling monkeys sat in the topmost branches, and at night belched out their howls, making the forest tremble as if a band of lions inhabited the trees. At night, too, vampire bats fastened to the horse's neck, and left him jaded when Roberto had most need of him.

Finally he came to more or less civilised parts where he found villages and little towns; and after weeks of travelling and studying the country and its prospects, he unsaddled near Asunción, on the ranch belonging to a countryman of his, a certain Dr. Stewart.

Owing to the disastrous war, the country was desolate and uncultivated, with the male population so reduced that there were thirteen women to a man, and the few men who had survived were either mutilated war veterans, or boys of fourteen or fifteen years of age. Many of the Paraguayans he met exhausted all the adjectives of Spanish and of Guarani, to express their hatred of Francisco Solano Lopez, who, in many instances, had tortured their fathers, brothers, wives and sisters and then, when human nature could endure no more and the poor, half-starved wretches lagged behind during the retreat into the northern forests, had them lanced, or their brains beaten out with rifle butts.

The Brazilians and the Argentines who had remained behind in the army of occupation confirmed to Roberto all that the Paraguayans told him about the dead tyrant, whom they called the "Monkey-Tiger." Many of the wretched people who had endured starvation and bad treatment all through the five years that the war had lasted, were still afraid to speak, and if the name of Lopez happened to be mentioned, would look round apprehensively, as if they were not certain he was dead.

The country's only export of real value was the leaf of the Ilex Paraguayensis, the substitute for tea which is known as *maté*. The poorest people had their plot of ground in which they grew sufficient maize and *mandioca* (a long, potato-like root), for their simple wants. Round every house there was a grove of orange trees, which even grew wild in woods, forming great thickets.

Obviously, Roberto thought he was about to strike oil, for among the letters he wrote at the time—in almost illegible scrawl—he sent the following to England:

> "Asunción,
> "Paraguay.
> "Dec. 20th, 1871.
>
> ". . . I am coming home at once on business. I think I am going to drop in for a pretty good thing, for I have got a concession to make 'yerba' from the Paraguayan Government. I have just returned from inspecting it, rather thin and a good deal bothered with the 'rhoomaticks,' but otherwise in good health. . . . Please try to find a writing master for me, as I intend to do all I can to improve my hand when I arrive. I expect to be only a few months in England. I have a two and a half miles gallop to catch the steamer, and thirteen minutes to do it in. . . ."

As will be seen later, enthusiastic Roberto had counted his chickens before they were hatched, for although he had taken part in an Argentine revolution, he knew but little or nothing about South American politicians, on whose promise of a concession he pinned his faith.

Leaving his faithful horse, "Bunny," with Dr. Stewart,

69

Roberto boarded a river steamer bound for the Argentine where, before sailing home, he went to the Province of Entre Ríos to visit his old friends, the Macks.

On his return to the ranch he found that things had been happening during his absence. Cattle had been stolen, the foreman had been carried away by the grippe, and the younger Mack was locked up in a shed where he roared like a lion with delirium tremens, or the "tiddly-ums," as an English neighbour, who had come there to help, called the complaint. Among the letters Roberto found waiting for him was one from his mother, who informed him that his father's health was giving anxiety, and she also expressed a wish that her eldest son should return home.

Talking matters over with the elder Mack, Roberto and he decided that the best thing to do with his brother was to take him back to England. Accordingly, after a few belongings had been packed and the invalid had calmed down sufficiently to be able to travel, the two took the steamer down the River Paraná, and after having stayed in Claraz's hostelry in Buenos Aires for a few days, they boarded a vessel bound for Liverpool.

Mack was practically normal again when they reached Rio, but there, somehow, he managed to slip away from his guardian who, after a long hunt through the town, found him locked up in a gaol, where he raved worse than ever he had done before. According to reports, Mack had been drinking furiously, but fortunately the authorities released him, and with the help of several sturdy sailors Roberto managed to take him back to the ship, where he had to be kept in irons until his violence abated. After two days, when he was again allowed to wander about the decks, he had to be carefully watched, for on several occasions he tried to throw himself overboard. Finally, however, the invalid arrived safely on his father's estate in the north of England, and although he continued to drink heavily, he never had a recurrence of delirium tremens, and lived, happy and well, until he died at the ripe age of eighty-one.

Proud of his long hair, which flowed down to his shoulders, Roberto had not been able to make up his mind to have it cut, and it can easily be imagined how his people must have stared when a tall, bronzed and long-haired man arrived at Gartmore, and when they recognised this veritable Robinson Crusoe as their eldest son.

CHAPTER IV

THE boy, Roberto, had grown into a tall young man, so from now on I shall call him "Don Roberto," the name by which he was known to all his friends throughout life.

Having spent a few days with his parents at Gartmore, he journeyed to London, where he vainly tried to form a company to grow *yerba maté* (from which green South American tea is made), in Paraguay. As no one was interested, or willing to invest money in an enterprise, out of which vast fortunes have been made since those "early" days, the enthusiastic young man decided to return to Paraguay, and there to make a fortune on his own. However, before he returned to his new El Dorado, he made a trip to Nova Scotia. His brother Charles, at the time a midshipman in H.M.S. *Royal Alfred*, was stationed at Halifax. On the way out, Don Roberto was so sea-sick that, in order to cure him, he was hoisted up aloft.

When the two brothers met they did not recognise one another. Although Don Roberto did not like shooting as a sport, he was an interested spectator on a moose-hunting expedition. (Moose were "called" with a birch-bark trumpet, with which the hunters imitated the call of female moose.)

After a stay that lasted a month, he boarded a ship bound

for New York, where he remained for some three weeks. It was a filthy autumn day in 1872 when he drove in a jolting horse-cab along the rough cobblestone streets to a wharf, to go on board the *Alps*. The S.S. *Alps* was a type of ship well known in the 'seventies, but now obsolete.

Vessels—long, iron-built, flat-sided and coffin-like—of the *Alps* type, held an indeterminate position between the modern "tramp" and the liner of those days. The American agent had informed Don Roberto that the fare from New York to Glasgow was ten pounds, and that the vessel was a Scotch boat which might reach Glasgow in twelve days. Once on board, Don Roberto found that he was the only passenger, and that the decks were an inch deep in coal-dust. The vessel went to sea at once. Leaving Sandy Hook they encountered the full force of a north-westerly gale, and the lone passenger retired at once to his bunk, to be miserable and endeavour to read the *Faerie Queene*, his only book, and the only book on board except a Bible, and some professional works. For weeks, as it appeared to him, he heard nothing but the rattle of ropes, racing of screw, banging of portmanteau as it washed to and fro in a foot of water in the cabin, roaring of the wind, shouting of boatswain, pattering of naked feet upon the deck; then a fitful dozing, broken but by the rare visits of the steward with a "cup of arrowroot and whisky, sir," to tell that everything was battened down, and that the skipper had been sixteen hours on the bridge and looked like Lot's wife when she enjoyed her last wistful glance at Sodom.

After the seventh day, no cooking, galley fire put out, and cabin steward staggering in drunk, white-faced and frightened, rubber sea-boots on, and a plate of cold salt horse and biscuit, and, of course, more whisky.

At last, Don Roberto on deck, with Rathlin Island on the starboard beam, steaming towards the Mull; no boats, bulwarks all washed away upon the weather side, doors torn

off the hinges, the "fetched loose" smoke stack, coated white
with salt, and stayed up in a clumsy fashion with some chains;
rigging a mass of tatters, the Captain haggard and red-eyed,
the officers all cheerfully profane, the crew going about like
men after a long debauch.

At home, ten days flew past with theatres, dress-clothes,
good dinners, uncontrollable fits of temper of Don Roberto's
father, the unaccustomed feel of comfort; ten days amongst
beloved faces; and then back again to the *Alps*, ready to
return to South America in search of a fortune. The Glasgow
docks: rain, fog and coal-dust, and the lights of whisky
shops that glared like ogres' eyes upon the crowd. The decks
of the *Alps* were filthy, the crew either half drunk or else
disabled by disease; the skipper sulky, mates thinking about
home and surly, the boatswain almost inaudible through a
bad cold, and the poor draggled drabs upon the shore looked
like animated rag-shops in the December gloom. Scuffling
and cursing, creaking of blocks, throbbing of the screw, and
then the vessel slid out into the foul-smelling, muddy Clyde.
Out in the Irish Sea she dipped and rolled, and after three
days anchored outside Pauillac, where the warm sun cheered
up the traveller. Emigrants were taken on board, to be
crowded into bunks, fitted up in tiers, after the fashion of
vans in which sheep make their railway journeys. Tugs
crammed thick with people came alongside the *Alps*; men
and women who carried bags, bundles, and the inevitable
bird-cage.

A bell rang, and the quartermasters cleared the ship;
the friends who went ashore held their dirty handkerchiefs,
wet with tears, to their red eyes; the friends on board waved
their greasy hats, and neither tried in the least to keep their
feelings in, but wept lustily after the primitive and natural
fashion which relieves a man and makes him feel that tears
wash away his grief.

Then on to Lisbon, where, again, the ship took in another freight of human cattle, this time chiefly peasants from the Galician hills. Then out into the "roaring forties," followed by a rising gale. Hell down below amongst the emigrants, and no one on board who could speak French or Spanish, still less Portuguese, except Don Roberto. So through those alley-ways he weltered, sick to death, when difficulties arose, and jabbered with the unlucky peasants, who bore their sufferings manfully, sitting on the deck, all jammed together like sardines, from the grandmother to the new-born infant. And then the gale subsided and the old "tramp" lurched at nine knots before the following seas, till in a day or two they struck the north-east trades. Christmas Day (1873), caught them near Rio. The emigrants performed a sort of mutilated Mass upon the deck, a Biscayan schoolmaster mumbling from a prayer-book, and the faithful gathered in a crowd a little aft of the fore bitts, whilst the Scotch crew pushed through them now and then to trim the sails, or make their way to the forecastle.

New Year's Day—the great Scotch festival—found the *Alps* off Fernando Noronha, the little island off the coast where the Brazilians had a penal settlement. The day broke hot, and as the ship passed the island it loomed low, the palm-trees standing in a sort of mirage, so that they seemed to have no roots and to float above the land like parasols, between the sand and sky.

How the crew got the liquor no one ever knew, but before twelve o'clock the ship was like a pandemonium. From the stokehold came the sounds of "Auld Lang Syne," the watch on deck were stupid, and the emigrants scattered before them like chickens before the gambols of a large Newfoundland pup. When, finally, the emigrants became angry, things began to look ugly. The captain, who since early morn had been boiling with fury, growled like a bear, knocked down a seaman, and had him put in irons. By this time the decks were filthy, men falling down and being sick all over them, the mates and engineers working like slaves, punching and kicking, driving the drunken crew below, until at last they were all got into the forecastle, and a man planted at the door, armed with a hand-spike to keep them in. Till night fell, the mates, the passengers, the doctor, and such of the emigrants as were able, were forced to work the ship; the doctor and Don Roberto steering occasionally, and putting the helm invariably hard up, when it should have been put hard down, keeping the vessel yawing about as if they wished to write their names upon the sea. Next morning decks were washed, black eyes and broken heads attended to, the prisoners let out on promise of amendment, and a search made to find out how the men had got the drink. Nothing, of course, came out, and they pursued their voyage until, one fine morning, the *Alps* finally anchored outside Monte Video.

The following letters were written by Don Roberto during this voyage. Fortunately his mother preserved a great many of his communications, some of which I reproduce in this book. Most of the letters to his mother are signed: "Your affectionate son, R. Graham Bontine."

"S.S. *Alps*,
"Nearing Rio de Janeiro,
"December 26th, 1872.

"MY DEAR MOTHER,—

"After leaving Pauillac I was in bed for five days, but have been pretty well since, with the exception of a day or two now and then. I am sitting writing in a cabin on deck, with four windows open and the thermometer at about 86°. The voyage has been great fun as there are many French and Spanish emigrants, and no one

76

speaks their languages on board but myself. The Scotch sailors and the emigrants express themselves freely and strongly in their respective languages, and I always have to interpret when there is a row, which happens about three or four times every day. As yet the emigrants have confined themselves to showing their knives, but there seems every chance of a jolly row. One of the French passengers drew his revolver on me for enticing him up the rigging. However, he was promptly disarmed, and on being threatened to be put in irons he promised better behaviour, so we went to *boire une coupe*, and have been *mon brave* and *mon cher* ever since. He now makes valiant attempts to get as far as the top gallant yard. The captain said, somewhat disconnectedly, it was a good thing that the Frenchman had slowed off when he did, as he (the captain) was afraid I might hurt him. The force of this observation I did not at once perceive, as I was quite unarmed, and the Frenchman was flourishing a loaded revolver at my head. Afterwards I accounted for it by supposing the captain thought every Scotsman could fight an unlimited number of Frenchmen. Some of the scenes in consequence of the misunderstandings due to language difficulties have been wonderfully funny. I have had a great deal of practice, and now speak French as well as when I left Brussels. However, it is rather trying to have to call over a hundred names before all the ship's company, and ask every man and woman their height, weight, ages and possible chances of valuation, as I had to do the other day when they wanted to make out a list for the Argentine authorities. . . . A little English barque has just passed. She looked very jolly, the sails white and the vessel newly painted, homeward bound. . . . I have been in the fore rigging all the morning, watching two eagles fishing

77   G

among shoals of funny-looking little fish, close to the
ship. . . ."

"Monte Video,
"January 6th, 1873.

"Arrived here safely yesterday. . . . Of course, on
New Year's Day—as this is a Scotch ship—all hands
were drunk, or, I should say 'a wee bit overcome,' and
fighting prevailed to a large extent. Among rather
unpleasant scenes, a very amusing one took place.
The purser, who is generally a quiet man, got drunk and
came up to where I was sitting, talking with a Spaniard.
When the purser offered to fight us both, we laughed, and
when he got nasty, the Spaniard, who is an immensely
powerful man, carried the purser downstairs and locked
him into his cabin. . . . I will tell you the story of an
old *compañero* of mine, a story which, for wildness, beats
anything of Bret Harte's. Bill Rice had been forty years
in this country, and was the best fighter with the knife
in this part of Spanish America. A year ago, previously
to my going home, he gave me a letter to post in England.
This letter which I posted for him, was the first one he
had written for forty years. He received an answer,
telling him he had had some money left him, so he
decided to go home to Dartmouth. . . . Before leaving
he was heard to say that he would never forget the
young chap as posted that 'ere letter for poor old Bill
Rice. Just before he went home he was going round
the camp, bidding good-bye to old friends. (I must add
that he had made a vow to kill no more men before he
went home.) In the course of bidding his friends good-
bye, he happened to go to the house of one Reyton, an
Irishman who happened to be drunk, and was going to
indulge himself in the national luxury of beating his wife.

Bill interfered, and was remonstrating when the Irishman seized his knife and stabbed him to the heart, killing him instantly. Such is life in the River Plate. I was sorry for poor old Bill who was a very good fellow, in spite of his man-killing proclivities."

In Monte Video the ship was quarantined for six days, and when some of the emigrants had been landed in boats, the *Alps* proceeded up the River Plate towards Buenos Aires.

If by any chance a case of fever occurred, all the passengers were herded together, like sheep in a pen, in the *lazaretto* on Flores Island. For this privilege the unfortunate victims had to pay four pesos per day, and often they were kept there for eight weeks or even longer.

In due time Don Roberto landed in Buenos Aires, and after having spent a few days among old friends and acquaintances, at Claraz's hostelry, he boarded a primitive river boat, in which he sailed up the mighty River Paraná, towards Paraguay.

All day the steamer ran between the myriad islets of the yellow muddy river. Sometimes it seemed impossible that she could thread her way between the mass of floating water vegetation which clogged the channel. Now and then the branches of tall trees swept the deck as the vessel hugged the shore. On every side a mass of vegetation, feathery palms, horny mimosas, giant cacti, all knotted together with lianas like cordage of a ship.

Now and then wild horses came into sight and snorted as the steamer passed; or a gaucho, with flowing hair and floating poncho, cantered along the plain where the banks were low. In the slack water, under the lee of the islands, alligators lay like trunks of trees, and basked. In the trees, the monkeys and parrots chattered and howled, and humming-birds flitted from flower to flower; and once between the islands a jaguar appeared swimming in pursuit of some water-hogs. The air was full of the filmy white filaments like cobwebs which the north wind always brings with it in those countries, and which clung to every rope and piece of rigging, making the steamer look as if she had run through a cotton manufactory. In every cabin mosquitoes hummed and made life miserable.

On board the steamer everything was "moderno" (according to the natives), but no door would shut, no bolt would draw, and nothing made to slide would work. The captain was from Barcelona, the crew, Italians and Spanish Basques; the pilot, from the north of the Argentine, equally at home in the saddle or in a schooner, and knowing every turn and bend of the river in the nineteen hundred miles from Buenos Aires to Cuyabá.

The passengers, also, were a mixed lot, consisting of Paraguayans, Brazilians, Argentines, a few merchants, a gambler or two in pursuit of their daily avocation. Among the chattering crowd of passengers were two or three dusky couples with innumerable children, and a few gauchos with their foreman. Keeping apart from the rest, they enjoyed the journey, playing with cards which were as greasy as bits of hide, drinking *maté* or talking of horses and discussing cattle brands which they scratched on the decks with their long knives.

Like Don Roberto, who had joined this group of herdsmen, they slept on their saddles, on deck, in preference to being shut up in a stuffy cabin with a crowd of men who spent the nights snoring melodiously, or smoking black, rank-smelling cigars and spitting twice to every puff.

One of the gauchos had a guitar, and sang to it for hours in the moonlight, but in such a fashion as to disturb no one. His songs were chiefly of melancholy love affairs, or of the prowess of famous horses.

Thus the days passed until, at last, the boat arrived at its destination.

Roberto went to stay with Dr. Stewart, where he found his horse, "Bunny," sound and well. His enthusiasm about the concession soon grew less, as can clearly be seen in the following letter he wrote to his mother:

"Asunción,
"July 16th, 1873.

". . . To fill up time, till I hear something definite, I am going down to the Argentine province of Corrientes to fetch up a troop of mules for Dr. Stewart who, by the way, has been excessively kind and civil to me, and at whose *quinta*,* about two miles out of Asunción, I am at present staying. This, of course, is a great saving of expense to me. I am very glad I have come up to Paraguay, for I think there is a great deal to be done here. I hope to make some money by the mules I bring for Dr. Stewart. . . . It is not very easy to get a concession, and a good deal depends on whether the President is in a good humour or not, as he is a fool, and quite in the hands of the Brazilians who still occupy the country. I find Portuguese very useful to me up here, as it is almost—if not as much—spoken here as Spanish. I have only learnt a very little of it as yet. . . . The people of the country are not gauchos like the Argentines and Orientals (Uruguayans); far otherwise, although they wear the same sort of clothes and have a fair number of horses. They are, in general, quite duffers on a horse, and few of them throw the lasso any better than I can myself. 'Bunny,' I think, is the tamest horse I ever saw in South America. The Brazilian soldiers who have got to know me and him pretty well—as I am almost all day

* Country residence.

81

about the Government offices, trying to see someone or other who, of course, is always 'enfermo' (ill), or 'siestiando'—always call out: 'Ola Jose Maria, aqui ven Dom Roberto com o Bonee!' and some fellow always answers: 'Si Jose Antonio, cabale muite bein.' 'Bunny' is rather lazy, which is always considered a good sign of a horse's endurance in these parts. He follows me about and comes when he is called. I am very glad to hear Mallie [Don Roberto's brother Malise who at the time was a student of theology] has won a race. Let him continue to do so, and he will probably be an ornament to his state of life, some day, if not eventually, Archbishop of Canterbury. . . ."

(In most of his letters, Don Roberto shows a keen interest in everything going on in England, and in other parts of the world; art, politics, literature, current events. Some of the remarks he makes are gems of sarcasm and wit; but as most of the names of people and certain events have by this time been forgotten, I refrain from quoting.)

How he managed to communicate with his old gaucho friend Angel Cabrera (who fought with him during the revolution in the Argentine), I do not know, but in due time the two ex-revolutionary companions were re-united, forty mules were bought, a few gauchos were hired to act as drivers, and the animals were driven from Corrientes to Asunción, a distance of some five hundred miles. For a month or two, Cabrera thought he had arrived in a paradise, for, as we have already seen in the previous chapter, owing to the war, men were at a premium in Paraguay, and the women literally waylaid travellers of Cabrera's type. However, he soon got tired of this social novelty, and was glad to take a ship down-river and to return to his roaming life in the Argentine.

For some time, whilst waiting for his concession, Don Roberto made his headquarters on the property of Dr. Stewart, who was well known in Paraguay. Nature seemed to have made the place impregnable. On three sides of the land, which measured eight or ten miles in length on every side, forks of a river ran, and at the fourth they came so close together that a short fence, not half a mile in length, closed up the circle, and cattle once inside were safe, but for the jaguars, which at the time abounded and which had grown so fierce by reason of the want of population that they sometimes killed horses or cows close to the door of the house. A short cut through the wood of about a quarter of a mile in length, led to the gate. Through it Don Roberto often rode at night, alert, with a pistol in his hand. One night when close to the gate—which consisted of bamboo bars stuck through two thick posts—he heard a grunt. Thinking his last hour had come he quickly turned round, fired a shot at a shadow in the undergrowth, and when he knew that he had brought something down he carefully approached and found that it was a peccary. Tearing the bars of the gate down in a hurry, he leapt on his nervous horse and galloped nine miles to the house, thinking each moment that the herd of peccaries was close behind and panting for his blood. (Peccaries, when left undisturbed, are harmless, but if one is shot or hurt, the whole herd attacks, at once.)

On every *estancia* in Paraguay, jaguar traps were constructed; structures resembling enormous mouse-traps, made of strong bamboo poles.

Sick and tired of waiting for the decision of the President —who was much too busy with his *politica* to be bothered with concessions and such trifles, out of which he could make no easy money—Don Roberto set out to see the country and to study prospects.

Having started from Dr. Stewart's place near Asunción, he

83

entered the old Jesuit Missions from the north, riding his light grey, "Bunny." He travelled a fortnight, swimming the rivers, sleeping in native huts, or sometimes alone by his horse out on some little plain, for it was dangerous to approach a wood, as jaguars swarmed. The country was almost uninhabited, and if he met a stranger, he was usually one of that kind one does not care to meet alone, unless one has a horse such as "Bunny" was, who could turn on a handkerchief, as the old gaucho saying goes, and stop in two or three sharp bounds when at full speed. Mounted on him, Don Roberto felt confident, for a good horse imparts his spirit to his rider, just as a bold rider gives his courage to his horse.

When he arrived at a settlement which is now called Posadas, he met a Brazilian officer, and as the two crossed the River Uruguay, on a flying bridge, the Brazilian, whose horse fairly blazed with silver trappings, suddenly jumped him from the bridge into the water, which, at the time, was only some two feet in depth. When the animal felt the water he started bucking; but the rider sat like a statue in his saddle, holding his gun in his right hand. Don Roberto could not resist the temptation, and also spurred his horse off the bridge. These were the humours of the trail in those days.

The country he travelled through was that in which the Jesuit Missions once flourished. In all the mission towns, unlike most other parts of South America in those days, a man was perfectly secure, both as to life and property. Crime was unknown, and although sexual morality was lax, the old chapels might be said, even in those days, to be Arcadian, even if ritual was somewhat neglected.

All classes and both sexes smoked continually. Cigarettes were practically unknown, for all the Paraguayans smoked cigars. The countrywomen, when journeying in companies

through woods, smoked cigars as thick as ordinary bananas, lighting them at a torch always carried by their leader. Men smoked cigars of a smaller size, and women were said to be able to smoke stronger tobaccos than were the men.

Sometimes, in country districts, a stout Indian wench would take a leaf or two of raw tobacco, tuck up her chemise-like garment, and with a dextrous roll or two upon her thigh, make a cigar which she handed to the intended smoker with a smile. Gourmets used to say this gave a peculiar *Bouquet d'Indienne* to the cigar, and rendered it sweeter. Referring to this belief, Don Roberto wrote: "It was not vouchsafed to me, sinner that I am, to see that the operation made any difference to the tobacco. Some, no doubt, when angels have alighted at their door, have been too dull to recognise their celestial visitors."

By tracks that led through thick woods, he came to some of these neglected Jesuit villages, inhabited by Indians dressed in white and wearing a cloak of scarlet baize, or cloth, according to their rank. The women dressed in a shift, cut rather low, and a short petticoat, their long, black hair hanging down their backs and spread upon the forehead, like a horse's forelock.

Upon arriving at a Jesuit village in the woods, Don Roberto felt a sort of calm, as if he had come to some place that he had seen in dreams. The great chapel, the largest in the Jesuit Reductions, was built round a huge square, almost a quarter of a mile across. Upon three sides ran the low, continuous line of houses. Each dwelling was of the same design and size as all the rest. Rough tiles made in the Jesuit times, but now weathered and broken, showing rafters tied with raw-hide in many places, formed the long roof. A deep verandah ran in front, stretching from one end to the other of the square, supported on great baulks of wood which, after more than two hundred years and the assaults of the weather and the all-devouring ants, still showed the adze marks where they had been dressed.

The church, built of wood cut in the neighbouring forest, had two tall towers. Bells of great size, either cast upon the spot or brought at vast expense from Spain, hung in the towers, and as it was the feast-day of the Blessed Virgin when Don Roberto arrived, they jangled ceaselessly, the Indians taking turns to haul upon the dried lianas that served instead of ropes. Though they pulled vigorously, the bells sounded a little muffled, as if they strove in vain against the overpowering Nature that rendered any work of man puny in the Paraguayan wilds.

Inside, the church was dark, the images of saints were dusty, their paint was cracked, their gilding tarnished. On the neglected altar, the Indians had placed great bunches of red flowers, and now and then a humming-bird flitted in through the glass windows and hung poised above them; then darted out again with a soft whirring sound. Over the whole chapel, in which at one time several thousand Indians had lived, now reduced to seventy or eighty at the most, there hung an air of desolation. It seemed as if man, in his long protracted struggle with the forces of the woods, had been defeated and had accepted his defeat, content to vegetate, forgotten by the world, in the vast sea of green.

On this particular day, the annual festival of the Blessed Virgin, there was an air of animation, for from far and near, from straw-thatched huts lost in the clearings of the primeval forest, from the few cattle ranches that then existed, and from a little town fifty miles away, the scanty population had turned out to attend the festival.

Upon the forest tracks, from earliest dawn, long lines of white-clad, bare-footed women, had marched as silently as ghosts. All of them smoked great, green cigars, and as they marched along, their leader carrying a torch till the sun rose and jaguars went back to their lairs, they never talked.

Soon the square filled, and a few men arriving tied their horses in the shade. Bands of boys came trooping in, accompanied by crowds of women and of girls, who carried their belongings, for as most of the men had been killed off in the past war, the youngest boy was at a premium amongst the Indian women, who fought for male stragglers like unchained tigresses. Then a few gauchos from the North of the Argentine arrived, dressed in their national costume of loose black merino trousers, stuffed into long boots, whose fronts were all embroidered in red silk.

The *plaza* filled up imperceptibly, and the short grass was covered with a white-clad throng of Indians. The heat increased, and all the time the bells rang out, and at a given signal the people turned and trooped towards the church, all carrying flowers in their hands.

As there was no one to sing Mass, and as the organ long ago had been neglected, the congregation listened to some prayers, read from a book of Hours by an old Indian, who pronounced the Latin—of which most likely he did not understand a word—as if it had been Guarani (an Indian language of Paraguay).

As everyone except the gauchos went barefooted, the exit of the congregation made no noise except the sound of naked feet, slapping a little on the wooden steps, and so the people silently once again filled the *plaza*, where a high wooden arch had been erected in the middle for the equestrian sport of running at the ring (*Sortija*).

Sellers of food, alcoholic drinks and trifles such as no one in the world but a Paraguayan Indian could possibly require, now removed from the middle of the square, taking their wares under the long verandah.

Just about twelve o'clock, despite the heat, a band got ready in the church porch, playing old instruments, some of which had probably survived from Jesuit times, or, at least, had been copied from the originals which had decayed. Sackbuts and psalteries and shawms were there, with serpents, gigantic clarionets, and curiously twisted oboes, and drums whose canvas hung all slack and gave a muffled sound when they were beaten, and little fifes, ear-piercing and devilish, were represented in that band. It banged and crashed "La Palomita," that tune of evil-sounding omen, for to its strains prisoners were always ushered out to execution in the times of Lopez.

Then the Argentine gauchos and a few Paraguayan riders gave a dashing display of horsemanship. The winners received a prize in the shape of wineglasses filled with gin and, with compliments as to the order of their drinking, emptied them solemnly, and the crowd went off to breakfast at tables spread under the long verandahs, and silence fell upon the square.

The long hot hours during the middle of the day were passed in sleeping. Some lay face downwards in the shade while others swung in white cotton hammocks, keeping them in perpetual motion till they fell asleep, by pushing them with a naked toe upon the ground. At last the sun slowly declined, and white-robed women began to come out into the verandahs, slack and perspiring ¡after the midday struggle with the heat. Then bands of girls sauntered down to the river, from whence soon came the sound of merry laughter as they splashed about and bathed.

Night came on as it does in those latitudes, no twilight intervening, and from the rows of houses came the faint lights of wicks burning in bowls of grease, whilst from beneath the orange-trees was heard the tinkling of guitars. Enormous bats soared about noiselessly, and white-dressed couples lingered about, and men stood talking, pressed closely up against the wooden gratings of the windows, to women hidden inside the room. The air was heavy with the languorous murmur of the tropic night, and gradually the lights, one by one, were extinguished, and the tinkling of the guitars stilled. The moon came out, serene and glorious, showing each stone upon the sandy trails as clearly as at midday. Saddling up their horses, the gauchos and Don Roberto silently struck a trail, and bands of women moved off along the forest tracks towards their homes, walking in Indian file. The shrill neighing of a horse seemed as if it bade farewell to its companions, and noises that rose from the forest sounded mysteriously.

From one of these old Jesuit villages, Don Roberto wrote the following letter:

"Misiones,
"Paraguay,
"Sept. 9th, 1873.

". . . I am being detained at this place by a strain received in riding a wild horse. I am now all right, and shall march to-morrow, I had just returned, at about 7 p.m. from a thirty-mile ride, when, to my horror, I was told the postman was to saddle up at daybreak; and I have many letters to write. I shall do this after having fed my horses, and probably just retire to sleep on my saddle at daybreak when the infernal postman is starting for his ride of 140 miles. I have a new horse now, a 'doradillo' (light brown), a very useful beast, but a fearful kicker. He has already lamed one fellow, and has done his best to do the same to others, besides fighting with, and beating, almost all the other horses in the place. 'Bunny' has turned out to be one of the best horses I ever had. I can saddle him by 9 p.m. and be about 50 miles by morning. I have to take great care of him on account of the jaguars of which there are a great many here. One killed a bullock the other night. I think that with care I may be able to make a good thing out of this Paraguayan business. It is just the thing to suit me. . . ."

How much Don Roberto travelled through this difficult country is clearly shown in another letter, written in Asunción. The "Alto Paraná," or the headwaters of the River Paraná, is at least five hundred miles north of the Jesuit missions. Most of his long journeys were made with the object of finding suitable land for planting Ilex Paraguayensis (the plant from which the green tea, *maté*, is made.) Evidently he was still optimistic about reaching an agreement with the Paraguayan Government.

"Asunción,
"November 4th, 1873.

". . . I have just returned from the Alto Paraná. I had a very interesting and somewhat pesky journey to the Pelata concession. It rained tremendously, and I had the rheumatism all the time, and had to be helped on and off my horse, added to which I slept out in pouring rain every night, and had nothing to eat except oranges and mandioca (a kind of potato-like root). 'Bunny' has come back in first-rate condition, but a little lame in the off hind leg. When he had done about 650 miles, I had to get him shod, as his hoofs were a good deal worn away. In Paraguay, travelling is very hard on horses, not like on the splendid turf of the Banda (Uruguay), and Entre Ríos. 'Bunny' spent a whole day trying to pull off his shoes against posts and things, but now he is reconciled, and, in fact, rather proud of them. The country of the Alto Paraná is magnificent; only the scarcity of food is rather pesky. If I had not

met a very nice Italian on the frontier, who lent me a
gun (of course, I had left my rifle in Asunción, when I
wanted it), I should have eaten very little meat on
the journey. The Italian was a sort of gentleman, and
had served in the Crimea. He spoke English fluently.
The country down there is very fine, the trees, jaguars
and tapirs being abundant and of large size. I fired at
a jaguar three times with my revolver, quite close, but
could not hit on account of 'Bunny's' expressing his
strong disgust of the proceedings. We then (I had an
Indian guide) were preparing to attack him with lances,
but he quietly walked away, wagging his tail. The ferns
were splendid, and some tree ferns of enormous size.
The flowers were lovely, acacias and mimosas abounded,
and the lagoons were covered with Victoria Regis. . . .
I care very little about the Menteith peerage, as long
as no one else gets it. Of course, if I had it, I should be
a sort of Lord C——, and sit at rich men's feasts, in a
sort of second-hand way, as he does. However, as to
that agreeable sort of entertainment, I would rather
share a handful of maize with Bunny out on the
plains. . . ."

After the long war in Paraguay, the railway (built by the
tyrant Lopez, from Asunción to Paraguarí, only thirty miles),
fell into semi-ruinous condition. It still performed a journey
on alternate days, and staggered along a rough track, almost
unballasted. Many sleepers had been taken out for firewood
by the country people and most of the remaining had
decayed. The line was quite unfenced, and now and then a
bullock strayed upon it and was found sleeping on the track.
If the engine-driver saw the animal in time, he blew his
whistle loudly, the passengers all started, and if the bullock
refused to move, got down, and stoned it off the line. The

bridges, luckily, were few, and were constructed of the hard, imperishable woods so plentiful in Paraguay. They had no railings, and when after the downpours of the tropics, the streams they crossed were flooded, the water lapped up and covered them to the depth of several inches, so that the train appeared to roll upon the waters, and gave the passengers an experience they were not likely to forget.

The engines, that burned wood, achieved a maximum speed of ten miles an hour, but no one minded, for that was greater than the speed of the bullock carts to which they had been accustomed all their lives.

Certainly that little line through the primeval forest, with now and then breaks of open plain dotted here and there with dwarf scrubby palms, was one of the most curious and interesting the world has ever known. The trains, in general, started an hour or two behind the time that they were supposed to start, picking up passengers who waved coats or handkerchiefs, or in some cases a green palm leaf, to the engine-driver. Sometimes a man on horseback, urging his mount up to the train, would hand a letter or a little packet to the engine-driver or to some travelling friend.

In little townships through which the train crawled, the stops were lengthy. Women in long, white sleeveless smocks (their only garment), went about selling a kind of bread made of mandioca flour, flavoured with cheese, pieces of sugar-cane, oranges, bananas, etc. After a longer or shorter interval, the station-master, generally well-dressed in white, his head crowned with an official, semi-military cap, his bare feet shoved into slippers, and smoking a cigar, would appear on the platform, elbow his way amongst the crowd of women, pinching them and addressing salacious compliments to those he deemed attractive. When he reached the guard or engine-driver, he gossiped a little with him, and presently signalled to a female porter to ring the starting-bell. Then the engine-driver sounded his whistle shrilly, and the train, in a long series of jerks, as if protesting, bumped off from the platform in a cloud of dust.

One day Don Roberto had to send an urgent letter, and as by a miracle the train started punctually, he missed it. Borrowing the station-master's horse, he galloped after the train, which he overtook some ten miles down the line. He gave the letter to the engine-driver, who, wishing the rider good luck on the way home—for night was falling—opened the throttle and made the train move along as fast as it could.

At last, after a long interview with the President, Don Roberto realised that the capital he was prepared to put into the *maté* business was not sufficient to run the concessions the "one-man government" was willing to grant him. Still convinced that the project was sound, he wrote out an extensive report, on the strength of which he hoped to form a company in Buenos Aires where, unlike in Paraguay, many people had money which they sought to invest in profitable enterprises.

Accordingly, he left "Bunny," with Dr. Stewart, and took the first river boat down to the Argentine. He had been in Paraguay for nearly a year, and early in 1874 was back at Claraz's hostelry in Buenos Aires. Although he submitted his report to many prospective investors, no one was willing to put money into anything connected with Paraguay, and, therefore, he finally decided to take it to England, where he arrived late in 1874. Another disappointment awaited him in London, for there, like in Buenos Aires, no one took an interest in his Paraguayan scheme.

During idle moments, as he wandered about, or rode in Rotten Row, he occasionally saw Madame Lynch getting into her carriage at a house she had near Hyde Park. She had been the ambitious Irish-born mistress of General Lopez, the ruthless dictator of Paraguay, and it was largely due to her instigations that that country had been involved in the disastrous war to which I have already referred, and about which, in 1933, Don Roberto wrote in his book: *Portrait of a Dictator* (Wm. Heinemann, London). After Lopez's death (March 1st, 1870), during his hurried flight through the jungle, Madame Lynch managed to escape from South America, and for some time lived in London, but finally died in poverty in Paris, the Municipality paying for her funeral.

Sick and tired of walking in and out of stuffy offices and interviewing "soft, white-kneed" gentlemen, as Don Roberto called them, he went to Scotland, where he stayed at Gartmore with his people; but not for long, for soon after the restless young man went to visit his mother's relatives in Spain (Cadiz), and from there moved on to Paris, where he spent his time visiting art galleries, riding in the Bois de Boulogne, and fencing. The appearance of a tall rider, with a flowing mane of hair and a dashing black sombrero, created quite a sensation in Paris at the time, and in fencing circles the name of "Bontine" soon became famous, for shortly after his appearance, this mysterious stranger challenged, and defeated, the best fencers in the City of Light.

As suddenly as the now much discussed "Bontine" had appeared in Paris, he vanished, for upon receiving news that his brother, Charles, was in Gibraltar with the English fleet, Don Roberto hurried south to pay him a surprise visit.

CHAPTER V

SINCE the two brothers had met in Halifax (Nova Scotia), in 1872, they had not seen one another until, in June 1875, they were re-united in Gibraltar.

Fate had a great deal in store for Don Roberto, for among the naval officers he met in Gibraltar was a Lieutenant George Mansel, who immediately befriended the extra-ordinary visitor who, for hours on end, was made to recount some of his amazing adventures in South America.

Lieutenant Mansel was about thirty-five years of age, tall, dark and nervous, with round, prominent eyes, and a skin tanned by the sun to a brick-dark-red. His hair was cut short, or, as he called it, "all the same dog's back." At the first glance, even when he was dressed in plain clothes, one saw that he was a sailor, for the sea had left its marks upon him. Rough-tongued, hot-tempered, he was one of those who, in their dictionaries, had never come upon the verb "to fear." Whilst slave-cruising off the coast of Africa, Mansel had taken to drink. "Albert Van Hoytema Palm Tree Brand" was a favourite gin in those days, and Don Roberto's new friend could drink a whole bottle without turning a hair.

At that time a new retiring scheme came into operation in the British Navy, and when Mansel became enthusiastic about South America he proposed to take advantage of this retiring scheme—whereby he would receive a considerable sum of money—and to join Don Roberto in order to settle in the dangerous Indian territory south of Buenos Aires. (Although Mansel had been a sailor for many years, he knew horses and cattle well, for he was the son of a country squire who owned an estate in the South of England.)

He immediately sent in his papers, but as the settling of his official and private affairs was a matter of several months, and Don Roberto had nothing in particular to do in the meantime, Mansel introduced him to the captain of a certain barque. The three men met in a sailors' tavern, and after having discussed one or two points to which the captain seemed to attach great importance, he agreed to take Don Roberto on his next cruise.

The captain—who had an abundant crop of flaming red hair and a pointed beard and dashing moustaches of the same colour—was a famous character. Though his reputation was not an enviable one, he was often to be seen in the company of British naval officers, who liked him for the sake of company. He traded along the African coast, from Mogador to Mossamedes, where barbarism had its last entrenchments.

When Don Roberto got on board his barque, he found it laden with rum, gin, "gas-pipe" muskets, cotton goods, brass dishes, musical boxes, beads, bells, mirrors, etc.

Being short-handed, at Palmas they shipped a gang of Krooboys, healthy, tall and active pagans who could speak a jargon called "Blackman English." The Krooboys' faces were tattooed on either temple with a triangle from which a line of blue—which started below the hair—ran down to the

97

nose, giving them, when they laughed, a look of having two distinct faces.

Krooboys shipped for a cruise, and then, on returning home, reverted to paganism, and invested their wages in the purchase of more wives. English sailors gave them the most extraordinary names, of which the darkies were very proud— "Jack Beef," "Sam Coffee," "Small Fish," etc.

The captain knew the coast by day and by night, and was familiar with every harbour, inlet, mangrove and swamp.

Life on board the trading barque was easy. The skipper sought cargo as he sailed down the coast, picking up palm-oil, ivory, gold-dust, ostrich feathers, always on the barter system, and by direct dealing with the native headmen. Together with Don Roberto the skipper visited them, or they came on the ship to trade. Invariably the chief argument was gin. When the captain went ashore, he went with an armed guard, and the Krooboys carried the merchandise. The skipper's greatest joy was to get a native girl to dance for him, and whilst the negress danced to the accompaniment of a tom-tom and a flute, bending her body about like a snake and turning her eyes back till the pupils were almost invisible, he drank gin which he sweetened with orange marmalade.

Although slavery had officially been abolished, whenever he had a chance, the skipper kidnapped natives and threw them into the hold, and later sold them to Brazilian slavers who shipped them to South America as "rolls of tobacco."

At the end of this cruise, on which Don Roberto saw and learnt much, but wisely held his peace, he returned to England, where he spent Christmas with his family.

In the meantime Mansel had settled his affairs, and early in January 1876, on a cold and dreary day, the two sailed from Southampton—the twenty-four-year-old Don Roberto and his partner Mansel, who was his senior by eleven years, were on the way to their "Promised Land."

The first news Mrs. Bontine received came from St. Vincent.

"S.S. *Douco*,
"Jan. 19th, 1876.

". . . Mansel and I dined on board the *Black Prince* at Lisbon. Three of Mansel's old friends came off and had breakfast with us on board the *Douco*. Leaving, we steamed through the Fleet, passing right under the stern of the flagship. All the fellows were on deck, waving to us, and the last thing we saw of them was when they ran up 'ADIOS' to us in the signals. . . . We fence every day, and Mansel has cut his hair like the top of a match which delights the Portuguese. . . . At dinner I sit opposite to a Brazilian lady who, at every mouthful, pushes her knife, right down to the handle, into her throat. This shows me what I might attain with practice. . . ."

After a wretched passage down the Brazilian coast, they touched at Rio, where they saw a soldier on a fine black horse. As Don Roberto and Mansel were going to the Argentine to make their fortunes, they asked the soldier what such a horse was worth, and where the Brazilian Government got their remounts. Learning that in Rio a good horse cost five to six gold ounces, a golden future rose before their eyes, for Don Roberto knew that in Uruguay a horse such as the trooper rode might be worth an ounce (roughly £3 15s.). What could be easier than to go to Uruguay, buy horses and drive them overland to the Brazilian capital?

They were so confident of the success of their scheme that they counted every hour till the boat put to sea once more, and as they steamed out of the Bay of Rio, they hardly noticed its almost over-powering beauty.

During the voyage to the River Plate, they planned the business well. First of all they would investigate the land on the Indian frontier in the Argentine, and then, having selected the spot where to build a ranch house, they would go to Uruguay, buy horses, drive them eleven hundred miles to Rio, sell them at enormous profit, and then return to the Argentine, having at least doubled their capital.

The business looked so attractive and simple that several young passengers with whom they talked it over envied the two adventurers, for ranching and making a quick fortune out of horses were much more attractive than going to work in banks and counting-houses in Buenos Aires.

Whilst in quarantine outside Buenos Aires, Don Roberto wrote to his mother:—

"February 8th, 1876.

". . . Mansel is getting on very well with his Spanish, and says he will soon be able to make himself pretty fairly misunderstood. There is a Spanish bullfighter on board. He is the brother of a celebrated matador in Spain. He is an Andaluz, a most amusing fellow. He always sings drony Spanish songs, compared to which the tedious journey to Van Dieman's Land (Van Dieman, a favourite brand of gin) might be called lively. He has taken a great fancy to Mansel, and says he would soon turn him out a complete torero. . . . Anglo- and Franco-Spanish flourishes on board to a great degree as there are some French passengers. Complete peace reigns in the Banda Oriental (Uruguay), but I hear that lately a general—with a following of about fifty men—met another gentleman (also attended) at the door of the Solis theatre in Monte Video, and, in the words of the newspapers, 'a serious affray ensued.' This reads nicely, but does not seem to give much promise of a

permanent peace, as I had been led to suppose. . . .
Quarantine is one of the times in a man's life when he
can read Chaucer all through. . . ."

From Buenos Aires, the two prospective millionaires rode
to Bahia Blanca, a journey of about five hundred miles. A
great part of the territory they traversed had just been invaded
by Indians. Near almost every burnt-down house a man or
two lay dead, but Don Roberto and Mansel counted it as
nothing, for they were confident that their fortunes were
assured.

During this trip Don Roberto wrote home:—

"Fonda de Los Catalanes
"Azul (Provincia de Buenos Aires),
"Frontera del Oeste,
"March 4th, 1876.

"MY DEAR MOTHER,—

"Mansel and I came down here yesterday to see if we
could buy some cattle to sell the people who have lost
theirs in the last Indian raid. There has been a tremendous invasion of Indians who have carried off some
100,000 head of horses and cattle, and who have burnt
the camp for miles.

"This is a very curious little place. Formerly a tribe
of tame Indians lived just outside the town, but when the
wild ones invaded the other day, the 'Mansos' (tame
ones) all retreated into the desert with them. This is a
pity, as they are said to have looked very picturesque,
galloping about the town, trailing their spears after them.

"Mansel has taken tremendously to South American
life, and spends all day on a horse. By the bye; I have
got a chestnut, a pretty good horse, but not tame like
old 'Bunny.' I heard rather an amusing conversation the

other day, among some gauchos who were talking about a steam-boat. One of the men, who had been up to Rosario on one, said that an ordinary steam-boat carried twenty-five thousand passengers. One of the gauchos then remarked: 'Jesús! Qué lindo caballo!' (Jesus! what a fine horse!)

"Last night, Mansel, not understanding the bill of fare, passed it to another fellow to translate for him. On the list were sausages, blood-pudding and tripe. The man told Mansel they were beefsteaks, cutlets, etc; so he at once ordered them all. His feelings can be imagined.

"A large expedition started from here yesterday, to extend the frontiers. The general opinion is that they will lose all their horses in the desert, and that the Indians will 'eat them up.'

"Last night the people here performed the ceremony of burning 'Carnaval.' A large procession walked round the *plaza*, with a sham priest at their head, imitating a mock service. It was rather pretty as the night was lovely.

"Believe me,

"Your affectionate son,

"ROBERTO GRAHAM."

For several weeks the two adventurers rode over the southern pampas. They heard the music of the wind in the dried grasses, spent long days behind cattle on tired horses, with heels a-jogging ceaselessly against their mounts' sides, the ache between the shoulders growing intolerable as the slow hours moved on. The pampas stores they came to at long intervals were all fortified, ditches were dug around them, and the houses were built behind stockades. In those days, if a traveller's horse tired, and he came to a *rancho*, he was sure that a good animal would be loaned to him to reach his destination. "Just turn him loose at night," the owner would recommend, "no matter how far you take him, he will soon find his way back here."

The recommendation to let loose the horse at night, was because homing horses on the plains could be distinguished readily by their travelling in straight line, obviously with a purpose, stopping to graze but rarely, and when cantering along, carrying their heads high as if they sought to explore the horizon for the way.

When a rider arrived at a *rancho* he was told: "The meat is hanging up there; go and take as much as you want." If there was none, sometimes the rancher said: "Take that horse there, the one with the lasso tied to his saddle, and go out and kill a steer or a sheep." Before continuing their journey, the kind host would recommend: "Ride on to the lone tree on the horizon, then bear a little to the right, and if you can keep the line you cannot miss the stockade, for the barking of the dogs will guide you, if it falls dark." And then came evening, the travellers still urging on their horses, straining their eyes, and cursing every time their mounts stumbled or shied at seemingly nothing. When sleeping out in places where there were no trees or bushes, horses were fastened up for the night by scraping out a hole in the ground. When this had been done, a bone, or a piece of wood (carried for the purpose), was inserted into it, and forced into a horizontal position at the bottom of the hole. To the bone or piece of wood was fixed the lasso to which the horse was tied. Then the hole was filled with earth, which was stamped down and usually the riders, for more security, lay down to sleep over the place where the horse was, as it were, "anchored." If anything frightened the animal during the night, the sleeper was awakened by its snorts and by the jerking of the rope. After a meal of jerked meat and biscuit, one or two black cigarettes were smoked, and, if they ran the risk of making a fire which might attract marauding Indians, they lay down on the sheepskins of their saddles, hands on their rifles, boots turned towards the blaze, sleeping fitfully and rising oft to view the horses feeding quietly under the stars, or standing with heads held high, ears pricked up and nostrils dilated, if a faint noise was heard in the distance.

Having found a place where they thought of settling down after the trip to Rio with horses, Don Roberto and Mansel returned to Buenos Aires, whence they took a river-boat to Monte Video.

"Hotel Oriental,
"Monte Video,
"June 21st, 1876.

". . . Mansel and I are on our way to Rio with horses for the Brazilian cavalry. We expect to make a good thing out of it.

"The other day, in Buenos Aires, I was photographed at a 'Fotografía Artística'! ! ! Enclosed is the result. The man pulled my hat into the position that it assumes in the diagram, saying it looked 'más artístico.' If one takes the two artistic photographs (I mean the one with Olde Bunny in it, taken in Paraguay, and this one), I think I would prefer to be 'fotoged' by an artist who has studied his profession as a shoeblack. . . . If Mansel and I get safely up to Rio with the horses, we intend appearing on board H.M.S. *Volage* just in our travelling rig, which, I think, will astonish them not a little. In Buenos Aires I saw the President going to 'un meetin'.' I had expected to see a fellow in a long motley coat bordered with yellow, but I must confess I was surprised. Four whites, a glass coach, a nigger driving, President in his boiled shirt, white necktie, claw-hammer coat, tube hat (rituallest, please), sitting in state like a wapmah 'chez Tussaud's.'

DON ROBERTO, 1876

(Photograph referred to in letter. See page 104.)

"The other day, at the opera, a horse was introduced, led carefully by four men. He plunged a good deal, and an unfortunate French super had to ride him. The gaucho, like the English sailor, is always delighted to see himself on the stage. With rapture, a gaucho and a sailor, a miserable creature in a striped jersey, climbed on to the stage to assist the unhappy super. At the end of the scene I observed eight or ten gauchos, who had previously sat unmoved, get up in a frenzy of delight, insisting on having the horse brought before the curtain. The excitement was immense, and the horse crowned it all by violently breaking away from the trembling French supers and escaping behind the scenes where, apparently, judging by the noise I heard, he smashed up everything. Almost all my old friends here are dead (drink shot or married). . . ."

After a short stay in Monte Video the two companions journeyed to Durazno, a little town in Uruguay where horses and mules were cheap. About a league outside the town, in a wooded elbow of the River Yi, lived an old friend of Don Roberto's. When the two travellers arrived there was great rejoicing, and when Don Roberto explained what had brought him there, his friends liked the scheme, pronounced it practical and businesslike, and, to show goodwill, despatched a boy to town to bring a demijohn of rum back at full speed, instructing him not to delay upon the way, and to be careful no one stole it at the crossing of the river.

Next day Don Roberto and Mansel mounted on horses which were lent to them, and began to scour the land. Gauchos, Brazilians, negroes, cattle-drovers, farmers, each man in the whole district had at least a horse to sell. Singly, driven, led, pulled unwillingly along with raw-hide lassos, and sitting back like obstinate lapdogs, the horses came.

They bought them all after much bargaining, and then began to hunt about at farms, *estancias* and fields, and to enquire on every side where horses could be got.

Uruguay had been a prey to civil war for fifty years. The two great parties of the *Blancos* (Whites), and the *Colorados* (Reds), whose only aim was to seize power and place their friends in office (of course disguising their aims under the usual plea of liberty, progress and freedom, and other catch-words that mankind should be ashamed of using), had made the country a perpetual battlefield. The inhabitants were chiefly *gauchos* who lived on horseback, free as the ostriches and deer of their own plains, and as ungovernable. No race of men resembled them, for they had no kind of tribal organisation. Religion had but little hold upon them, though nominally they were all Catholics. The few who had been married with the sanction of the Church in a distant town were said to have been "married in Latin." Others were often married by some ambulatory priest, usually after their children had been born.

For some time Don Roberto and Mansel passed their days in the neighbourhood of Durazno, collecting horses of every shade and hue, wild and tame, and then, before starting, had to go to *la justicia* to get a passport with the horses' attributes and marks. The mayor could not read, but was so far advanced towards culture as to be able to sign his name and rubricate, which means, drawing a complicated flourish, such as many people place under their signature. His rubric was most elaborate, and when he had finished it he looked at it sideways with pride and informed Don Roberto that a signature was good, but that he thought a rubric more authentic.

"Durazno,

"August 5th, 1876.

"MY DEAR MOTHER,—

"Mansel and I are just on the eve of starting to Brazil (Rio), with a lot of horses. If anything turns up and I am wanted homeward, communications must be sent to the English Consul in Rio where I expect to be in about two months—that is to say, if the journey is possible by land. Many people say it is not, so you had better write to old Munroe, the Consul in Monte Video.

"Mansel has been getting some tremendous falls, but by degrees he is becoming more 'gaucho.'

"There has been one incessant rain for the last three weeks, and all the rivers are flooded, or else we should have started some time ago. We have a fine lot of horses, about seventy, some of them pictures of a wild horse, with tails down to the ground and tremendous manes. Mansel is tormented by a desire (which, I am afraid, will cause his early death), to ride some of the wild ones. . . . There was an old German here the other day. He told me: 'Bismarck, I have seen him sentry stand on a bridge in Berlin during thirty years ago.' I thought of George Washington's little hatchet. . . . I should not be afraid of what Sir Walter Raleigh says: 'And be sure of this; thou shalt never find a friend in thy young years whose conditions and qualities will please thee after thou comest to more discretion and judgment.' Neither Mansel nor I being in our young years—except in the ordinary sense of the word—or having, either of us, any discretion or judgment to speak of.

"A Scotsman called Graham stole my horse and *recado* (saddle), the other day, and I had to pay thirty dollars to the *Alcalde* (mayor) before I could get it back again. 'En el más pobre siempre se cae el rayo.'

107

(Lightning always strikes the poorest). A fellow murdered an Italian recently. Of course, they were going to let him off, but every one went and petitioned to have him shot. . . ."

All being ready, and some gaucho assistants being found with difficulty, the usual revolution having drained off the able-bodied men, they made ready for the start, and early one morning, after some trouble with the wilder of their beasts, took to the road.

Days followed one another, and nights still caught them upon horseback, driving or rounding up their horses. Mountains and plains, they passed and rivers fringed with thick, hard, thorny woods; they sweltered in the sun, sat shivering on their horses during the watches of the night, slept fitfully by turns at the camp-fire, ate dried meat (*charquî*), and drank *maté*. Then they emerged on to the plain, which, broken here and there by rivers, slopes towards the southern frontier of Brazil. But as they had been short-handed from the first, the horses had got into bad ways. A nothing startled them, and the bad example of the wild horses they had bought led the others astray, and once or twice they separated, and gave hours of work to bring them back.

Nearing the Brazilian border, they drove to what, in South America, is called a "pass," that is, a ford.

The trail that they followed to the pass was steep and sandy, and cut by the passage of animals into deep ruts. Great cactuses with their flat leaves, white, gaunt and sere, stood here and there, and seemed to guard the road. They had an almost human look, and report said that not long before Don Roberto passed, a band of robbers had stripped themselves, and, standing naked by the whitish stems, were so invisible that they were able quietly to kill some travellers, who rode right into them before they were aware of their presence. Therefore Don Roberto and Mansel rode with care, and now and then hitched their pistols nearer to their hands as they urged on the troop, swinging their whips about their heads, and pressing close upon the horses to prevent their cutting back or separating when they came to the "pass." At fords the horses usually took the water well, and the men stood back to give them space, so that they should not crowd upon each other and get choked.

The animals' heads lay flat upon the stream, their backs made lines in the swift current, their tails spread out, and all swam a little sideways. Their eyes were fixed upon the bank and in their wake a little wave as of a boat washed to the shore. The men stood and gazed, watching a piebald mare, who led the troop.

Just as the men were thinking about entering the stream themselves, having taken off their clothes and piled them on their heads, cinched up their saddles a little forward and hung their boots and pistols round their necks, the spurs inside the boots, one of the peons cried out that the mare was drowning. Don Roberto, saw that the current had swept her on her side. Little by little she appeared to sink, her quarters dropping perpendicularly, and the water creeping up round her neck. For one moment her fore-feet emerged, battling for life, her eyes blue with terror; and then with a loud snort she disappeared.

The men crossed, the water lapping up almost to their mouths at the first plunge, and on the other side, they drove the troop into an open glade, and, dismounting, spread their clothes to dry.

The horses, after rolling, began to feed, guarded by a man who rode naked but for a light poncho. The others sat in the shade and boiled a kettle to make *maté*, in the lee of a fire of smoke wood to keep the flies away. To pass away the time the gauchos, squatting on the ground, discussed revolutions, all the time drawing horse-brands in the dust, with their fingers. Presently, in high-pitched, falsetto voices, they sang a *triste*, and when they were tired of this they merely sat and looked at the horses. Without warning and for some unknown reason, one of them shied at something, and before the gauchos could prevent it, the whole troop set off at a mad gallop.

When the men had got the horses turned and were riding slowly round them with the sun blistering their naked backs, they noticed that their feet were bleeding, for they had mounted barebacked in the hurry of the fright, and ridden through the thorns. However, this was all in a day's work, so no one took much notice.

To the north, the frontier lay, and there the Brazilian Government had guards, but Don Roberto and Mansel, being "business men," intended to smuggle their horses across the border in the night. In order to find a reliable guide they had heard about, and also to see how the land lay, Don Roberto left his companions with the horses, and galloped off to a border village.

Whilst he halted at a *pulpería* (saloon), a Brazilian rider arrived. Spaniards and Portuguese never saw eye to eye and this old hatred still existed between Uruguay and Brazil. (Spanish is spoken in the former country, Portuguese in the latter.)

The Brazilian leapt off his horse and ordered a glass of rum. He left his horse near the door, untied, with the reins thrown down; and when he was about to depart, an Uruguayan policeman told him to hobble his horse, or to tie him up. Without a word, the stranger gathered up his reins, sprang at a bound upon his horse, and, drawing his mother-of-pearl-handled pistol, fired at the policeman almost as he sprang. The shot threw up a shower of sand just in the policeman's face, and probably saved the rider's life. Drawing his pistol, the policeman fired back, but the Brazilian, with a shout, was off like lightning, firing as he rode, and zigzagging across the street. The policeman's shots went wide, and the rider, turning in his saddle, fired again and missed.

By this time men with pistols in their hands stood at the doors of all the huts, but the Brazilian passed so rapidly, throwing himself alternately now on the near side, now on the off side of his horse, hanging by one foot across the croup and holding with the other to the mane, that he presented no mark for them to hit. As he passed the local town hall, where the mayor and his friends were sitting smoking just before the door, he fired with such good aim that a large piece of plaster just above their heads fell, covering them with dust.

Drawing his second pistol and still firing as he went, he dashed out of the village, in spite of shots from every side, his horse bounding like lightning as his great silver spurs ploughed deep into its sides. When he had crossed the border—just as a patrol of cavalry appeared—a band of men from his own side of the border came out to meet him. He stopped, and shouting out defiance to the Uruguayans, drew up his horse, and lit a cigarette.

After a short search, Don Roberto found the guide whom he had come to interview, and towards evening, accompanied by this man—who was a noted smuggler—returned to the place where Mansel and his men were waiting.

Immediately after sundown, the horses were driven ahead once more. The smuggler showed the expedition the way, guiding it by devious paths, through a thick wood to a ford known to him, and only just practicable. This they passed, swimming and wading, and struggling through the mud. The river wound about through beds of reeds, trees grew thickly on the banks, and as the travellers passed, water-hogs snorted; great fish leaped into the air and fell with a resounding crash into the stream, and in the trees was heard the scream of

III

vultures, as, frightened by the passage of men and horses, they rose and weltered heavily through the thick wood.

By morning they were safe in Brazil, passing through a thick cane-brake, where they left several of their best horses, since to pursue them when they straggled was impossible without running the risk of losing all the rest. The crossing of the ford had brought them into another world, for the river had set a barrier between the peoples. True, in Uruguay, especially in the north, many Brazilians had settled, but living amongst the gaucho population, they had adapted themselves to the customs of the land. That is, they practised hospitality after the gaucho fashion, taking no money from the way-faring man for a piece of beef; they lent a horse—usually the worst they had—if one came to their house with one's horse tired; their women showed themselves occasionally; and not being able to hold slaves, they were obliged to adopt a different tone to men in general from that which they practised in Brazil. But in those days, in their own country, they still carried swords, slaves trotted after the rich landowner's horse, the women of the family never sat down to table with the men, and if a stranger chanced to call on business at their house, they were as jealously kept from his eyes as if they had all been Turks.

The *fazenda* (ranch) houses had great iron-studded doors, often a moat, and not infrequently a rusty cannon, a relic of bygone times. The traveller fared much worse than in Uruguay, for save at the large cattle farms it was impossible to buy a piece of meat. Admitted to the house, the traveller rarely passed beyond the guest-chamber: a room with four bare, white-washed walls, having for furniture a narrow hard-wood table with wrought-iron supports between its legs; chairs cut, apparently, out of the solid block, a tin bucket or a large gourd in the corner, with drinking-water; so that his sojourn at the place was generally brief, and his departure a relief to all concerned. Still, on the frontier, the gaucho influence made itself a little felt, and the people were not so inhospitable as they were further in the interior of the land.

Two or three leagues beyond the river there was a little town, towards which Don Roberto and Mansel drove their horses, assisted by their gauchos, who were beginning to be dissatisfied, partly because they disliked travelling in Brazil, and partly because the weather had suddenly turned windy, wet and cold.

Soaked to the skin and without food, they came to a ranch where they spent the night, and twenty-four hours later they were caught out in the open, a south wind blowing, and the rain-drops congealing as they fell. Three of the men, muffled in ponchos, rode round the horses, whilst the others crouched at the fire. Midnight came, the riders rode to the fire, stretched on the wet mud, and tried to sleep, whilst three other men took their places, guarding the horses. Day came at last, and miserable they looked, wet, cold and hungry, the fire out, matches all damp, and nothing else to do but march till the sun rose and made life tolerable. When they came to a hut where they obtained some food, a difficulty cropped up with one of the men. Don Roberto had told him to catch a horse which looked a little wild, but the disgruntled gaucho answered that he was not a horse-breaker, and told Don Roberto to ride the beast himself. This he promptly did, and when he dismounted he sarcastically asked the man if he knew what a wild horse was. Hearing this, everybody laughed, and this so infuriated the bad-tempered gaucho that he drew his knife and rushed at Don Roberto, only to find himself looking down the barrel of a pistol which Mansel with some forethought had produced. This brought things to a crisis; for a few minutes later all the gauchos cantered towards their homeland, leaving the two partners with the troop of horses on their hands.

Several Brazilians having volunteered, they took them, bought a tame horse, accustomed to carry packs, procured a bullock, had it killed and the meat "jerked," and, making bags out of the hide, filled them with food.

So one day told another, and each night found them on horseback, riding round the drove. Through forest, over baking plain, up mountain paths, through marshes, splashing to the saddle-flaps, by lone ranches, and again through herds of cattle dotting the plain for miles, they took their way. Day followed night without adventure, save when a horse suddenly threw its rider and a Brazilian peon uncoiled his lasso, and with a jangling of spurs against the stirrups, sprang into life, and in a moment the long snaky rope flew through the air and settled round the runaway just beneath his ears. Once in a clearing, as they plodded on, they saw a deer jumping into the air, and coming down again on the same spot repeatedly. The Brazilians explained the mystery, saying that the animal was fighting with a snake.

One day, having crossed some hills, they came to a plain at the end of which a little town with flat-roofed houses and sandy streets appeared. At the west corner of the square was situated a store: the chief emporium, mart, and meeting-place of the whole town.

To this commercial centre Don Roberto rode, leaving his partner with the peons riding round the troop of horses in the plain. Dressed as he was, in the clothes worn by the gauchos of Uruguay, he made a blot of colour in the place.

Half an hour's talk with the boss of the store shattered all his plans, for it appeared that to take horses on to Rio was impossible, the country further on being one dense forest; and even if the horses stood the change of climate, the trip would take a year, thus running away with any profit which might be expected. Moreover, it appeared that mules were in demand throughout Brazil, but horses, till five hundred miles ahead, but little valued, and almost as cheap, though much inferior in breed, to those bred on the plains of Uruguay. The boss also told Don Roberto to lose not one day in teaching all the horses to eat salt, for without that they would not live a month, there being in the pasture some malign quality which salt alone would cure. Naturally, being a good business man, he had some excellent cheap salt to sell. After a short council of war, Don Roberto and Mansel decided that the horses were too thin to take them further without a rest, so they set about to find an enclosured pasture where the animals could feed.

After much talk with a retired slave, who was now a mule-dealer, they agreed to pay him a certain sum of money for the use of his fenced pasture, and for their own maintenance during the time they stayed.

This ex-slave was known as "Tío Gancho" (Uncle Hook). Although eighty years of age, he was still a great rider and very active, and, being very amusing and witty, he was famous throughout Southern Brazil. He was an African from Angola, and had arrived in Brazil as a child. When he was a young man, his former owner had broken his two big toes, to make it easier for him to catch the stirrups, and later when the two toes began to resemble hooks, the unfortunate slave was nicknamed "Tío Gancho."

Slaves in Rio Grande were treated well on the whole. Some worked among the cattle, and were relatively free, but the household slaves were often ill-treated.

Finding that the horses, after the long journey and change of water and of grass, daily grew thinner, making it quite impossible to move them forwards or back, and after having vainly tried to sell them, or change them for mules, or sugar, Don Roberto and Mansel, having paid off the peons, settled down to loaf.

Slaves of many hues were to be seen about, the girls

doing but little work, all the time chattering volubly. An official kept, by virtue of his office, a whipping-house, to which slaves who had committed some offence were sent.

So the days passed, and the would-be horse-dealers no longer worried, but just took things as they came. Now and then they rode to a confectioner's shop where they ate cakes, and drank innumerable glasses of sweet Malaga; laid in a store of cigarettes, frequented dances, far and near, joined in cattle-marketings, races, and anything which happened in the place.

Just when all hope was gone, and they thought seriously of leaving the horses to their fate, and pushing on with some of the best of them towards Rio, a man appeared upon the scene and offered to buy them, half for money and half in exchange for silver horse-gear; for he turned out to be a pawnbroker who had an enormous stock of these articles in his house. After much bargaining they closed for three hundred dollars and a lot of silver bridles, spurs, whips and other stuff, after reserving four of the best horses for themselves to make their journey back. At the head of so much capital, their spirits rose, and they determined to push on to Paraguay, crossing the rivers Uruguay and Paraná, and to ride to Asunción (the capital of Paraguay), where Don Roberto had friends.

Among the many old letters I have been fortunate enough to find, he wrote the following to his mother. The paper he wrote on was pink, and the handwriting almost illegible.

> "Cruz Alta,
> "Rio Grande (Brazil),
> "December 27th, 1876.

"MY DEAR MOTHER,—

"Mansel and I have just succeeded in selling the last of our horses, and we are just going to strike the back trail, cheerful, but flat broke. We managed to sell the last of the horses after we had almost lost all hope of ever getting rid of them, on Christmas Day.

"It is exactly four months since I have looked on print, except an old almanac, in Portuguese, that I know by heart now. I could read anything, even to 'Good Wishes,' and would enjoy the stories of the pious corporal, and the Table Talk of all the people in the known world, the Scotch not excepted.

"The Brazilians are the most disagreeable, mean, thievish mendacious lot of brutes I ever came across. Cruz Alta of itself is lively, but the pomposity of the people surpasses all belief. Tell Grandmamma that, although I now speak Portuguese well and quite as fluently as I do French, she shall never hear any more of it from me. Last week we had nine days of praying and singing to herald the anniversary of our 'Blessed Lad's' birth. It was rather amusing, as all sorts of old horses turned up. Here the people are so ignorant that what they don't know would fill a library. (One of those with the 'bookes' in glass cases, and brass wire in front of them. I think there can be litel wisdom in such bookes, or they would not be so closely guarded, wisdom not being so rife.)

"One man asked me if 'aquelle Londres não era parte da Europa.'* I said I thought it was, and then he asked me if 'todo Ingles não sabia alguma coisa de "bosa".'† I was beat, when he put himself into an extraordinary position and explained that 'bosa' was a mode of fighting, practised among the English, and that, after having used the hands for a while, the English were accustomed

---

* If that London was not part of Europe.
† Did not all Englishmen know something about "bosa."

to 'pegar-se um puntapé no rostro.'* I then understood it was 'Boxe Française' he referred to.

"I wish I had Shakespeare with me, but I did not anticipate being so long away. Our clothes are like Robinson Crusoe's, but the horses are in 'grate estate.' We could do nothing but smoke, sleep, bathe and walk, and could not get through the days. I never was so glad to leave any place. It is raining in torrents.

"A lawyer died here the other day. As is usual, they placed his body in an open coffin before the altar. In the morning his body was missing. The people thought the devil (here there are no doubts of his personality), had taken it away. In the meantime it turns out that the lawyer owed a great deal of money, shammed dead, and bolted out of the coffin in the night. . . ."

Don Roberto and Mansel paid their debts, bid good-bye to the friends they had made during their stay in the neighbourhood, and, next day at daybreak, started on the road.

By easy stages they journeyed on, descending gradually towards the River Uruguay, passing through country almost unpopulated. Sometimes they camped at lonely *ranchos* inhabited, in general, by free negroes; or they camped, choosing some little cove in a wood where they tied the horses. Having done this, they built a fire and concocted a vile beverage made of birch leaves. Their food consisted of pieces of hard "jerked" beef which they moistened with orange juice to make it palatable.

After several days' travelling they reached the River Uruguay. Nearly half a mile in breadth, it flowed sluggishly between primeval woods. Over all a darkish vapour hung, blending the trees and water into one, and making the "ferry-boat"—made of inflated hides of oxen—as it laboured

* Give one another a kick in the face.

across to the other side, look like a contraption of another world.

Having ridden through a desert of tall grass for a whole day, they camped by a wood about a quarter of a league from a lonely *rancho*. Just at even-fall they were astonished by the arrival of the owner of the hut, mounted upon a half-wild horse, a spear in his hand, escorted by two ragged sons on half-wild ponies, holding in their hands long canes to which a broken sheep-shear had been fixed with strips of raw-hide. After a formal greeting the man said that the object of his visit was to enquire if Don Roberto and Mansel had seen a tiger which had killed some sheep; but the man's suspicious glance made the travellers think that he suspected them of having designs upon his cattle, and had come to reconnoitre them. However, an offer of some of the vile birch-leaf tea soon made the two parties friends, and after drinking almost a quart of it, the leather-skinned, bearded and long-haired visitor said: "*Muy rico*" (very good), and, together with his two boys, rode back to his hut.

When the two adventurers came to a little town they disposed of their spare horses, bidding them good-bye as if they had been old friends. They then had the other two shod for the first time in their lives, an operation which took the united strength of half a dozen men to achieve, but which was necessary, as their feet, accustomed to the stoneless plains of Uruguay, had suffered greatly in the mountain paths. In this little town, for the first time in many months, the two friends sat down to a good meal, drank wine of a suspicious kind, and almost thought they were in Paris, so great the change from the wilds, and the nights passed in the lone *ranchos* of the hilly district of Brazil.

Ferrying across the River Paraná (there more than a mile broad), they soon found themselves in quite another world. The little Paraguayan town of Ytapua lay upon a plateau above the stream. The houses, built of canes and thatched with straw, differed extremely from the white houses on the other side of the river. The people's dress, the vegetation, and the mode of life, differed still more in every aspect. The Paraguayan, with his shirt hanging outside his white duck trousers, bare feet, and cloak made of red cloth, his broad straw hat and quiet manner, was the complete antithesis of the high-booted, loose-trousered gaucho, with his long knife and swaggering air: the latter a horseman of the plains, the former a footman of the forests.

Here, too, the language changed, and Guaraní became the dominant tongue of the natives, though the Government officials and people of the upper classes spoke Spanish, but with a strange accent.

The wanderers passed two days in Ytapua, resting their horses, and Don Roberto renewed his friendship with the Italian whom during his former visit to Paraguay he had mentioned in a letter to his mother.* He kept a saloon, and, being a born fighter, his delight was when a row occurred, for on such occasions he cleared the place by flinging empty bottles from the bar. A handsome, gentleman like man, but terrible with a bottle in his hand, whether as a weapon of offence or for the purpose of drink; withal well educated and an upright character.

Not far outside the village a butcher had his shop, a little straw-thatched hut, with strings of fresh jerked beef festooning all the place. Whilst talking to the owner, an Argentine gaucho from the southern plains, Don Roberto's eye fell on a fine, dark chestnut horse which stood underneath a shed, saddled and bitted in gaucho style. The animal somehow seemed familiar to him, and the gaucho, seeing him look at the horse, asked if he knew the brand, but Don Roberto answered that he failed to recognise it. Suddenly, however

* See p. 92.

an incident that had happened during his previous trip to Paraguay, three years before, just as he was about to return to England, flashed through his memory.

One night, journeying through a marsh in the company of a German whose only means of communication with Don Roberto was a jargon of Spanish mixed with "Plattdeutsch," they met a gaucho, and as their horses drowned the sound of their approach by splashing with their feet, this sudden meeting startled both parties. Frightened, the gaucho drew his knife, Don Roberto a pistol, and the German lugged out a rusty sword, which he wore stuck through his saddle-girth. However, the first surprise over, explanations followed and no blood was shed, and then the three drew aside to a dry spot where they sat down to smoke cigarettes and have a chat, as travellers often did in those lonely regions. Now, the place where the gaucho said he had come from was a three days' journey distance on an ordinary horse, and as the man said he had come from there that day, Don Roberto and the German wondered why he had ridden his horse so hard and almost incredibly far.

Now, three years later, that is to say when he passed through Ytapua with Mansel, and was talking to the butcher, Don Roberto recognised the horse he had seen that night when he had travelled through the swamp with the German, and just at the same time the butcher recognised Don Roberto. When the two men had shaken hands, the gaucho butcher took Don Roberto aside, and, laughing, said that when, three years before, they had met in the marsh, he was "retreating," having killed a man. On that occasion, his horse (a dark chestnut), had covered a three days' journey in less than one day, and later, when the storm had blown over and the murder was forgotten, the gaucho settled down and became a butcher in the settlement.

Continuing their return journey towards Buenos Aires,

Don Roberto and Mansel struck right through the then desolated regions known as Misiones; skirting by forests where red macaws hovered like hawks and parrots chattered, they passed through open plains, or splashed for hours through wet marshes. Finally they reached Asunción where, after having visited Dr. Stewart and Don Roberto's old favourite horse, "Bunny," they awaited the arrival of a Brazilian mail-boat.

Both Don Roberto and Mansel were sorry when they had to part with their horses, which they sold to Dr. Stewart. Two days later the companions were on board the primitive vessel, slowly steaming down the sluggish yellow river, on their way back to Buenos Aires—not richer, but wiser for the disappointing experiences they had had.

CHAPTER VI

CLARAZ'S hostelry in Buenos Aires was still flourishing,
and "camp men" continued to make it their headquarters when they came into the city to spend their
hard-earned money.

Until funds arrived from England, Don Roberto and Mansel
stayed at Claraz's, the former doing a great deal of reading
whilst the latter preferred to mix and make merry with those
who "painted the town red."

A "camp man" who happened to be in town, informed Don
Roberto that his old revolutionary companion, Angel Cabrera,
was still roaming about in the Province of Entre Ríos, so he
promptly made efforts to communicate with him.

Some time passed, and then money arrived from England,
and Don Roberto and Mansel were just making final preparations to set out towards the Indian frontier in the South when
Cabrera appeared. He still looked exactly as he had when
Don Roberto first met him in the camp of the revolutionary
soldiers in Entre Ríos, and when asked what he had been
doing with himself since the trip to Paraguay with horses, he
gave one of his usual answers, that is, he quoted a favourite
gaucho saying: "The cow which does not roam from one

region to another, never gets fat." The first greetings over, and Cabrera duly introduced to Mansel, the unexpected visitor said that he had heard all about Don Roberto's plans to settle in the South, and that he had brought with him an old friend who was looking for a job. The man, Cabrera explained, was waiting outside the hostelry, and before he called him in to introduce him to his future *patrones*, he said that they would find him most useful, the man being a great *rastreador*, that is, a track-reader. (Such men—who came from the North—were often employed to track down strayed animals. They could perform feats that Europeans would look on as impossible. The best came from the upper provinces, some of which have difficult names, such as Catamarca, Jujuy, Rioja, etc. Highlanders are known as "arribeños," "arriba," meaning "high" or "above.")

As Don Roberto and Mansel followed Cabrera to be introduced to the *rastreador*, he whispered with a meaning wink that his good and trusty friend had left his beloved home-regions after a slight bother with the authorities, due to a minor incident he had had with a friend who did not see eye to eye with him. "The poor fellow died," Cabrera said, sadly shaking his head, and then added with a sigh: "When a poor man goes on a spree, something is sure to turn out wrong with him."

The *rastreador* was a fine-looking gaucho, about thirty years of age. When he expressed his willingness to accompany Don Roberto wherever he went, his services were immediately accepted.

Near Tandil, about two hundred miles south of Buenos Aires, Don Roberto and Mansel bought cattle and horses which they intended to drive down towards a region near Bahia Blanca where they intended to set up a ranch.

Whilst they were buying cattle, a number of their horses were stolen. "Let us mount," the *rastreador* said, after he had walked about smoking a black cigarette without, apparently, having looked at anything. Followed by a few gauchos who had been hired to help drive the cattle, the *rastreador* galloped across the pampa, stopping every now and again to say what the thieves had done at certain spots.

After having ridden many leagues, without being in the slightest aware how the human bloodhound in front recognised certain tracks among the masses to be seen everywhere, he rode into a village where he stopped in front of the house belonging to the local judge, in whose corral, behind the house, the missing horses were found. Needless to say, the judge told a most dramatic story about how he had taken the animals from some cattle thieves, and, after having accepted a "tip" for his service, Don Roberto and his men drove the troop away. The track-reader—who had been as silent as an owl in the daytime, since he had tracked down the horses—suddenly startled his companions by saying: "The judge may know something about our laws, but he knows nothing about tracks, for just here I can see where he dismounted to tighten the girth of his bay which was in the corral with our horses. He had four men with him when he passed here with the stolen animals, and two of those men were sitting with him, drinking *maté*, just as we rode up to his house."

Having bought as many animals and other necessaries as they could afford, the expedition set out towards Bahia Blanca. First they traversed the southern section of the prairie of Buenos Aires, between the mountains of Tandil, with their famous landmark, a huge balancing rock, resembling a gigantic mushroom.

The suffocating north wind blew hot and fatiguing. Nothing to break the brown eternity of the pampa but here and there a green *ombú* tree, like an umbrella, or a straggling line of pampas grass, which marked the edges of some watercourse. If by any chance travellers approached in the opposite direction, the cattle and horses were driven together. Holding their pistols or long knives, some of the men advanced, halted a stone's throw off the strangers, and shouted their salutations. If all seemed right, they then advanced and asked for news about Indians, for all the country had been laid waste, the houses burnt, men killed, and women and cattle carried off, about a week before. The few houses Don Roberto and Mansel came to were still smouldering, and the bodies of the owners lay near them, swollen horribly and festering in the sun.

The travellers had to beware of "smokes" (the Indians' smoke signals), and whenever they came to little hills, they dismounted and crawled up to scan the horizon well before they descended.

One evening they reached what, in those days, was called a "fort," that is, the place had a shallow ditch all round it, and the house had a flat roof, on which was a rusty cannon.

A strong corral of hard-wood posts, all bound together with strips of hide, and a few posts to fasten horses to, formed the outworks of the place. The latter posts marked the boundary to which wayfaring men, if not fools, could venture on their horses. To pass beyond these posts uninvited, especially at night, exposed one to the chance of a casual shot, or, at the least, to the assaults of a pack of dogs. In those days it was customary to approach any ranch slowly, and, still sitting on one's horse, to clap the hands and at the same time to call: "Ave María!" Attracted by the noise, the owner would then come out, and when he was satisfied that there was no danger, he would say *"Sin pecado concebido"* (conceived without sin). Religion and politeness being thus satisfied, the traveller was asked to dismount, to tie up his horse, and to enter the kitchen where he could seat himself on a horse's skull beside the fire.

Outside the fort where Don Roberto, Mansel and their men arrived they saw many horses which were tied to wheels of bullock-carts, to posts, to tufts of grass and bones half buried in the ground. It puzzled the travellers why, after an invasion of the Indians, so many people had come to visit the place.

Soon the owner came out, asking the tired wayfarers to dismount, and recommending that they hobble the bell-mare and carefully tie up a horse. After minute inquiries as to the health of every man's family (of whom he knew no member), he said: "We have *un angelito* (a little angel), in our poor house; that is, his body, for his soul is with the blest." (In those days, whenever a child died, it was the signal for a dance.)

In a long, low room, lit by a score of candles, made of tin-moulds, and smoking blackly, were assembled some fifty people, gauchos, ranchers, a Basque or two, and the ubiquitous Italian with his organ, who in those days used to pervade the pampa.

The women (in many cases only dressed in a cotton gown) sat, when not dancing, in rows on chairs along the wall, waiting patiently for any man to dance with them.

The *angelito*, dressed in his best clothes, sat in a chair upon a table, greenish in colour, and with his hands and feet hanging down limply—horrible, but at the same time fascinating. Over his head a cheap Italian lithograph of the Madonna hung by a strip of hide from a deer's horn stuck into the wall. On either side a pious and frightful German print, one of the Prodigal amongst his swine, another flanking it setting him forth in better circumstances, seated in pomp between two German ladies, monstrously fair and fat.

Just underneath the *angelito*, sat an old gaucho playing the guitar with a fatuous air with which musicians in countries such as South America invest their trade. Two or three men of the richer classes, as their silver-handled knives and spurs made plain, smoked in a knot apart; whilst in a corner sat some old men talking of horses' marks, and illustrating any difficulty by "painting" the mark in question on the table with their finger dipped in gin.

The younger people danced various pretty native dances, or one of those slow valses with much balancing of hips affected by the South Americans. Evidently they had been drinking to the fair passage of the new angel into the realms of bliss. Above the rasping music, the rattle of the dancers' spurs was heard, and now and then the man at the guitar broke into a shrill falsetto song, in which the company took part. Stretched on a crude camp-bed lay a man wrapped in his poncho, with a deep lance-wound in the groin, given by an Indian a few days before. To keep the blood in, and in order to heal his wound, he ate great pieces of beef cooked in the hide, and smoked incessantly.

On passing opposite the body, the girls occasionally snatched loose their hands from the clutches of their partners and crossed themselves, and then, as if ashamed of thus indulging in a religious exercise in public, broke into laughter.

At pampas stores, the owner sometimes begged or bought the body of a child just dead, to use it as an *angelito* to attract the country people to revel at his store. The body was put in a cool, dark room to keep it from the flies, and was brought out at night. Where this peculiar custom came from—whether from Europe or from the Indians—seems to be unknown.

As Don Roberto and Mansel proceeded south with their cattle they had ample opportunity to see what an Indian raid meant, and although they heard many rumours about the chief Namuncurá and his hordes of fierce Tehuelche Indians, they forged ahead until they arrived at their destination.

The ranch they had bought was known as "Sauce Chico" (Little Willow). The house had been burnt down by Indians in a former raid, and the owner, who had managed to escape, was only too glad when he found someone who was willing to buy the ruins.

For some time everything went well with the new settlers.

The gauchos rebuilt the house, the old stockade was mended and strengthened, the ditch surrounding the place was dug deeper and wider, and the cattle thrived. Soon other settlers began to arrive in the region, and, as the Indians had retreated south, beyond the Rio Negro, peace and a golden future seemed assured.

Cabrera—who had been appointed foreman of the "Sauce Chico" ranch—was the life and soul of the place. Everybody, far and near, knew him as a courteous, kindly man who could ride even the most rebellious horse. During idle hours he often played on a cracked guitar, occasionally stopping to recite a gaucho saying. He was, however, as obstinate as a mule, and could never see a stray, unbranded animal without putting the "Sauce Chico" brand on it. (In Western Texas such an animal was called a Maverick, after a certain Colonel Maverick, who, as the legend goes, looked on all animals as potentially his own.)

The neighbours used to laugh and said that either the grass in Don Roberto's camp was the sweetest in the whole district or else his foreman used a *lazo* made from the hide of a very long cow.

"Justice, but not in my house," says the proverb, and as Don Roberto knew her to be blind, and half suspected her of deafness in most cases, he did not wish to fall into her hands. So when a good-sized calf or colt, with the skin peeling off a half-healed brand upon its hip, mysteriously appeared amongst his animals, he used to lecture Cabrera on the error of his ways.

The foreman promised faithfully, swearing upon his children's heads (he had seven of them, somewhere), that he would never lift a lawless *lazo* on an animal again during the whole of his life.

Don Roberto doubted that Cabrera took him for a fool, for the foreman was one of those who, had he owned even a yoke of oxen, would soon have had a plentiful supply of calves from them. So, in despite of all that Don Roberto could say, he found his cattle and his colts increasing mightily, especially when he had been away for a month or two.

When Don Roberto remonstrated and reproached him for having broken faith, Cabrera used to look at him with a sly glance out of his eye, just as a mule that kicks at the stirrup as you are mounting him, and say: "If a man happens to be born with a big belly, it is of little use to bind a sash round it." So with the best grace Don Roberto could assume he let him ride his hobby, recognising how difficult it is to teach old dogs new tricks.

The two partners might have ended their careers as great cattle kings for men have lived, who, starting life from just as small beginnings as theirs in the Argentine, finished up millionaires, but with this difference, that they required no foreman to brand other people's cattle for them. Fate, however, willed otherwise.

After some months of peace, when Prosperity began to smile upon the brave settlers, rumours of a new Indian invasion reached "El Sauce Chico."

The chief "Namuncurá" of the Tehuelches, and the chief "Catriel" of the Pampas Indians, had crossed the Rio Negro to concentrate their savage hordes near Bahia Blanca, then just a small mud fortress with a ditch round it.

Occasionally the Indians broke in among the ranches, spreading terror among the settlers. All but the chiefs (who had saddles) rode upon sheep-skins, carrying lances of bamboo, fifteen to twenty feet in length. Fastened to the shaft, just underneath the blade or point made of hard-wood or iron, was a tuft of horse-hair, an ornament which looked like a human scalp.

Each warrior led a spare horse, taught to run beside him, thus leaving the rider's hand free for the spear.

When charging, the Indians now and again struck their hands upon their mouths to make their war-cry, a loud prolonged "Ah, ah, ah—a—a" or "Hee, hee, hoo—oo——," more wild and terrifying.

Each warrior carried round his waist two or three sets of *bolas*. Many had long knives or swords, which, as a rule, they shortened—for convenience of carriage—to about the length of a bayonet, wearing them stuck through a narrow woollen sash made by their women. All the warriors were smeared over with a coat of ostrich grease, though never painted. Their fierce cries and strong smell were terrifying to horses used to white men, making them mad with fear.

More than once Don Roberto found himself alone upon the plains when he saw the ostriches and deer running, or dust arise without a cause. On such occasions he hurried his horse to a hollow where he muffled up the animal's head in a poncho to stop him neighing. Then, covering his own head with grass, in order to make himself invisible even to the eagle eyes of the Indians, he watched them pass in the distance, almost holding his breath until the rumble of the horses' feet had died away in the far distance. With his heart thumping, he cautiously stole up the hollow, and, if all was clear, leapt on his horse and touched him with the spurs to make him race, brushing through the high grasses with a noise as of a boat crashing through reeds. When he came to a house he shouted: "Los Indios!" a cry which brought every man running to the door.

Quickly the tame horses would be driven up and shut in the corral; all the old arms loaded and furbished up; for the gauchos of the south had nothing but an old blunderbuss, or a pair of flint-lock pistols.

The Indians themselves, having no arms but spears and *bolas*, were seldom formidable, except on the plain. A little ditch, not five feet deep and eight or ten across, kept a house safe from them. As they never left their horses, they could not cross it, and as they came to plunder, not especially to kill, they wasted little time upon such places, unless they knew that there were young and handsome women shut up in the house. "Christian girl, she more big, more white than Indian," they would say, and woe betide the unlucky girl who fell into their hands!

Hurried off to the *toldos* (tents)—often a hundred leagues away—white women fell, if young and pretty, to the chiefs. If not, they had to do the hardest kind of work; but in all cases, unless they gained the affections of their captor, their lives were made a burden by the Indian women, who beat them and otherwise ill-used them on the sly.

Such were the Indians on the war-path, in regions that were then deserted, or, at the best, roamed over by herds of wild horses.

A chain of forts was supposed to hold the Indians in check; but in reality did little, as they slipped through to plunder whenever they felt like it.

Their skins were of a coppery colour, they were not tall, but well proportioned, all but their legs, which were invariably bowed by their lives passed on horseback from their youth. Both sexes wore their hair long, cut square across the forehead and hanging down the back, and both had rather flat and brutal faces, and all the men had restless eyes, perpetually fixed on the horizon as if they lived in fear.

When the Tehuelche and the Pampas Indians were joined by the fierce Araucanians and the Ranqueles, raids became more frequent and dangerous. Twice "El Sauce Chico" was attacked, but on both occasions the savages were successfully beaten off.

In the South Pampa, below Bahia Blanca, within a three days' ride from Don Roberto's and Mansel's ranch, upon a stony ridge, stood a low, gnarled and twisted tree. This tree was a famous landmark, and was known as the "Gualichu Tree."* Gualichu was the evil spirit of the Indian tribes, and no native ever passed this tree without offering something, hanging his gift to the spirit on one of the branches. Later the gauchos did as the Indians had done before them, until the Gualichu tree looked like a sort of everlasting Christmas tree, adorned with bits of cast-off saddlery, ostrich feathers, empty bottles, old bridles, stirrups, lance-heads and all the flotsam and jetsam of roaming gauchos and Indians who offered to their deity only those articles useless to themselves.

After Indian raids, human heads, a hand or a foot, were hung on the tree, and sometimes a long tress of hair, cut from some captive Christian woman's head.

An ostrich-hunter who had hired himself to carry mail-bags to the furthest settlements in the south, offered up his life beneath the boughs of the Gualichu tree.

As all the country which he travelled was exposed to Indian raids, and as he generally, when chased, had to throw off his saddle and escape barebacked, by degrees he found it too expensive to make good the saddles he had lost. So all the 250 miles he rode barebacked, use having made him part and parcel of the horse.

An ostrich hunter from his youth up, aware that one day he would die the ostrich-hunter's death, by hunger, thirst, or by an Indian's lance, well did he know the great green inland sea of grass in which men used to sleep with their faces set towards the way they had to go, knowing that he who lost the trail had forfeited his life, unless by a hard lucky chance he reached an Indian camp, there to become a slave.

One day, between the first well and the Rio Colorado, the mail-carrier's horse must have tired with him, for a track-reader discovered afterwards that he had made for the second

---

* Darwin mentions this tree, close to which he camped. The tree was famous all over the South Pampa, from Tandil to Patagones.

well which was dry. Then, after long hours of thirst, he must have sighted the Gualichu Tree, and made for it, and, having hung his mail-bag on it to keep it safe, wandered about and waited for relief. Then, his last cigarette smoked, and thrown aside, he had sat down stoically to meet the ostrich-hunter's fate.

His horse had struggled on, instinctively, a league or two, making for the distant Rio Colorado. Like his master, the animal had done his best, but the track-reader found the noble beast in a circle of brown withered grass, which the last dying struggle of a horse makes.

Both Don Roberto and Mansel had several narrow escapes from Indians, and one night they lost most of their cattle, which were driven off by the savages. The two friends were seriously thinking about giving up the ranch when a prospective settler arrived, and offered them a good sum of money for the place. They did not waste time, and as soon as the deal had been settled, packed a few possessions on horses, and, together with Cabrera, set out towards Buenos Aires.

One night, whilst they were sleeping under the southern stars, the horses—which were staked down near them—became restive, and, upon listening, the three travellers heard the trampling of many hoofs. Indians were approaching. Hastily the three men leapt on their horses, barebacked, leaving the other animals, saddles and belongings behind, and raced hell for leather towards a tiny fortified settlement, called Mar del Plata. They were hardly inside the stockade when the Indians came on, yelling and brandishing their spears. When a small brass cannon was fired, the attackers kept at a respectful distance, and finally disappeared into the night. In those days Mar del Plata (to-day a luxurious seaside resort) consisted of a few huts, and two or three primitive stores. A few soldiers were stationed there, and occasionally seal-fishers called at the settlement.

Following the coast—which was safer than the interior—the three travellers arrived in Buenos Aires. Cabrera returned to his roaming life, and Don Roberto and Mansel were so hard up that, until funds arrived from England, they joined a gang of road-builders, and worked in the outskirts of the town. This they did, partly, to occupy themselves, and partly for adventure. In due time the two companions decided to cross the river to Uruguay and to go into the cattle business.

When they arrived, there was great excitement in that country, for a railroad was being extended to new parts. The workmen had to be armed because people stole the rails and sleepers to make corrals.

The two friends were doing quite well in the cattle business when Don Roberto received news that his father's health was failing badly. Thus, just when—for the first time in his life—Dame Fortune smiled upon him, he had to hurry away from the lands which, in spite of the hardships and disappointments he had suffered there, he had grown to love.

For some time Mansel continued to do very well in the cattle business, and later went to Buenos Aires where he made a great deal of money on the Stock Exchange; but finally lost it all. When his mother died he returned to England, where, with the inheritance of the family estate, he became a country squire. Until his death—at the age of seventy—he continued to drink heavily, and whenever Don Roberto visited him, and asked what he would do if he could start his life over again, Mansel always answered: "I'd drink less, and I'd pay more attention to the ladies."

For several years Cabrera used to write to Don Roberto, that is, he got a Basque who was the owner of the nearest saloon to do it for him.

Droughts, floods, dances, Indian incursions, locusts and the like Don Roberto learned of after he had laboriously spelled out the Basque's calligraphy and phonetic rendering of the tongue.

These letters ceased after one saying that certain malicious people had falsely spread a rumour that Cabrera killed his neighbour's cows on nights without a moon. "You know my heart," he wrote, "and how repugnant to my sense of honour such a deed would be. Moreover, such things are difficult to prove, for were a man to demean himself to such an action, he would be sure to cut the brand out of the hide and certainly on his way home would lead his horse on the bed of some stream or other, to cover up the trail."

That was the last Don Roberto ever heard of his old foreman, Cabrera.

CHAPTER VII

EARLY in 1878 Don Roberto was home once more. Doctors had been unable to do anything for his father, whose old injury, caused by the accident in the hunting field, grew more and more serious. The splinter of his skull affected his mental condition to such an extent that, at times, he was not responsible for his actions. Finally the family decided to send him to a shooting lodge where he was looked after by a trusty old man-servant who was the only person whom the invalid obeyed.

His wife had taken a house in London where she spent most of her time, for Gartmore was too big and gloomy a place for a solitary lady to live in.

The re-union of mother and son was a happy one, but after having spent a few weeks, attending to family matters, going to theatres, and visiting old friends, Don Roberto again grew restless. His mother—who was intelligent and understanding—advised him to go to Paris for a while, and there to mix in intellectual circles—with which she was well acquainted—as well as to practise the art of fencing.

Accordingly, Don Roberto once more returned to Paris, where he took fourth place in an international fencing contest in which the crack swordsmen of France, Italy and other countries competed. (Whenever Don Roberto spoke to me about this contest he said: "I only managed to take fourth place.") Unable to stay in one place for long, he then decided to go to Spain and, incidentally, to visit his brother Charles, who happened to be stationed at Gibraltar. The interest Don Roberto always took in Spain and her history, is clearly shown in the following extract from a letter written whilst cruising along the Spanish coast on his brother's ship.

"With the Fleet, North of Vigo.
"June 21st, 1878.

". . . After seeing the north of Spain, I begin to understand Pizarro and Cortes better than I did. . . . The northern Spaniard, tho' not nearly so amusing, is much more of a man for a colonist or soldier than a Southerner . . ."

From Spain Don Roberto once more returned to Paris, where he had many friends and interests. One day he rode a horse which gave him a certain amount of trouble, and when the animal suddenly began to prance about wildly, it nearly knocked over a young lady who happened to be near. Don Roberto immediately dismounted to apologise, and, being somewhat embarrassed, he inadvertently spoke to her in Spanish. To his surprise and delight she answered in the same language, and then, for a while, the two chatted and arranged to meet again next day. As this was a case of love at first sight, things happened quickly.

The dark-haired and soft grey-blue-eyed young lady, whose name was Gabrielle de la Balmondière, was eighteen years of age. Born in Chile, of a French father and a Spanish mother, she had, as a child of twelve, come to Paris, where her aunt had put her in a convent. When Don Roberto heard that she was unhappy and lonely, he did not think twice, and suggested that she elope with him to England. No sooner said than done, and thus it happened that, a few days later, without the knowledge of Don Roberto's family, or of

Gabrielle's aunt, the two lovers contracted marriage in a London Registry office, on the 24th of October, 1878, Don Roberto being twenty-six years of age at the time, and his newly-wed wife just nineteen.

How surprised Mrs. Bontine must have been when her son suddenly appeared with a wife is best left to imagination. Although she did not approve of the marriage, and the informal manner in which it had been contracted, she was much too tactful to express her opinion to her son, but, finding his youthful wife most intelligent and charming, she received her kindly, though evidently with a certain reservation.

Gabrielle, having spent her early youth in Chile, spoke Spanish fairly well, but not correctly, nor without some difficulty, for her parents had always conversed in French, which, therefore, was her parental tongue. Where and how she learnt English is unknown to me. When she met Don Roberto in Paris, she had a remarkable knowledge of this language which, however, she spoke with a slight accent, neither French nor Spanish, but most attractive and charming, as foreign accents sometimes can be, especially with ladies.

The Gartmore estate had been badly neglected for some years, and therefore Don Roberto and his youthful wife decided to spend their honeymoon on the old family estate, where a great deal of work had to be done.

Gartmore stands at the point where the Lowlands end, and the great jumble of the Highland hills begins. The house itself, buried in the woods, stood lonely, and grass grew rank in the avenues when the couple arrived.

During the evenings, and until late at night, the two lovers sat in a long, low Georgian room where they talked about business, adventures in far-away lands, and, probably, about the future, whilst from the walls, likenesses of ancestors, painted by Reynolds and Raeburn, seemed to look down and listen to the conversation. In the corridors and in the hall were many curiosities from South America: whips, spurs, lassos, guns and the saddle Don Roberto had used in his long and perilous journeys.

Don Roberto and his wife, a studious woman, but yet with an adventurous strain, lived quietly as was befitting to their narrow circumstances, due to the fall in agricultural values, which, in those days, had just begun. Time often hung a little heavy on their hands, especially during the long spells of rain which visit Scotland.

At such times, when old favourites had been read, re-read, and put away, the two went into the drawing-room where, with their dogs about them, they sat in the semi-darkness, watching the half-green logs of wood seethe and splutter in the grate, and listened to the low belling of roe-deer, and the hooting of owls outside.

As the power of attorney was still in Major Bontine's hands, Don Roberto could do but little, and so, finally, disheartened by the prospects of the future, but determined to save the family estate, he and Gabrielle decided to try their luck in Texas, where, according to rumours and reports, fortunes could be made quickly.

Accordingly, with the necessary capital to start a ranch, they sailed from Liverpool during the month of April, 1879.

The following extracts from the first letter, written after having arrived in his new "Land of Hope," are typical for their keen observation, sarcasm and wit.

> "City Hotel,
> "New Orleans.
> "May 10th, 1879.

"My dear Mother,—

"We arrived here yesterday, having had a splendid passage with not a rough day all the way. It is very hot, but New Orleans is lovely though quite flat. The trees

GABRIELLE DE LA BALMONDIÈRE

[Portrait by Jacomb Hood; Hands by Whistler.

are splendid; all the town needs is a few white Spanish
houses. The wooden houses are all very well, but as soon
as a rich citizen builds a mansion, the old Anglo-Saxon
vulgarity steps in, and Ionic columns, with Doric capitals,
the whole finished with a Gothic (strangulated) spire, is
the order of the day.

"This is a completely ruined place. Before the war it
was the rival of New York, and had about six hundred
thousand inhabitants, but now there are only one hundred
and eighty thousand. The town covers an immense
extent of ground, and the magnolias and oleander, etc.,
are splendid.

"I think here one realises the South more than anywhere (I mean in opposition to the Northern States) long,
lank faces abound, feet are elevated (on chair), high
above the head, and everyone chews. To speak to they
are decidedly better than the northern people. There is
no enormous quantity of 'Nigs' to be seen in the streets.
Quite as much French as English seems to be spoken.

" 'The Brownsville boat, Sir, sails on Thursday, Sir,
and takes about three days.' Thence, I think, my next
move will be to Hidalgo, about eighty miles off.

"The horses are not good here, but the mules are very
fine. I shall like horses out here, as it is too hot to
walk . . . I see the Boers have sent a petition for freedom. Please write to Post Office, Brownsville, and tell me
all about the Grand Vizier and his little wars . . . The
British Sabbath reigns here with all its accustomed horror
and want of charity. When I add that the principal
church (I have not yet seen the Roman Catholic cathedral)
has a yellow Gothic door, with sham iron clasps on it, I
think you will understand the extreme respectability of
the city . . ."

The next letter I found, was written in Brownsville, Texas, and is dated June 2nd, 1879.

"We have been here about a week, after the most awful passage from New Orleans via little flat-bottomed steamboat. The people are a little like the gauchos, but do not wear long hair, nor do they dress in any particular kind of costume. The only curious thing they wear is a hat with a large band of silver and flowers embroidered on it. There are about four hundred soldiers here, all very well mounted, but I should think they were about as effective as the Trades Union in Zululand.

"I am trying to get a small place for breeding mules, from a man called Casimiro Tomazo, a curious old chap who speaks just like a gaucho. There is a good wooden house on the property, and also a garden, which is a great thing.

"Matamoros, a large Mexican town of about 15,000 (souls), is about a mile from here, on the other side of the Rio Grande. It is very picturesque, the *plaza* and streets quite Spanish, the same aimless officers, in red trousers, wandering listlessly about with a burnt-out cigarette in their mouths, wondering whether either the Government will ever pay their arrears of pay (due eighteen months), or if they will meet a friend with a match about him. In either case they are quite resigned; in the one to steal the first box of matches they can find, and in the other to rob the first person handy of a dollar, 'for God's sake.' To go to Matamoros is like getting into another world. The people all ride about on good horses and silver-mounted saddles, while here, in Brownsville, the hair rope and old moke is all they afford. It is, however, far too dangerous on the other side of the Rio Grande, to think of living there . . ."

Brownsville had a bad reputation in those days, for, being near the frontier, it was a favourite haven for outlaws, "road agents," gamblers and other undesirable characters.

Having investigated the possibilities and prospects offered by a mule-breeding establishment, and after a "serious incident with a certain gentleman who came out second best," as Don Roberto modestly put it, he decided to try his luck in another place from where he wrote the following letters, to friends and to his family:

"Corpus Christi, Texas.
"June 17th, 1879.

". . . We left Brownsville as it was too uncivilised a place to live in. This is a quiet little town on the sea. A large portion of the people are Mexicans, and are the pleasantest half of the population to deal with.* I am addressed, habitually, as 'Judge,' and have a very commanding aspect with the revolver you gave me. My horse here is a black one, as ugly as possible, with most of his tail eaten off by the cows, but he is a good beast, and came up from the frontier very well. Almost all the way, we travelled through sandy desert, and although the country is said to be dangerous, we only saw a prairie wolf or two. If you see Mr. R . . . , please tell him there is a good opening for a barrister in Corpus Christi, if he is a good shot, swimmer and horseman . . ."

"Corpus Christi, Texas.
"June 17th, 1879.

". . . We left Brownsville on account of its being too dangerous a place for settling in, as it is so near the

---

* In the U.S.A. Mexicans were known as "greasers," because many worked as stevedores in American ports (chiefly in California). As there was a great deal of grease on the hides, the Mexican labourers' clothes and bodies were covered with this evil-smelling substance, and therefore they were nicknamed "greasers."

Mexican frontier. Corpus Christi is on the sea, and, like in Brownsville, most of the people are Mexicans, but they are much quieter than on the frontier.

"I think there is a street here that would lay over anything on 'Red Dog.' It is very like one of Bret Harte's places—the same loafers, horses, Mexicans, etc., and the same intermixture of Germans and French. If this is *cuerpo de Cristo, donde esta enterrado el alma del licenciado?**

"My horse came up the hundred and sixty miles of almost desert country very well indeed, and now he is eating outside the window. 'Jack,' a stray little dog I adopted in Brownsville, came about fifty leagues and then had to be brought in the stage coach.

"Texas is not nearly so nice as the River Plate, but some of the old Mexicans are very much like the gauchos. Most of the land about here belongs to two men, King and Kennedy, both of whom came here without a cent. Both, I believe, are unmitigated rascals, but, of course, 'a mask of gold hides all the deformities,' or, perhaps, as it is Texas we live in, 'a lasso of gold . . .'

"The first time I ever heard myself addressed as 'Judge' was the other day when a mulatto said to me: 'I reckon, Judge, that's a right lively-looking horse of yours.' Please tell F . . . a coyote is the image of him: half bold, half timid, yet lazy all through.

"There are about ten different 'choches' [churches] here; all hating one another for the love of God, in the usual style . . ."

Together with Gabrielle, Don Roberto inspected land in the neighbourhood of Corpus Christi, for he felt sure that by breeding a superior type of horse, a great deal of money

* A sarcastic remark about the name "Corpus Christi," difficult to translate into English.

could be made. For some time, also, he took an interest in a proposed shipping concern which, however, came to nothing.

The letters he wrote from Corpus Christi show how keenly he observed things, and that, although he had travelled in far-away lands ever since he had been a mere boy, he took an interest in, and kept in touch, with art, literature and even international politics.

> "Corpus Christi, Texas.
> "July 25th, 1879.
>
> ". . . Here it is awfully hot. There has been no rain for eight months . . . The horses are not so strong as in the River Plate . . . What a disgraceful affair the Zulu war seems to be turning into, a sort of perpetual 'Battle of the Spens.' On what date was Lord Sir Wolseley advertised to appear in Pieter Maritzburg? Did it state in the posters if he was under the distinguished patronage of Mrs. Victoria Guelph, her Grand Vizier and all the nobility?
>
> "I enclose a scrap, culled from the *Galveston News*, 'a "dimokrat" publication, Sir.' "

The cutting Don Roberto enclosed reads:

> "Mr. Henry Irving, the tragedian, has given a chain which he has worn in *Hamlet* for a hundred representations to an enthusiastic lady admirer, who sent him another in exchange. This, too, is to be given to somebody after a hundred wearings. The exchange from which we glean this information does not name the 'enthusiastic lady admirer,' but we suspect it is the Baroness Burdett-Coutts, who for many years has sent Mr. Irving a cheque for fifty guineas ($262), every time he has a benefit. The chain business is an advertising

dodge worthy of the actor. If he would confine himself
to such trifles the public would excuse him; but when he
takes, as he constantly does, unwarrantable liberties with
the sacred text of Shakespeare, well—'the judicious
grieve.' "

Don Roberto continues his letter:

"Words are inadequate for the citizens about here;
their meanness, hypocrisy and assassination being beyond
bounds. I don't believe in Italy, in the Middle Ages,
there was so much assassination as there is in Texas
to-day. Every day one or two persons are murdered, and
such a thing as a fair fight is unknown. If you enquire
how So-and-so was killed you are told: 'I guess, Sir, he
waited for him in the chaparral, and shot him in the
back, Sir.'

"The Baptist is the most prevalent form of Christianity.

"Two Texans, called respectively 'Broncho Bill' and
Sam (cognomen unknown. 'Broncho' is only an
'aguomen'), met on opposite sides of a river. Being unable
to shake hands, Broncho remarked: 'Say, Sam, it's a pity
we can't shake hands. Let's go down-stream a bit, and
have a friendly shot at one another.' At the first fire, Sam
called out: 'Hello, ol' man, you've broke the pummel of
my saddle!'

" 'Demmit!' remarked Broncho, 'you went better than
that; you got about two inches into my left arm. Well,
old fellow, good-bye, tell the folks at home I met you and
we had a good time together . . .' "

"Corpus Christi.
"August 3rd, 1879.
" . . . I am thinking of moving to San Antonio, as this

146

place is not very healthy, and is rather dangerous to live in. (You must remember I have my wife with me.) 'Times' are very bad, worse than ever. I saw them at their worst in the River Plate. The country is very ugly, all covered with dense scrub, and not such a thing as an open pampa. The people, of all the people I ever came across, are revolting and mean to a degree. The Mexicans are the only redeeming feature; and they are not, strictly speaking, agreeable, as they are chiefly thieves and murderers exiled from Mexico. However, they are civil to speak to.

"The frightful wooden houses are most repulsive, and I long to see some of the white Spanish houses of the River Plate. They say San Antonio is the most endurable place in Texas. The ruins of the old Missions are there. I wish I had gone down to Mexico instead of coming into Brownsville.

"My horse is getting very fat. Horses are cheap here, as cheap as in the River Plate, but on the average a little smaller, and not so strongly built.

"Corpus Christi is not adapted for shipping, as the harbour only admits small schooners. In fact, all down the coast the harbours are bad, and the Norther very violent one time of year. Therefore, unless shipping were started on very favourable terms, I don't think it would succeed.

"Sarah Bernhardt, indeed, seems to be spoilt. I wonder what language she is to act in in America, as French is not much understood.

"I suppose the Afghan affair is over by this time. What a curious turn things seem to be taking in Egypt . . .

"There are many people near here who 'have got religion'—Methodist form—and really seem as if they worshipped God for spite . . ."

(The rest of this letter is quite illegible, owing to age and difficult handwriting, but, apparently, deals with opera singers and actors of the English stage.)

Obviously, about five days after having written the above letter, Don Roberto and Gabrielle left Corpus Christi for San Antonio where he sent the following:

"San Antonio de Bexar,
"Texas.
"August 27th, 1879.

"MY DEAR MOTHER,—

"I arrived here two days ago, after a journey of seventeen days from Corpus. The distance is only 150 miles, but I came in a wagon on account of the luggage. It came on to rain, and we had to camp several times at the different rivers. We stuck in the mud several times and had to get extra horses to pull us out. Once I went into a wood to look for the horses, and got lost, and wandered about five hours in the most intense heat. At last I lassoed an old horse, and, while riding him, met a vaquero who put me on the right road.

"We stopped three days at a little Irish settlement called (of course) San Patricio. It was a grant in the time of the Spaniards, to a colony of Irish. The settlement has not much advanced since those days, except, I should think, in the depth of the mud. The people are a mixture of Irish and Mexicans, and are as dirty, civil and lying as Irishmen are in other parts of the world, for, as Holy Writ has nicely put it, 'the Ethiopian cannot change his spots.'

"San Antonio is by far the most picturesque place in Texas. In the time of the Mexicans it must have been wonderfully quaint. It is intersected in all directions

148

by the river, and by little irrigation canals, like certain places in Spain. The town was built by the Duke of Bexar who was governor here, and imported a great many families from the Canary Islands.

"The old Missions, like the churches in the town, are mostly in ruins, but in the street next to this (Calle de las Salinas) there is an old Spanish church which is being restored. A stone tablet sets it forth to be the first Presbyterian church! The cross has been taken down and an effigy of the New Samuel B. Edwards has been placed in its stead. The pulpit, according to universal Presbyterian use, has been placed in the chancel, and is about twenty-five feet high, with sounding board and red velvet (cotton) cushions, and long tassels hanging. Also, according to primitive use, though the church is large, and the worshippers but few (all their friends and relatives having been consigned to the pit), a gallery is in contemplation. . . .

"How disgracefully the Tories seem to be bidding for popularity about the Turkish question.

"Eventually, what has been done about the Prince Imperial, and what acrobat has replaced him before the public? . . .

"I use, exclusively, the twelve-shooting Winchester, and find it a very good weapon. In Texas no one stirs without his rifle. . . .

"I saw a Mexican Methodist preacher the other day. He was on horseback, and, of course, wore black clothes, white tie, and a Mexican hat. A bulge at his back indicated that he had, either a small Bible, or a pistol there . . ."

For some two months Don Roberto prospected in the neighbourhood of San Antonio, and during this time he wrote a number of letters, extracts from which I reproduce:

"San Antonio de Bexar,
"September 29th.
[Year not stated. Presumably 1879.]

" . . . How delighted the Parliament folk must be to get loose at last. I am afraid Parliament is getting inadequate to express the wishes of the English nation, as expressed through the mouth-pieces, Lord R. Churchill, Mr. Parnell, Mr. Chaplin and others, and, I am also of opinion, Mr. Chamberlain. Something like a Bear Garden with every member paid two shillings and three pence ha'penny a day, and chosen for power of lungs, would be about as much fun. . . .

"The revolution has stopped, for the moment, in Mexico, owing to two rival Presidents having abdicated in opposite directions, with all the available money.

"Brownsville, I believe, was almost entirely destroyed by a hurricane. The pious clearly see 'His' hand in the destruction, as a great many gamblers had refuged there on account of it being a frontier 'city.'

"Of all the odious American nomenclature, Smith's, Brown's and James' Ville, I think, are the worst examples. I much prefer Skunk's Misery, Tear Shirt, Powder Horn, Horse Bend, etc., and I think the Indian names are far better. However my heart turns longingly to Fraile Muerto [Dead Friar], Los Ballesteros [The Crossbowmen], Indio Muerto, etc . . ."

"San Antonio de Bexar,
"October 10th.
[Year not stated. Presumably 1879.]

" . . . Here there is no particular news, except that cotton is low, wheat hard and plentiful, Hancock for

Vice President, the coloured population of Limebury have just hanged a Baptist minister, the Republican interest is again rising, the usual thing is Wall Street, on the 'fronteers' the Indians are out again, Sitting Bull, the Sioux Chief, after being converted by a Universalist missionary, has just had him scalped, etc . . ."

"San Antonio de Bexar,
"October 21st.
[Year not stated.]

" . . . The *Spectator* comes with the greatest accuracy now, since I made a row about it at the Post Office where they used to steal every second or third copy. I only found it out by seeing in the *San Antonio Democrat* (!!) that 'the *London Spectator* says . . .'

"On visiting the editor—who was seated in a small bullet-proof room, with a Winchester and a six-shooter on the table before him—he at once owned to the fact of the *Spectators*, from which he had quoted, being mine.

"Elections are going on lustily, and what are called shooting scraps or musses, are very frequent. . . .

"I believe I am perfectly qualified for a Queen's Messengership, as I can speak French and German (badly), ride, and have no political or religious convictions that cannot be promptly altered . . ."

"San Antonio de Bexar,
"November 1st, 1879.

" . . . There is a very tolerable library in San Antonio, that is to say, for Texas where the book is rather out of repute. . . .

"The Mexican hats are very pretty, some of them weigh eight and nine pounds, with gold and silver braid and ornaments on them. The pants ('trousers' is too low a word for Americans to use) are comely, much like sailors' trousers, of velveteen or deer-skin, and have rows of buttons down the sides. Mexicans are splendid horse-men, as good as the gauchos, but they have not the wild look, nor the easy seat, nor the open and pleasant ways of my friends in the pampas. The Mexicans are rather fanatical, very treacherous, and, though splendid riders, sit rather stiffly in the saddle; but perhaps that is some-what on account of the clothes that are tight. . . . When does Disraeli Maccabees intend to take the field in person, at the head of our armies? My idea is that his plans for the subjugation of Asia are in revenge for the Babylonian captivity. What a pity he should be allowed to drag us into such trouble and disgrace. . . .

"The American mob and Press is even more indecently elated with an Indian victory than the English. If it were possible, as in the case of Major Harbryk's [name almost illegible] affair with the Utes [?]. Notices appear in the newspapers in large type: 'Horrible massacre of white men! Death! Blood! Scalps! The Indians again! Citizens to the front! Glory to God! Hallelujah!'

"Why is it that, in England and America, when white troops win, it is a 'victory,' and when beaten it is termed a 'horrible massacre'? I always thought 'massacre' meant when those who were killed could not resist . . ."

CHAPTER VIII

HAVING spent over four months in San Antonio, Don
Roberto still could not make up his mind where to
settle down, or what to do; and then, one day, when he
heard that cotton was in great demand, and fetched good
prices in Mexico City, he and Gabrielle decided to buy mules
and carts, load them with cotton, hire men, and make the long
hazardous overland trek to the capital of Mexico where, they
felt sure, they would easily double their capital which had
already dwindled considerably.

Accordingly, excited with the prospect of adventure, Don
Roberto got busy buying covered wagons with huge wheels,
and when he had acquired harness, cooking utensils and other
necessaries for the journey, he bought mules and hired a
number of men. The cotton purchased at not too low a
price, and everything in order, the expedition was ready to
start.

Gabrielle (Mrs. Cunninghame Graham), in her book of
short stories, *The Christ of Toro*, published by Eveleigh Nash,
London, 1908, so well describes how the wagon train set out
from San Antonio, that I cannot do better than to use a
part of her own account:

" . . . The excitement is unbounded as we leave San
Antonio, 'outward-bound' for San Luis Potosí; and it

153

reminds one forcibly of a vessel clearing out of London docks. Men say good-bye to their wives, children and sweethearts, or shout and swear fiercely at their restive mules; dogs bark, and the mule-boy, a sort of savage, brown and ragged, his hair coming through the crown of his tattered, silver-embroidered hat, and iron spurs on his dilapidated boots, which have evidently belonged to some bigger man than himself, drives the spare mules furiously hither and thither to the barking of all the curs in the neighbourhood. The men have donned their best go-to-meeting clothes for the occasion, and swell about, clanking their spurs and showing their clean frilled shirts and gaudy sashes, with great complacency.

"By the side of the wagons rides the *capataz* or overseer, directing the muleteers, with much unnecessary gesticulation and cracking of a long whip. The suburbs of San Antonio are not very extensive, and we soon emerged into the flat, bush-covered plains, and the mules, of which many are half broken, and some in harness for the first time, now steady down into a soberer pace, although one of them kicks himself free and escapes into the bush. After an exciting chase of about a mile and a half, he is lassoed, and brought back kicking vigorously and we all feel much enlivened by the incident. On the first day it is customary to make a short stage, as nothing is as yet in good working order, and so we halt for the night on the banks of a small creek, the overseer having first ridden forward to ascertain if there is wood, grass, and water—the three requisites of a camping ground. We reach the camp, the wagons are formed into a square, the interstices between them being secured by hide ropes; the harness is taken off the mules with marvellous celerity, and placed neatly underneath the wagons. Round the inside of the square a portable manger, filled with Indian corn, is speedily erected, and the mules fall into line to eat. As it is the first night out, the grass bad, and the mules near home, we have brought hay for them, and they are not let out of the square all night. On other occasions it is general to let them pasture loose under a guard, the wildest being hobbled. The camp-fires are next lit, the Mexicans having all the dexterity of the Indian for lighting fire in all weathers; wind, rain, sleet or damp wood, does not make a bit of difference—the fire is always lit, and that soon. Then the coffee is boiled, beans put in a pan to stew, bacon fried, and the cook mixes a rough sort of bread, which is baked in covered iron pots called by the Texan cowboy a skillet, made of maize flour. We enjoy our frugal supper, then we gather round the fire to smoke our cigarettes, and, as the evening is chilly and threatens a Norther, indulge in a stiff glass of hot toddy. Our sleeping arrangements are simple; rolled up in blankets as we go to roost, some round the fire, others on top of the bales of cotton with which the wagons are loaded, and some underneath; and as we are so near the town no watch is kept.

"Seven days of monotonous, uneventful travel through rolling prairies, and we reach the frontier town of El Paso del Aguila (Eagle Pass), on the northern side of the Rio Grande. On the other bank, facing the American settlement, is the small Mexican town of Piedras Negras, having a pretty *plaza de armas* and a ruined church. The town is a den of smugglers, thieving custom-house officers, and mongrel Americans, kept in order by a beggarly, bare-footed crew of soldiers, of which seven hundred, cavalry and infantry, are always in the barracks.

"The Rio Grande is the boundary between two countries as distinctly separate from each other in every respect as Western Europe is from Asia. From the

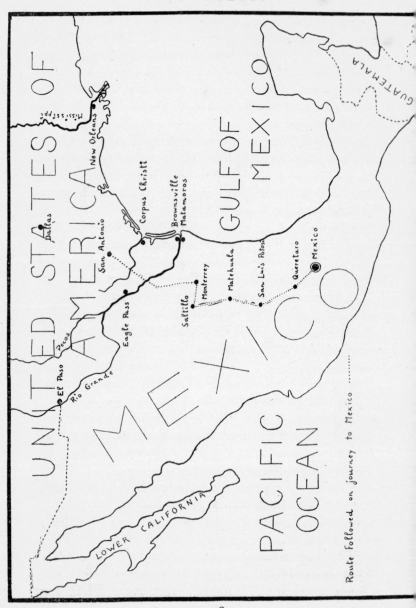

wooden shanty of the American, in all its appalling ugliness, his tinned meats and universal shoddy, we come upon a country where the schoolmaster is not yet abroad (excepting always in the capital itself), where the towns, with their flat-roofed houses and huts built of baked mud, date mostly from the time of the old *conquistadores;* a country where the artist may luxuriate in almost perfect specimens of Hispano-Mauresque architecture, and the people, idle and thievish, are brown and picturesque, and have all the Southern love for the *dolce far niente*, and all the Southerner's materialism. They like lounging about in their *plazas*, dressed in wide white drawers, a multi-coloured cloak thrown carelessly over the shoulders, glowering suspiciously at the stranger, and gloomily calculating what amount of profit might possibly accrue from a quick stab of the knife dexterously driven home into that stranger's shoulder. All day they lie on the benches, enjoying in a dull, sensual way the scent of flowers and the dreaming invoked by lying in the sun watching a fountain splashing. . . .

"The country outside Piedras Negras is wild and romantic, and as we go further on, the flat waste plains, covered with short wiry grass and sage bush, slope gradually up to the horizon; a barrier of rocky and precipitous mountains shuts them in. On these wide desolate prairies range herds of deer and antelope, and we saw numbers of these animals who, raising their gracefully poised heads for an instant as they smelt danger, scudded away in the distance with all the velocity of the wind. Troops of wild turkeys defile across the trail, and once or twice wild hogs with bristling crests and white tusks glare cautiously out from among the brushwood. Of bears and wolves there are plenty amongst the mountains. Little black pigs run squealing and

M

grunting about every hut, hens and chickens peck about the road, the dogs and cats lie sleeping in the sun, and even the miserable *pelón* (tiny hairless Aztec dog, called Chihuahua), with its pink body and hideous face, finds some happiness in life. . . .

"The outskirts of these villages are all more or less dangerous, as though on the frontiers of Mexico there are no regular highway robbers, as in the interior of the country, yet, on the smallest suspicion that the unfortunate traveller carries money, several of the principal householders of the village would be sure to band together and follow him out. In fact, it may be said that the whole population are thieves only kept in check by their own phlegmatic temperament, not a shadow of law existing.

"Near a pool of stagnant water where we stop to light a fire and have our midday meal, a flock of scraggy goats and sheep are feeding, guarded, or rather accompanied, by a shepherd asleep under a bush. These shepherds lead a hard life. Sent out in charge of from two to three thousand sheep or goats, they often pass three or four months away from their homes and families, out alone in the plains. About once a week they kill a sheep; sometimes, if short of clothes, fashioning the skin into a jacket; and occasionally a ragged urchin on a donkey brings some coffee and tobacco. At the sound of the wagon wheels crashing amongst the brushwood he looks up sleepily, but does not ask for news of any kind. We tell him that Indians are about, but even this fails to arouse him from his apathy. We ask him if he is not afraid that they will come upon him suddenly some day and kill him, alone as he is, without even a dog to give him warning. He answers that he has given a candle to Saint Rufino; and pointing to an ancient firearm, bell-mouthed and worm-eaten, and warranted at least to miss fire five times out of ten, he observes, with a touch of vanity: '*Y pues, señor, yo tengo mi rifle.*' [Oh well, sir, I have my rifle.] The poor fellow takes the cigarettes we offer with a brightened eye, and is thankful for the dry beef and beans the overseer hands to him. Suddenly his lean, brown finger points far away to a cloud of dust in the mountains, and he remarks quite casually: '*Los barbaros con una caballada.*' . . . . [The barbarians with a troop of horses.]"

From Monterey Don Roberto wrote the following letter to his mother:

"Monterey, Mexico.
"January 19th, 1880.

"MY DEAR MOTHER,—

"This is the first time I have been at a respectable place since leaving San Antonio. The journey has been very difficult on account of the winter having set in, and the cold being awful.

"Monterey is wonderfully picturesque, much more Spanish than the River Plate towns. The place is quite shut in by a chain of the Rocky Mountains, and has a very pretty little river flowing through it.

"I started from San Antonio with a train of cotton wagons, but had a dispute with the men, and had to wait a week with the most awful cold I ever experienced. However, we finally reached the frontier, and had to wait a fortnight to get on, and finally came with the Captain who was coming here to pay the frontier troops. All the way there was *novedad de los Indios* [news of the Indians], which culminated one day in a place called 'El Taruman,' by our meeting two men who had seen some horsemen galloping away among the rocks, and supposed they were

Comanches or Lipanes. However, nothing happened, although five days before they had killed a whole family, leaving only a little child that hid itself in some bushes.

"Some days after that I by accident discovered that the captain was making a plot to kill us, and take our arms, boxes, horses and mules, so I came here, and am now waiting till a stray party starts for Mexico. The journey from here takes about twenty days.

"Since leaving Bexar I have not slept in a bed, nor, in fact, much at all, for there has been so much *novedad* (news) on the road.

"I still have my black horse who looks fine though he was so miserable when I bought him in Brownsville. . . . I carry a revolver, a Winchester carbine of twelve shots, a sword and a knife, and I am not safe for a minute, and have to sleep with my horse tied at my head. . . .

"Here in Monterey the remnant of the Kickapoos are living. They fought their way from far up in the States down to here, having been at war with white men for the last 150 years. About twenty years ago they came down here, and, after having made peace, established themselves. They are a curious people (rather like gypsies), and ride or walk through the streets, one after another, in Indian file, without speaking. They have fat little horses with feathers on their heads, and even tied to their eyelashes. Whenever the Indians walk about the streets they wear moccasins and always carry a rifle. There are only about a hundred of them left, but there are a few more in a place called Santa Rosa.

"These Indians are of a much finer type than the low-class Mexicans who are of the Aztec type, short, stout and flat-nosed. The Mexicans are not in the least like the gauchos, or half as nice, for they are sullen and very treacherous, but they take great care of their horses which they wash and comb all day.

"As to what is going on in Europe, I have no idea whether the Home Rulers have put Ireland up to auction, and made Parnell Chief Auctioneer, or if England is still engaged in any colossal war with African potentates, or even if the Queen and Trix still walk as usual, on the slopes, and H.R.H. rides out with Colonel Teesdale in waiting (what for?); even the momentous question as to whether or not crinoline shall be worn with eucharistic vestments, has lost its interest for me.

"Of one thing I am quite sure—that I am very glad to be out of Texas.

" 'Jack,' the little dog I got in the dogs' home in Brownsville, runs all the way, and has desperate battles with tortoises and things. He is a little thin now with the journey, but has saved the horses from being stolen several times.

"At the frontier I saw a Mexican bull-fight. It is a very curious affair; neither the horses nor bulls are killed, and the whole thing is done by private people, for their amusement. The bull rolls them about like ninepins. . . .

"Upon arriving at Juarez, we found that the savage Mescalero Apaches had on the previous night murdered a family in the neighbourhood and burnt their hut. The mother was pierced through by a lance; and a boy—a rickety-looking little fellow about two years old—was found amongst the bushes, where he had crept for safety. His brothers and sisters to the number of ten were all killed.

"We talked over the dismal occurrence at night over the camp-fire, the coyotes howling dismally in the distance, as we sit round smoking cigarettes and endeavouring to chew hunks of tough, dried meat, before wrapping ourselves in blankets and going to sleep. We knew we were in wild and dangerous country, where there was a chance of Indians, and before turning in every rifle was put ready to hand, in case of alarm, and the animals were carefully staked. Before morning there was a false alarm. The horses and mules were restless, and snorted every now and then; and as the first method of attack by Indians is to stampede the horses, an extra guard were roused up so as to be on the alert. Nothing else occurred, however, to give cause for apprehension. Long before daylight we had left our night's camping ground far behind, and at dawn are skirting the *Sierra Madre*.

"It is a very beautiful sight which meets us as we rub our eyes and gaze drowsily out. But drowsiness soon passes away as we watch the delicate opaline lights playing on the faces of the cliffs, amber deepening into gold through every phase of hue, which again changes into a faint flush of rose colour, gradually deepening into the lightest, tenderest shades of purple. The sides of the mountains become like jewels where the light subtly plays amongst the shadows, whilst their base is lost in billowy clouds of dense white mist.

"After many miles of fatiguing and dusty travel through the blistering heat we were glad to see the *Cerro de la Silla* [Saddle Mountain, so named because it has the exact shape of a Mexican saddle] looming in the distance . . ."

Through a gorge* between high mountains, the wagon train slowly wound its way up to the main *meseta* of Mexico.

The country here is wild beyond description. Mist often covers the far-away mountains beyond which, when Don

* During his ride from Buenos Aires to Washington the writer of this "Life" rode through the same gorge.

GIANT CACTUS NEAR THE RIVER GILA ON THE MEXICAN BORDER
Reproduced from "Report on the U.S. and Mexican Boundary Survey"
by W. H. Emory, 1857.

Roberto's wagon train passed, lay the Indians' country, known as *país desconocido* (unknown land), a desert, uninhabited save by the Red man and the buffalo. Here and there, like emblems of the strange and weird solitariness, rose lonely palms, the slim shapes and fantastic heads of which gave them an almost human appearance.

Shortly before the travellers arrived, Mescalero Indians had raided a settlement in this neighbourhood, and in the ensuing encounter with well-armed white men forty Indians were killed. Eight were captured—six warriors, one woman and a boy. These were chained together, caged like wild animals, and taken to Mexico City in a wagon where they were to be put on show at Chapultepec. The captives had a little dog who followed behind the cart, refusing to be driven away by the white men.

Soon the country changed again, and Don Roberto's wagon train passed once more through sandy plains covered with sage bush, and inhabited by prairie-dogs—shrewd little animals, who sit on their burrows and watch the wagons pass, occasionally giving a sharp yelp like that of a new-born pup. The travellers noted many mounds covered with heaps of stones, a wooden cross stuck in the middle, or a square plaster niche containing crucifixes and faded chaplets of flowers. They were the graves of people killed by Indians or robbers. It was a custom for every traveller to add a stone to the heap as a tribute of respect to the dead lying beneath; for who knew what was to be his own fate in this lawless country where life and property were equally insecure? A larger heap of blackened stones and another cross was pointed out by one of the muleteers as "a settlement burnt by the barbarians." It seemed that the Indians had come down out of the mountains on to the lonely settlement, which they had burnt down, with all its inhabitants.

Sometimes Don Roberto's "outfit" camped within the walls

of *haciendas*—big farming estates which were a kind of oasis in the desert. Most of them were built when the Spanish *ranchero* made his house a kind of fortification to repel the attacks of Indians. Sometimes the courtyard was of immense extent, often a quarter of a mile in diameter, and in it were the owner's house, the *mayordomo's* (overseer's) hut, a flour mill, a store where the bookkeeper paid the people employed on the *hacienda*, a church, a house, called *meson*, where travellers stopped, and the mud huts of the labourers, who sometimes numbered above a hundred.

Near Matehuala, a town where the silver was brought from the mountains of Catorce, the convoy taking the silver to the capital passed the wagon train. A heavy old-fashioned coach bore the conductor, and after him came lumbering ambulances travelling with him for safety, and a heavy cart containing the chests of silver, guarded by sixty cavalry and some foot-soldiers, all small men, round-shouldered, but hard walkers, in dirty brown uniforms and bare feet, with or without sandals.

Being in more inhabited parts now, the travellers met the stage-coach that used to do the journey from Mexico to San Luis Potosí in four days. These stage-coaches were the favourite prey of bandits. Shortly before Don Roberto and his wife arrived in these parts, bandits had made an attack which, however, had not turned out as successful as they had hoped, for the robbers found that they could neither drag the iron chest (bearing their prize), away from the road amongst the bushes, nor could they force an opening anywhere. Fires were lighted round the chest, but without effect; and eventually the authorities recovered it almost uninjured.

After a short halt in San Luis Potosí, the wagon train followed a wide, dusty track which led towards the ultimate goal. The dust flew up in clouds, and muleteers, animals and wagons lost their natural colour, and became a dingy white.

On either side the travellers saw nothing but scorched plains, covered with many different kinds of cactus and thorny brushwood, and in the far distance dim blue mountains were visible, but the chief feature in the landscape were innumerable cactus plants. They met trains of donkeys loaded with pottery and articles of the country, whilst their bare-footed drovers ran beside the animals. Troops of Aztecs passed, every man or woman carrying on his or her back about eighty or ninety pounds weight of large pots and vessels of baked clay.

During the journey, "Jack," the little dog, probably saved some of the travellers' lives. One night after the wagons had been placed in the usual formation, to make a square, everybody squatted near a fire to chat and smoke before going to sleep. Suddenly the dog started to bark furiously, and the mules and horses snorted, obviously frightened at something. Immediately a bucket of water was thrown on the fire, and Don Roberto, armed with a sword and a revolver, crept out of the square, in the opposite direction in which the dog barked. Crawling on all fours, he then slowly and cautiously worked his way round the camp in a semi-circle. As the night was pitch-dark, he could see nothing, and so, after having crawled about for some time, he returned to the camp.

In the meantime the dog and the animals had calmed down, and in the morning, when the men went to investigate the surroundings, they could clearly see by the tracks in the sand that Don Roberto had crawled close up to an Indian who had approached the camp on all fours, obviously with the intention of dispatching an arrow or two. A few hundred yards away, in a hollow, the travellers saw the marks in the sand where the Indian had left his horse.

A few hours later, as the wagons slowly rolled along, a number of arrows suddenly came whirring through the air, but although the travellers were taken by surprise, only one man and a mule were slightly injured. Whilst the terrified animals snorted, stamped and reared up, rifles cracked, for in the meantime Indians had appeared from behind cactus plants where they had been hidden. In a few moments they vanished —obviously to fetch their horses, which were hidden in a hollow, for soon they re-appeared, galloping wildly round the wagon train, yelling and raising a cloud of dust. Again rifles cracked, but as the attackers kept at a respectful distance, no damage was done. Suddenly the mount of one of the Indians turned over like a shot rabbit, but the rider picked himself up at once, and with great agility leapt on to the pony one of his tribesmen was riding, and sat behind him. Finding the white men's firing too hot, the Indians suddenly wheeled about, like a flight of birds changing direction, and soon disappeared in the distance.

Finally Don Roberto's wagon train safely reached the capital of Mexico, where another bitter disappointment awaited him and his brave wife.

The price of cotton had fallen so much that he had to sell his bales at a loss, and by the time he had paid off the men, and sold all the mules, horses and carts (keeping only his favourite black horse), his capital had shrunk considerably.

Finding Mexico City very interesting, he and his wife decided to stay there for some time, but as they did not want to spend their capital, they decided to combine study and pleasure with business. Thus it came about that Don Roberto, under the name of "Professor Bontini," opened a fencing academy, whilst his wife, who was a very gifted woman, taught French, painting and the art of playing the guitar.

The couple spent their free time reading and studying the history of Mexico, visiting old Spanish churches, famous houses and landmarks.

One thing fascinated Don Roberto more than the natural beauties of the city, the snow-capped volcanoes (the

INDIANS ATTACKING A WAGON TRAIN
From a contemporary print.

Popocatepetl and the Ixtaccihuatl, Aztec names meaning: "Smoky Mountain" and "Sleeping Woman)—the old floating gardens of the Aztecs, and the beautiful Spanish churches and buildings. Whenever he had time he hurried to the castle of Chapultepec upon its rock and surrounded by the giant cypresses which were old even when the Spaniards first arrived. In the small courtyard of the castle, ironed and guarded, were kept the eight Indians who had been made captives after the massacre he had witnessed in the far North of Mexico during his long and fruitless trek with cotton towards the capital. The six warriors, the woman and the boy, and the faithful little dog who had followed them some twelve hundred miles to captivity, sat in their fetters, silent, stoical, not speaking once in a whole day, only communicating by signs. Naked except the breech-clout, they looked at the gaping white people as though without sight, but seeing everything.

Although Don Roberto always took some food and smokes to the wretched captives, only once did one speak, and this when he was asked if he was a Mescalero. For a moment a gleam shone through the Indian's eyes as one of them answered: "Mescalero-hay." The soldier at the gate said they were *brutos*, all sons of dogs, infidels, and that for his part he could not see why the government went to the expense of keeping them alive.

Although Don Roberto and his wife had only been in Mexico City for some eight months, they had managed to save a certain amount of money which, added to their modest capital, was sufficient to start a small ranch where land would not be too dear.

Finding that Mexico offered few possibilities, they decided to return to Texas, and there, once more to try their luck. "Professor Bontini's" fencing academy had become a favourite meeting-place for the aristocracy of Mexico, and therefore

Don Roberto made a very good thing out of it when he sold the establishment to a Frenchman who was a *Maître d'Armes* of sorts.

During the month of October, 1880, Don Roberto and his wife joined a mule train which was starting out from Mexico City for the distant Rio Grande, the Texan border.

After the first day's trekking, when everybody was grouped round a fire, a traveller came dashing up and excitedly reported that the Mescalero Indians had broken loose from the castle of Chapultepec, after having slipped their fetters, and murdered two of the guard, and that the infidels were said to be in the neighbourhood, on their way towards the recesses of the mountains of the Santa Rosa range.

Needless to say, this put everybody almost beside themselves, and this in spite of the fact that everybody was so loaded down with arms as to resemble walking or riding arsenals.

Next day the rumour spread that the escaped Indians had got ahead of the mule train, and that they were obviously making towards the north. Two of them, it appeared, had made themselves bows with sticks, the string being twisted out of palm fibre, and the other six were armed with clubs. What delighted Don Roberto most was to hear that behind the Indians was seen their little white dog who trotted along joyfully, as if realising that his masters were once more free. Outside San Juan del Rio—a neat little town the mule train reached upon the second day—people said that in the night the homing Mescaleros had stolen a horse, and that two of them, mounting upon him, had ridden off, leaving the rest of the forlorn and miserable band behind. How they had lived, so far, in the scorched alkali-covered plains, how they managed to conceal themselves by day, or how they steered by night, no one could tell, for white man knows nothing of the desert craft, and has no idea that there is always food of some kind for an Indian, either by digging roots, snaring small animals, or as

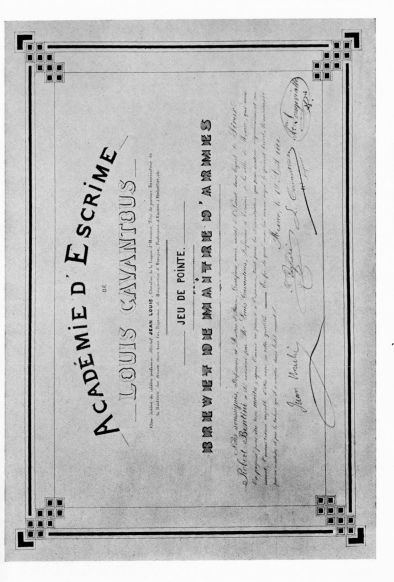

DON ROBERTO'S DIPLOMA AS A FENCING MASTER

the last resort, by catching locusts or any other insect he can find.

Days followed days as in a ship at sea; the wagons rolling across the plains, and Don Roberto jogging upon his black horse, half sleeping in the sun, or stretched at night, half dozing on a tilt. Near San Luis Potosí the travellers heard that two of the Indians had been killed, but that the four remaining were still pushing onward, and in a little while the caravan met a body of armed men carrying two ghastly heads tied by their scalp-locks to the saddle-bow.

As the days passed, the Indian fugitives were forgotten by the muleteers, but Don Roberto followed their every step in his mind's eye. One day, crossing a sandy tract, the overseer drew up his horse, and, pointing to the ground, exclaimed: "Viva México!—look at these footmarks in the sand. They are the infidels; see where the men have trod; here is the woman's print and this the boy's. Look how their toes are all turned in, unlike the Christians'. This trail is a day old, and yet how fresh! See where the boy stumbled—thanks to the Blessed Virgin they must all be tired, and praise to God will die upon the road, either by hunger or some Christian hand."

At a ranch the mule train stopped to pass the hottest hours in sleep. Suddenly there was great excitement; men came in, their horses flecked in foam; others were mounting, and all armed to the teeth. "Los Indios! Sí señor," they had been seen, only last night. No chance of sleep in such a turmoil of alarm; each man had his own plan, all talked at once, but when Don Roberto asked dryly if they had thought of following the trail, a silence fell on all. Just then upon the plain a cloud of dust was seen. Nearer it came, and then out of the midst of it horses appeared, arms flashed, and then nearing to the place five or six men galloped up to the walls, and stopped their horses with a jerk. "What news? Have you seen anything of the savages?" The chief rider of the band, getting off slowly, and fastening up his horse, said, with an air of dignity: "Four leagues along the road you will find one of them. We came upon him sitting on a stone, too tired to move, called on him to surrender, but Indians have no sense, so he came at us as he was, and we, being valiant, fired, and he fell dead. Then, that the law should be manifest to all, we hung his body by the feet to a *huisaché* tree." Compliments broke out: "*Vivan los valientes!*" "*Viva México!*" "*Mueran los Indios salvajes!*"

Leaving the noisy crew drinking confusion to their enemies, Don Roberto's wagon train once more rolled over the plain. Four dusty leagues, and the *huisaché* tree came into sight. To a branch, covered with bullet-wounds, the travellers saw the Indian hang. Half-starved he looked, and so reduced that from the bullet-holes but little blood had run; his feet were bloody, and his face hanging an inch or two above the ground was distorted; flies buzzed about him, and in the sky a faint black line on the horizon showed that the vultures had already scented food.

They left the nameless warrior hanging on his tree, and continued over the sterile plateau which spread out like a vast sea. All trace of the remaining Indian fugitives was lost; no one had heard of them, and the mysterious party, now reduced to three, left no more trace of its passing than water which has closed upon the passage of a fish. Then the plateau of Anáhuac finished abruptly; in a day the caravan descended by a rough path from the plateau to a land of palms, of cultivation, orange groves, of fruit trees, olive gardens, a balmy air filled with the noise of running waters. Beyond the vast plains stretched towards the Rio Grande and Texas. Soon Monterey became a memory, and when the *Cerro de la Silla* had vanished in the distance behind, the mule train moved through a veritable ocean of tall, coarse grass. Out of the thickets wild boars peered, rattle-snakes sounded their note of warning, or lay basking in the sun; at times an antelope bounded across the track, and the rare settlements were fortified with high mud walls, for the region was subject to invasions of the Indians, and no one rode a mile without the chance of an attack. When solitary travellers met they zigzagged to and fro like battle-ships in the old days, striving to get the "weather gauge," holding their horses tightly by the head, and interchanging salutations fifty yards away. If they happened to be Texans and Mexicans they only glared, or perhaps yelled an obscenity at one another in their different tongues.

On reaching Navas, Don Roberto found the village astir, knots of people talking excitedly, and upon asking an in-habitant what all the fuss was about he was told that the Mescaleros had been seen passing about a mile out of the town.

Towards some foothills, not fifteen miles away, rose the dark mountains of the Santa Rosa chain where the three Indian survivors would be safe, for the whole range was Indian territory. However, it was not to be, for as the wagon train continued on its journey, a ranch was passed where a Texan settler proudly informed the travellers that he had "tumbled" the young "buck." He added that his *vaqueros* had buried the corpse a little further along the trail, and that because his gun had jammed, the other "buck" and the squaw had managed to get away.

Under a palm tree, not far from the house, the young Indian's grave was dug, and upon it, wretched and draggled, sat the little dog who had refused to leave his human friend, even after death. Don Roberto and his wife offered a reward for the dog, but neither the muleteers nor the *vaqueros* could lasso him, as he was very shy and ran away when anyone approached.

As the travellers continued, the little dog came out of the tall grass, ran to and fro as if he sought for something, howled dismally, and, after scratching in the ground, squatted

171

dejectedly on the freshly-turned-up earth which marked the young Indian's grave. Don Roberto hoped that the other two safely reached their beloved wild homeland, to tell the story of their feat to their friends, and to surfeit themselves, amid great rejoicing, with meat of the buffalo.

During the return journey to Texas, Don Roberto lost his favourite black pony in a curious way. The animal was staked out near the camp when a troop of wild horses stampeded past, a few hundred yards away. Hearing the trampling of many hoofs and the neighs of liberty, the pony tugged at the rope, which snapped. The last thing Don Roberto saw of his favourite animal was when it joined the herd of wild horses and, together with them, disappeared in the bush, towards Indian territory where it would have been foolhardy to follow them. As the following letter shows, the travellers arrived in San Antonio towards the end of May 1881:

"San Antonio de Bexar,
"May 28th, 1881.

" . . . We have just got back. The journey was not so bad as going, and we passed through some lovely frontier country on the other side of the Rio Grande.

"I am sorry to say I lost my horse, for he was a splendid animal, and in excellent condition after such a journey. (52 days.)

"San Luis Potosí I liked better than Mexico City, for it is a very curious old town. However, the people are most disagreeable, and to me it is very unpleasant not to be able to go outside a town alone. In nearly all parts of Mexico it is too dangerous to do so, and every one travels in company of ten or twelve, at least, all well armed. San Luis Potosí is especially dangerous. . . .

"Everything is very quiet here. No Indian or Mexican raids, lynchings, elections, negro agitations, or anything, not even a revolution in Mexico; in fact, nothing worth mentioning, except a riot in our good town Monterey, between the police and the military, in which, after much battle that lasted for a few hours, most of the police were killed, but I understand there has been no *novedad* [news] since, and all is serene. . . .

"My reason for using this writing paper* is twofold. First, to avoid wilful waste, always so productive of want, and second, that it may remind you of letters you received from the wilds of South America . . ."

In another letter Don Roberto says:

"San Antonio de Bexar,
"[Date not mentioned.]

" . . . The Texans all voted against Garfield, as most of them are Democrats, and the State belays, I think, to the 'Solid South.' I did not vote, though I might have done so. If I had, I should have voted for Hancock, as I see no possible advantage in the cohesion of any number of States to one another, when, as is the case of America, there is no one who could possibly attack them. Also, Hancock, though he represents a corrupt party—as regards bribery, the tricks with the coinage, etc.—is a Free Trader.

"The Lord Archie and his son and daughter must be having quite a time in California. . . . Spelling seems to be a great stumbling block to scions of the Aristocracy. I daresay they will enjoy themselves very much, as California is the best State in the Union for rich people.

"Tom Hughes ought to be hanged for decoying so many people out to Tennessee with his High Faluting and Scholl Days. I fancy they will not much care about a

* The letter is written on a sheet of pink packing paper.

Tennessee winter when it once sets in. About that time Mr. Hughes will, no doubt, have urgent family affairs to call him to Europe, and will have to sell the shooting boots (mentioned in one of his articles) at a considerable reduction, and pack up a paper collar or two, a flannel shirt, and a pocket Bible, and wend his way home to pose as a sort of religious Sir Walter Raleigh with the chill off. . . .

"The prosecution of Mr. Dole seems very hard. I liked when he said he had food enough at present, and asked for some books. I am sure he said 'mental papulum.'

"The persecution of the Chinese in Columbo is analogous to that of Mr. Dole, on account of their vestments, chiefly. It is a horrible shame, and reflects very badly on the Americans. A copy of *Wan Lee the Pagan* and *The Last Chinese Outrage* ought to be circulated, free of cost, to everyone in the States. Here books are very dear . . ."

CHAPTER IX

ROBBED AND RUINED BY INDIANS—DON ROBERTO BECOMES
STORE ASSISTANT, HORSE-TRAINER, TRIES HIS HAND AT
JOURNALISM, JOINS A GANG OF CATTLE-DROVERS, AND ACTS AS
INTERPRETER ON BUFFALO HUNTING EXPEDITION—MEETING
WITH BUFFALO BILL AND AN OLD ARGENTINE REVOLUTIONARY
COMPANION—RETURN TO ENGLAND—GENTLEMAN FARMER—
THE PURCHASE OF "PAMPA"—DON ROBERTO BEGINS TO TAKE AN
ACTIVE INTEREST IN POLITICS AND BECOMES A MEMBER OF
PARLIAMENT

BACK in San Antonio, Don Roberto met a Mexican-Greek who was looking for a partner to start a ranch, somewhere near the border. As the man was an experienced rancher, and generally impressed Don Roberto as being a trustworthy person, things happened quickly. Pooling their respective capital, the two men acquired land, built a rough wooden house, and bought cattle and horses. One day the two partners left the new establishment in charge of the foreman and a number of hands they had hired, for business called them to San Antonio, where Don Roberto's wife was staying with friends whilst the ranch was being put into running order.*

When the two men returned to the border, they found that during an Indian raid all their cattle and horses had been driven away. All that was left of their house, wagons and personal belongings, was a smouldering heap of ruins.

Obviously the men had defended themselves bravely, for

* Unfortunately I am unable to state exactly where the ranch was situated. "A week's hard riding from San Antonio," is the only clue I possess.—A. F. T.

in the course of the fight they had put up during the unexpected nocturnal attack, they had killed several Indians whilst, on the defenders' side, only one man was slightly wounded.

Completely ruined, Don Roberto rode back to San Antonio to tell his wife about the misfortune, and whilst his partner tried to sell the land and the few things which had been saved, husband and wife discussed the future.

Don Roberto could easily have written home for more money, but this he refused to do, being loth to acknowledge defeat. In his letters to his people he never mentioned his plight, but wrote cheerfully, as if everything were going splendidly with him.

About a hundred dollars, his horse, saddle and clothes, was all he possessed after the latest disaster which had befallen him. For some time he and his wife worked as assistants in a store, and when they grew tired of so monotonous an occupation, Don Roberto joined a gang of men and helped drive cattle from Mexico into Texas. Gabrielle returned to New Orleans where she taught French, Italian, music and painting. Thus, for some time, everything went fairly well.

In those days cattle-driving in the Mexican border countries was exciting and often interesting. Once, in the Sierra Madre, whilst looking for some horses which had strayed, Don Roberto and his companions came upon a little shelter made of withies and covered with one of those striped blankets woven by the Navajo Indians.

The little wigwam, shaped like a gipsy tent, stood close to a thicket of *huisaché* trees in flower.

On every side of the deep valley towered hills with great, flat, rocky sides, on some of which the Indian tribes had scratched crude pictures: records of their race.

In one of them an Indian chief, surrounded by his friends, was setting free his favourite horse upon the prairies, either

176

before his death or in reward of faithful services. The little group of men cut in the stone (most probably with an arrow-head) was life-like, though drawn without perspective, which gave those figures of a vanished race an air of standing in the clouds.

The chief, naked except the breech clout, but wearing his feather head-dress, stood with a bridle in his hand. A bow was slung across his shoulders and a quiver hung below his arm, and with the other hand he kept the sun from his face as he gazed upon his horse. All kinds of hunting scenes were there displayed, also others, such as the burial of a chief, a dance and other ceremonials.

Somehow the little wigwam had an eerie look about it, standing so desolate, out in the flowery wilds.

Inside it lay the body of a man, with the skin dry as parch-ment, and his weapons beside him—a Winchester, a bow and arrows, and a lance.

One of the men, taking up an arrow, and looking at it, said that the dead man was an Apache of the Mescalero band; and then, looking upon the ground and pointing out some marks, added: "He let loose his horse before he died, just as the chief did in the picture-writing."

During his subsequent wanderings through Texas, New Mexico and Arizona, Don Roberto schooled horses for wealthy people, teaching the animals "manners" about which the rough-riding cow-boys knew nothing. At, or about this time, he met Buffalo Bill at the "Horsehead Crossing," and once, as he cantered over a plain, he stopped to speak to another lone rider who, to his astonishment and joy, turned out to be none other than "Pancho Pajaro" (Frederick Vogel), his old revolutionary companion from the Argentine. Whilst the two men rode side by side, Pancho recounted how he had left the Argentine because the killing of his own brother haunted him, and he told Don Roberto about his wanderings among Indians with whom he had traded for some years. What happened to Pancho after the two men parted will probably never be known, but obviously, in his case, the curse the gauchos believed in had come true.

Once, for some time, Don Roberto went as Spanish-English interpreter with a buffalo-hunting expedition in the "Staked Plain." Owing to the Indians this was dangerous work, for the herds which were getting small, numbering between two or three hundred head, had to be sought in territory which the Indian bravely tried to defend against the white invaders who were, however, so well armed that the natives—who chiefly relied on bows and arrows, and a few very antiquated rifles—had but little chance in an open fight. But woe betide the buffalo-hunter who strayed too far from his companions, especially if his horse was tired after a long gallop.

Occasionally Don Roberto returned to San Antonio where he collected and wrote letters, and during some of his visits to the town (between 1880 and 1883), he wrote articles for a newspaper. (Unfortunately, so far, I have been unable to trace any of these articles which must have been his first writings to have been put into print.)

Although he had led a rough life, often far away from civilisation, he always travelled with a book or two in his saddle-bags, and, thanks to his mother, he was kept in touch with happenings and current events in England.

Below I reproduce extracts from two letters written from San Antonio. They are dated July 3rd and 15th, but the year is not mentioned.

"San Antonio de Bexar,
"July 3rd.

" . . . I have tried two or three times to make a magazine article out of the Mexican journey, but find I have no talent whatever in that line. I am thinking of trying an essay on the Elizabethans, but find it difficult. I think I have no literary ability whatever . . ."

"San Antonio de Bezar,
"July 15th.

" . . . The 'Bookes' are, at last, bailed out of the customs house. They cost me (for bailing out), £3 3. o.

"They are splendid, especially the Shakespeare, Isaac Walton, etc. Dodsley is magnificent. When I am a Congress man I shall have my portrait done in full suit of black, satin vest, fly hat, diamond studs, and my hand resting on Dodsley on a small table, or, perhaps, on the top of a small pillar, with a red curtain as background.

"It is a pity that Jehovah, Bradlaugh, Labby* and the musical glasses are taking up all the time of the House. . . .

"The best 'Cavalia Protestante' is the negro Baptist (Hard Shell) Church. The noise made by the regenerate, on Sunday evening, almost rivals the sweet modulated thunder of the bar next door to the church, or the cries and shouts of the *monte* players (chiefly Mexicans, or, 'Mexhinglis' as they say when they are 'spikkiting de Inglis') on the opposite side, and the row of bands in German beer gardens behind the church. . . .

"Poor Jack (the little dog), is stolen. I have advertised for him . . ."

(Note: Although Don Roberto offered a big reward, and searched for several days, he never recovered the dog.)

Early in 1883, he received news that his father was seriously ill, and as his mother urged him to return home as soon as possible, he hurried to New Orleans where, after having

* Labouchere.

joined his wife, he took the first boat to leave for England. Both he and Gabrielle had managed to save a certain amount of money, but they left the country without a penny of the capital with which they had arrived, about four years before. However, what they had lost in money, they had gained in experience and adventure, such as few men or women ever saw, even in those days.

Shortly after the couple arrived home, Major Bontine died,* leaving debts amounting to over £100,000 which the young couple courageously started to pay off.

Knowing but little about farming on a large scale in the region in which Gartmore is situated, Don Roberto studied the intricacies of this science, whilst his wife undertook the task of keeping the books; and thus the two struggled bravely against the inevitable.

Gartmore House had an air of belonging to a family fallen fortunes. Under the arch which led to the stable yard, stood dilapidated kennels, disused, but with some links of rusty chain still hanging to them, as if they waited for the return of the dogs, dead years ago. The evenings and nights seemed long to Don Roberto and his wife, and often they felt as if they had been marooned upon some island.

Without a horse, he was like a navigator without a ship, and therefore, as soon as he settled in Gartmore, he bought two or three good saddle-horses.

One day, whilst walking through the streets in Glasgow, he saw a horse in the traces of a tramway car. Evidently the animal was unaccustomed to the work, and, therefore, gave the driver a great deal of trouble. Approaching to give a helping hand, Don Roberto recognised the beast as an Argentine mustang, and upon closer examination discovered that on its hind-quarters it bore a brand which he remembered

---

* In 1876 Major William Bontine published a booklet containing over fifty light poems and verses. (Robert Anderson, Glasgow, printers.)

as that of Eduardo Casey of "Curumulan," a ranch he had known during his stormy days in the Argentine.

This discovery so delighted him that he immediately went to see the director of the tramway company. When Don Roberto heard that the horse had only arrived from South America two days before, and that it was one of the most troublesome the company had ever tried to handle, he offered fifty pounds for it. As this was about three times the sum the company had paid for it, the deal was made at once, and when the tramcar came back, after having completed a journey, Don Roberto himself unharnessed the animal, put a saddle on him, and after a wild tussle in which the mustang came out second best, rode him to Gartmore.

"Pampa," as he called the horse, turned out to be the best and highest spirited he ever possessed, and, as we shall see later, one of the pride and joys of his life. (One of the finest pictures Sir John Lavery has painted, is that of Don Roberto seated on "Pampa." This beautiful painting is now the property of the "Museo de Bellas Artes" in Buenos Aires.)

Don Roberto was devoted to his mother, and whenever he had time he hurried to London where she had a house in Chester Square. "Number thirty-nine" was a meeting-place of great ladies, painters, artists and writers, and there many interesting conversations and discussions were held.

Don Roberto soon evinced a strong interest in home politics. His experiences in foreign lands had led him far from the conventional traditions of his ancestors, and to the dismay of his friends he proclaimed himself a Radical, though, occasionally, he made sympathetic allusions to some dogma of the Tory faith. Being a thorough-going democrat, he even shocked Radicals when he spoke about universal suffrage, abolition of the House of Lords, free secular education with a free meal, triennial Parliaments, graduated income-tax, nationalisation of land, Sunday opening of museums, abolition of mineral royalties, disestablishment and direct veto of the liquor traffic, eight-hour working day, etc.

The life of a land-owner, riding about and supervising his huge estate and various farms, was not varied enough to satisfy his restless spirit. In Scotland and in London he frequently attended Socialist meetings where William Morris, George Bernard Shaw, H. M. Hyndman, Keir Hardie, John Burns and others spoke. However, being entirely unaffected by the herd instinct, so prevalent amongst the vast majority of men, he was never a member of the Fabian group.

The first time he spoke in public was when he addressed a meeting outside the church in Buchlyvie, a little village near Gartmore, in Stirlingshire. Shortly after this he took up politics seriously, and wherever he spoke, startled his audiences, to put it mildly. He proved to be a born speaker, and remarkable for the fact that he appealed to uneducated people who were accustomed to "mob oratory." Although he never prepared his speeches, and therefore used no notes, his sentences, spoken in a very powerful voice, were always precise and elegant. Even when he spoke in a rage or with vitriolic scorn, he never hesitated or wandered off the subject. Sometimes, probably due to the Latin blood in his veins, his gestures were rather theatrical, but always elegant; and yet, he never acted, but was always quite natural. Most of his speeches startled his listeners for their complete departure from convention, for he was in advance of the "planks" of the most advanced platform. However, a great deal of what he said, including his humour, went over the heads of most of his listeners, and some of the answers he gave to numerous questions were hardly helpful for a successful election.

In those days (and even now), a candidate's church connection was of serious account, especially in Scotland. "What kirk do you belong to?" somebody asked him during one of his speeches. Instantly, with a courteous bow, Don

DON ROBERTO AND "PAMPA"

[*From a painting by Sir John Lavery.*

Roberto answered: "Sir, I am a Christian—unattached."

Again, when invited to give his views on the maintenance of the Army, he replied: "I have a hereditary regard for the ancient and honourable profession of arms; but I would like to see the time when no soldier would be seen, except, perhaps, a stuffed specimen or two in a museum."

Perhaps he was too passionate in his enthusiasms, and unmerciful in the scorn he poured upon the objects of his attack. His lively wit and readiness in repartee made him more than a match for any heckler.

In Leeds, a Scottish Trade Union leader spoke on the same platform as Don Roberto who, in differing from the speaker on some point, added: "This shows that Scotsmen are not clannish." In the same speech he told a story of wrong and suffering in Russia, and used the phrase "infected with syphilis." At that time this common disease was never mentioned in public, and the effect of the phrase on the audience was stinging, as if a whip had been drawn across its face.

Once, when a political opponent interrupted him and asked if he were a descendant of the Sir Robert Graham who killed King James I—(he was)—he flashed back: "Go to hell and ask him yourself!"

Again, after having addressed a stormy meeting, he showed his sardonic sense of humour by thanking the audience for the manner in which it had showed its appreciation by "contributing a large quantity of loose building material."

In many ways he was quite as sound a Tory as any. He was no partisan, except as a fearless champion of all underdogs. Could anybody better express a political philosophy than he did when he wrote: "I hold that the best right that a man can have is to be happy after the way that pleases him best."

Tousled and red-haired, Don Roberto made a strange

picture, striding up and down the platforms in local assembly halls (with audiences consisting chiefly of grimy miners and poor people who had never been away from their home regions), proclaiming politics, Socialism, books, Scotland, Spain, America, Shakespeare, Socrates, Cervantes, or anything chance suggested to his energetic and versatile mind.

On one occasion, when speaking in support of a candidate, his verbal fireworks were such that his listeners became uneasy and even hostile. When he finished he turned to the candidate he had spoken for and said: "Well, I calculate I have lost you at least two hundred damn fool votes."

David Lowe, in *Souvenirs of Scottish Labour*, gives a very interesting description of Don Roberto speaking at a meeting in Kinnaird Hall, Dundee, at the time the largest hall in the town. Keir Hardie, sturdily built, and with a brown-red bushy beard flowing over his broad chest, was also on the platform, and so were Shaw Maxwell and Chisholm Robertson. Mr. Lowe writes:

" . . . I entered the hall alone, and discreetly took a back seat. The arena was not particularly well filled, and the audience sat stolid and undemonstrative. It was almost exclusively a working-class audience, and over the scene there seemed to hang a grey cloud of weariness. The arrival of the platform party did not help matters, the handful of men on the spacious platform making a miserable show.

"The chairman, having finished his introductory remarks, called upon the speaker of the evening. From his side arose a tall, spare man, dressed in a brown suit of Melton cloth. The suit was fashionably cut, and the double-breasted jacket fitted his lithe figure to a nicety. It was an interesting presence: a personality which would have seemed quite at home in a picture by Velázquez.

Standing uprightly on somewhat long feet, he looked at the gathering with burning intuitive eyes, which seemed to instantly diagnose the human material on which he had to work, and then after running his thin hands swiftly backwards through a thick crop of upstanding dark* hair, he began to speak. There was a touch of hesitance and difficulty in his pronunciation at first, but soon it passed away. The long thin face, with its high narrow forehead and pointed beard, glowed with animation, and from his mouth came rapid sentences which vied in brilliancy the light of his eyes.

"It was Graham!

"The audience gave no sign of being impressed: not a cheer; not an interjection; not a sound. With impassioned periods Graham portrayed the helplessness and misery of the poor, and urged them to send men to Parliament who knew their needs and aspirations. The dour, cold, human mass was irresponsive. Then came a change over the speaker. He ceased to urge and to exhort. The expression of his countenance altered, and he poured over them a torrent of satire and cynicism. In so many words he told them they were not men at all, and that they had not the heart to feel for their kind, nor the intellect to vote and work for their own protection. His cutting remarks became unbearable, I could see men begin to shift in their seats, a few interjections were made, and all at once there came over the audience a wave of fierce resentment.

"Again there was a change in the speaker's expression, and in kindly words, mixed strangely with pride, banter, and humour, he told them how glad he was to see their manhood emerge. From that point onward the minds of the meeting was open to receive Socialist

* This is not correct. His hair was dark-red.

ideas, and the opportunity was not allowed to pass unseized. I sat listening and observing as if it were a drama . . ."

On one occasion Don Roberto was asked to introduce Keir-Hardie at a meeting in the Camlachie constituency, in one of the slums of Glasgow. In the vicinity of the large hall in which the meeting was to be held, lived a very rough Irish element, and as the people did not know Keir Hardie's attitude towards Irish Home Rule, a great number of roughs invaded the hall to break up the meeting.

When Don Roberto stepped on to the platform pandemonium broke loose, but this did not worry him in the least; in fact, he enjoyed it. Going into a little ante-room behind the platform, he called two of the door attendants and asked them to hurry and bolt and bar all the doors leading into the hall.

This done, on a given signal he then stepped on to the platform for the second time, but before he did so he picked up a dummy six-shooter which he had seen lying among the belongings of a theatrical company in the ante-room. Pointing the formidable-looking weapon at the noisy crowd below him, he bellowed for order. Silence fell as if by magic, and then he told his startled audience that the doors had been locked, and that, if anyone moved from his seat, or interrupted a speaker, he would blow his brains out. "I am going to speak for half an hour," he announced, "and then I shall introduce my friend, Keir Hardie, and until he has finished his address, not a man will interrupt him, or try to move, unless he wishes to be carried out of the hall as a corpse!"

For a moment one could have heard a pin drop, but then, the audience having a sense of humour, roars of laughter broke out and everybody applauded the solitary figure on the platform, and when Keir Hardie appeared, immediate silence reigned in the hall.

When the listeners heard that both Don Roberto and the principal speaker strongly favoured Home Rule for Ireland, they acclaimed wildly, and when the meeting was over, the two speakers were chaired out of the hall, but not before Don Roberto had explained where he had found his formidable-looking gun.

He took a great interest in the sufferings of the Scottish miners. Together with Keir Hardie, "the only genius, probably, that the Labour Party has ever produced," he often investigated conditions under which the miners had to work. Once the two crept on hands and feet through a long, subterranean passage to the opening where a man, stripped to the waist, was working alone. When the two friends came out into the fresh air once more, Keir Hardie said: "Graham, there's no muckle in our ceevilisation after a'."

When Don Roberto contested the North-West Lanark seat, a bitter political opponent asked him if it was true that he did not send his children to Sunday school. "Yes," replied the candidate. A tense silence fell upon the audience, for religious feelings ran high at the time. "Well, will you kindly inform this meeting why you do not send your children to Sunday school?" the heckler then demanded, knowing that he had picked on a subject that was very prejudicial to the success of the Socialist candidate. An uproar greeted this question, but when Don Roberto had silenced the crowd he replied: "In relation to this question being answered, Madam Graham, who is present here, is the best capable person to give a reply, and the most culpable party; from the fact that she has not as yet presented me with any children. So it is, indeed, very difficult to send them to Sunday school." The heckler left the hall amid a roar of laughter, and took good care never to attend another meeting.

When Don Roberto contested North-West Lanarkshire, at the General Election of 1885, he put forth a programme which made the Radicals stand aghast; and, accordingly, was defeated by a majority of 1,103, but a year later was returned for the same constituency, and on the same programme, with a majority of 332. And so Robert Bontine Cunninghame Graham of Gartmore, big-hearted Scottish laird, ex-revolutionary soldier, gaucho, rider of wild horses, rancher, horse- and cattle-dealer, prospector, frontiersman, fencing-master, store assistant, buffalo-hunter, explorer, keen reader of books, lover of art and historian, became—a Member of Parliament! It needs no great effort of the imagination to realise the effect produced when the handsome aristocratic new member marched into the House of Commons to disturb the stuffy atmosphere which was one of its characteristics in the 'eighties. The frock-coated and severely "respectable" occupants of the green benches were at first not a little shocked by the outbursts of their new member. But soon stout-hearted Tory gentlemen, who at first had been shocked by the ideals for which Don Roberto fought so valiantly, came to like him for his unexpected qualities. Here was a fiery democrat of aristocratic ancestry and looks, who not only spoke Spanish, French, Portuguese and Italian and had an affection for Arabic, but a Velázquez reincarnation which rode down to the House on "Pampa," his fiery Argentine mustang which he had brought down from Gartmore.*

If nothing else, Don Roberto soon became at one and the same time the *enfant terrible* and the spoiled child of the House of Commons—a combination which requires qualifications as much as to be Prime Minister, or, as his friend G. K. Chesterton wrote in his Autobiography:

Don Roberto's youngest brother, the Rev. Malise Cunninghame Graham, died on the 26th November, 1885, aged 25 years.

* Several Members used to ride into the New Palace Yard. The mounting-block (which Don Roberto never used, for he leapt into the saddle), still stands close to the entrance of Westminster Hall. Stables were provided in those days.

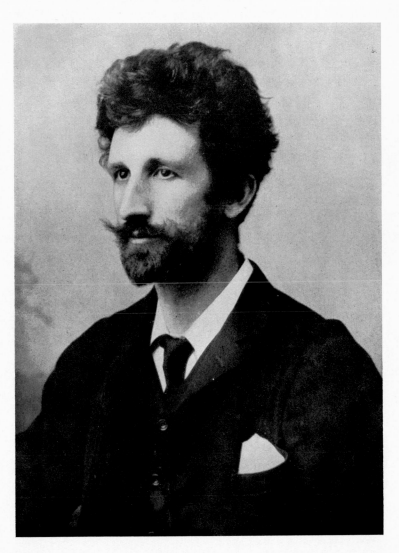

AT THE AGE OF 34

"Cunninghame Graham:—A splendid specimen of the sort of Scot who, even when he was interested in politics, would never really be allowed in practical politics. . . . No Cabinet Minister would ever admire his Parliamentary style; though he had a much better style than any Cabinet Minister. Nothing could prevent Balfour being Prime Minister or MacDonald being a Prime Minister, but Cunninghame Graham achieved the adventure of being Cunninghame Graham. . . ."

Disinterested, Don Roberto—whose brief was the case of the underdog—looked upon the House of Commons as a tilting ground, and to him a debate was merely what a joust used to be to a knight of olden days. In the House he often used "strong" words, which, had he used them under different circumstances, he would have apologised for; but in the House he never apologised. He distinguished himself by his witty speeches, and seemed to take a special delight in lampooning noble lords and baronets who sat on the Government's side, and he was strenuously opposed to the election system, which he considered degrading to the candidate, and demoralising to the electors. He wished for abolition of all canvassing, and advocated prohibiting the candidates to subscribe anything in the constituency.

He used to dart up to his place in the House of Commons as if he were projected by means of a spring, but his voice was not so sharp as his looks, and there was not an atom of humour conveyed in his facial expressions, yet his speeches scintillated with the queerest of imagery, and the most curious epithets.

An article, signed "Young Parliamentary Hand," which appeared in *United Ireland*, in 1888, gives an interesting pen picture of Don Roberto, the new M.P.:

"From the beginning Cunninghame Graham was regarded as one of the most remarkable men in the new Parliament. His appearance alone singled him out from the ordinary run and ruck of new members who huddled (timidly) together in the lobbies of Westminster. They stared in amazement at the stranger who always seemed to be in a hurry. Had Cunninghame Graham only carried himself a little less erectly, if his closely-knit frame had been a little less sinewy, and his movements less limber, he might very well have passed muster as the representative of a certain school of art. . . . But anyone who carried investigation beyond the cursory glance soon noticed muscularity in the body which never came from wielding the paint-brush, a tan upon the firm flesh which never was due to the cool light and shade of stuccoed studios. In fact, the critical observer noted something about Cunninghame Graham that was of a soldierly smack, and not quite soldierly either. That the man was a mighty rider was obvious to the experienced eye in a little, but his movements were not of a cavalryman: they were freer, less stiff, simpler.

"London, more eager than Athens of old for something new, was pleased, at the time, to take a great deal of interest in that curious production of American frontier life, the Cow-boy. Buffalo Bill and his merry men were the heroes of the hour, and in certain circles, while the craze lasted, little was talked or thought but the Cow-boy. The Cow-boy fever ran its course and died away as all such frenzies do in a great capital where people hunger and thirst after any new excitement.

"If Cunninghame Graham had been content to call himself 'Mexican Jack' and to sport a *sombrero*, he would have obtained what the French call a *succès fou*, but he was a man with a mission, and languid London does not love men with missions. He was a Radical in the true sense of the term—a Radical with that touch of Quixotism without which few reforms would ever come to anything. He saw that there was work to be done, and he set himself to do it with the same fiery energy and indomitable determination which he had shown during his former travels in wild lands. He entered Parliament not to play the part of the silent member, but to plead vehemently for all the causes dearest to his heart.

"It is needless to say that he made himself at once amazingly unpopular with all the 'classes,' with advocates of things as they are, and that if there was one individual whom the average Tory hated almost as much as any Irish member, it was the impetuous, red-haired Cunninghame Graham."

CHAPTER X

O N the 1st of February 1887, Don Roberto made his maiden speech in Parliament. The opportunity was an ideal one for a man such as he was, and he took full advantage of it, rising with an elegant gesture to make his address in answer to Queen Victoria's Speech. With unique courage and conviction he spoke, his stentorian voice ringing through the House, and his words startling and shocking the Members who had rarely heard such an eloquent flow of language. It can easily be imagined what the effect must have been when he started:

"A debate on the Queen's Speech forms the best occasion for a new Member to loose his political virginity, and, therefore, I cast myself at once on the forbearance and the generosity of the House.

"On glancing over the Queen's Speech, I am struck with the evident desire which prevails in it to do nothing at all. There is a similarity in its paragraphs to the *laissez-faire* school of political economy. Not one word is said in the Speech about lightening the taxation under which Her Majesty's lieges suffer; not a word to make that taxation more bearable; not one word to bridge over the awful chasm existing between the poor and the rich; not one word of kindly sympathy for the sufferers from the present commercial and agricultural depression—nothing but platitudes, nothing but views of society

192

through a little bit of pink glass. . . . It is not to be expected that Her Majesty's Government will vouchsafe to the House any idea of when the British troops might be withdrawn from Egypt. . . ."

Continuing his startling speech he proceeded to attack what he styled "our latest filibustering exploit in Burmah . . . with arms of precision shooting down naked savages." Then he went on, sarcastically: "When telegrams come from Burma we slap our hands on our chests—quite regardless of damage to our shirts—and talk of British gallantry, and laugh like parrots at a bagpiper, when we look at the sketches in the illustrated papers depicting natives running away from our troops. . . ."

Going on, probably smiling inwardly at the expressions on the faces looking at him, he referred to Liberals as "crutch-and-toothpick gentlemen," and then, sweeping a pointing finger at the assembly, at the same time looking round the House, he said that this Government reminded him of Pope's flies in amber:

"Things in themselves, though neither rich nor rare,
One wonders how the devil they got there."

Then, referring to the resignation of Lord Randolph Churchill, he continued: "The noble Lord's resignation has saddened me as children are saddened when they see a rocket spout up, and are all unaware that it will fall down a stick, as well said by Ben Jonson:

'He was a child that so did thrive in grace and feature,
As Heaven and nature seemed to strive which owned the creature.'

here is the noble Lord now?" Don Roberto exclaimed.

"Yesterday he was, to-day he is not—gone like the froth on the licensed victualler's beer. . . ."

Touching on the Irish Home Rule question he astonished his listeners by saying: "With regard to Ireland, I have eminent qualifications for dealing with that subject, for many reasons. First of all, I have never been there, second, because I am sitting next to Nationalist Members, and then because I have once known an Irish commercial traveller who imparted to me various facts quite unattainable by the general public. . . ."

Raising his voice more and more, and looking, sometimes even pointing at Members, who wriggled with indignation, he wound up his speech by attacking society in general:

"... The society in which one man works and another enjoys the fruit—the society in which capital and luxury makes Heaven for 30,000 and a Hell for 30,000,000, that society whose crowning achievement is this dreary waste of mud and stucco—with its misery, its want and destitution, its degradation, its prostitution, and its glaring social inequalities—the society we call London—that society which, by a refinement of irony, has placed the mainspring of human action, almost the power of life and death, and the absolute power to pay labour and to reward honour, behind the grey tweed veil which enshrouds the greasy pocket of the capitalist."

What effect this maiden speech must have had upon the assembly is best left to imagination. Before the bewildered Members had finished staring at each other, he strode out, leapt on his mustang "Pampa," and cantered towards his London home to attend to his many new duties.

A full account of his Parliamentary speeches and activities would fill a volume, so I must limit these memoirs to some of the most typical things he said and did during the stormy six years he was in Parliament.

As time went on, Members who considered him an eccentric, began to like him as a man, though, as a Member of the House he was a nuisance, always giving trouble and interrupting speeches with the fiery indignation of a Swift. His presence must have been all the more a nuisance because he was quite incorrigible, and, above all, incorruptible. When he quoted poetry, Gladstone (whom Don Roberto despised with all his heart and soul), looked at him amused and at the same time interested. The bluff old country members fancied him an original poet, but the men who make history gave him credit for what he was—namely, the true friend of the people, the one who dared to force the Labour questions to the front in the House of Commons. In the eyes of those who found fault with his mannerisms and Quixotism, he was a Spanish Don whose weakness it was to tilt at windmills.

Certainly he was more at home with poets, gauchos and frontiersmen than with statistics, facts and figures.

The so-called Labour Members did not agree with him, for his chivalrous nature led him to champion the cause of those they wished to consider "outside politics." This he did, single-handed, from the day he set foot in the House of Commons. Forlorn hopes attracted him, as did any man who was down and out, and personal ambition was too vulgar to have influenced him. He was not a man who lived on theories, and, although his position in Parliament brought him in contact with Socialists, Anarchists and other "ists," and all these people spoke well of him, he instinctively kept them at arm's length with an excess of politeness, for at heart, although he did not realise it, he was the perfect aristocrat, which, however, did not prevent him from being an ardent and sincere democrat.

Once, when a man from London went to a miners' meeting in Scotland, he spoke to some of the black, grimy and weather-beaten constituents who, after the meeting, had gathered in groups to discuss the "toozled-headed darling" they had sent to represent them in Parliament.

"What do the London men say of *our* Graham?" the man from the South was asked by one of the miners.

"Oh, they say he is rattle-brained, and needs ballast," was the reply.

A complete silence fell on the men, and presently an old miner, with tears rolling down his black cheeks, spoke.

"When you go back to London," he said, "you tell the London men we *love* our Graham."

Whatever Don Roberto has achieved, or not achieved, as a Member of Parliament, no nobler epitaph could he have earned than the words of the grimy old miner.

English people could hardly be expected to have understood him, for he had the manners and mentality which represent two nations. His first—and strongest—was that of the Spanish Don; and his second that of the Scottish nobleman, and a more curious mixture would be difficult to find.

Besides the startling "plank" which gained him election, here are a few of the items he brought before the House, not to mention many emphatic protests, interruptions and numerous "slaps" he directed at Members.

Protection of pit ponies:

". . . I have such a high opinion of the animal I desire to protect," he said in connection with this, . . . "one effect of shortening the hours of labour among men cannot but lessen to some extent the barbarities now practised upon beasts of burden. Pit ponies of South Wales work up to nineteen hours. A haulier said that he had to take a horse out of the stable though it had been working day and night in succession for six days. The haulier remarked that the animal, immediately on its being brought out of the stable trembled, dropped down, and cried like a baby. It actually cried. To do such work the poor animals are compelled by brutality of the most revolting kind: they are kicked, beaten and whipped. . . ."

Don Roberto compelled the Home Secretary to send out a circular, calling upon Inspectors of Mines to pay special regard to the welfare of these dumb sharers in man's toil.

Among the many other items and protests he brought before the House were the following I mention but briefly:

Overloading of cattle ships.

Opposed construction of a railway in Lake District.

Opposed capital and corporal punishment.

Furious attacks on the sweating system.

Asked for leniency in cases of severe sentences.

Prison reform.

Pleaded that mercy be shown to two Zulu murderers. (In connection with this he said: "In time the natives become subject to those blessings which civilisation affords both natives and Europeans, namely, drunkenness and immorality.")

Defended the Right of Public Meeting.

Fought for illegitimate children. (The law as it was, inflicted serious hardships on such children, and Don Roberto asked that the law be amended so as to remove the legal disabilities of children born out of wedlock. In Scotland eight per cent of the children were illegitimate). Etc., etc.

Once, when rising to speak on one of these subjects, he began: "Even at the risk of being as tedious as a king, I feel it necessary to bestow my tediousness upon the House. . . ."

Writing to a friend about political programmes, Don Roberto said: "A programme should be:

1. Short.
2. Definite.

197

3. It should not *argue* or endeavour to meet objections. *Nail* the flag to the mast."

Conditions among the nail- and chain-makers of Cradley Heath ("Hell Hole," as Disraeli called it) were appalling; in fact, for 150 years the condition of the nailers—who were "sweated"—had been wretched in the extreme. The average earnings, for twelve to fifteen hours' hard work per day were six shillings per week, and women, most of whom worked naked down to the waist, earned less than half that amount.

Don Roberto had paid several visits to Cradley Heath, and when he pressed the House for an inquiry into conditions among the nail- and chain-makers, a Conservative Member put down what is called a "blocking motion," in order to prevent a debate on the subject.

Don Roberto then asked the First Lord of the Treasury if, before the end of the session, he would give a day to discuss the motion.

The First Lord of the Treasury answered that the subject to which Don Roberto had drawn attention was receiving the earnest attention of the Government, but that, owing to the pressure of Public Business, he could not make any further disposition of the public time.

Leaping to his feet, Don Roberto flashed back: "May I remind the Right Honourable Gentleman that he has not in the least degree answered my question. I asked a definite question: Whether he would afford facilities for the discussion of a Motion of one of his own supporters? If he does not do so, I characterise that Motion as a dishonourable trick to avoid discussion."

Mr. Speaker: "Order! Order! The Honourable Member is conducting himself in a most unusual and un-Parliamentary manner in making use of language of that kind. I must request him to withdraw the expression he has made use of."

Don Roberto: *"I never withdraw!** I simply said what I mean."

Mr. Speaker: "I must ask the Honourable Member to withdraw the expression 'dishonourable trick,' which is a strictly improper and un-Parliamentary expression."

Don Roberto: "Mr. Speaker, I wish, as on former occasions, to acquit myself of an intentional discourtesy to you; but I am compelled again to characterise the action taken with regard to this Motion by the Honourable Member for Dudley as a dishonourable trick."

Mr. Speaker: "I must again ask the Honourable Member to withdraw so improper and un-Parliamentary an expression."

Don Roberto: "I refuse, Sir, to withdraw it."

Mr. Speaker: "Then I must ask the Honourable Member to withdraw from the House."

Don Roberto: "Certainly, Sir, I will go to Cradley Heath."

And so he did, taking the midnight train. This naturally annoyed the Member for Dudley, in whose constituency Cradley Heath was situated. The displeasure at Don Roberto's intrusion into his constituency he aired in a later Session in the House, to the great joy of Don Roberto.

To-day, most people are unaware, and will hardly believe it when I state from statistics that in those days (1888), on the North British Railway Company, its servants worked:

in 6,142 instances over 13 hours.
„ 6,028 „ „ 14 „
„ 3,808 „ „ 15 „
„ 1,999 „ „ 16 „

and there were over 1,300 cases of works being carried on for even longer periods.

Don Roberto maintained that leisure was essential if the level of culture was to be raised, for men had only time to work and sleep, and no mental relaxation, if they had minds

---

* See what G. B. Shaw says about this remark. Pages 262–263.

at all; never having had a chance to acquire or cultivate minds of their own. However, whenever he asked the House if there was any possible chance of discussing the Eight Hours Bill, his question was greeted with roars of laughter.

In 1890, in answer to the Queen's Speech, he said: "There is a pleasing air of concord and agreement hanging over the first day or two of the present session of the House of Commons. It is a little dull while it lasts, and it is fortunate that it does not continue for long. Not infrequently it is my unfortunate task to break in on the concord of the House with a discordant note. . . ."

And certainly he often did break in on the concord of the House with discordant notes, as will be seen by the following utterances he made in the House during the six years he sat in it. In making reference to a Member's speech he once sarcastically said: ". . . That difference of opinion that makes the life of debate . . . I do like thoroughly a good contradiction, especially when it comes on the heels of an opinion expressed with force a short time before. It must show the country the extreme steadiness of opinion that prevails in this legislative chamber. . . ."

And, answering to a proposal that women be not eligible for election as County Councillors, "I will put it straight across this House to the Lord Advocate, whether he thinks that the functions of women are to be confined to their ball of thin cotton and a number eight needle, and the production of little sinners. . . ."

A Member referred to a previous speaker's tone and language and reproached him for having imported into the debate an element which it would have been better to leave out.

(The previous speaker had compared an Amendment with a clergyman found drunk in the street.)

This was a great chance for Don Roberto who immediately

rose and said: "Of course, personally, I do not care very much whether a clergyman is found, once or twice drunk in the street. I merely wish to say that I differ from the Honourable Member who has just sat down in what he has said about the tone and language which have been imported into this debate. I am very much obliged to the Honourable Gentleman who made use of that language for introducing that tone. I cannot say that I would have adopted it myself, but I must say that if you want to have the attention of the public fixed upon a matter like this, it is by importing a tone of acrimony into a debate that you most effectually fix it. . . ."

The previous speaker: "I do not wish to imitate the Honourable Member who has just sat down."

Don Roberto: "I quite absolve you."

The effect of the following words can easily be imagined, when he said to the House: "I have never attacked the Queen or any Member of the Royal Family outside the House, and, therefore, I do not come to the House with nauseous pretensions of sham loyalty."

On one occasion he referred to Kings and Queens as "Creatures of Parliament."

In connection with regulating the traffic of white people invading the Solomon Islands and the New Hebrides with coloured labour, he shocked the House by having a slap at the bishops. He said:

"I do not know that I have hitherto had a great deal of sympathy with bishops or missionaries. I respect missionaries who go out to savage countries in order to reclaim the people there; but I need not remind the Committee that when the debates for abolition of slavery in the West Indies took place in the other House [House of Lords], almost every bishop voted for the retention of such a sacred institution. When, also, the question of continuing the practice of pigeon shooting was under consideration, nearly every bishop voted in favour of its continuance. Therefore I am not inclined to attach much importance to the testimony of bishops. . . ."

As might be expected, he created several uproars in the House, and on various occasions was suspended. Once he greatly annoyed the assembly by saying: "I have not that infantile or elephantine faith in Governments, and I am not engaged in swallowing my life's convictions, and, putting myself up for auction for a place in either of the two Governments. . . ."

And then again he made the following statements:

"The occupants of the Front Bench sit like so many stuffed figures at Madame Tussaud's, making no observations whatever, but occasionally run out to look at the telegraph tape to see what news is coming from Connemara or other parts of the world out of which they might be able to make political capital. . . ."

"I do not wish to be oppressed here by the grunting of innumerable swine, even though they are of Guinea. In the House of Commons one would rather expect to sit amongst choice company, unelbowed by a gamester, pimp or player."

"That pillar of our civilisation, the Hotchkiss gun."

"There is a Darker Continent east of Temple Bar than that through which the Zambezi, the Congo, and the Limpopo flow. Those who explore it are not commonly awarded honours by County Councils. You see, the people who live in it are not negroes, only Englishmen, the cheapest, most submissive animals ever created."

On one occasion, interrupting his old friend (though political opponent), Mr. Asquith, who spoke on a Local Authorities Purchase of Land Bill, he shouted: "Perhaps the Honourable Member will explain how shareholders in swindling companies——"

(Cries of "Order! Order!")

Don Roberto: "Oh, I am not going to be put down!"

(Cries of "Order!" and "Name!")

Don Roberto: "It is a matter of no importance to me whether I am named or not."

Mr. Speaker: "Order! Order!"

Don Roberto: "What I want to know is, how do swindling shareholders in a company derive their funds?"

(Shouts of: "Order! Name!")

Mr. Speaker: "Order! Order!—The conduct of the Honourable Gentleman is such that I must name him to the House. I name, you, Mr. Cunninghame Graham."

Don Roberto: "All right! I am simply named for standing up for Socialism in this House in the face of a swindling speech endeavouring to draw ridiculous distinctions. That is why I am named."

The Secretary of State for the Home Department: "I beg to move, in the terms of the Standing Order, that the Honourable Member be suspended from the service of the House."

Don Roberto: "Suspend away! . . . I do not care a damn!"

(Shouts of: "Order! Order!" as Don Roberto strides out of the House.)

John Burns once said of Don Roberto: "He is a Social Reformer."

I feel inclined to agree with this remark, for the only statement of Socialism Don Roberto ever made in the House—as far as I have been able to trace—was when he said:

"We look confidently for the time when the Government

will take possession of the mines and machinery of this country, and work them for the benefit of the country, and not in the selfish interests of capitalists." (1887.)

That Don Roberto took up politics, as the French would say, *pour faute de mieux*, but nevertheless quite seriously, seems obvious, and that he often spoke with his tongue in his cheek, is just as certain. He himself admitted that "during the babble of the House of Commons, when, in the hot summer nights the Members were hard at work substituting the word 'and' for the word 'but,' and leaving out all the words from 'whereinsoever' down to 'which in so after,' in some senseless Bill, I often wandered back in my mind to the Pampas."

The House of Parliament he called the "Great Thieves' Kitchen, manned with magnolia-scented cooks, too fine to cook," or the "National Gas Works."

According to him, the Members were "Gentlemen raised on weak lemonade and seed-cake," and he said that he saw no difference between Liberals and Conservatives, "except the better cut of the Conservatives' boots."

"All that is required of a man, in order to make him an efficient Member of Parliament," he once remarked, "is that he has a good pair of legs to enable him to trot in and out of the Division Lobby at the call of the Party Whip."

More than once, coming out of the House, he was heard to say: "Business done: None. England saved again!"

To me he said that the House of Commons, with all the bald heads, crowded together, always reminded him of a huge ostrich nest; with the only difference that these "eggs" were either empty or addled.

"If a hat were dropped from the House of Commons on the Liberal benches," he wrote during what might be called his "Parliamentary period," "it would fall on the bald head of a millionaire."

In writing about the Liberal Party he was vitriolic beyond

measure, referring to it as "an amorphous crowd of Non-conformists, Temperance Reformers, Deceased Wife's Sisters, Mono-maniacs, and Single Taxers, with all the faddist and dried fruit of outworn Liberal politics which the tide of Liberalism has left like jelly-fish and seaweed, stranded and dying on the beach. And what a beach it is, strewn with the dead remains of Leagues and Federations and Societies, mostly composed of Treasurer and Secretary, long-haired and stammering speakers with their theories of prompt regeneration for the body politic, and a collecting-box to shove beneath the public's nose."

The literary world must be thankful that Don Roberto became a Member of Parliament, for if this had not come about, the chances are that he would never have written.

One day, after he had made a remarkable speech in the House, a Member who was interested in a Labour newspaper, went up to him and asked him to write the speech he had made. At first he refused to do so, saying that he had no literary ability, but finally gave in, with the result that his article* caused quite a stir among the critics and writers of those days.

It has been said that Frank Harris, one time editor of the *Saturday Review*, "discovered" G. B. Shaw, H. G. Wells, Max Beerbohm, Cunninghame Graham and other writers. This may be so, but not in Don Roberto's case, for his first story, published in the *Saturday Review*, appeared late in 1895, under the title of "Ras Doura."

(Between 1895 and 1914, he wrote no fewer than 117 stories and sketches for the *Saturday Review*. Some of these were later published in book form.)

The amount of work dynamic Don Roberto did whilst he was in Parliament is almost incredible, for besides masses

---

* *Economic Evolution*, later published in pamphlet form. (Printed in Aberdeen, 1891.)

of long political articles, letters to editors, attending, and speaking at meetings and looking after his estates, he still found time to do a great deal of reading, and at the same time he kept in touch with his numerous friends. He never employed a secretary, and wrote everything by hand.

Among the many amusing things that happened owing to his bad hand-writing was when, on one occasion, from Scotland, he sent a short note to a fellow Socialist in London. Unable to read the scrawl, the receiver of the note asked a friend if he could make out what the short communication was about. Unable to make head or tail out of it, the friend then suggested taking the note to a chemist who surely was used to deciphering even the worst hand-writings. Accordingly, they sent a servant, and when she returned from the chemist who, by the way, was a staunch Liberal, and therefore disliked Don Roberto's political views, she brought back a small glass-container filled with—mercurial ointment! When Don Roberto came to London and heard about this joke he called on this chemist and congratulated him on an excellent joke, and, until the man retired, always patronised his shop.

Before going further with Don Roberto's Parliamentary career, let me acquaint the reader with just a few things he said and wrote at the time.

He referred to Mr. Gladstone, Lord Salisbury and others as "political cheap-jacks."

. . . . . .

". . . this jolly old roast-beefy, plum pudding, dunder-headed port-wine-and-Bible old country of ours."

. . . . . .

"*Something must be done.* Ill-omened phrase to whisper to a Parliament—People's Parliament. If it had been, *something must be SAID*, or better still, *left unsaid*, then, indeed, there would be probability enough of Parliament attending.

But done! perish the thought; a *fico* for it; done, done, no do's in Parliament."

.   .   .   .   .

"I am a man of peace. I am a man who would at any time a good deal rather run than fight. All violence is hateful to me, because I see so much of it. I see society based upon violence, and I know that many in their heart of hearts are longing for a chance to use the glorious instruments which bolster up our civilisation."

.   .   .   .   .

"The strife of parties means nothing, but rotation of rascals in office."

.   .   .   .   .

"The proletarian has no country; all are equally prisons to him alike."

.   .   .   .   .

"I must confess, with shame, that till lately one's idea of a typical Scotchman has been: a stout, skunk-like, hypo-critical, broad-clothed, money-bagged, constant in church and smart; ever anxious after having duly diluted the sugar with sand to call all his household together to praise 'Gawd.'"

.   .   .   .   .

"I cannot believe that the natural state of man is one of war. I hold that war can be subdued by reason. It does not seem as if a state of things in which the country resounds with constant struggle can be satisfactory. It does not seem a state of things in which the men must always lose should be considered by them as definite."

.   .   .   .   .

"Surely it is a matter of much self-congratulation, much handshaking, much rubbing of pious noses—and stomachs— much food for declamation, that our Parliament alone of all its imitators has the tradition of true gentility.

"I do not deny that in the days of your clouded cane, your

amber snuff-box, small-sword, good manners, peach-coloured coats and Steinkirk ruffles, a gentleman performed a pleasing and almost useful function in the State.

"He it was whose mission was to be a thing of beauty, to set the tone in good society, to lead our armies, die for his country—and he often did so—and generally disport himself as if he were a mixture of bulldog and butterfly. Peace to his snuff-box! May the earth lie lightly on his clouded cane. May his bloom-coloured coat and small-clothes in the town museum serve to remind us that in his time shoddy and machinery were unknown and yet men lived. . . ."

. . . . .

"Never in the history of this thrice-blessed world have Bibles been so cheap. Think of that, man! A starveling in his garret may read the Holy Scriptures—if his eyes can stand the print—for twopence. Selah!"

. . . . .

On the Press: "It is, perhaps, a cruel thing to say that the press is nobbled, and now, instead of being an instrument of freedom, it has become a reptile of the basest sort. The function of the Press is to chronicle small beer, to tell us who is dead and damned, or hanged, or married, to print the lists of shares, to let the public know what theatres are open, and when the glove fight and the football match comes off, and if her gracious Majesty in the east wind has deigned to walk upon the slopes. In fact to be a pimp of news for the public at a penny.

"Render to Cæsar what is his'n, and to the editor his penny, but give him not your conscience in his keeping. . . . A lie becomes almost true in type. . . ."

. . . . .

"That cowardly quantity called public sympathy."

. . . . .

"To look at the average Englishman, with his mutton-chop

whiskers, cleanly shaven chin, short legs, well-developed profile below the waist, and generally prosaic habit of mind, body and estate, one would not be likely to imagine that a certain tendency, a delicacy of mental vision—if I may so call it—was one of his leading characteristics. I think, though, that—without the aid of the smoked glass, so necessary in eclipses—I can detect, and more than that, show the existence of the microbe of Rose-Pinkism in the tissues of his well-fed frame, and perhaps somewhat sluggish-acting mind. I know that many will deny this with an oath, exclaiming perhaps, if they be Scotchmen, as did the Johnstone, Thirwall and a', after the death of Albany Featherstonehaugh, 'Hoot awa' lads, hoot awa'.'

"Nevertheless, I do most confidently assert that a most roseate hue of pink is what does prevail in the mental vision of most Britons. Furthermore, if there is no rose-pink in nature, they will seek to beautify and paint the London fog, the streets of Whitechapel and the lives of the poor, all of that colour.

"Chiefly, perhaps, when treating of reforms, does the tendency exist."

.   .   .   .   .   .

"Do not for a moment imagine that I care in the smallest degree for business as such. The business generally understood, seems to be the acquisition of money by a man living in the suburbs, taking a morning train into the City, turning over a few letters, eating a heavy luncheon, and returning home in the evening, carrying a parcel containing a special titbit for the dinner-table. Understand, I respect this man's ability in precisely the same way that I dislike the imbecility of the community for allowing money to be made off their labour by such a process. . . . I am content to admire this business, standing far off, like a publican, but no more seek to inquire into its inner workings than I would seek to inquire if the bloom on the actress's cheek were real, or if, when the unctuous bishop hid his face in his hem-stitched 'wipe,' he really was dissolved in tears for human frailty, nor only blew his nose. . . ."

.   .   .   .   .

"I protest against the practice of sending down a man into the constituency labelled—'Gladstone 2s. 6d.'"

.   .   .   .   .

"There are enough tears shed in this England of ours to float a number of the Queen's battleships."

.   .   .   .   .

Mr. Peel, the Speaker, was the son of Sir Robert Peel, the repealer of the Corn Laws. During a debate, when Don Roberto was subjected to interruptions by Liberals and Conservatives, he pointed a finger at the Speaker and exclaimed:

"To the son of the man who gave the people Free Bread, I appeal for Free Speech."

.   .   .   .   .

"Gentlemen, I shall be brief but tedious."

In attacking the "Co-operation dummy," he showed unique imagination in making the following comparison:

"You have seen little boys work their wicked will with their sisters' dolls. Those of unartistic mind will flatten out the wax features, poke the glass eyes and scalp off the golden wig. But little boys of refined and cultivated tastes will make a tiny hole in the foot of his sister's idol and watch with unholy glee the sawdust run out, until nothing is left but a piece of rag surmounted by a waxen bust that would not deceive a baby, and every one can see that the doll was a fraud, and a very poor fraud, too."

.   .   .   .   .

"If I cannot be epigrammatic in my dissatisfaction, I can at least be brutal. . . . How shall brutality offend, when all are brutal? The brutal ——, well stuffed with meat and drink, common and vulgar in his pleasures. The brutal lord at the Pelican club; the brutal lady at the pigeon match or pheasant battue. The brutal man of business, caring not a fraction if all the world should come to ruin, so that his brutal firm should flourish. The coarse and brutal doctrine of the Gospel shop, reward and punishment, or profit and loss. The brutal treatment of wives, horses, children, dogs and all the weaker animals that God has sent (a brutal God!) into the world for man's behoof. The thought of all this, and the thought that it is all to go on unchanged till a thousand or more years are out, robs me of my gladness in the contemplation of the Glad New Year." (1891.)

. . . . .

A typical example of Don Roberto's humour when he spoke in the auctioneer's rostrum in a Scottish cattle market. He described the place as a "pure fountain of truth and honour," to the immense enjoyment of the "ring."

. . . . .

A meeting of Lancashire and Yorkshire Socialists was to be held on a certain spot on the bleak moorland near the border of the two counties. Don Roberto and the Yorkshire contingent—for whom he was to speak—were first to arrive at the meeting-place. Some time later, when the Lancastrian party wound its way up the steep hill, led by the redoubtable H. M. Hyndman, who wore a long frock-coat and whose patriarchal beard fluttered about in the wind, Don Roberto, raising one arm, with a flourish exclaimed: "Behold, here cometh Moses and the Israelites."

. . . . .

A certain gentleman who disliked Don Roberto for political reasons travelled on the same train from Glasgow to London. During lunch the two were seated at the same table. The gentleman, who had a very delicate palate, carried in his hand-bag some specially nutritious and delicious bread which his wife had baked for him. As he sat down, he placed one of these rolls in front of him.

Don Roberto was reading a book, and as the lunch did not arrive, and, feeling hungry, he stretched out his hand towards the conjugal roll.

"Sir!" cried the gentleman, making all the other passengers turn their heads, "Sir, you have tried to take away my character, but you shall never take away my bread!"

"Your bread?" echoed Don Roberto.

"Yes, Sir, my bread—the bread my own wife has specially baked for me, the bread I brought here in my own hand-bag."

"Your hand-bag!" shuddered the Spanish Don.

"Yes, Sir, my own hand-bag."

As if horrified Don Roberto dropped his book on his knee and hurriedly produced his pocket-handkerchief.

"Steward!" he called, as he wiped his well-shaped strong fingers—"steward, some *clean* bread, please!"

. . . . .

Money given to the Church he called "Fire Insurance."

. . . . .

A Scotsman he described as "a slave of the hopeless sort, who thinks he is free, and hugs his party chains, and chains of *kirk*, and of respectability, and says: 'Look at me, and see how free I am.' Just as free, indeed, as the squirrel turning in his cruel cage, free to turn round, but not come out."

. . . . .

In 1886, "the aristocratic Socialist and cow-boy dandy," (as *The Times* called Don Roberto), together with his friend Keir Hardie, joined the Scottish Home Rule Association, and it was also together with him that he founded the Scottish Labour Party, which later merged with other groups and has now become an important factor in English politics.

However, he was regarded with some suspicion by some

of his Socialist companions, for they could not help feeling
that he was so different from themselves.

In 1889, in Glasgow, in the office of Bailie Shaw Maxwell,
the Independent Labour Party was founded. Among others
present were Keir Hardie and Don Roberto.

Not cut out to be a "party man," he gradually drifted away
from those with whom Socialist propaganda brought him
into contact, and became what suited him best: a free lance.

As readers must be aware, the vexing Irish Home Rule
question was the sore spot in English politics at the time,
and was to remain so for several decades longer. Besides
Gladstone and Parnell the Irish cause had two sturdy
champions in Wilfrid Scawen Blunt, poet extraordinary,
wealthy Catholic squire, traveller and bitter anti-English
imperialist, and Don Roberto who soon became his life-long
friend.

Naturally both were the great favourites of the Irish
Members of the House, and often Don Roberto and Parnell
were to be seen sitting in a coffee-house in Westminster.

As might be expected, people thought they must be talking
politics, or even plotting, but Don Roberto assured me that,
outside the House, they never once mentioned politics, but,
instead, always talked about horses, about which Parnell
knew very little or nothing.

CHAPTER XI

THE "BATTLE" OF TRAFALGAR SQUARE, OR "BLOODY
SUNDAY"—TRIAL AND CONVICTION AT THE OLD
BAILEY—LIFE IN PENTONVILLE PRISON

LATE in 1887, William O'Brien, Member of Parliament,
and other Irish patriots, had been imprisoned in Ireland
because they had caused trouble in demanding Irish
Home Rule, and at the time Wilfrid Blunt was also in gaol.

Things soon came to a crisis in London, and when the
"Metropolitan Radical Federation" planned a meeting to
demand the release of O'Brien, Sir Charles Warren, head of
the London police, prohibited the meeting which was to be
held, on Sunday, November 13th, 1887, in Trafalgar Square.

On Saturday, November 12th, Don Roberto and his wife
were sitting in a little hotel in Stoke-upon-Trent where he
had addressed a meeting. Whilst reading the *Morning Post*,
he saw that the Trafalgar Square meeting had been banned.
Jumping up, he exclaimed: "I am sure that not a single M.P.
is to be found who will protest! By Jove! I'll go!"

At once he packed his portmanteau and made the journey
towards London where a great deal of trouble was in store
for him.

Arriving in the metropolis, he was delighted to hear that,
determined as the authorities were to prevent the holding
of the meeting, the demonstrators and orators were equally
determined to carry out their intentions. (Mr. John Burns,
with whom I spoke recently, still maintains that Sir
Charles Warren had no right to stop the meeting, and
he affirms that in doing so he (Sir Charles), and
those with him, committed a serious legal blunder.)

214

Already early in the morning of the day (which was to be known as "Bloody Sunday"), clouds of unrest drifted over the London sky.

In order to keep Trafalgar Square "clear for the Queen," 1,500 constables were posted all round it, in single and double files, and at certain strategic points they even stood in fours. Mounted police patrolled, circling round, and 2,500 constables were kept in reserve to break up the processions which were to start from various quarters of the metropolis. Thus the Chief of Police had no fewer than 5,000 men on duty.

Early in the afternoon the various contingents of demonstrators set into motion. William Morris, the poet-socialist, led one, and with others marched a number of famous men, including Prince Kropotkin.

Acting upon orders issued by Sir Charles Warren, the police broke up most of these processions at selected points *en route*, and therefore they never reached the Square where a vast mass of humanity arrived from all directions, like a tidal wave. People hooted when the mounted police rode among them, and as the crowd grew there were incidents every now and again. Gradually the excitement increased, and so did the incidents, as the mounted police vainly tried to drive away people.

When things began to look really ugly, 300 Grenadier Guards arrived on the scene, and, shortly after, these were followed by 300 Life Guards, their cuirasses and drawn swords shining. A grey-suited man in a top-hat, rode at the head of the Life Guards, between two officers. This was the stipendiary magistrate from Woolwich, who carried the Riot Act in his hand.

The Grenadier Guards now fixed bayonets, and the mounted police charged, using their batons freely, knocking down and injuring many people.

In the meantime John Burns—who had arranged to meet several leaders who were to speak in the Square—waited vainly for his friends outside Charing Cross Station. Evidently the outlook was not to their liking, for not one appeared, although a number had made a vow that, no matter what might happen, they would speak from the foot of the Nelson Column, at 3 p.m.

Burns was sadly disappointed, but suddenly he saw a figure appear, immaculately dressed, striding towards him. It was Don Roberto! Burns wondered where and how on earth his friend had heard about this secret meeting-place, for he had nothing to do with the organisation of the demonstration; in fact Burns thought he was still in Stoke-upon-Trent.

Said Burns: "It is three o'clock." "So it is," Don Roberto answered, pulling a silk handkerchief out of the breast pocket of his coat, with an inimitable flourish.

Burns then explained that it would be most difficult, or even impossible to reach the Square, for the side from which they would have to force their way through, was guarded by three or four rows of mounted police, behind which stood a line of foot constables.

After a short council of war Burns exclaimed: "Now for it! You come along, Graham, you know how to handle horses." "Yes, but what about you?" Don Roberto asked. "With your help I'll get through under them," answered Burns, and with this the two hurried towards Trafalgar Square where, for a while, they were mixed up in the dense, angry crowd. Having pushed their way through the seething mass of humanity, they reached the mounted police, and whilst Don Roberto gently caught horses by the bridles, Burns slipped through the ranks, followed by his friend, without the mounted constables being aware that the two were "enemies." In fact, probably owing to their boldness, the policemen took them for officials. The two dare-devils were just about to pass the last obstacle (a line of constables on foot), when one of them recognised the sturdy and bearded figure of Burns.

Immediately a crowd of policemen attacked the two, batoning and kicking them unmercifully. Don Roberto's head was cracked open, and Burns, who was an excellent boxer, valiantly shielded his badly injured friend from further harm, for the constables still kept on battering him. Finally a number of strong arms held the two captives, and just then an excited Superintendent of Police came running up, shouting: "Burns, you rascal, we heard you were coming, and here you are!" and with this struck him several times.

"All right, old fellow," the helpless Burns replied, "I like to keep my word; you keep your temper."

Don Roberto's wound was bleeding terribly, but although he felt faint, he pretended not to be in distress.

From the crowd who had witnessed this incident, there came a roar of disapproval, followed by a rush which, however, was repulsed. When temporary calm had been restored, Don Roberto was allowed to go to a fountain in the Square where Burns, filling his bowler hat with water, poured it over his friend's head.

Gabrielle, who had watched the scene from a window of a hotel overlooking the Square, thought her husband was dying, but as soon as he was able, he sent her a note stating that he and Burns were detained, but that they were "all right."

Presently the two captives were taken up some steps, leading out of the Square towards the National Gallery, and as they passed through the Grenadier Guards, stationed there with fixed bayonets, a sergeant, prodding Burns with the butt-end of his rifle, said: "You're a well-plucked 'un."

Shortly after 6 p.m. order was restored, but this only after many people had been injured, one so severely that he died.

Among the innocent people who were accidentally knocked about by the police, was M. Andreux, an ex-Ambassador of France who was hit on the head and prostrated when, as the mounted police were charging, he happened to be walking out of the Hôtel Métropole.

No doubt, as usually happens on such occasions, a number of roughs were among the demonstrators, and when the police broke up the processions, sticks, bricks and similar weapons were used, and pickpockets had a good day. Naturally, the Irish element was very strong, and full of the national love of a good row. Seventy-five men were arrested, most of them in Parliament Square where the fighting was particularly severe.

Don Roberto and Burns were taken to the cells of the Bow Street Police Court where, although the former was badly injured and bleeding profusely, he was not allowed a doctor or water. Mr. Asquith and Colonel Hope, V.C.—an uncle of Don Roberto—offered bail, which was only granted after twenty-three hours.

Don Roberto had not gone to the Square as a sympathiser with the Socialists. His sole object had been to speak in favour of O'Brien's release from prison. In fact, since the meeting had been arranged by the Metropolitan Radical Federation, he had no knowledge that the Socialists were taking part in it until he heard that Burns was to meet a number of allies outside Charing Cross Station.

Whatever may be thought of Don Roberto's and Burns's opinions, they had enough conviction to risk their skins for them, although they showed a determination that was—perhaps—silly, and courage that was grotesque; but it must be remembered that, from a worldly point of view, they had everything to lose and nothing to gain. Anyway, considering that Burns was only armed with a return tram ticket, and Don Roberto with a silk handkerchief, they had, as Mr. Burns recently told me, "the satisfaction of having had what probably is the biggest escort in English history."

Confined in their cell, next to one in which were two drunken prostitutes, and another in which three young men from the slums used language that was "painful, frequent and free," Don Roberto (who at the time was Justice of the Peace for three counties and a Deputy-Lieutenant for Dumbarton-shire), sat, together with John Burns, who was to become one of Britain's most remarkable Cabinet Ministers, a post he held for nine years.

During the night they heard groaning and scuffling close to their cell, and listened to a moaning voice: "You need not give a fellow such a doing."

Though badly battered about the shoulders and arms, Burns passed away time by singing snatches out of the "Mikado" throughout the night, whilst his companion, with only the help of his handkerchief, tried to stem the flow of blood which still oozed out of his wound.

In the morning they saw go past their cell men with bandaged heads, who, the night before, had had nothing wrong with them.

Towards noon, when Don Roberto's mother was allowed to visit the prisoners, she took with her a basket filled with food and drink. Sorely distressed, she found her son sitting on the edge of his bunk, his mop of hair clotted with congealed blood.

Having kissed him and John Burns, whom she thanked for the brave manner in which he had defended her son, she produced the food which the two hungry men welcomed with joy. Noticing that his mother was still very distressed, Don Roberto said with a laugh: "The condemned men ate heartily," whereupon the three laughed together. Presently he was allowed to go into the yard where, at a pump, he washed his head. Shortly after, when a friend arrived and asked him how it felt to be locked up, he said: "Oh, I have been locked up once before, in the Argentine, but this is a strange and curious experience, on the whole not an unpleasant one."

Later in the day, when the two prisoners were brought before the magistrate, the tribunal was crowded with persons very different from those who ordinarily frequent a police court. Mr. Haldane, Mr. Asquith, Mrs. Pankhurst and a number of other prominent suffragettes, several members of Parliament, Oscar Wilde and other literary men, as well as Don Roberto's mother and wife, filled the benches.

When the door, on which was painted in large letters: "FOR PRISONERS ONLY" was opened, Mr. Burns and Don Roberto walked into the court, attended by two constables. Burns, familiar with the formula, made directly for the dock and took his seat, and Don Roberto who was positively overwhelmed by complimentary attentions, followed suit. He was very pale, and his head was bound up in a bandage which indicated the severity of his wounds. His handkerchief—which he frequently used to wipe away drops of blood which trickled from under the bandages—was one congealed mass of blood. In spite of his situation and sufferings, he comported himself with great bravery, and at the close assented to go on the bail of Mr. Haldane.

Released on bail, he stayed at the Hôtel Métropole where he was kept under constant guard, a police sergeant and a constable in plain clothes being placed in the hall and entrance to the hotel. Naturally, the Tory Press attacked him, saying that the crime of resistance to lawful authority is infinitely greater in the case of a man of education and social standing than in the case of the ordinary street ruffian. One or two papers suggested that Don Roberto, having lived the life of a cowboy in America, required to be taught that Londoners would not endure the "brutal turbulence that prevails in more or less savage societies."

TRIAL SCENES AT THE OLD BAILEY. FROM A CONTEMPORARY SKETCH.

During the trial at the Old Bailey, the historic, stuffy and dingy court-room was uncomfortably crowded. The importance of the case had attracted crowds of barristers, as many as fifty being in the lobby of the court, and the public gallery was packed with many famous people.

Charged with "Unlawful assembly, assault of the police, along with other 'evil-disposed' persons, thereby endangering public peace," both prisoners pleaded "Not guilty."

Mr. Asquith (who later became Prime Minister and Lord Oxford) defended Don Roberto, but Burns refused legal aid.

During the trial, which lasted several days, Don Roberto —who was immaculately dressed and wore a gay buttonhole— looked about the court-room with lofty indifference. Sometimes, when he had an opportunity, he chatted gaily with everybody within his range of hearing, and held, in fact, a sort of levee from his position in the criminal dock.

At the outset of his defence which he conducted himself, John Burns stated that he wished to assume entire responsibility for what he said in the court. He asked the jury not in any way to connect his co-defendant with acts of his. He said among other things:

"I emphasise this because he is not identified with me in any of the views I hold, or with the method advocated by me, of securing their realisation, other than a general belief in the right of public meeting in Trafalgar Square and other places, and the necessity of preserving rights that it is the common lot of all to defend. *He is a Social Reformer. I am a Socialist.* This explanation is due from me to Mr. Graham. As for myself, I do not wish to seek shelter behind a man of his social position—a Member of Parliament —or anything else other than the justice of my conduct on Sunday, November thirteenth. . . ."

When the Court adjourned whilst the jury retired to consider the verdict, Don Roberto went to a nearby coffee-house

CONTEMPORARY CARTOON SHOWING IRISH POLITICAL PRISONERS, AS WELL AS
MR. JOHN BURNS AND DON ROBERTO (LAST IN ROW OF CONVICTS).

to take some refreshment. As he pushed his way through a
crowd of supporters, admirers and curious people who had
assembled outside to hear the result of the trial, a boy came
up to him and pushed a piece of paper into his hand. When,
inside the coffee-house, Don Roberto unfolded the slip of
paper, he read: "It's all right, a Graham is the foreman of
the jury." (His name was J. Mann, but probably he was in
some way connected with the Graham clan.)

The court-room was packed when the verdict was
announced, and after Mr. Justice Charles had pronounced
the sentence of six weeks' imprisonment, Don Roberto rose,
and with a smile bowed to him.

Immediately after the trial, when the two prisoners had
shaken hands with their relatives and a number of friends,
they were taken to Pentonville Prison, in a "Black Maria,"
drawn by two horses. The first night they spent together in
the same cell, vainly trying to sleep on a hard plank-bed.

Burns, who for months past had over-taxed his strength
and energy by working for the Socialist cause which was so
dear to his heart, now began to feel the reaction. In addition
to this, the "skilly" they were given to eat on being admitted
to the prison, upset his stomach badly. (The food for the first
few days, consisted only of very watery boiled potatoes which
were calculated to act as a purge, the effects of which
weakened and demoralised even the most rebellious prisoner.)

During the first night in Pentonville, Don Roberto and Burns agreed on a certain code of signals, for they knew that from the morrow on they would be separated, and that conversation between prisoners was forbidden.

Next morning they were examined by a doctor and clad in the then customary dark-brown arrow-suits, and whilst Don Roberto was sent to his cell to pick oakum, Burns, owing to his weak condition, was admitted to the prison hospital where he stayed until his release.

In those days old ropes were weighed out to prisoners every morning. These bits of rope were supplied by waste dealers who gathered them from all sorts of queer quarters. Oakum was used for caulking wooden walls, and portions went to the fishing ports, but most of it was re-spun into ropes.

On the first visiting-day, when a friend called on Don Roberto, he smilingly looked at his hands, which were rough and stained with tar, and said: "I am well and very jolly, and my present ambition is to beat the record at oakum-picking."

During his term of imprisonment he saw the Governor once, and he was never sick or sorry, nor did he complain about anything. On being released he told a friend: "I used to think, when I lay awake, listening to the clock striking hour after hour, that if I were Home Secretary, I would not send a brother Member of Parliament to sit solitary in Pentonville, but that's all."

The plank-bed, was nothing to him, and solitude was no new thing for a man who, in the past, had often been, for weeks, all alone out in the wilds. Prison life affected him little; in fact, he regarded it as a curious experience. He missed his cigarettes, but was of a more phlegmatic disposition than most people imagined.

The skilly, or "glue" as the prisoners called it, was of a consistency such as even a bill-sticker would despise, and the bread was brown, hard and dry, and, on the whole, the

Mr ROBERT BONTINE CUNNINGHAME CUNNINGHAME GRAHAM M.P.
Claimant to the Earldom of Monteith and Airth.

IN PRISON GARB

[*From a sketch by Tom Merry.*

prisoners were never given enough to eat, so that they were always more or less hungry.

Don Roberto greatly enjoyed the compulsory exercise, racing round and round in circles with his fellow-prisoners. Being in excellent condition, and a very fast runner, he could keep it up longer, and used to outrun all the others. Often, as he spun past thieves, they used to say to each other: "If we could run like this 'ere Member of Parliament, we'd not be in this bloody 'ole."

In his cell, of course, Don Roberto had an "official" Bible, prayer and hymn books, but besides these he had only one book during the five weeks he was in Pentonville. It was Simon Patrick's *Parable of the Pilgrims*, in the reading of which the prisoner took a considerable interest. (This book was published in the reign of Charles II, about eight months before the publication of *The Pilgrim's Progress*, and is a kind of High Church *Pilgrim's Progress*.)

Don Roberto spent most of his spare time reading the Bible. Ecclesiastes was his favourite book.

Burns and he only met in chapel where speaking was not allowed. As I have already mentioned, whilst the two had been together during the first night of their imprisonment, they had arranged certain signals. Thus, for instance, when Burns stroked his moustache with his left hand, it meant: "How are you?" When Don Roberto stroked his upper lip with the right hand, that indicated: "All right." A touch on the bridge of the nose meant: "Are you weak?" etc. Although they were only a few feet apart in chapel, they were carefully watched by warders who were placed there to see that no verbal communication between the two was possible. When the system of signals was detected, they were immediately placed in different parts of the chapel where they could not see one another. Obviously, for the benefit of the two, the chaplain, in every sermon preached against sedition,

riot, etc., to the great amusement of the other prisoners.
In a sense we should be grateful that Don Roberto spent
six weeks within the walls of Pentonville Prison, for otherwise
his masterful sketch: *Sursum Corda* (Lift up your Hearts),
would never have been written. In order to acquaint the
reader with conditions and life in an English prison in those
days, I reproduce parts of what Don Roberto has written:

". . . a whitewashed cell, with windows of Dutch glass,
gas and a Bible, table, chair, little square salt-box,
wooden spoon, tin pan, schedule of rules, men with hell
in their hearts, a pound of oakum in their hands, condemned to silence and to count the days, pricking them
off under the ventilator with a bent nail or pin!

"Well was it said, the only humanising influence in a
prison comes from the prisoners. Let the officials do their
duty as they think they should, the governor be humane,
the doctor know a little of his work, the chaplain not too
inept, still prisoners of whatever rank or class, imprisoned
for whatever crime, offence or misdemeanour, look on
each other as old friends after a day or two within the
prison walls. Day follows day with 'skilly' exercise,
with chapel, with dreary dullness, and with counting
hours. Night follows night, and when the light goes out
the tramping up and down the cells begins, the rapping
and the mysterious code by which the prisoners communicate, sound through the building like an imprisoned
woodpecker tapping to be free; tremendous nights of
eight-and-forty hours, a twisting, turning, rising oft, and
lying down to rise again, of watching, counting up to a
million, walking about, and touching every separate
article; of thinking upon every base action of one's life,
of breaking out a cursing like a drab; then falling to a
fitful, unrefreshing sleep which seems to last but for a

minute, and then the morning bell . . . in the yard, exercising . . . the circling miserable ring of lame folk, aged men, those on the sick list, and the rest, who in the prison yard revolve in a small circle round a post, too feeble to keep pace with the robuster rogues at exercise in their long shoddy greatcoats, thin, pale, abject as dogs, purposeless, shiftless, self-abased, down-eyed, and shuffling in the prison shoes; expectorating, coughing, and a jest to those who trot round the ring stamping and cursing underneath their breath, what time the warders stand blowing their fingers, side-arms belted on, stiff and immovable, on the watch to pounce upon a contravention of the rules. . . .

"The dull week over, oakum all duly picked, cells well swept out, the skilly and brown bread discussed, beds all rolled up, the inspection over, faces all washed, with clean checked handkerchiefs (coarse as the topsail of a sugar drogher), duly served out to last the week, the terrors of the bath encountered, the creepy silence of the vast unmurmuring hive is broken by the Sabbath bell. Then cells give up their dead, and corridors are full of the pale, skilly-fed shuffling crowd, each headed by its warder, and every man with something of anticipation in his eye, ready to march to church. To the vast chapel streams the voiceless crowd, and soon each seat is filled, a warder duly placed at each end to see that the wor-shippers do not engage in speculations as to the nature of the Trinity, but stand and kneel and sit, do everything in fact other congregations do, omitting only the due dumping of the threepenny-bit into the plate, and not forgetting that when two or three are gathered thus to pray, their Creator stands amongst them, although they are thieves. And thus assembled in their hundreds, to make their prayer before the God of Prisons, the congregation sits—prisoners and captives, shut within themselves, and each man tortured by the thought that those outside have lost him from their minds.

"The chapel built in a semi-circle, with the back-seats gradually rising, so that all may be in view, the pulpit made of deal and varnished brown, the organ cased in deal, and for all ornament, over the altar the Creed, Lord's Prayer and Ten Commandments, and those last look at the congregation as if ironically, and seem designed to fill the place of prison rules for all mankind.

"Furtively Bill greets Jack and 'Enery, George: ' 'Ow are yer, blokes? Another bloomin' week gone past.' 'I ain't a-talkin', Sir, 'twas t' other bloke,' and a mysterious twitch makes itself felt from bench to bench till the whole chapel thus has said good day. Loud peals the voluntary, the convicted organist—some thievish schoolmaster or poor bank clerk having made (according to himself), a slight mistake in counting out some notes— attacks an organ fugue, making wrong notes, drawing out all the stops alternately, keeping the *vox humana* permanently on, and plays and plays and plays till a grim warder stalks across the floor and bids him cease.

" 'Dearly Beloved,' seemed a little forced, our daily skilly scarce a matter worth much thanks, the trespasses of others we forgave thinking our own were all wiped out by our mere presence in the place, the Creed we treated as a subject well thrashed out, 'prisoners and captives' made us all feel bad, the litany we roared out like a chant, calling upon the Lord to hear us in voices that I feel He must have heard; epistle, gospel, collects we endured, sitting as patiently as toads in mud, all waiting for the hymn. The chaplain names it, and the organ roars, the organist rocks in his chair, on every brow the perspiration starts, all hands are clenched, and no one dares to look his neighbour in the eyes; then like an earthquake the pent-up sound breaks forth, the chapel quivers like a ship from stem to stern, dust flies, and loud from every throat the pious doggerel peals. And in the sounds the prison melts away, the doors are opened, and each man sits in his home surrounded by his friends, his Sunday dinner smokes, his children all clean-washed are by his side, and so we sing; lift up our hearts and roar vociferously (praising some kind of God), shaken inside and out, yelling, perspiring, shouting each other down. Old lags and forgers, area sneaks, burglars, cheats, swindlers, confidence-trick men, horse thieves, and dog stealers, men in for rape, for crimes of violence, assault and battery, with 'smashers,' swell mobsmen, blackmailers, all the vilest of the vile, no worse perhaps if all were known than are the most immaculate of all the good, made human once more during the sixteen verses of the hymn, and all the miseries of the past week wiped out in the brief exercise of unusual speech. The sixteen verses over, we sit down, and for a moment look at one another just in the same way as the worshippers are wont to do in St. Paul's, Knightsbridge, or St. Peter's, Eaton Square.

" 'Does you good, Number Eight, the bloomin' 'ymn,' an old lag says, but for the moment dazed by the ceasing of the noise, I do not answer, but at length deal him a friendly kick and think the sixteen verses of the hymn are all too short. . . ."

CHAPTER XII

WHILE Don Roberto was in prison his wife received many vile and even threatening letters from anonymous writers. Having heard about this, his chief anxiety while he was in prison, was lest any harm should come to Gabrielle.

The six weeks soon passed. In order to circumvent any attempt at organised demonstration outside the prison, Don Roberto and Burns were released at 6.30 a.m., instead of 8 o'clock, which was the customary hour to set prisoners free. When the two emerged from a private side door, they were greeted by a number of admirers who cheered them, for, guessing that their friends would be released early, they had waited near the prison since 5 a.m. There was a great deal of handshaking, and although the ex-prisoners were not hungry, they had to eat meat pies and other things offered to them. A local baker distributed hot loaves to anybody who cared to have one. Then everybody crowded into "Evans's" little coffee-shop which faced Pentonville Prison up the Caledonian Road, overshadowed by the grim walls. "Evans's" was a favourite meeting-place for released gaol-birds, but as it was a small establishment all the victuals were soon eaten up.

Don Roberto looked well, though for a few days past he had suffered from a bad cold which affected his throat and chest; however, the short imprisonment told upon Burns who had lost weight, and looked very pale.

When the news spread in the vicinity, and more admirers, friends and reporters with open note-books came rushing into the coffee-house, there was a great crush. Presently Don Roberto's mother and brother arrived, and after she had kissed Burns and her son, happy scenes ensued.

Asked what he thought of the prison, Don Roberto said: "Oh, it's all right, but I wouldn't send a friend there." However, the reporters were not satisfied with this, and as he knew that they had to earn a living, and had not come out so early on a cold morning for pleasure, he made a few statements. About the prison he said:

"It is very dull and monotonous. And at night how some of the prisoners howl! Last night, for instance, one of my neighbours kept up a dreadful howl all night through; he can never have slept. He was by no means the only one who indulged in similar eccentricities. The howling and groaning that used to echo along the corridors were sometimes quite ghastly. Sometimes, the only noise I heard, was that of a man who had stolen a wheel-barrow. He was in one of the cells adjoining mine, and used to pass away the time by singing Sankey's hymns. I was sandwiched between a horse-stealer, whom we should have hanged in Texas, but who was a very fine fellow, and a man who was in for committing an assault of some kind. They were very nice fellows, and very seldom passed me on my way to chapel or exercise ground without a kindly word: 'Cheer up, old fellow, you'll soon be out,' for they could tell how long I was in for by the card on my prison cell. . . .

I only saw the chaplain once, but never had any talk with him."

When interviewed, the chaplain said that he did not think a gentleman of Mr. Graham's education would have any need for his services, so he had sent a substitute. (The "substitute" wisely kept away from Don Roberto who never even saw him.)

To an interviewer's question as to what Don Roberto had brought out with him from gaol, he answered:

"First, a deeper sense of the misery of the lives of many of our poor people, since many of them prefer, when the cold weather comes round to commit some offence to qualify for imprisonment rather than remain at large and enjoy the sweets of liberty, which, in their case, are equivalent to starvation and privation of all kinds. Secondly, I would not send my political opponents to prison. Thirdly, I think I would allow even the worst prisoner the use of writing materials and an increased quantity of bread. The prison has not changed my views as to the necessity for decentralisation of administration, and I am strongly against any increase of the authority of Governments. But these ideas I had before; I am just as I was, for six weeks have passed pretty much as they would have if I had been on a sea voyage or in a ranchman's hut in the Far West."

When asked why he had gone to Trafalgar Square, he said:

"I went simply to assert the right of free speech, and not as a Socialist or as a Radical. I should have done the same thing had the meeting been one of the Primrose League. I am a believer in the theories of Karl Marx, to a great extent, but, both as regards Christianity and Socialism, I care more for works than mere faith."

A vast crowd of supporters and admirers—consisting chiefly of poor people—followed the cab in which he drove towards the House of Commons. Arriving there, one of the first men he met was the Prime Minister, Lord Salisbury, who, with a friendly smile, asked: "Well, Mr. Graham, are you thinking where to put your guillotine?" Laughing heartily, Don Roberto answered: "In Trafalgar Square, of course, for water is plentiful there."

Whilst he walked to his seat, a cry of welcome and good cheer was raised from the Irish benches, where almost every man had served a term in prison for political reasons, but the majority of the House jeered him, and some went as far as to cat-call him. Instead of being annoyed, Don Roberto was delighted with the scene, and although he had not intended to speak, he rose, and, when he could be heard, told the House that for what he had considered his duty he had been beaten and assaulted in the sight of London, and that he had been put to great inconvenience and expense, as well as having had to serve six weeks' imprisonment.

A roar of laughter greeted the last remark, and when he could again be heard, Don Roberto continued:

". . . I appeal to anyone who has followed the social and political movements of the day to say that the proletariat of London is not well able to judge upon social circumstances as the proletariat of Russia. They are not deceived by phrases. They estimate a cheat upon the Stock Exchange and the Turf with the habitual criminals in gaols, and they fail to see the difference between the titled whore of Belgravia and the poor prostitute of Regent Street, except as regards sympathy and censure.

I do not wish to say that the trial and sentence passed upon me were not perfectly fair and legal from the judge's point of view; but it requires more than a finding of a judge and jury to lay at rest for ever the question of free meeting in the capital of the British Empire. I have been tried on three counts: assault on the police, causing riot, and illegal assembly. However, the good sense and honesty of a British jury acquitted me instantly on the counts of 'assault' and 'riot,' and therefore I fail to see how any fair-minded man can come forward with a stale argument of riot having been caused by my action or that of the working men in London. I challenge anyone to say what Statute or unwritten law I broke on that occasion. I was found guilty of the obsolete offence of illegal assembly. . . . It has been charged against me that I have stirred up a lot of ignorant men to dash their heads against a wall, and it has been charged against me that I have spoken sedition and I am a revolutionary. If to be a revolutionary is to wish to ameliorate the condition of the poor, to wish for a more democratic form of government, to wish that Members of Parliament should be paid for their services, to wish to pass Liberal measures of a similar nature, then I am a revolutionary."

After many noisy interruptions, Don Roberto wound up his speech by sarcastically thanking the Members for the courteous way in which they had listened to a man struggling with weakness. Whilst speaking he had frequently coughed, for at the time the cold he had caught shortly before leaving prison bothered him a great deal.

For some time after his release he was kept very busy attending meetings where, together with other ex-political prisoners, he had to speak, and for several years after, loafers —who called him the "Toff of Pentonville"—frequently came sidling up to him as he walked through the streets. Speaking through the corners of their mouths, they would say: "Gawd bless yer, Mr. Graham, chuck us arf a pint; I was in with you in that crooil plaice." Although Don Roberto knew that most of these beggars did not speak the truth, he always gave them a shilling to relieve their thirst.

A few days after his release, business called him back to Scotland, and when he arrived in Glasgow, the Central Station was packed with a dense crowd, from end to end. This was to be expected, for in that town the Liberal element was very strong. At Buchlyvie, he was met by another crowd of friends and sympathisers, and at Gartmore the explosion of fog signals and rockets heralded the arrival of the train. When Don Roberto and his wife stepped on to the station platform they were almost mobbed by friends and tenantry from miles around. Speeches were made, and pipers played "The Gallant Graham." When, finally, they got into a carriage to drive to their estate, enthusiastic men, young and old, took the horses out of the shafts and pulled the carriage towards Gartmore.

One of the most daring things Don Roberto did, was on the occasion of Queen Victoria's visit to Glasgow. On learning when the Royal train was due to arrive at St. Enoch Station, he promptly called for a mass meeting of miners, to be held in St. Enoch Square, with the result that when the Queen arrived, countless ill-clad and grimy men were crowded together in front of the station, listening to Don Roberto, who made a fiery speech in their defence.

Whilst in Scotland, attending to his estates, he received a letter asking him to attend a mass meeting of policemen in London. (They were protesting against the long hours of duty, and asked him to speak.) However, as he was too busy to attend, he wrote a witty letter in which he expressed his regret at not being able to be with them. Having wished them success and "more power to their elbows," he added that he wondered if it was wise to break the lieges' heads with cocus wood, whilst there was still "so much good oak running waste in England."

Not long after, on returning to London, when most people thought the Trafalgar Square incident was but a memory, Don Roberto infuriated the House by giving a sarcastic moral lecture. Pointing towards the Ministerial side of the House, he said as an aside in a speech:

"There sit, on the Ministerial side of the House, many representatives of the nobility and aristocracy of the nation. There is an ancient and obsolete phrase that *noblesse oblige;* but how is it that when, some time ago, I spoke on the question of Trafalgar Square, Members so far forgot that antiquated adage as to treat in the way they did, a man whom they knew had been severely injured in the Trafalgar Square meeting, and who had had the opportunity of recuperating his strength by the salutary and palatable diet extended to prisoners in Her Majesty's prisons. I venture to say that from the most violent working men, honourable gentlemen opposite would not, under the circumstances in which I stood, without ten men on my own side to back me up, and without the command of my voice, have received the unworthy treatment I received from those who should remember that *noblesse oblige.* . . ."

For some time after the Trafalgar Square incident, whenever the opportunity presented itself in the House, Don Roberto pretended to be taking a lively interest in matters connected with the police force and prison welfare, and on several occasions he spoke about life in prison, referring to convicts as "we." Among the many matters he brought before the House were, respite for a murderer, alleged assault by a policeman, arrest of an innocent woman, a lunatic put in gaol to the annoyance of the prisoners, dissatisfaction in the police force owing to unfair promotions, unfair dismissal of twenty men in the police force. On one occasion, in speaking about the Chief of Police, Sir Charles Warren, he characterised him as a "psalm-singing, sanctimonious swashbuckler." When a Member raised the question to change the constables who had regularly been in attendance in the House, a privilege which excited jealousies among their fellow-constables, Don Roberto seized the opportunity, and, jumping up from his seat, asked: "As this is a matter of privilege, will the Home Secretary cause any of the heroes of Trafalgar Square to be appointed to serve in the House?" This gibe evoked cries of anger, and from the Speaker, "Order! Order!"

When Mr. Gladstone was Prime Minister, Don Roberto made some violent speeches among the poor, in the slums in the East End of London. One day, Mr. Gladstone sent for the incorrigible rebel, intending to give him a moral lecture.

When trying to intimidate or impress a man, Gladstone usually received him in his office alone, and after having kept the caller waiting for some time alongside his desk, he rose from his chair and for some time stared at him, at the same time tapping his desk with a finger.

This trick may have produced the desired effect in most cases, but not so when Don Roberto faced him. When the Prime Minister rose and began to stare, Don Roberto, did likewise, pushing his head closer and closer, until, at last Mr. Gladstone lowered his eyes. The interview lasted but a few minutes, for Don Roberto was uncompromising. He departed with a polite bow, smiling to himself.

Don Roberto never appeared before an English King or Queen, although, indirectly, he was asked to do so. His brother, Charles—as mentioned in the opening chapters of this book—commanded Queen Victoria's yacht, the *Osborne*,

R

and later became a groom-in-waiting to King Edward VII and later to King George V.

Not only in the House of Commons, but also outside it, Don Roberto was a nuisance and a trouble-maker, for he took an active part in the organising of several strikes. The Clyde shipowners addressed a memorial to the Home Secretary, drawing attention to the speeches made by him and Keir Hardie. These speeches were described as inflammatory, and the memorial stated that matters were becoming serious. Over and over again, in political speeches, Don Roberto warned his listeners against "these men who wriggle into Parliament at Election times, by pretending that they are going to do things which they take good care never to do when they get into the House of Commons."

Shortly after he had been mobbed, kicked and thrown into a canal by a number of young political opponents, he wrote the following letters to a friend, Councillor Henry Reid of Coatbridge.

"February 24—1888.

". . . Formerly every Reformer was dubbed 'Atheist,' now the most convenient epithet the Tories find for us is 'Socialist.' I am not, as far as I know, more than a Reformer wishing to relieve the hard lot of the poor. If some of my methods are Socialistic, then all justice is Socialistic. You need never fear me joining a Socialist Society, as I hate all fixed dogmas and am well aware that in the Socialist Party, for one Owen and Morris, you may find twenty rogues and villains. . . . I am, I regret to say, far from well as you will see by the *Mail*. The kicks I received on the 19th, having brought on an affection of the bladder, very painful and exhausting."

"May 10—1888.

". . . I will be at the meeting. . . . Personally I am so much accustomed to opposition that it matters little or nothing to me. The other day I addressed a large out-of-doors meeting against the Compensation Clauses. The Drink Party was there in full force and howled all the time. It seems that with both Tories and Liberals I shall have a lively time. . . . I do not care an atom what the meeting is like as I shall not probably have to fare worse than I have done in the House of Commons when speaking for the benefit of the working classes. . . . I have attended five meetings in London in the last two days. . . . Rheumatism and overwork have tired me out a good deal. . . ."

"December 1—1888.

". . . I fear I shall have to retire from Parliament entirely as I find it too expensive. . . ."

The enthusiastic crusader, Don Roberto, not only limited his sphere of activity to England and Scotland, for on May Day, 1891, he went to Paris to take a prominent part in a big demonstration which was held in spite of a prohibition by the French authorities. However, the demonstration was promptly stopped by the police, and when indignant Don Roberto attempted to hold a meeting of protest, he was warned that he would be arrested. Accompanied by a few leaders of the French Labour Party, he then directed his steps towards the Chamber of Deputies, where the party was admitted to the office of the President's Secretary who, however, in spite of their protestations, refused to deposit a petition they had brought.

In the evening the Federation of Paris Working Men's Syndicates and Clubs met, and among numerous speeches made, Don Roberto delivered an address. Although the meeting passed off quietly, it was later rumoured that Don Roberto had been arrested, but that he had succeeded in escaping from the hands of the police.

At Fourmies the disturbances were serious, three persons being killed and several seriously injured when the soldiers and gendarmes were given orders to fire upon the crowd of disorderly demonstrators.

Whilst Don Roberto was in Paris, his wife went to Madrid where she spoke in favour of an eight-hour working day, and she also informed her listeners that the English Socialist Party was opposed to a general strike.

On the 4th of May, Don Roberto was back in London where, in Hyde Park, together with Messrs. John Burns, Tillett and Dr. Aveling, he spoke in favour of a legal eight-hour working day. On the 11th of May, he returned to France to attend a Labour meeting in Calais. In his speech he denounced the French Government, the officials and soldiers for the shooting down of workmen at Fourmies. Speaking in French, he proposed to organise a procession to lay a wreath of immortelles on the grave of one of the victims, killed in the May Day riot at Fourmies, and later buried in Calais. The authorities issued orders not to let the demonstration be made, and thirty policemen with a squadron of dragoons, guarded the gate of the cemetery. After vain protests the demonstration proceeded to a public hall where Don Roberto made a speech, the violent character of which led to his arrest and expulsion from French territory. At the moment of his arrest he was at the Hôtel de la Cloche, waiting for the steamer which was to leave at 1 a.m. At about midnight the Chief Commissioner walked in to inform him that he was under arrest, and that a warrant for his expulsion had been issued.

Once he addressed a Liberal meeting with an ex-Cabinet

Minister in the chair. He made an extraordinary speech which contained unconventional doctrines to address to a Liberal audience, presided over by a Liberal lawyer.

Here are some of the points:

There had been brought before Parliament an Eight Hours Mines Bill, but it had never been discussed. But both parties had shown the most surprising alacrity in putting aside those questions which went to the root of the capitalistic system and tended to raise the social condition of the working classes. In order to discuss the people's matters they elected to the House of Commons middle-aged men whose lives had been devoted to getting money, whose lives had been spent in ruining the lives of the working men, their wives and children, and whose lives had also been devoted to cheating, starting speculative limited liability companies and making tramways to pay so that they could keep the money in their breeches pockets. (Laughter and cheers.) There is an old Scotch proverb: "Hawks never pick out Hawks' een," and these members, no matter whether they were Liberals or Tories, landlords or lawyers—(laughter)—he begged the chairman's pardon—(renewed laughter)—he did not mean to be personal—would do nothing which was diametrically opposed to their own interests.

On one occasion, whilst his old friend and co-prisoner, John Burns, happened to be in Scotland on political business, Don Roberto invited him to stay with him at Gartmore, an invitation Burns gladly accepted because he badly needed a rest. One day, the host proposed to show his visitor the region, and when the latter said he would love to see the beauties of the surrounding country, Don Roberto ordered two horses to be saddled at once. Burns explained that he was no horseman, having only ridden a donkey or two at the seaside, but his friends assured him that the horse he was giving him to ride

was like an arm-chair, and very gentle. After some difficulty
Burns managed to get on the horse which, fortunately, was very
tame, though extremely sturdy. Mounting on his fiery
"Pampa," which accompanied Don Roberto whenever he
went to London, he led the way, followed by Burns, who, after
a while, began to enjoy the jaunt. The two friends had ridden
for several hours, when, calling at a lonely store for some
refreshment, Don Roberto suddenly remembered that his
old housekeeper at home was not feeling well. Thinking that
port wine would do the old lady good, he purchased a bottle,
and when he noticed the roomy pockets in Burns's jacket, he
asked him to be kind enough to put the bottle into one of
them. Burns, who had been a teetotaller all his life, did not
exactly like the idea of carrying the port wine, much less
because he found riding quite difficult enough without so
cumbersome a cargo as a bottle. However, he said nothing,
and after having mounted, with Don Roberto's assistance, he
did his best to keep up with him, steadying the bottle as it
bumped against him with every stride of the horse. For nearly
twenty miles the two rode at a fast canter, Burns miraculously
sticking on his horse, though he bounced up and down on the
saddle, like a sparrow hopping across a road. When the two
arrived at Gartmore, and Don Roberto jumped off his horse,
poor Burns was so stiff, sore and bruised that he dare not
dismount for fear of falling and breaking the treasure he had
so successfully carried all the way back. "Here, Don
Quixote," he shouted to the ex-gaucho and cowboy, "please
take this bottle from your Sancho Panza!" (Mr. Burns tells
me that this was the first and last time in his life that he carried
alcohol.)

Don Roberto was an idealist and a humanitarian, and
therefore he was out of place among politicians. His
incorrigible idealism he clearly showed when, in speaking on
the Eight Hours Bill, he said: ". . . I wish to see an extension

of the most precious boon men can give one another, namely, sympathy. . . . As long as I have the honour of a seat in this House I shall continue to press this question, and if I succeed in awakening the public conscience on this matter I shall feel that I have had my reward."

In 1890, when, in the United States of America, the soldiers made a punitive expedition against the Sioux Indians in South Dakota—at the same time as England sent out various similar expeditions to her colonies—he wrote three letters which are masterpieces of irony, especially as they had a double meaning at the time.

"THE REDSKIN PROBLEM.

"BUT 'TWAS A FAMOUS VICTORY.

"By R. Cunninghame Graham, J.P.

"To the Editor of the *Daily Graphic*.

"SIR,—

" 'Our special correspondent' at Pine Ridge, Dakota, whose dispatches I have read with such heartfelt pleasure for the last month, has had the opportunity lately of assisting in one of the most healthy manifestations of the spirit of civilisation that it has been the lot of any special correspondent (out of Africa and Egypt), to chronicle for many years. I freely admit I am dense, and density is as the sin of witchcraft, but be that as it may, I never yet was able to discover why it is, when a body of white troops, well-armed with all the newest murderous appliances of scientific warfare, shoot down men whose ignorance of their proper calling clearly proves them to be savages, the act is invariably spoken of as a 'glorious victory.' There are some things which be too hard for me, and the way of the serpent on the rock is as easy of comprehension in comparison to it, as is the fact that the particular political party to which I choose to belong is composed of upright, righteous living, whole-souled patriots, and that the other fellows are all either rogues or fools, or an amalgam of the two.

"If, though, the previous fact is difficult of comprehension to me, how much more so is the converse fact that, if the aforesaid braceless, breechless knaves, in precisely the same manner, shoot our 'glorious troops,' their proceeding become a 'bloody massacre,' a 'treacherous ambuscade,' or something of a low-priced nature of that sort.

"I should have thought that sauce for the Indian savage was also sauce for the white rowdy who swarms in all frontier corps, even if the latter worthy was acquainted with the priceless boons of boiled shirts and plug hats, and worshipped his fetish in a stifling meeting-house instead of an open prairie. Still, that in no wise alters the case that there has been a glorious victory of the American troops at Pine Ridge. Very pleasing to read that after three centuries the good old racial feud between Indians and Whites is being fought out in the good old way.

"Let it be once granted that there is no good Indian but a dead Indian. Does that apply, though, to Indian women and children? I see that our 'brave troops' remorselessly slaughtered all the women and children, and our special correspondent, in estimating the 'bag,' remarks that by this time probably not more than six children remain alive out of the whole Indian camp.

"Can anything more miserable be conceived than the forlorn position of the wretched Indians, when at the break of day they found their camp surrounded by troops, when, at the same time, we remember they were probably half-starving, and that the recent severe weather is as summer compared to the winter of Dakota? I cannot imagine anyone reading (always from our special correspondent), and not feeling the profoundest pity for the wretched Indians.

"The spectacle of them sitting silently in a semi-circle, one would have thought, would have appealed to anyone but an American frontier soldier. We are told that the Indians planned an ambuscade, but it would seem a curious kind of ambuscade that 120 men should allow themselves to be surrounded by 500, backed by artillery. That many of the Indians—now so fortunately dead—had murdered settlers and fired ranches I have little doubt. That the whole Indian question (like the question of the unemployed in London), is a most difficult and piteous one no one will deny. Still, though, hardly anyone who knows Indians can refrain from thinking that in this instance there seems to have been a deliberate attempt to goad them to fury in order to shoot them down. Any old Indian fighter will agree with me that to attempt to deprive Indians of their arms by surrounding them at daybreak with troops, was certain to produce a conflict. The Indian resents nothing in the world like an attempt to deprive him of his weapons.

"He is almost born with them. His little bow as a child grows with him, becomes strong and tough with him, and is buried with him.

"It is no more his fault that generations on generations have been accustomed to go armed than it is the fault of a mustang, born a pacer, to refuse to trot.

"It is as ridiculous to expect an Indian to love work, as it would have been to expect a Highlander of the time of the '45 to take to typewriting rather than cattle lifting as a means of subsistence.

"Indians will (and experience, both on the Pampa and prairie, has taught me this), only deliver up their arms

245

at a time of solemn treaty or in the presence of an overwhelming force. Five hundred men were enough to destroy, but not enough to overawe one hundred Indians.

"No one should have known this better than the officer in command of the troops.

"Therefore I believe the whole affair was arranged beforehand by men who knew perfectly well what would happen.

"One's very soul revolts in disgust from the account of the cruel butchery, the shooting down of fleeing savages with Gatling guns, the useless and cruel slaughter of the women and children.

"The only consolatory feature of the whole affair is that the Indians seem to have fought like demons and inflicted severe loss on the troops before they were exterminated.

"I had hoped that the matchless pen of Bret Harte would have raised a protest against the doings in Dakota; if the protest had been made it would have run through the American Press like wildfire, and surely must have produced some good.

"Soon, I suppose, we shall hear of some more glorious victories of the same kind, and then the ghost-dancers can all dance together in some other world, where we may hope there may be neither Gatlings nor any other of pillars of civilisation to annoy them. It seems a pity, too, to waste so many good Indians who might have been so advantageously used to turn honest pennies for enterprising showmen, if no other method of utilising them occurred to the great American Republic.

"However, I may be permitted to make my moan over the women and children at least, for I doubt much if they had committed any weightier crimes than the unpardonable one of living.

"Now that they are dead they will furnish an excellent repast for coyotes; and, for the Indians, they would have died hereafter; and, after all, what does it matter? For, as Montaigne says: 'Quoi, ils ne portaient pas des haults de chausses!'

(Signed) "R. B. Cunninghame Graham."

I do not think that many people read this letter, and the few who did, probably yawned and turned over the pages to look for important news, such as stocks and shares, football and other sporting events, or, may be, an interesting divorce case, or a horrible murder.

Shortly after the publication of the above letter, Don Roberto wrote two more on the same subject. Mr. Morley Roberts, in his book on W. H. Hudson, says: "I remember best one thing of his [Cunninghame Graham's], about a Ghost Dance. [See following letter]. Hudson spoke of that and many other things the man had written. How should such a man "succeed"? "Impossible," said Hudson, knowing that failure was often the sign of great success, as he of whom he spoke knew well enough."

When one considers that Don Roberto had had some most unpleasant experiences with Indians, both in South and North America, his defence of them is all the more remarkable.

"THE AMERICAN INDIANS.
"GHOSTS DANCING.

"By R. B. Cunninghame Graham, M.P.

"SIR,—

"The special correspondent of *The Sun* at Pine Ridge, Dakota, keeps us informed of the movement of the Indians now massing their forces at Cherry Creek.

"Glancing over the evenings papers we see that the Sioux are dancing the Ghost Dance, and learn that in the opinion of the perspicacious correspondent the settlers expect to be robbed and murdered. Some of us may say: 'Confound these Indians, they ought to be shot down.'

"Yes, smokeless powder is your true civiliser after all. There is no good Indian but a dead Indian, which we know is true, for have not American humorists declared it, and has not a true-hearted public in two continents affirmed their declaration with a laugh? Artists wish they could be present to see the ceremony. Those who, in pursuit of money, have been in the 'Territory'—the whisky-sellers, the Bible pedlars, the land speculators (having caught the phrase from some frontier man)— tell us 'Indians is pizin', and, like Peter, seal the lie with an oath. The general public glances over the telegrams from Omaha and hopes that there will be no bloodshed, then turns to discuss the recent political scandals and the prurient details connected with the private life of party leaders, which, of course, we all know are of vastly more importance than the extermination of legions of heathen Indians.

"Still there are a few who really realise what is going on in the snow of Cherry Creek, what the Messiah really is the Indians are looking for, and who the ghosts are who are dancing. A Ghost Dance to the Sioux is what the Holy War is to the Mohammedan, what the Last Prayer (faith present or faith absent), is to the Christian. The Sioux can stand no more; therefore, they are dancing to the Ghosts of their forefathers to arise and help them against their enemies. Only an Indian superstition. Looking for a Messiah. Waiting for the Las Casas who will never come.

"I wonder if the British public realises that it is the Sioux themselves who are the Ghosts dancing. Ghosts of a primeval race. Ghosts of Ghosts who for three hundred years, through no crimes committed by themselves (except that of being born), if it be not a crime to love better the rustle of the grass than the shrieking of the engine, have suffered their long purgatory. Ghosts who were men. The Messiah these poor people are waiting for, our poor people here in London also look for. But both will look in vain. Justice will not come either to Cherry Creek, no, nor yet to Whitechapel.

"The buffalo have gone first, their bones whitening in long lines upon the prairies, the elk have retired into the extreme deserts of Oregon, the beaver is exterminated to make jackets for the sweater's wife. The Indian must go next, and why not, pray? Is he not of less value than the other three? Let him make place for better things —for the drinking shop, for the speculator, for the tin church. Let him realise that in the future, where he changed his pelfries for beads and powder, two gills of whisky shall be sold for a quarter. Men say the change is good (but good is merely relative), perhaps good enough for him, but death, indeed, for all Ghost Dancers. Civilisation, perhaps, one day will remember them when the civilised Indians, which commercialism is creating, are dancing around the flames of European capitals.

"But Rocky Bear and Little Wound, Short Bull and Sleeping Water have had enough, they have taken horse, mounting lightly as drops of water (from the offside), silently, in single file, never stopping but to squat and pass the pipe around, each man holding his pony by the mecate, they are marching on Cherry Creek.

"But the Kiowas, the Cheyennes, the Arapahoes, the Comanches have braided their horses' manes. They (who before civilisation loved one another as the dwellers in Liddesdale and Bewcastledale did of old), are friends.

"They have mounted their best horses, they are

coming through the day, they are coming through the night, across the frozen prairie (the dry grass hardly crackling beneath the broncos' feet), they are passing the whispering red woods, passing the lonely canyons, marching silently as the Ghosts on Cherry Creek, across the lands that once were theirs to take counsel with the ghosts of those their former owners.

"Better that they should come and smoke and dance, 'dance for ten days without food or water,' better far that they should die fighting, than by disease and whisky. Outrages they will commit, of that there is a certainty, but all they do can scarce atone for all that they and theirs have suffered. Tricked by all, outwitted, plundered by the Christian speculator, better far that they should die fighting, and join the Ghosts who went before them. This I want the world to recognise, that even Indians do not contemplate their own extermination without centuries of suffering. We might have taught them something, they might have taught us much, soon they will be all forgotten, and the lying telegrams will speak of 'glorious victories by our troops.'

"Once more sin will be committed in the name of law and progress. It is a hard case to decide on, no matter from what side you approach it; these men have lived too long, better, therefore, they died fighting. No one will regret them (but myself)—except, perhaps, their ponies, who may feel their new owner's hands heavy on their horsehair bridles. The majesty of Civilisation will be vindicated, one more step towards universal hideousness attained, and the Darwinian theory of the weakest to the wall have received another confirmation to strengthen those who want to use it against the weakest here in Europe.

"Yours obediently,

(Signed) "R. B. CUNNINGHAME GRAHAM."

"SALVATION BY STARVATION.
"SITTING BULL.

"The American-Indian Problem.

"To the Editor of the *Daily Graphic*.

"SIR,—

"The first act in the concluding of the Existence of the Sioux Indians is played out. Apparently, in direct violation of the President's express orders, the Indian police arrested Sitting Bull, with the natural consequences that a rescue was attempted and a fight took place. In the fight, Sitting Bull, who was heard giving his orders in a loud voice, fell pierced by a bullet. This is an old trick, well known in Spain and in Mexico, and throughout the frontiers of the United States.

"The escort appears at the frontier town without the prisoner. Officer reports prisoner endeavoured to escape, and in the struggle that ensued, was accidentally shot. Quite so; that is to say one of two things happened— either the prisoner was offered a supposititious occasion to escape, and shot in the attempt, or else he was deliberately murdered in order to save time, legal expenses, and the problematical Spanish-American or Uncle Sam's justice. [*sic*].

"This would seem to have been the end of Sitting Bull —deliberately murdered to stop him from asking food for his tribe. 'Minds' in Boston, 'First Families' in Virginia, and that notorious product of civilisation, the Anglified American, the man who secretly laments that there is no peerage in America will talk of Cortés and Pizarro. The editors of Western papers will write about the safety of the settlers being at last secured by the removal of Sitting Bull, and, worst of all, the American public, as a whole, will believe them, and think a piece of poetical justice had been performed.

"Poetical, no doubt, but as for justice—as far removed from anything connected with it as was the other specimen of American 'justice' executed three years ago in Chicago. . . .

"Whether in Patagonia, on the Pampas, or on the prairies of the North-West, the treatment that the whole Indian race has received, whether at the hands of Spanish or English Americans, is a disgrace and a scandal even to that disgrace and scandal facetiously called civilisation—in which the doctrine of whether the iron pot strike the earthenware pot, or the earthenware pot float against the iron pot, bad for the earthenware pot had become a gospel. . . . I write not as a sentimentalist who takes his Indian (coloured) from the pages of Fennimore Cooper, but as one who has passed many a night staring into the darkness watching his horses when Indians were about. . . . I am one of those who think that the colour of the skin makes little difference to right and wrong in the abstract, and who fail to see so much difference between an Indian sitting over a fire gnawing a piece of venison, and a tailor in the East end of London working in a gas-lit den sixteen hours a day for a few shillings a week. It does not much matter though the bulk of mankind declare that a prairie with corn growing on it, and a log house or two with a corrugated iron roof, is a more pleasing sight than the same prairie with a herd of wild horses on it, and the beaver swimming in every creek.

"That is their opinion, and they will not, I am sure, deny me the right to express mine, that, as the Spaniards say: '*Hay gustos que merecen palos.*' [There are tastes which deserve sticks.]

"But the gain to civilisation. You would not surely allow these rich lands remain for ever in the hands of a few wandering savages? Again, I say, to me that the mere accident of a little more colouring matter in a skin does not alter right or wrong, and that the land was theirs, no matter to what uses they put it, centuries before the first white man sneaked timidly across the Atlantic. . . . Those who are loudest now (the settlers in Dakota), for the final extermination of the Sioux fail to grasp that when Dakota is all settled they themselves will in the main become as dependent on the capitalists as the Indians now are on the U.S. Government, and that the precedent of rigorous measures with the starving Indians will be used against themselves.

"I would, even at the eleventh hour, secure the Indians in a fertile territory, and prohibit any white man from settling among them, except he were a man of proved good character. I would in that territory make it a criminal offence to supply drink to any Indians.

"I would exclude all missionaries except those of the Roman Catholic faith, for in my experience of missionaries and Indians, the Roman Catholics alone have seemed to me to understand them.

"Lastly, I would endeavour to set up cattle ranches among them, for in my experience of Indians this is the occupation to which at present they are best suited. My frontier friends may smile at my idea of Indians as ranchers, and exclaim with expressions that I spare your readers, the Indians would eat all the cattle in a week. All I can say is, I have seen the Indians in the Gran Chaco,* and on the frontiers of Chile, no whit less savage than the Sioux, make first-rate ranchers when drink was away.

* Paraguay.

"At least we owe the men from whom we have taken their all, replacing doubtfully the beaver and the buffalo with whisky and smallpox, some reparation besides a small-bore bullet. Even in America, where public opinion is, perhaps, more brutal than in any other country of the world, surely a flush of shame must rise to the faces of honest men when they receive the telegrams from Dakota. It puzzles me to think, except the horse, what benefit the Indian race has gained from civilisation.

"Perhaps, though, it is better that the evil should come quickly, for it will come at last.

"In the next generation or so they will be gone, and then the Americans will organise picnics on a grand scale to visit the historic places in Dakota and Montana, where the curious and picturesque peoples (*vide* advertisement to cheap circular trips from New York to Dakota), who once inhabit our continent, lived and smoked their red calumets.

"Yours obediently,
(Signed) "R. B. CUNNINGHAME GRAHAM."

Don Roberto, as we have seen before, was very fond of quoting passages out of poems in his speeches in the House. Once Parnell told him that he wished he could do likewise, whereupon Don Roberto immediately offered to help his friend whose memory for poems and verses was not good. When Parnell had informed Don Roberto what his speech was to be about, the latter jotted down several suitable quotations on a piece of paper, and then Parnell proceeded to learn them by heart. However, when he tried to use them in his speech, he got himself into such a muddle that what he said made no sense, and when he met Don Roberto after the debate, he told him that never again in his life would he try to quote poetry.

When Parnell was in trouble over his affair with Mrs. O'Shea,* and even the members of his own party ignored him in the House, Don Roberto, who happened to arrive late one day (November 28th, 1890), walked up to his friend's seat, and whilst everybody watched him in silence, shook hands with him, and when the scandal first started, Don Roberto wrote an open letter which I here reproduce:—

"January 25th, 1890.

"PARNELL.

"Yes, I know. 'Thou shalt not commit adultery.' That is to say: Thou shalt not be found out committing adultery. Now, I do not express any opinion on the Parnell–O'Shea case. I have no opinion to express, and if I had one, should not express it. I neither know nor care whether Mrs. O'Shea was Mr. Parnell's mistress or not. What can it matter to me? Still less, what can it matter to the cause of Home Rule for Ireland? I hear that amongst the ranks of the 'unco' guid,' an attempt will be made to damage his political reputation through the aspersion on his private character.

"Is this as it should be? Perhaps Mr. Stead will say 'yes.' Perhaps the great Nonconformist Party will say 'yes.' I say: 'no.' Do I mean, therefore, that the private character of a politician is not to be taken into account when we consider his public actions? Do I mean that adultery is a venial crime, and to be made light of? Certainly not. There are crimes that warrant the public in withdrawing all confidence from the man who com-

---

* In December, 1889, Captain O'Shea filed a petition for divorce on the ground of his wife's adultery with Parnell. Parnell and Mrs. O'Shea were married in June, 1891. The life he led, the agonies he endured and the labours he undertook from the beginning of 1891, travelling weekly to Ireland, would have broken down a much stronger man. He was found to be suffering from acute rheumatism and general debility. He died on the 6th October, 1891, at his home in Brighton.

mits them. There are actions—actions considered, I am
well aware, perfectly legitimate on the Stock Exchange
and in the office—that should be sufficient to hunt a man
from public life. Is this one of them? I say, 'no.' It
seems to me that the offence charged against Mr.
Parnell is merely the offence of being found out. That
is to say, if he *has* been found out, for of that we know
nothing yet. Look round the House of Commons, look
at the well-fed, idle, rich men in it, and then ask me to
believe they are all earnest practisers of social purity.
If this is so, and if the public knows that even St.
Stephen's harbours a fair proportion of offenders against
the Seventh Commandment, and knowing, tolerates
them because they have not been the objectives of public
scandal; why, therefore, this tone amongst so many
Liberal papers of affecting to treat Mr. Parnell as a
criminal? Has he been an obscure member of the Irish
Party, some McHafferty, or O'Rafferty, or some member
for Ballyshaughuttery, is one to suppose anyone would
have cared a farthing? It is because on the Liberal
posterior the imprint of the Parnellite boot is so clearly
to be traced, even without the aid of smoked glass, that
this freezing tone has come over so many of his quondam
allies, assuming for the sake of argument the O'Shea
thesis.

"Has, therefore, Mr. Parnell altered his political convictions? Are the funds of the Irish National League
likely to be less justly administered? Are the paid
members of the Party the less likely to receive the £2
a week, or whatever it is, with less punctuality? Had
the offence with which Mr. Parnell is charged been of a
different nature, had he been accused of taking shares
in a Company which paid a dividend of 25 per cent;
then I can well understand the feeling of repugnance

256

that must inevitably have crept into the hearts of his allies. Is it not a well-ascertained fact that the Liberals are men of principle, and that the Tories are hounds? Is it not matter of public notoriety that no good Gladstonian Liberal ever accepts more than two and a half per cent return on his money? I should think so; for if not, what do their public mouthings mean? If a man commits a crime that disposes people to think that on account of it he is unreliable in his dealings with them; then, if he is a public man, we are right to take our oyster shell and write quickly on it: 'Banish him.' If on the other hand the offence is one that the vast majority of men take pleasure in committing as long as there is no danger of being found out—is one which two-thirds of the House of Commons are in the habit of doing— why then, I say, let him who is without sin, put out his well-gloved hand, and rushing in front of the steamroller, let him seize a jagged flint and hurl it at the Liberator's head. If then he feels qualms of conscience, let him rather retire in haste to the Liberal meeting and spout there on Freedom of Contract.

"This whole affair is evidently the specious plot of some knaves calculating to play upon the well-known hypocrisy of the British nation. Taking into consideration moreover, the help that they will receive from Tories of the baser sort, and not forgetting the delight that will be caused in the Liberal camp if the strong man who has rubbed the weak noses in the dirt can be brought to confusion. I have referred to Sir Charles Dilke. Now I am not concerned in the least to defend him. All that I say is, that Sir Charles Dilke was not treated with justice. Does anyone believe that the political principles of the man are altered? It is because a set was made against Sir Charles Dilke by men and women who were likely enough no better than himself, that I am constrained to write these few words on the Parnell–O'Shea incident. If we push this mania to its logical sequence, we must assure ourselves that the Judge before whom the case comes for trial is a man of absolutely pure private life. If he be not—why, how is he any more fitted for the Bench than is Parnell to be the associate of Brunner, Balfour, Gladstone, Churchill, myself and other wealthy men who live on the labour of others? In no other country in the world but England would it, I believe, be possible to get up a cry against such a public man on such a question. This is, as I understand it, no question of seduction of a young child; no case of unnatural perversion of appetite such as that of the so-called West-End Scandals. The Bible applies another and plainer word, if I remember rightly, to the offence. This is simply a case of the natural affection of two grown-up people, for I understand Mrs. O'Shea has also arrived at years of discretion. Now what I contend is, that in no other country in the world would it be possible to ruin a public man on such a question. Should it be possible in England? Yes, if—if all our people were pure themselves—if such a thing as a Divorce Case was unknown in the land. However, when I take up a newspaper (which I confess I do as seldom as I can), I find whole columns and columns are devoted to divorce. When I look up lives of statesmen who have been honoured in this land, I find some of them were notorious offenders in this respect, and that no one thought of doubting their political principles on that account. Are we, then, so much better than our fathers? Well then, I say, that it is impolitic, unjust, and thoroughly hypocritical to try to raise a cry against a man for an offence which, if it hurts anyone, assuredly does not produce a tithe of the misery, poverty and ruin that a single morning's speculation on the Stock Exchange often entails on humanity.

"What! hunt an adulterer from public life, and take a sweater to your chaste arms? The thing is ridiculous in a state of society in which marriage itself is too often a clerical-absolved prostitution—in a society in which we see a Prince marry his daughter to a boon-companion in his adventures, and no one raise a word of disgust and contempt—a society in which every day we see mothers eager to marry their youngest and fairest to old, painted, padded, lecherous baboons, simply because they have rank or wealth. If the Liberals are to banish, and the Tories are to persecute Mr. Parnell for his alleged connection with Mrs. O'Shea, what are we to do with H——, and S——, and Z——, and all the others whom we know are guilty of similar offences? Let us form a huge Vigilance Committee, and whilst the bulk of the population are delivered over to long hours and low wages, let us leave the consideration of such matters to fools, and let us, as practical men and women, turn our attention to practical matters—such as the one I have been writing on."

. . . .

Don Roberto's enthusiasm for the Labour Party began to wane in the early 'nineties, but not his enthusiasm for the Ideals. What he thought of the Leaders of the Social Democratic Federation, of the Socialist League and Trade-unionism, he expressed in no uncertain words when, in 1891, in an article he accused them of being "all Tories in disguise, trying to get their nozzles into the State swill; men of straw, the bottle-washers of the capitalists."

Personally, I cannot help feeling that his waning enthusiasm was due to the fact that the Socialist Party was beginning to gather strength; and he was one of those rare men who could never fight on the side of strength. He was one who enjoyed a losing fight, provided that fight was one he considered worthy of his support.

When the Labour Party became strong, and a number of "big" men joined its rapidly growing ranks, he characterised the leaders as "p—— pot Socialists, a lot of disillusioned Lords and Baronets, surrounded by the most bigoted bunch of bourgeois and social climbers."

"If a workman becomes a '*leading man*,' " he once said in speech, "he becomes at once the obedient slave and faithful tool of his employer, to lead the rest after the soap bubble of mere party welfare."

Finally he grew so tired of Socialism, as preached by most leaders of the Party, that he prophesied ironically of the time when "all shall sit, apparelled in one livery, at little tables, drinking some kind of not too diuric table-water, approved by the County Council, and reading expurgated Bibles."

In later years, when, on one occasion, I discussed socialism with him, he told me: "Toryism is a mental attitude that will continue to exist as long as man is man. . . . Like the Liberal Party, which was ground out between the Tories and the Socialists, so is the Socialist Party doomed to be ground out between Tories and Communists."

This statement made me think that, perhaps, the Socialist Party originally attracted him because he subconsciously had a feeling that it would finally end in failure.

Don Roberto's Parliamentary career ended in 1892. Let us listen for a moment to his last speech. He rises, and after having looked round the House, speaks with a voice that rings with vitality. This is his swan-song to a group which never met him half-way, men he had often shocked or cynically amused with his honesty and straight statements. He spoke on Parnell:

AT THE AGE OF 40

. . . "He was human, like the rest of us. He had his faults, as we all have; but when time has blotted out his faults, and when his qualities, which I consider great, undoubtedly, have been more clearly discerned, when the present unhappy dissensions among the Irish Party have been removed, as they will be removed some day, the present generation will undoubtedly say that a most remarkable man, whom those in the House, if they did not all respect, very largely feared, has been taken from us; a man with whom I myself was acquainted on terms of friendship, and whose death, under the unfortunate circumstances which occurred, I shall always deplore, as having deprived this House of the most remarkable man who has sat in it this century. . . ."

This shows Don Roberto, the man who never deserted a friend, even though he was down, and every one was glad to be rid of him.

Thus ended the Parliamentary career of one who, probably, had achieved nothing but the amelioration of conditions among the wretched chain-makers of Cradley Heath.

And thus a man made his final bow to the House where, in one of his first speeches he had said:

". . . I feel like one of the Governors of Mexico who, when Charles the Fifth asked him what he most felt when he undertook the office he held, replied 'the sense of my own unworthiness.' It is no light task for any young Member of this House, standing alone as I stand, to come before this House and ask Honourable Members to consider a question [an eight-hour working day], so vast in its importance and so far-reaching as this of the social condition of the working class, but I claim to be as good a patriot as any of my colleagues, and I maintain that Great Britain has always been a pioneer on all these questions. . . . I came to this House, not from the merchant's office or the lawyer's court, but straight from the prairies of America, where want is unknown, so that the sight of such misery as exists in London was brought home to my mind with exceptional force. . . ."

Perhaps, during the six years he had fearlessly fought for the weak, the lowly and the oppressed he had paved the way for other crusaders who were to follow him; but one thing is certain, and that is that in his disinterested fight he had been uncompromising (a rare quality among politicians), and that he had only struggled for others, in spite of the fact that he fully realised that, personally, he had nothing to gain but everything to lose.

He left the House to roam elsewhere, and Mr. G. B. Shaw sums up Don Roberto's parliamentary career in *Three Plays for Puritans*, in a footnote on the Trafalgar Square riots—which, by the way, he witnessed as a spectator. Mr. Shaw writes:

". . . On that occasion civilisation, qualitatively his inferior, was quantitatively so hugely in excess of him, that it put him in prison but hadn't sense enough to keep him there. Yet his getting out of prison was nothing compared to his getting into the House of Commons. How he did it I know not; but the thing certainly happened, somehow. That he made pregnant utterances as a legislator may be taken as proved by the keen philosophy of the travels and tales he has since tossed to us; but the House, strong in stupidity, did not understand him until, in an inspired moment, he voiced a universal impulse by bluntly damning its hypocrisy. Of all the eloquence of that silly Parliament, there remains only one single damn. It has survived the front-bench speeches of the 'eighties as the word of Cervantes survives the oraculations of the Dons and Deys who put him, too, in prison. The shocked House demanded that he should withdraw his cruel word. 'I never withdraw,' [see pages 198-199] said he; and I promptly stole the potent phrase for the sake of its perfect style, and used it as a cockade for the Bulgarian hero of *Arms and the Man*."

Shortly after Don Roberto left the House of Commons, he wrote to a friend: ". . . I have been foolish enough to soil myself with the pitch of politics, and to have endured the concentrated idiocy of the Asylum for Incapables at Westminster for six years. . . . Now I think I may do my fooling alone, and leave the stage for younger fools. . . ."

CHAPTER XIII

GABRIELLE'S BOOKS—FRIENDSHIP WITH W. H. HUDSON—
SEARCHING AN OLD ROMAN GOLD-MINE IN SPAIN—DON
ROBERTO'S FIRST BOOK—TRAVELS THROUGH SPAIN AND
MOROCCO

WHILST Don Roberto had been in Parliament,
filling in his spare time speaking at meetings in
every corner of the United Kingdom, and writing
innumerable articles for the Socialist Press,* his wife had
taken care of the estates in Scotland, a difficult task in which
he had taken a hand whenever he was free for a few days.

Gabrielle was a great reader, fond of painting and writing
verses, but, above all, she was a mystic, though she followed
no particular faith.

In 1885, when, during the winter months, she had visited
Spain, she engaged as a companion a tall Galician servant,
Peregrina Collazo. Together with Peregrina, Gabrielle
returned to Gartmore, and for a number of years after, this
witty and amusing Galician servant was her constant companion, and a source of great amusement to Don Roberto
who took a delight in the masses of Spanish proverbs and
adages (which reminded him of Angel Cabrera), she quoted
whenever she made a statement.

Already before Gabrielle had attained the age of twenty-
five, she had written several stories and sketches, among them
the description of the journey she and her husband made

* In 1887, he wrote to a friend: "I am at last forced back on *Justice*
again, as no paper will take anything from me. Fancy the *Yellow Book*
refusing a thing of mine on the ground that it was *immoral*. Cretins, liars,
etc."

from Texas to Mexico City, a description, parts of which I have quoted in a previous chapter. (See pages 153–159.)

These stories, including two of her translations of the great Spanish writer, Begner, were published under the title of *The Christ of Toro* (Eveleigh Nash, London, 1908), at the same time as her *Father Archangel of Scotland* and a book of her poems.

Whilst Don Roberto was in Parliament (1886–1892), his wife and her servant, Peregrina, travelled through Spain during the summer months, for Gabrielle endeavoured to live over again the life of the Castilian saint, Teresa, about whom she had made up her mind to write a book, a monumental and scholarly work which, under the title of *Santa Teresa: Her Life and Times*, gained the *Permissio Superiorum* of the Court of the Vatican.

In a later chapter I shall again refer to these books.

Dynamic Don Roberto must have been glad when, once more, he was free to do as he pleased. He was now forty years of age, but yet remained as vigorous and active as he had been at the age of twenty.

He had not allowed his political activities to interfere with his private interests. In fact, despite the hurricane life he had lived during six years, he still had found time for reading, and during his parliamentary career, though he had made a number of political enemies, he made many new friendships, chiefly in the literary and artistic world. Among them was W. H. Hudson who, lost in the commercial whirlpool of London, poor, ill and friendless, found in Don Roberto the moral support and encouragement he so much needed and appreciated. From the time of their first meeting they understood one another. It was through Don Roberto that Hudson later met Joseph Conrad who described him (Hudson) as a "son of nature, an almost primitive man who was born too late," whereas about Don Roberto he said that he was

"living half a century, or even more ahead of his time."
Hudson once described Don Roberto as "the first and last
nobleman in England."

Early in 1890, one of Hudson's articles on the Argentine
had appeared in a magazine, and Don Roberto who happened
to read it was so delighted with it that he immediately wrote
to the author, who sent the following reply:

> "40, St. Luke's Road,
> "Westbourne Park,
> "London, W.
> "March 10, 1890.

"DEAR SIR,

"I am much obliged for your letter which I found on
my return home last evening.

"It would be strange indeed if I did not know the
Pampa, seeing that I was born there; and as I have the
feeling for it which each one of us has for 'his own, his
native land,' it is always a rare pleasure to meet with
anyone at this distance with whom I can compare notes
about it.

"I should be glad indeed to have a talk with you;
but my rather bad health prevents me from going about
much so that my excursions are usually limited to walks
in this neighbourhood.

"If you can spare the time, and are not afraid to
travel into such a desert as this, with macadam and
mud for *paja* [grass] and smoke, or something dark,
for *cielo* [sky], I should be very glad to see you any
day. By dropping me a postcard beforehand you would
make sure of finding me in.

"No, I have not seen the French book you mention.

"After reading your letter it suddenly occurred
to me that I had heard of your having been a

resident in Buenos Ayres, but I forget where I got
the information.

"I am, dear Sir,

"Yours very truly,

(Signed) "W. H. Hudson."

Another letter:

"40, St. Luke's Road,

"Westbourne Park, W.

"April 15th, 1890.

"Dear Mr. Cunninghame Graham,

"Thanks for your note of yesterday; also for copy of
Time, containing your pampas article, which I found
most interesting. There is much information in it which
is fresh to me; and the paper is fresh in another sense:
you observe and judge for yourself. Most persons who
write are satisfied to mix a teaspoonful of original stuff
with about a quart—in some cases a gallon—of borrowed
matter.

"By the way, why did you not give the English of the
Gaucho proverb—'Caballo ruano para las putas.'*

"I trust you will be able to get a laugh out of the
Purple Land; but I really know less of the country it
relates to than yourself, as you will probably find out
on reading it.

"The chief difficulty I find is that the flavour of
Gaucho talk is lost in translating. One is compelled to
make a sort of imitation, which must seem rather
poor to a reader who has a knowledge of the real
thing.

"However, I shall by and by attempt to spin

---

* *Ruano* is the gaucho term for a light bay with a white mane and tail.
A horse of this colour was considered weak and of little resistance, hence the
proverb: "*Ruano* horse for the harlots."

another little yarn, entitled *El Ombú*, for Mac-
millan's, for which I have some tempting materials.
"Believe me,
                 "Always cordially yours,
                          (Signed) "W. H. HUDSON."

Within a short time the two new friends dropped the
formal "Sir" and "Mr.," and until Hudson died, on the 18th
of August 1922, the two were often together and exchanged
numerous letters, passages out of which I shall quote later.

The life of a Scottish "laird" soon became too monotonous
for Don Roberto, who, like his wife, felt that Britain was too
small for him.

In 1893, the two went to Spain where they spent weeks
reading up historical documents in archives, for Don Roberto
had made up his mind to write a book on Spanish colonial
history. The more he read, and studied Spanish people, the
more he felt that, in order to understand them thoroughly,
it was necessary to cross the Straits of Gibraltar and to become
acquainted with the people in Morocco. Accordingly, the
two students made the trip to Tangier where, for some
time, they made their headquarters. Accompanied by
guides, Don Roberto made several inland journeys, visiting
places which were hardly safe in those days.

However, business called the two travellers back to Scotland
where a great deal of work was to be done on their estates
which were doing far from well, for agriculture was in a bad
state at the time.

Throughout the days, whilst her husband inspected his
vast property, mounted on his favourite horse, "Pampa,"
Gabrielle kept the accounts and books, and her spare time
she filled in reading through, and assorting, old family documents, or working at her bulky manuscript of *Saint Teresa*.

Gabrielle, who had been fond of smoking for some years

past, gradually became a slave to this normally harmless vice. As time went on, she became so heavy a smoker that she could never be without a cigarette in her mouth. She was in the habit of doing her work, sitting on the floor, with the books and papers placed around her in a circle, and after she had sat thus for a while, burnt-out or smouldering cigarette ends lay all round the room. Even during the nights, whenever she woke up, she smoked two or three cigarettes in rapid succession, inhaling the fumes. By degrees the nicotine affected her nerves, but although doctors asked her to limit her smoking to twenty cigarettes per day, she never smoked less than fifty, and frequently she consumed more than a hundred in twenty-four hours, and there were days when she performed the almost incredible feat of reaching the two hundred mark.

Time often hung a little heavily on Don Roberto's hands, especially in the long spells of rain which visit the District of Menteith. At such times, far from a town, when old favourites had been taken from the bookcases, and when they had been read, re-read and put away, he set about exploring some of those books that all men have upon their bookshelves, which they have never read, and yet know the outside, the binding, and the lettering on the backs so well that they have but to shut their eyes to see them in their own particular place.

Among a number of old books was a two-volume folio bound in sheepskin, with the name on the back done with a thick quill pen, the lettering setting forth in Spanish that the two bulky volumes were the works of Pliny.

Don Roberto soon got tired of reading, and made the works over to his wife. She read and annotated, after her custom, and in a day or two asked him if he remembered hearing of a Roman gold-mine in Galicia, upon a journey they had made.

The thing had slipped his memory, though when she spoke

of the mine, he thought he had heard something of the sort, in a vague kind of way.

So she took up the book and read him out a passage, in which the writer talked of a gold-mine in Lusitania, which, in Pliny's days, comprised Galicia. Then Don Roberto remembered how the country people used to go down to the sands upon the River Sil and wash for gold, and an infinity of stories he had heard. As the two talked, Gabrielle perceived the connection between Pliny's account of the old Roman gold-mine and the tales of the Spanish peasantry, and nothing would content her but that her husband should go at once and find the mine. After having talked the matter over for a while, Don Roberto began to think there was something in his wife's arguments, although he was still unconvinced about the mine.

In the evening, several days later, when they were sitting in the long drawing-room, in semi-darkness, they fell a-talking of the passage Gabrielle had found, and after a while the two agreed that Don Roberto should go and find the place where, according to Pliny, the Romans had drawn much of their gold in Spain.

Having settled the thing in their minds, the next step was to get a mining engineer, for Don Roberto understood nothing about mines. Gabrielle, however, knew of an English engineer whom she had once met in Spain. In due time, in answer to a letter, the engineer wrote that he would meet Don Roberto at Orense.

A few days later our prospective Crœsus found himself on board a steamer bound for Vigo, with a treatise upon placer-mining in his bag. In reading it he could not help smiling at himself, and when he found that he could make little of it, he took out his pocket-book and read through the passage he had copied out of the book which had given him hopes of becoming rich overnight. Now as he read, he found it

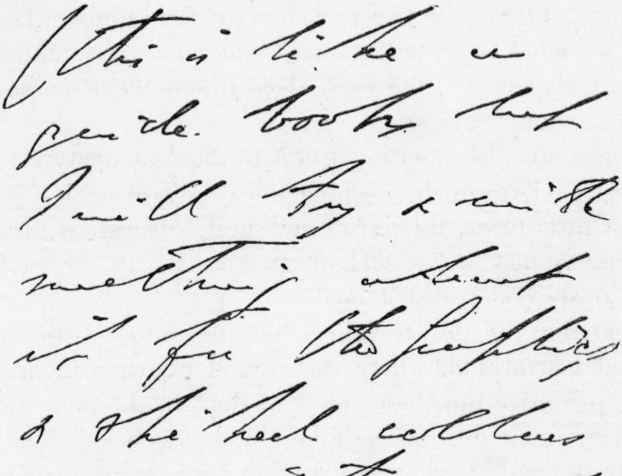

HAND-WRITING 1894.

vaguer in the full light of day than it had seemed at home in the semi-dark. However, there was nothing to be done, and in a twinkling, as it seemed, the vessel ran into the Bay of Vigo. From there he took a train for Orense where he had arranged to meet the mining engineer, and that night, after having dined, the two talked about the Roman mine until the small hours.

Dawn saw them jolting towards the Val de Orras in a diligence. Late in the evening the primitive vehicle jogged into a little town, the horses and mules dead-beat, and the passengers shaken like walnuts in a sack, stiff, bruised and sore, dusty and travel-stained.

Next day the two travellers bumped into a little village named Carraceido, where they found quarters in an even more primitive inn than they had slept in the night before.

After a most uncomfortable night, during which they tried vainly to sleep on mattresses stuffed with dried maize leaves (and fleas), they started to explore the surrounding country. In the far distance rose the Asturian mountains, whilst a small river, running near the inn, tinkled amongst the stones.

The Roman mine was a tradition of the place, well known to everyone, and in the River Sil, after a flood, people occasionally washed out a pan or two, and got a little gold. This set the engineer afire, and all day he wandered about, jotting down what he heard in a crushed note-book, greasy and dog-eared, in order, as he said, "to strike an average of the lies when he had panned them out."

By degrees the whole fantastic scheme took hold of Don Roberto, and he began half to believe he was about to make a fortune, half to believe he was a fool. Never in all his life had he heard so much mining talk. Pay-dirt and bed-rock, gold in the quartz, in placer-diggings, and many other terms of which he had no real idea of the true value, were always in his head.

One morning the engineer came rushing in, roaring: "Eureka!" and when he had cooled down sufficiently to speak he explained that he had found a man who knew the Roman mine, that it was three leagues off amongst the hills, and by the account must have been a great placer-working in the old Roman times.

So excited were the two that they arranged to start about an hour before the sun went down, and camp amongst the hills.

They left the village mounted on mules, with a man following upon a donkey carrying provisions.

Most of the inhabitants stood at their doors to see the prospectors start, for every living soul knew of the *expedición*, and the Roman mine had been a household word to all of them from their earliest youth, not much believed in, but still ever present to their minds.

With the grave cynicism of Spanish peasants, they looked on the two strangers as madmen; but with the materialism of their race were quite prepared to take advantage of the fruits of the prospective millionaires' brains. In the meantime, the hire of the mules had been a godsend to them, for in the village hardly any money circulated.

The heat was still sweltering as the little party followed a steep track through chestnut woods. About half-way, the light began to fail, and presently the moon rose, casting strange shadows on the wild path that they were now following. After an hour or two of struggling upwards, they came to a little open glade amongst some chestnut trees. The guide hobbled his donkey's feet, and, drawing his flint and steel, soon made a bright fire.

When they had made some tea and smoked a cigarette, they strolled across the little clearing, and a most wondrous view, made still more marvellous by the moon's glittering beams, lay stretched beneath them, for the green glade ended abruptly in a precipice, sheer down, seemingly unfathomable. It looked as if a monstrous bowl had been dug out of the earth about a quarter of a mile across.

So still was everything that Don Roberto and the engineer stood looking, awestruck, till the guide, advancing cautiously, said: "That is the Roman mine."

"A placer-working!" the engineer exclaimed. "What wonderful men the Romans were! To-morrow, when it is light, we must go down and get to work at once." Don Roberto almost had to pinch himself to be sure he was awake.

The night wore on, and just about dawn the howling of a wolf, deep in the hills, reached the three men's camp, startling both the mules, who strained upon their ropes and trembled, and would have broken loose had the guide not quieted them.

Early next morning the prospectors began their work, after having got down to the level of the great placer-digging by a winding path made by the goats in the hill-side.

At the first glance the engineer said that the place had been worked systematically, and he pointed out the cuttings, waterways and places where he said the Romans had their sluices. To all this Don Roberto said "Yes," and although he strongly suspected that he was on a wild-goose chase, he gradually became enthusiastic.

All day, on the edge of a small stream which ran through the middle of the working, they washed out countless pans of dirt, the excited engineer talking volubly about the prospects of success, how they would denounce the mine, and claim it for themselves. Each time they washed a pan he grew excited, swearing that this time they were certain to find "colour"; and when, each time, nothing but fine red sediment remained, mixed with some little pebbles, he was quite sure that the next try was certain to give something better, and so time wore on.

The first day was quite enough for Don Roberto whose back ached with washing out the pans, and he felt as if in all his life he had done nothing but wash out mud in a tin pan, and then begin again.

Finally, after some arguing, they decided to take some samples of the earth from parts which appeared to have been left untouched by the Romans, and to take them to Madrid to have them analysed. Accordingly, they loaded up a mule with two great sacks of earth dug from the hearts of several seemingly untouched places, and when, everything had been loaded on the beasts—remains of the provisions, pots and kettles, blankets and tin pans—they started on their return journey towards Carraceido, tired, eaten by mosquitoes, sunburned, with their hands blistered, and in that state of mind in which a man will quarrel with his dearest friend about the colour of a mule.

Soon they drew near the village, and if their setting out had been received but coldly, nothing could well have been more cordial than their welcome on returning. When the villagers saw the laden mule, the wildest rumours as to the success of the expedition were set about at once. The little street was full—women stood at the doors, and children ran about like rabbits, whilst men stepped forward to congratulate the sunburnt and dog-tired men on having found the mine.

The innkeeper hailed Don Roberto and his companion as the saviours of the district, and a sort of deputation of the chief inhabitants, with the priest at its head, appeared to interview them on all they had seen.

Everybody sat down in the *patio* of the inn, and called for wine, after having sent out for some cigars. The priest stepped forward, and, taking off his hat, harangued briefly on the ancient Romans, on British energy, and on the wealth he supposed would flow into the town when the mine was in order, and work begun. He said that, owing to bad government, the state of the parties, and the lack of confidence existing betwixt man and man—so contrary to the principles of our holy faith—Spain had gone through a period of decay. This, as a patriot, he deplored, and trusted that with the well-known energy of Englishmen, the curse, that lay upon the land, would, at least be removed from Carraceido. He thanked both—Don Roberto for his public spirit, and his companion for that hard-headed shrewdness and engineering knowledge that distinguished him—and hoped that when a stream of gold had poured into the place, two of the streets of the new town that would arise should bear the Englishmen's honourable names.

The miller was more brief, and merely said that he knew the welcome visitors had found gold, for he had seen the sacks upon the mule. None could come to him, as he said, "with celestial music"; he was a practical and hard-working man, but seeing is believing, so he wished the two saviours of his beloved village luck, remarking that he cared little for the ancient Romans, who, he had always understood, were hardly better than the Moors; but in all cases, if they had been so foolish as to leave their gold up in the hills, it was a right and proper thing that Christians should profit by their carelessness.

When, at long last, the speeches were over they drank gravely to the health of England and Spain in a rough, heady red wine, and lighting their cigars, tilted their chairs against the wall and fell a-talking as they smoked. Much was said about the badness of the Government, the infamy of those in high estate, the price of bullocks, and other topics of the kind, till someone fetched the *música*, which consisted of a man who played on a shrill pipe called the *dulzaina*, to the accompaniment of a little drum, on which a man beat with his right hand, and with his left scratched the parchment with a stick.

When Don Roberto was left alone, he hastily wrote the following letter to his mother:

"July 22nd, 1894.

". . . . The mine is one of the most extraordinary. It would take pages to describe it. . . . There is no doubt the place is very rich, but I fancy it would never pay to work. It is of enormous size, and split by the action of water, into fantastic pyramids of yellowish reddish earth, the intermediate space is occupied by a chestnut wood. . . . On all sides are old workings. Wolves, wild boars and bears are quite common. The whole thing is so fantastic I seem to have seen it in a dream. My idea is that it would never pay, but as the engineer thinks it is without doubt very rich, we are taking specimens to Madrid for assay. It is a curious journey from reading a passage in Pliny at Gartmore. It will probably furnish a good magazine article, *et voilà tout*. I got up in the night and walked out to listen to a wolf. The sight of the peaks rising out of the chestnut forest I shall never forget. It was like the first view of Rio, or some of the places in Paraguay. However, I think with Darwin that perhaps the Pampas have charm greater than anything. It is strange that some of our friends and acquaintances should be inhabitants of the same world with the little, hard, lean, dour, square people, as material as the Moors and superstitious as the Scotch. 'Quien dice 'España' dice 'chinches y pulgas!' ''*

Next day, after many warm handshakes, Don Roberto and his mining expert packed their belongings—including the precious sacks—on the diligence, their destination being the Mining College of Madrid.

In due time, when the final process of the assay was made,

* He who says "Spain" says "bugs and fleas."

Don Roberto could not help smiling, but the engineer was enthusiastic until the firing down of the two sacks was completed, and nothing remained but a handful of red dust.

Again, from Madrid, Don Roberto wrote to his mother:

> "Madrid,
> "5, Horno de la Plata,
> "July 24th, 1894.

"MY DEAR MOTHER,

"After a long and dusty journey with a whole troop of bullfighters, I arrived here this morning. Madrid is, as per usual, the same: noise in the Puerta del Sol and the selfsame Newfoundland puppy (grown younger), for sale. Apart from that, as many coaches as ever, as much poverty (*bajo capa**), and a *petit vent traître* from the Guadarrama, in spite of the heat.

"The stuff is assayed, but it will take a day or two, and I believe firmly that it is not worth a penny. But the trip has been an interesting one. . . . In Vigo I met a Peruvian Indian. His whole amusement was to walk about and talk to me about Peru (where I have never been), and refer to me as an authority. My old engineer has also been in Peru, so that between him and the Indian I shall shortly be an authority. . . ."

The humour of this adventure lies in the fact that Don Roberto thought the whole thing a huge joke and that, according to what he wrote to his mother about making a magazine story out of it, he later did so, and eventually included the story in one of his books, but instead of stating that it is autobiographical, he put the adventure down to a man whom he named "McFarlane." (I have freely reproduced parts of Don Roberto's own story.)

* *Bajo capa*, meaning "under cloak" or *hidden*.

From Madrid Don Roberto made another quick trip to Morocco. The ship he travelled on ran into a terrific storm and was nearly wrecked. Upon landing in North Africa, in describing his lucky escape in a letter to a friend, he wrote, among other things, ". . . as we were being battered about I wondered how it would look in the newspapers, 'Amongst the passengers on the ill-fated vessel was Mr. Cunninghame Graham. We regret, etc. . . . career . . . wasted opportunities . . . peculiar views, etc., etc.' . . ."

Shortly after his return to England he received a letter from James Connolly,* proposing that he should stand as a Socialist candidate for Central Edinburgh. In his answer, Don Roberto said:

". . . Many thanks for asking me to stand. However, I have no money, I am sorry to say, and this is the third or fourth offer I have been obliged to decline. Even if anybody paid for me (which is a thing I think I might get done) I could only attend the 'Den of Thieves,' now and then, as my affairs are in a bad way. . . . On re-reading your letter, I see you have an election fund. Under these circumstances I could not accept such a sacrifice from you. I am not a working man, and I could not accept such a sacrifice from you. . . . Pray thank the Branch very much for me and say that I am very sensible of the high compliment they pay me, but though much as I should like a fight, I do not see my way to enter it on account of want of funds, and I cannot, and will not, be a burden to anyone. Please say that I will do my best to help anyone else who may be selected. . . .

"I am the worst candidate in the world, as I hate elections, and soon get tired of meetings on my own account. . . ."

* James Connolly was then a Socialist propagandist, and afterwards the well-known Labour leader who was executed as one of the leaders of the Insurrection of Easter week, 1916. (See *Life*, by Desmond Ryan.)

In 1895, Don Roberto wrote his first book which, under the title of *Notes on the District of Menteith, for Tourists and Others*, was published by A. and C. Black. It is probably the strangest guide-book that ever appeared, but it is so well written and bristling with wit that it ranks among works of a more profound nature than the title suggests.

Don Roberto shows his humour in the following notice on the first page of the little volume: "All rights reserved except in the Republic of Paraguay."

This book, to quote the author's own words, was written, "half in idleness and half out of that affection which is common to a man and trees for the soil in which they have been for ages rooted."

Don Roberto had always been opposed to "progress," as most of us interpret the word, and, having a fondness for "characters," he dedicated his book on the *Shadowy District* to a "shady" character who, at the time, was famous in those regions. The dedication reads:

"I dedicate this little work to Mr. Wilkie, of Balfron, known to the world as 'Trootie.' This I do because, being himself a shadow of the time before the railway snorted across our moors, he should know most of the shadows as they come and go over the countryside. Already the shadow of St. Rollex's chimney, so to speak, reaches almost to Inverness, and in the time to come there will be no place for such as 'Trootie' in the land."

("Trootie" usually poached on Gartmore estate which was not fenced in in those days. The peasantry and visitors were allowed to roam over this vast property at will, with the exception of the private precincts of the house.)

This book was followed by over a hundred short stories and sketches which, at intervals, during a number of years, appeared in the *Saturday Review*. These were all written without reference to one another. A great many of these articles treat of Spain or South America—two parts of the world little written of in England. Neither of the two is capable of being dealt with in the modern spirit, for neither in Spain nor Latin-America do men act, or look at things (men, actions and events), in the way of England.

Don Roberto never wrote for material gain. Writing was never his profession, but the medium of expressing himself, and this is why his works suggest reality, for he has the apparent carelessness that veils consummate art: Velázquez with a touch of Gainsborough. His stories and sketches are for those who seek to understand a little of what passed in the writer's mind, and, as the cowpunchers of the Far West used to say, the reader must be "rarin' to go" before he mounts the bucking bronco.

What he thought of writing as a profession he made clear when he once wrote: "It is, I think, by accident that most writers begin to write. Few men in their right senses set out deliberately to live by literature, and most of those who do, repent when it has become too late for them to learn another trade. Think what an uneventful life a man who lives by literature condemns himself to pass. Others are preaching, praying, cheating and lying, fighting, exploring, inventing, risking their lives, and sailing on the sea. Whilst they are up and doing, the writer sits at his table cudgelling his brains."

When the editor of a magazine wrote to Don Roberto, asking him to write an article for him, he received the following reply from Spain:

". . . I cannot sit down to write an article *ad hoc*, but I have a sketch that I have written here, that might do if it is not too long. There are, however, one or two provisions that I should like to make, and would not send in the sketch unless these are accepted, in writing:

"1. The title, "Cámara de Lobos"
(it means the haunt of seals), must not be altered
or *explained*.

"2. The article must not be cut, even by a word,
or in any way altered, or divided into half for publication in successive numbers. I may add at once that there
is nothing of a blasphemous or indecent nature in it;
but I know the ways of editors, and the regrets they all
suffer from, by not having been born in the Garden of
Eden with the power to sub-edit the Book of Genesis. . . ."

Frank Harris—formerly editor of the *Saturday Review*—
writes, in his book: "Shaw" how, when William Morris died,
Shaw called to offer to write a special article on Morris, as
a prose-writer, Socialist and speaker. Harris was delighted,
for Arthur Symons was going to write on Morris's poetry,
and Don Roberto on the funeral, and so he hoped to have
three good articles. When they arrived he found that Symons
was very good indeed, and so was Shaw, but Cunninghame
Graham had written "a little masterpiece, a gem of restrained
yet passionate feeling; absolute realistic description lifted to
greatness by profound poetry." In his book (*Shaw*, page 129),
Harris says that Shaw was overwhelmed with admiration of
Don Roberto's story, and how, when he (Harris), praised:
"An amateur genius; it's a pity he hasn't to earn a living
by his pen!", Shaw cried: "And a good thing for us; he'd
wipe the floor with us all if he often wrote like that."

Don Roberto's handwriting was so bad that, very often,
he himself could not decipher certain passages of what he
had written. On several occasions, when I asked him to
read a particularly bad example of his own calligraphy, he
exclaimed: "Qué diablo! a man who writes like this deserves
a good beating."

An amusing anecdote is told in connection with the publication of his first book.

A Scottish compositor who, in vain, had often tried to decipher Don Roberto's weird hieroglyphics, declared that the manuscripts of the "Laird of Gartmore" were the bane of his life, and when he could stand the strain of trying to read them no longer, he packed up his few belongings and moved to London where he obtained a post on the *Saturday Review*. On the very first day, when he was about to start work, the foreman handed him an article written in the handwriting which had driven him from Glasgow. Gazing at it in horror, the poor compositor then exclaimed: "Michty me! An' to think that I fled from Glesca to get clear o' this mon."

Just about at this time, Hudson, in a letter referring to a note he had received from his friend, Don Roberto, wrote: ". . . I can usually read your writing easily as a printed page, whatever people say and the world to the contrary, notwithstanding; but this note has been rather a floorer. . . ."

As I shall deal with the writings of the "Laird of Gartmore" in a later chapter, let me continue with the account of his activities and wanderings after the publication of his first book and a number of articles, which created quite a stir in the literary world.

The supervision of his estates occupied a great deal of his time, but this did not prevent him from making prolonged stays in London, where he constantly visited his mother and numerous friends. Mrs. Bontine's house in Chester Square, was, as I have mentioned before, a favourite meeting-place of many famous writers and artists. During one of his visits to London, Don Roberto sent a note to Hudson, who answered as follows:

"DEAR GRAHAM,

"Thanks for your very kind invite, but I shall be away out of London, on business, not pleasure-bent, for the next two days. But if not absent it would be the same, since I could no more dine at Chester Square with you and your friends than with Fairies and Angels. Those beings do not really dine, they sup, but let that pass. The fact is, being poor I long ago gave up going to houses dining.

"One of the Apostles, a certain Paul, warned us against 'unequal' alliances, and Æsop touches instructively on the same subject in one of his parables.

"Besides being poor in this world's goods, altho', of course, rich in accumulated treasures where neither moth nor rust corrupt, I have for the last two or three months been afflicted with neuralgia of the eyes, which makes work 'with book and pen' wellnigh impossible; yet to live I must work. Do you remember Yeobright in Hardy's best work, *The Return of the Native?*—how when his eyes failed he took to cutting heath for an occupation, and was very happy in his rough toil? That would suit me better than writing.

"I send you a scrap (a rough proof), of a portion of a chapter in my London book, because your name is mentioned in it. Please do not tell me that I have told the story wrongly, as it is all set up in page now. And it is a good story! If you really want to see me about anything I shall be in London on Saturday, and could meet you that day at 3, Hanover Square, at any hour convenient to you (Zoological Society's rooms).

"Please give my respects and apologies to Madame Bontine.

"Always yours sincerely,

(Signed) "W. H. Hudson."

Although on this occasion Hudson did not accept the invitation, he later became a frequent visitor to No. 39, Chester Square, for Mrs. Bontine—who had been one of the first to recognise his genius—became one of his best and dearest friends in London.

In 1897, Don Roberto again became restless, and longed for adventure and sunshine. In order to avoid the raw and cold weather of an English winter, his wife, accompanied by her faithful Galician servant Peregrina, had left for Spain, soon after to be followed by Don Roberto who had decided to explore Morocco, a then little known part of the world which, ever since his first visit, had attracted and fascinated him.

Accordingly, early in September, 1897, the three left for Spain from where Don Roberto, alone, proceeded to Tangier, on the North Coast of Africa.

CHAPTER XIV

MOROCCAN JOURNEY—DON ROBERTO ATTEMPTS TO VISIT
TARUDANT, THE "FORBIDDEN CITY"—CAPTURED BY A CAID
IN THE ATLAS MOUNTAINS—VARIOUS LETTERS CONCERNING
CAPTIVITY—OTHER MOROCCAN TRAVELS AND INCIDENTS

DURING former visits, Don Roberto had done a great
deal of travelling in Morocco, and, therefore, knew
something about the people who, being primitive,
greatly interested him. He had ridden to Fez, and had made
several trips through country which was unsafe in those days.

In Tangier he had a number of friends, some of whom were
unknown to one another. Among them was a brigand,
known as "El Moro Valiente," the painter Crawhall, Berna-
dino de Velasco, Duke of Frías and Grand Constable of
Castile, Mohammed-el-Wad, a cattle-stealer, two poor,
illiterate Spanish anarchists, and several other characters
about whom he later wrote: "for fear the wind might blow
sand over such tracks as they made upon the world."

Crawhall and the Duke of Frías, together with a number of
others, used to play what probably are the most original
polo matches that have ever been played. Mounted on any
kind and type of horse or pony, and dressed in the most
original clothes, they played on a flat stretch of sand; and,
marvel of marvels, they even owned a pack of mongrels
which represented every combination of canine breeds, and
with this extraordinary pack of "hounds" they used to
sally forth to hunt à l'anglaise.

That Mrs. Bontine did not like her son to go to Tangier
she shows in the following letter she wrote to a friend:

"January 24th, 1895.

". . . I am looking forward to a visit of a few days from Robert who is going to Tangier. I am quite cross with him for going there again, instead of to Rome* to make notes for his history of the Jesuits in Paraguay; and when I had got him such good introductions to Monsignori and the Librarians etc., which will all be wasted! . . ."

However, in spite of everything, Don Roberto went back to Tangier, and, as we shall see later, he wrote about the Jesuits in 1901.

Often he could be seen on the beach, talking to the two Spanish anarchists who amused him immensely. Both were ex-convicts; one a cobbler, and the other a loafer and a petty thief. The former who could read, though with difficulty, earned a side income by teaching natives the mystery of the alphabet, but his heart lay in "Social Reform," about which he would talk for hours. Whenever Don Roberto asked him why he lived in such miserable surroundings, he shrugged his shoulders, threw out his arms and answered through the corner of his mouth: "Why do I live among so many fleas, lice and savages? . . . to push along civilisation!" ("la joya civilisación").

One day, Professor Westermarck, the well-known ethnologist, and Don Roberto were galloping along the sands near Tangier. A lady, who was in front of them, dropped a carnation, and Don Roberto, without stopping his horse, bent over the saddle, picked up the flower, and returned it to the owner with the grace and charm of which he had the secret.

During his previous visit to Tangier, Don Roberto had been

* Every winter, for a number of years, Mrs. Bontine went to Rome where she had many friends, including some at the Vatican. Her mother's family, the Alessandros, originally came from Rome. On several occasions Don Roberto accompanied his mother.

sitting on the sandhills, smoking a cigarette, when, all of a sudden, just below him, along the beach, there came a man upon a horse, who seemed to be in difficulties. The animal, evidently accustomed to the Moorish bit, was bridled with a snaffle, and therefore came tearing along with its mouth open, and its head high in the air.

Rising to his feet, Don Roberto threw his cigarette away, and as the rider passed him, hooked the reins with his walking stick, and stopped the runaway, causing the horseman nearly to fall upon his head.

Panting, the rider dismounted, and said with a smile: "Thank you, Sir; my name is Lavery."

The two men sauntered back to town, talking on this and on that, and thus began Don Roberto's friendship with the famous painter—a friendship what was to last until death parted them.

Soon after this meeting they made a long journey together, and Lavery had ample opportunity to see what a hardy and untiring traveller his new friend was, for even when tents failed at night, Don Roberto cheerfully parted with his spare blanket, and slept throughout the night, in spite of the penetrating chills of early morning, without, apparently, feeling the least discomfort, whereas Lavery snuggled up against the belly of his pony which, in Moorish fashion, had been trained to lie down and sleep with its rider.

During one of their journeys they passed through a famine-stricken part.

One evening, as Don Roberto sat before the tent, three or four figures came out of a palm grove, and dragging themselves slowly across the sand and grass, stood in a row before him, and pointed towards the sky with a mute gesture of despair. Famine had wasted them almost beyond semblance of mankind. Their sunken stomachs and protruding ribs made them look something like fossil fish embedded in the coal-measures, whilst their thin arms and legs scarcely sustained their feet and hands, which looked enormous in comparison with their shrunk, wasted limbs. Save for a wisp of dirty cotton rags about their loins, they were as naked as skeletons, and their parched tongues were rough and horny, like parrots'.

As Don Roberto stared at them, from every side—from hollows scooped out of the sand, from tufts of thorny shrubs—thin tottering figures rose and staggered to their tent. Women held children by the hand, and miserable boys supported aged men, whilst an old crone crawled on her hands and knees close to his feet, and then, raising herself a little, pointed a skinny finger to the sky. None of them spoke, but the mute glance of their beseeching eyes struck horror to Don Roberto's soul. When he could speak, he called for bread, and with his men cut it in slices, then, moistening it in water, passed it along the ranks. It vanished as by magic, but still the line grew longer, and in the moonlight the famine-stricken people looked like a troop of wolves that had surrounded some belated traveller on the plain. Some of the people snatched the barley from the horses and the mules, as they stood feeding whilst others struggled for the crumbs, fighting like starving dogs.

Don Roberto and Lavery called to their men and sent two of them to bring a mule laden with bread from town. When the food arrived, it disappeared almost as quickly as if it had been thrown into the sea. Night waned, and dawn still found the travellers' camp besieged with famine-stricken folk. Several days passed, and then the starvelings, having eaten, vanished as speedily as they had come, leaving no trace of their appearance. Then the travellers packed up their belongings, and once more proceeded on their way.

Fanatical Mohammedans frequently held up and even killed travellers. "Are you a Christian?" they asked in a threatening tone of voice. "Testify that Mohammed is the prophet of God, or. . . ."

On one occasion Don Roberto was held up by a gang of such fanatics, and when, at the point of long rifles and glittering knives, they asked him if he was a Christian, he immediately replied, raising his arms as if in horror: "No; I am a U.P.!"* The mysterious answer impressed, rifles and knives were withdrawn, and Don Roberto was left to wander on unmolested.

In 1897, when he arrived in Tangier, and told his friends about a journey he proposed to make to Tarudant, a "forbidden" city to which much mystery clung, their exclamations of "impossible" and "dangerous" merely had the effect of spurring him on.

Tarudant is the capital of the Sus, the southern province of Morocco. Polybius wrote vaguely about it, but as it was practically unknown to the outer world, all sorts of legends sprang up about the place which was said to be inhabited by demons and magicians, and, according to rumours in North Africa, everything strange and miraculous occurred there. In 1791, a French Army surgeon called Lemprière was chosen to cure the Sultan's son, and, accordingly, journeyed to Tarudant, but as far as was known, he was the first European who entered the city since the sixteenth century when merchants from Holland went to the annual fair. The British Vice-Consul in Tangier strongly advised Don Roberto not to venture into regions which were particularly dangerous at the time, because certain filibusters and international intriguers had tried to penetrate into them. Englishmen, in particular, were mistrusted and in disrepute in Southern Morocco, because a certain Major Spilsbury, assisted by a Jewish interpreter, and, it was reported, capital from David Sassoon tried to get concessions to trade in those parts. Two costly

* "U.P." meaning "United Presbyterian."

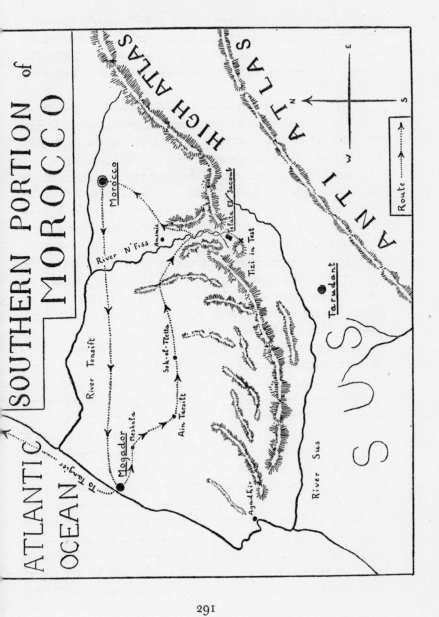

expeditions failed after shots had been exchanged. However, Spilsbury managed to escape in his yacht, but left behind four white companions and some Arabs who fell into the hands of the Moors, to be put in chains and sent to Fez to rot in dungeons.

In spite of the British Consul's warnings, and the unfavourable situation, Don Roberto was determined to penetrate into the Sus and to visit Tarudant, so he took no notice of what friends told him, and proceeded to carry out his plans.

Among his acquaintances in Tangier were two men whom he ran to earth after having made a number of inquiries as to their whereabouts. One was a Syrian, a certain Hassan Suleiman Lutaif, who spoke Arabic and various languages and dialects like a native. After he had agreed to join the expedition and act as interpreter, the two went to a hut on the outskirts of the town where lived the other man, Haj Mohammed es Swani: a Moor of the Riff pirate breed, short, strong, black-bearded, who spoke Spanish after the Arab fashion. When Haj heard about the proposed journey, he at once became enthusiastic, for he had accompanied Don Roberto on previous expeditions, and therefore knew his ways.

After a long discussion it was decided that Don Roberto should wear the necessary clothes to impersonate a Turkish doctor, travelling with his *taleb* or scribe. The project having been duly discussed, he bought a stock of medicines which consisted of quinine, mercury, some Seidlitz powders, eyewash for ophthalmia, and a few other simple drugs.

A few days later when a small ship, the *Rabat*, left Tangier, Don Roberto and his two companions were among the few passengers—a small League of Nations which consisted of Arabs, Portuguese, Berbers, Spaniards, Jews and Moors. When, after an uncomfortable, though uneventful, journey they landed in Mogador, Don Roberto found that the report had already spread that he and his two companions were agents of the British Government, or advance couriers of some filibustering syndicate. Fortunately, an old friend who was a missionary, in some way allayed the public fear, but, finding himself watched, Don Roberto and his two followers left the mission where they had been staying, and transferred their residence to a hotel, called the "International Sanatorium," about three miles outside the town, where he did his best to live down his filibustering character by going out shooting in the hottest time of day, collecting "specimens," such as butterflies and useless stones, taking photographs, classifying flowers, taking lessons in Arabic, and learning to ride upon the Moorish saddle.

Soon people began to believe that the "Turkish doctor," was a bona fide traveller, and then the time was ripe to look for a guide. The finding of a man, willing to undertake the journey proved to be very difficult, for no one cared to attempt the 150-mile trek beyond the Atlas Mountains, where Tarudant is situated. Arabs—who knew the way—were terrified at venturing into the territory of the Berbers who were giving a great deal of trouble at the time.

Several guides were approached, but all agreed that the journey was too hazardous. At last, however, a man named Mohammed el Hosein, came forward of his own accord. According to rumours, he was a slave-dealer, but the best muleteer in the country. He was thin and muscular, aged thirty-eight, a first-rate horseman, cunning and greedy, but to be depended on if once he gave his word. By nationality he was a Berber, with the flat face, small eyes and high cheek-bones of all his race.

The muleteer engaged, the choice of roads had to be discussed, for three were open to the travellers; the first along the coast. This road was flat and sandy, and followed close to the coast, right down to Agadir, and by it Tarudant could be reached within five days from Mogador. The disadvantages of following this road were three: firstly, they had to pass the town of Agadir, in which the Sultan had a governor; and secondly, Agadir once passed, they had to traverse the country of a tribe which bore an evil name for turbulence. Journeying, as Don Roberto proposed to do, two difficulties lay in his path. Firstly, he might be recognised by an official of the central government who would have turned him back at once. Again, supposing he dressed as a Moor, and were not discovered, he had to run all the risks a Moor must run in travelling, from robbers and from violence.

Just as he had decided to risk the journey by the way of Agadir, news came that a tribe inhabiting those regions was in rebellion, and that the road was shut.

Finally, he chose as his route a mountain pass through the Atlas, crossing the mountain at its greatest breadth. This route was longer, and much more difficult than the coast route would have been.

Hosein, the Berber guide, was a much travelled man who, though most trustworthy, was more attached to money than to his people and religion. When he unexpectedly—and quite blankly—said that no one would ever believe that Don Roberto was a Turkish doctor, he must have given him a rude shock. Finally, according to the guide's suggestion, it was decided that everybody should wear Moorish clothes.

With his beard and colouring, Don Roberto agreed that this was a capital idea, and it was decided that it would be better not to say what he was supposed to be, but to hope the natives would take him for a Shereef travelling with an escort. Accordingly, clothes were bought, and as Shereefs always rode on horses, a suitable mount was purchased, together with a Moorish saddle, covered with red cloth. When Don Roberto was disguised he was dressed in white, with a blue cloth cloak to cover all. His head was duly shaved, and he wore a fez and turban, yellow slippers, a

DON ROBERTO AS SHEIK MOHAMMED EL FASI

pair of horseman's boots embroidered with silk and silver thread, and across his shoulders was slung a leather bag.

The guide had his own mule, and another belonging to a fellow named Ali, who insisted on accompanying the expedition to see that his animal was not ill-treated. When mules had been bought for Lutaif, the interpreter, and Swani (the Moor), another animal was acquired to carry a small tent, just large enough to serve as sleeping quarters for Don Roberto and Lutaif. The other men, after the Moorish fashion, were to sleep by their mules, and, if it rained, to seek shelter under the lee-side of the tent. The cooking utensils consisted of a kettle and an iron pot, and besides these, as only luxury, a tea-tray, a pewter tea-pot, and six small glasses were added to the equipment, the glasses for drinking green tea flavoured with mint, and made as sweet as syrup. No forks or spoons were taken, for, being dressed as Moors, they would eat with their hands after the Moorish fashion.

Early in the morning, on the 12th of October, 1897, the little expedition set out, and soon after disappeared in the thick scrub. Ali—who had come to look after his mule—had no idea where he was going to, but when he found out, wished to return. However, he was prevented from carrying out his intention, and when he realised that to escape was impossible, he settled down and sang all day, dividing the night equally, smoking and sleeping.

Mohammed el Hosein (the guide), fully aware of the importance of getting the party accustomed to the Moorish clothes, gave instructions how to wear them, how to move, and many other details, for Don Roberto, in particular, knew nothing about this. Although he was accustomed to many kinds of saddle, the short Moorish stirrups soon cramped his legs. However, he refused to show that he felt the torture more and more, but when the party halted for a brief rest, he was glad when Swani gave him a good massage which greatly eased his discomfort.

Lunch despatched, green tea drunk, and cigarettes smoked, they mounted again and plunged into the forest where goats climbed upon the trees, and, here and there, camels browsed on the shoots. After about an hour the trees grew sparser, and the travellers emerged into a rolling country from where they had a last look at the sea.

Towards evening of the first day they arrived at a stronghold belonging to a Sheikh. The place looked rather like a "hacienda" in Mexico, surrounded by white walls, and at the gateway were two towers. Inside, the court—about two hundred feet across—was full of animals belonging to the Sheikh, and others which were the property of various travellers who had sought shelter for the night within the walls.

Accompanied by Hosein, Swani and Lutaif, Don Roberto must have felt uncomfortable when he met the Sheikh who conversed with them for a while. Don Roberto, who strongly suspected that he was recognised as a Christian, only occasionally said "yes" and "no," very low, in order to hide his accent. However, if the Sheikh penetrated his disguise he did not show it, for he was very courteous and showed the travellers the way to an upper room where they bedded down on the floor for the night. Before the Sheikh retired, he recommended them to bar the door, and then, turning away, said: "Sleep is Death's brother."

Having slept soundly on sheep skins, the travellers resumed their journey early in the morning. Towards noon, in the distance, the Atlas range appeared like a great wall of limestone capped with white. After having ridden for three hours over a hot desert of sand, stones and rocks, the little expedition came to a muddy stream by which the men lay, lapping the water like dogs.

In the evening they had to avoid a certain Caid's house, for if he had found out that a Christian was on his way towards Tarudant he would have caught him and had him escorted back to Mogador. This he would have done to avoid international complications, for if ever a white man was robbed or killed beyond such an outpost of civilisation, there was trouble for the Moors. Steering clear of the Caid's place, the travellers went to the house of a certain Sheikh who was known to Hosein, the guide. Until late at night they chatted with the Sheikh who lay on a divan in a room that was lit by a brass dish with a wick fed from raw mutton fat. Don Roberto, in order to avoid conversation and being discovered, pretended that he was feeling unwell. The Sheikh told them that a tribe had stopped the pass by which they intended to cross the Atlas Mountains, and warned his guests that to attempt to go beyond a certain point would be foolhardy and very dangerous.

When the little party was alone in the room which had been put at their disposal for the night, the guide and Ali (the muleteer) expressed great alarm, and even Lutaif and Swani admitted that they feared to go further. After a short whispered debate it was decided to stay in the place for a day, in order to obtain more information. Next morning, whilst Hosein went about, talking to different natives, Don Roberto prescribed for ophthalmia (inflammation of the eye), and handed out Seidlitz powders. As soon as it became known that a doctor had arrived, sick people came flocking to him, and many, who were unable to walk, were carried to the Sheikh's courtyard which Don Roberto used as consulting room.

In the evening Hosein, the guide, came back with the report that it was impossible to go through the pass, and that there had been an exchange of shots that afternoon when a troop of native cavalry had tried to pass. However, as Don

Roberto had no intention of turning back, it was decided to try another pass.

Next day they set out, and soon found themselves travelling along low hills which led upwards to the wall-like Atlas. Having jogged along for several hours, before they were aware of it, on going down a slope between some bushes, they found themselves in the middle of a crowded market. Men moved about, armed to the teeth; cows, camels and sheep were being noisily offered for sale; carcasses of sheep were being roasted inside ovens; crowds moved along lines of small brown tents, and the air was impregnated with the strong smell which emanates from a crowd of Arabs.

To ride through the market would have looked suspicious, for markets in Morocco form a sort of medium for exchange of news, and therefore all travellers stop to have a chat, even if only for a few minutes. Thinking and acting quickly, the travellers halted under an olive-tree, and Don Roberto lay down on the ground as if in agony. Hosein informed inquirers that the "Shereef" was ill, and when a small crowd collected, Don Roberto looked up slowly, and, raising one hand, muttered as indistinctly as he could that God was great, and that they all were in His hands. Until he was helped to mount, Lutaif talked almost incessantly to anyone he met, and when the little expedition was safely out of the place; Hosein was so pleased with Don Roberto for having acted as he had, that he congratulated him.

At midday they usually halted upon the open plain or under the shadow of a great rock. As it was too hot to eat, the travellers passed the time smoking and drinking from their water-jars whilst the animals rested.

After another long journey, and a night spent out in the open, heads upon their saddles and feet to the fire, the track got worse, until they entered a tremendous gorge, resembling a gigantic staircase. From this point on, travelling was

298

extremely hard on the animals which, however, were as willing and game as they had been when they had first set out.

Deep down below the river Wad el N'fiss boiled furiously amongst the stones. Descending along steep rocky mountain-sides and then slowly climbing up again, the travellers had to cross the foaming waters many times. Although they were not more than three feet deep, the current was so strong that they had to enter together in a group to keep their feet.

As they were toiling up a sharp incline, a shout brought their hearts into their mouths. Looking back, they saw two mountaineers rushing to intercept them, from a neighbouring hill. No time for any consultation, or do more than cock their guns and sit quite meekly waiting for the worst. On came the natives, bounding from stone to stone till they appeared on the track and blocked the travellers' way. Almost naked save for their long woollen shirts, their side-locks flying in the wind and with their long rifles and curved daggers these mountaineers looked most formidable, as they poured out at once a volume of guttural Shillah language which sounded menacing. Mohammed el Hosein, who—with Ali the muleteer—spoke Shillah, interpreted to Swani, who, half in Arabic and half in Spanish, informed Don Roberto what they said.

It seemed the desperadoes wanted the travellers to stop until a little boy brought down some Indian corn and milk, for it appeared it was the custom of these hills never to let a well-dressed Moor pass without some little offering. Of course, a poor man, or anyone to whom maize and milk would have been of great service, passed by unnoticed, as in other lands. Don Roberto promised to accept whatever gift these two men had to offer, and, in due course, a boy appeared, carrying a wooden bowl, from which he drank, and then passed it to his followers, after having said: "El Ham du lillah" (Praise be to God), the usual grace. The tribesmen would accept no money, but asked Don Roberto to say a word for them, about their taxes, which were not paid to their liege lord. Promising that he would do this, the little party once more proceeded.

The track gradually got worse and worse, so that Don Roberto rode, one stirrup brushing the mountainside, afraid that he would lose his slipper down the precipice, five or six hundred feet in depth upon the other side, which went sheer down into the river. Occasionally, the travellers had to call to trains of mules advancing to stop till they could get into one of the hollows scooped out, here and there, into the hillside, to allow people travelling in the opposite direction to pass. Now and again, a Sheikh's house, perched upon a hill and built like a castle, with turrets and battlements, all in mud, could be seen in the distance. Along the road, one constant interchange of "Peace be with you" was kept up, as they met other parties going or coming. (The route was obviously much travelled owing to the outbreak of hostilities in the other pass.)

Stumbling and tripping, leading their exhausted beasts, they came, long after nightfall, to a miserable house perched on a ledge of rocks over a river. Nothing was to be had, either for love or money, so the little party went to bed supperless, save for some green tea.

Next morning, on the twelfth day of their journey towards the "Forbidden City," and after several narrow escapes from detection, they were early upon the road. The animals had eaten well, as barley was carried by one of them. As on the day before, they started climbing staircases of rock, crossing and re-crossing deserted villages, and interchanging greetings with the various parties of travellers upon the road.

When Don Roberto's party passed near an inhabited house, Hosein went to see if he could get provisions. Luckily

300

TYPICAL SCENERY IN THE ATLAS MOUNTAINS

he obtained some, and the hungry adventurers sat down to enjoy what was to be the last square meal they were to have for several days. Proceeding once more, they passed several villages, all inhabited by well-armed and war-like people, and not infrequently robbers, who, being Berbers, would naturally rob any Moor passing, and without doubt kill any Christian whom they came across.

Having traversed a bare stony plain, on rounding a little hill, they suddenly came into full view of an immense castle. Presently, a man—obviously a messenger—came running towards them, and when he said that the Caid had heard Christians were travelling through the forbidden country, Swani said there must be some mistake. "Look at us," he exclaimed indignantly, "do we look like Christians? Christians burn their fathers."

Having apologised, the messenger returned towards the castle at a dog-trot, to the great relief of the party, all the members of which now felt sure that they would reach Tarudant. Joking about their latest escape, they continued their journey, and, after a long and steep climb, coming over the shoulder of a mountain, they saw another castle ahead. The guide explained that this was the guard-house of the Caid who lived in the other castle from which the messenger had been sent earlier in the day.

Just as Don Roberto and his party were passing the gate, a loud shouting from the zig-zag trail below them made them turn their heads. To their consternation they saw the messenger, accompanied by several armed men, bounding up the steep incline like mountain goats, brandishing their weapons and shouting wildly. Attracted by all the noise, armed men came rushing out of the castle, and others ran for their horses. Prepared for the worst, but ready to get out of the ticklish situation by bluffing once more, Don Roberto and his men stopped, and within a few seconds excited natives seized their animals by the bridles, calling out: "Arrumin!" (The Christians!), pointing their guns and fingering their formidable daggers. For a while things looked ugly, and when Lutaif and Swani explained who they were, the excited mob pointed to Don Roberto, and many throaty voices exclaimed: "This is the Rumi!" (Christian).

Finally, after the messenger had spoken to their angry and threatening fellow-tribesmen, they calmed down a little, for he explained that the Caid had given orders to take the party of travellers into custody, and to lead them back to the castle below. Followed by a hostile crowd, the captives were led away, and just as they turned to retrace their steps down the steep mountain, the sun broke through the clouds in the distance and Don Roberto had a glimpse of the tall towers and of the mosques of Tarudant: the goal he still hoped to reach.

It can easily be imagined what the feelings of the little party must have been, as, surrounded by dark wild-eyed natives, they were led back down the trail they had ridden over shortly before, confident that they would reach the "Forbidden City." To make things worse and more depressing, it started to rain heavily, and as they neared the Caid's castle, angry men, women and children collected and followed the captives, jeering and shouting. Having reached the enormous, mud-built stronghold, with its flat roofs and flat-topped towers, the prisoners were escorted to a tent where they found shelter from the torrential rain. Fortunately, the angry mob which had followed them, did nothing, and when Don Roberto and his companions were inside the tent which was guarded by several well-armed natives, many of the followers squatted down outside, in spite of the rain, and stared at the prisoners. Night came, and nothing happened, but torrential rain continued to fall, and, to make things more uncomfortable, the tent leaked badly. In spite of this, Don

Roberto slept soundly, and in the morning, when he awoke and looked outside, he was glad to find that the sun was shining brightly. This cheered him up greatly, but, looking up to the flat roof of the castle, he must have done a great deal of thinking, for there he saw gangs of heavily-chained prisoners tottering about whilst others were busy husking Indian corn. The poor creatures, he found out, were mostly members of a rebellious tribe who had fallen into the hands of the Caid.

Although he was very hungry, Don Roberto took a lively interest in everything that was going on near the castle, in and out of the gates of which armed horsemen continually rode. He was interested to see that the Berbers did not mock at the chained prisoners on the castle roof, but, on the contrary, sat with the blazing sun upon their shaven pates, talking to them, giving them bits of bread.

The hours crept on, and no food was brought to the captives in the tent, and whenever Swani or Hosein asked a member of the guard when they would be taken before the Caid, the answer was merely a stare. Towards evening, a little food arrived, but not nearly enough to satisfy Don Roberto's raving appetite. Shortly before sunset, the chained native prisoners were lowered, one by one, into a deep dry well, a mule revolving slowly round a crude kind of capstan, as, with esparto rope hitched in a bowline below their armpits, the captives were lowered beneath the ground. When all were down, four negroes placed a large, flat stone over the well.

Hungry and miserable, Don Roberto and his four companions sat in their tent, wondering what their fate was to be, but finally, one by one, they fell asleep. In the morning, curious to see the native prisoners being taken out of the dry well, Don Roberto approached the place, just as the negroes were lifting the stone. Judging by the terrible stench that rose from the well, he could well imagine what the state below must have been.

Three days passed, and still there was no sign of the Caid, and the detained party was beginning to wonder how long they would be kept in suspense before finding out what their fate was to be. Don Roberto, like his men and animals, was given next to nothing to eat, but, by degrees, the guards had become friendlier, and from them Hosein found out that the Caid was invisible because he had been wounded in a recent fight with an enemy tribe in the mountains. Fortunately, a travelling fakir arrived, and as he spoke Arabic, a language Don Roberto understood fairly well, he learnt much horse-lore from him, for the fakir was allowed to talk freely whenever he visited the tent.

Early in the morning, on the fourth day of Don Roberto's captivity, a starveling donkey was driven past his tent, carrying a dead prisoner who, it appeared, had tried to escape. The body of the man was thrown across the animal's back, and the corpse's feet and arms were dangling upon the ground.

In the evening, with the help of Swani, a native was bribed to take a letter to the British Consul in Mogador. Don Roberto retired to the tent where he hastily scribbled two notes, which, when they had been carefully wrapped up in string packing-paper, were tied round with palmetto cord. In the dead of night, the carrier crawled up to the tent, and when the letters were handed over to him, together with the bribe for his service, he made off as silently and mysteriously as he had appeared. For some time Don Roberto and his companions sat listening intently, for they knew that if the man were discovered he would immediately be shot at. The minutes passed as if they were hours, and when they were sure that the messenger was safe in the distance, he suddenly re-appeared, crawling into the tent, saying that his heart had failed him. Nothing would induce him to make the attempt, and so, having handed back the letters and the bribe, he left the disappointed captives who never slept a wink until daylight appeared over the bleak mountains.

Thanks to Swani, however, another man, willing to act as messenger, was found, and as the letters were to be slipped to him shortly before sun-down, Don Roberto re-wrote what he had written, and, in addition, added another letter for the editor of the *Daily Chronicle*. Although the situation he found himself in was far from pleasant, he obviously had not lost his sense of humour. With ample time for thought and recollection, he remembered a promise he had made to the editor of the *Saturday Review*, and probably, in order to pass away time, wrote the following letter which might well serve reviewers of books to "read and inwardly digest."

"Thelata El Jacoub, Kintafi,
"Atlas Mountains.
"22nd October, 1897.

"The Editor, *Saturday Review*.
"Sir,—

"It will, I fear, be impossible for me to review the work called the *Canon** about which I spoke to you. I hope, therefore, that you will place it in competent hands, for it is a well-written and curious book. You know that, as a general rule, I am reluctant to undertake reviewing, but in this case I should have been glad to make an exception to my usual practice.

"Before reviewing a book, I place a copy of it upon my table, and, after looking carefully at the outside of it, peruse the preface, glance at the title page, read the last paragraph, and then fall to work. On this occasion, title and last paragraph, even the preface (which I understand is worthy of consideration), are beyond my reach. Not

---

* After his captivity Don Roberto wrote a preface for a later edition of this book which deals with astronomy, mathematics and other branches of learning among ancient civilisations.

to be prolix, I may explain that for the last four days I have been a prisoner in the Atlas Mountain, at the above address, and that there seems no speedy prospect of my release. For details see the *Daily Chronicle*, to which I have addressed a letter, with one to our Ambassador at Tangier, which will, I hope, arrive some day, for when night falls our messenger is to endeavour to cross the hills to Mogador, our post-town, some two hundred miles away, and to inform the Consul of our case.

"I am, Sir, yours faithfully,
"R. B. CUNNINGHAME GRAHAM."

The other letter he wrote whilst he was being held by the Caid in the Atlas Mountains reads:

"Thelata El Jacoub, Kintafi,
"Atlas Mountains.
"22nd October, 1897.
"The Editor, *Daily Chronicle*, London.
"SIR,—

"It appears that, like St. Paul, I am destined to be in prison oft. Whilst endeavouring to cross the Atlas into the almost unknown province of Sus, I was arrested by the Governor of this province on October 19th, and have been detained here on various pretexts ever since. To-night one of our followers is to gird up his loins, tighten his turban, take his staff in his hand, pull up the heels of his shoes, testify to the existence of the one God, and strike across the hills to place this 'copy' in the hands of the British Vice-Consul at Mogador, about two hundred miles away.

"Though we are civilly treated, our position is the reverse of pleasant. We are allowed to walk about, but we cannot go far from our tent, and have no idea why we are detained. I spare you any remarks on the flora and fauna of the district, for Inshallah, I propose to inflict them on a harmless and much book-ridden public. I merely state briefly that this house, an immense castle built of mud, is situated in an amphitheatre of hills, all capped with snow, and that a brawling river, the Wad N'fiss, runs past our tent; goats wander the hills, tended by boys wild as their ancestors, whom Jugurtha led against the Romans. Horses and mules are driven down to drink by negro slaves, prisoners clank past in chains, knots of retainers armed with six-foot guns stroll about carelessly, pretending to guard the place; it is, in fact, Arcadia grafted on feudalism or feudalism steeped in Arcadia. The call to prayers rises five times a day; Allah looks down, and we sit smoking cigarettes, waiting for you to turn your mighty lever on our behalf.

"For my companion in adversity I have a Syrian Christian who acts as my interpreter, and who writes for reasons known to you. Should Britain fail us, we hope that the great prince, the Sultan Abdul Hamid (God hath given him the victory), will send his fleet to our assistance, for, as we know, each of his Christian subjects is a portion of his heart.

"Things look a little serious, as we are quite uncertain how long the Governor may keep us here. Therefore, I hope that this may go into your best edition, and be the means of making the Foreign Office act at once on our behalf, if we are not released.

"Yours faithfully,

"R. B. CUNNINGHAME GRAHAM."

"P.S.—

"Pray assure the public that we shall steadfastly refuse to abjure our faith. Having thus done all in my power to invoke the protection of the Nonconformist

Conscience (powerful amongst the noble Shillah race) for myself, and that of his Sultan for Lutaif, I recollected a business engagement, and wrote the following letter to excuse myself for non-completion of contract. I have ever held contracts as the most sacred of all the affairs of life."

For copies of the following letters, and permission to reproduce them, I am indebted to the authorities of the British Foreign Office who kindly helped me with my research work. As will be noted, the spelling of various names differs slightly in these letters.

"Tlata Yacoop, Dar el Kuntaff,
"Oued-en-Nafees.
"22nd October, 1897.

"DEAR MR. JOHNSTON,—

"I regret to say that having been unable to cross to Sus by the Imintaunt we were obliged to take the road from Aurzuiz to Tizi which follows the river Nafees. All went well till within four hours of Tizi. At this point the Kaid-li-Taib-ben-li-Muhammed-el-Gundafi arrested us on the 19th October. Under various pretexts we have been detained here ever since and there does not seem any immediate prospect of being allowed to depart. We think that he has written to the Sultan for instructions. This morning we saddled our mules with the intention of returning to Mogador, but we were at once ordered to unsaddle.

"Though we are treated with civility and provided with food and tent, the position is the reverse of pleasant, more especially as the Kaid will neither see us nor give us any explanation of why we are detained. Under these unpleasant circumstances I would be much obliged

if you would at once use every possible effort to procure
our release and communicate at once with Sir Arthur
Nicolson, stating the facts of the case.

> "I have, etc.,
>
> (Signed) "Cunninghame Graham."

If Don Roberto was apprehensive about the prospects of
his immediate future, he certainly did not show it in his
letters. Most travellers, under similar circumstances would,
no doubt, have written in a very different strain. The
British authorities immediately took the matter in hand, as
will be seen by the following communication.

> "Tangier,
>
> "November 7th, 1897.

"The Marquess of Salisbury, K.G.,

> etc., etc., etc.,

"Foreign Office.

"My Lord,—

"I received last night by special courier a despatch
from Mr. Consul Maclean, enclosing one from Mr.
Vice-Consul Johnston, informing me that Mr. Cunninghame Graham, the former Member of Parliament, had
been arrested, with his interpreter, a Turkish subject,
by a Kaid Gundafy at a place near Tizi, in the Atlas
Mountains and in the direction of the Sus district.

"Mr. Graham passed through Tangier some five weeks
ago, and told me that he was most anxious to visit
Tarudant in the Sus territory. I advised him to postpone
his project, as the Moorish Authorities were at this
moment extremely suspicious of any movement of
foreigners, and especially of British travellers in the Sus
district. Mr. Graham was unwilling to abandon his trip,

but said he would take every precaution, and gave me to understand that in any case he would follow my advice, and, on arrival at Mogador, acquaint the Governor of that place with his intentions and ask for the necessary escort. So far as I know this course was not adopted, and Mr. Graham has evidently endeavoured to carry out his journey on his own responsibility. Mr. Graham in a letter to Mr. Johnston, of which I beg leave to enclose a copy, is apparently well treated, and I have no fear of any mishap occurring to him. Mr. Johnston has despatched a messenger with a letter from the Governor of Mogador to the Kaid Gundafy requesting the immediate release of the travellers.

"I have also sent an express courier to the Grand Vizier with a similar demand, and I have little doubt that Mr. Graham will very shortly regain his liberty.

"Doubtless the Kaid has arrested him on suspicion that Mr. Graham is connected in some manner with commercial enterprises in the Sus; but he should not have prevented the travellers from returning to Mogador as they desired, and subsequently I propose to ask the Grand Vizier to obtain some explanation of the action of the Kaid.

"Mr. Johnston also warned Mr. Graham of the risks he would incur; but the latter is an adventurous traveller and difficult to dissuade from making journeys which he thinks will be interesting.

"I have the honour to be,
"With the highest respect,
"My Lord,
"Your Lordship's
"Most obedient, humble Servant,
(Signed) "A. Nicolson."

Even though the messenger had departed into the night with the letters, Don Roberto and his companions wondered if he really intended to take them to Mogador, or if he would throw them away and keep the bribe. At the very best, several days would pass before anything could be done for the prisoners, and therefore, next morning, determined to leave no stone unturned, Lutaif, who fancied himself as a man of letters, said he would write to the Caid to ask for an interview. So he lay upon his stomach in the tent for about an hour, scribbling on a flimsy sheet of paper with a small pencil-end. After great trouble he read his note aloud, evoking great admiration, both from Swani and Hosein who declared the communication to be a gem which, they felt sure, would have good effect. Knowing the respect the Moors attach to letters, Don Roberto hoped that, after it had been handed over to the keeper of the gate, it might perhaps bring an interview with the Caid; but nothing happened, and once more a gloomy night was spent in the tent.

In the morning, however, Don Roberto was pleased to find that, for the first time, ample supplies of food were brought to them. Towards midday the Chamberlain arrived with the happy news that the Caid would see the captives in the afternoon.

Delighted, they immediately got busy putting on their cleanest clothes, and early in the afternoon the Chamberlain, accompanied by a native, came for Don Roberto and his men who followed as majestically as they could. As they passed through several courts, they observed a wounded cream-coloured stallion which, they were informed, belonged to the Caid, and had been injured during the fight with the rebels in the mountains. Near the animal stood a little boy who flapped away the flies with a green bough. Then the Chamberlain led the way through a Mosque in which worshippers squatted in silence, and when they came to a door they were made to wait for almost half an hour, no doubt to impress them. Finally, at the intimation of their guide, Don Roberto and his companions slipped off their shoes, and entered the "Presence Chamber," a narrow room, vilely daubed in blue and dingy red, and with cheap gilding. The room was carpeted with fine, almost white rugs from Sus, all worked in curious geometric patterns. In a recess within a wall sat two boys who looked rather like hermaphrodites, and upon a dark red saddle-cloth, propped up by cushions, with his wounded leg stretched out before him, the Caid sat. Don Roberto's party advanced, and after having been presented by the Chamberlain, shook hands. The Caid, greeted quietly but courteously, and after Hosein and Swani had lifted his *selham* (cloak), and kissed it, all retreated and sat down, tucking their feet well underneath their clothes, according to Moorish custom. In the doorway stood two sentinels, two or three elders sat round the room, and two *talebs* (scribes) were writing letters.

For some time not a word was spoken, but it was evident that the Caid—who was about forty years of age, thick-set, dark-complexioned, with a black beard trimmed to a double point, and with rather small eyes—was taking mental note of Don Roberto.

By race and language he was a Berber, but as he spoke Arabic fairly fluently, he finally addressed the prisoners in this language. When Don Roberto, with the help of his companions, explained that the sole object of their journey was to visit Tarudant, this seemed incomprehensible to the Caid who obviously thought Don Roberto was a filibuster, or an English agent. Whilst coffee was being served by slave-boys, the conversation veered from one subject to another, but, on the whole, the subject which gave most scope for talk, was the Caid's wounded leg. Evidently Don Roberto's fame as a doctor had travelled before him, for the Caid, having explained that the bullet was still lodged deep in the flesh, asked him to examine the wound, and, if possible, to extract the ball. For a moment Don Roberto hesitated, thinking that if the ball was near the skin he would hazard the operation, and so earn the gratitude of the Caid who would surely send him to Tarudant with honour, and with an escort.

One look, however, dispelled all his hopes, for the wound was high up in the thigh, close to the femoral artery. Reluctantly he had to say he was unable to undertake so serious a case, but he advised the Caid to send for an English doctor, who, Don Roberto knew, was staying in Morocco City.

The interview having lasted some two hours, the little party of hopefuls who were sure that they would now be released, had a rude shock when they were escorted back to their tent by a guard of well-armed men. After the visit to the Caid, a great change came over everyone who had dealings with the prisoners, for even those who previously had hardly acknowledged their greetings, now gravely saluted them, and four men arrived bearing a sheep on a huge wooden dish, smoking and peppered so as to start Don Roberto sneezing. When the sheep had been torn into convenient portions, the prisoners ate like so many wolves.

Early next morning, the effects of Don Roberto's audience with the Caid began to manifest themselves. The sick, the halt, the lame, all besieged the tent, and he had to dispense his whole stock of medicines.

Day followed day, and finally, when nearly two weeks had passed, the Chamberlain arrived at the tent with the news that the prisoners could depart. Thinking that now was the time to make a last effort to go on to Tarudant, Don Roberto offered him a hundred dollars, but the Chamberlain merely shook his head and said: "What is the use to me of a hundred dollars without my head?" Shifting ground, Don Roberto said he could not think of leaving without a personal interview with the Caid to thank him for his hospitality. But here again the Chamberlain was ready with a message: "that it pained his Excellency not to receive him, but his wound had broken out afresh, and that he sent many salaams and wished him a prosperous journey back to the coast." As a last resource Don Roberto asked the Chamberlain: "What if I get on horseback, and ride straight on to Sus?" In answer to this, the Chamberlain asked gravely if Don Roberto thought he had the best horse in the valley, and if, supposing any tribesman was to fire, he thought his clothes were stout enough to turn a ball.

Seeing there was no earthly chance of going on to Tarudant, Don Roberto thanked the Chamberlain, and immediately ordered his men to make ready to depart. These worked like schoolboys packing to go home. As there were no medicines, food or barley left, the pack merely consisted of the little tent, a few rugs and utensils. Hosein, who had never thought to leave the place alive, ran about joyfully, Swani sang gay Spanish sailors' songs, and Ali, the mule-boy, felt his animal to see if it had suffered by the long exposure to heat and rain, with scarcely any fodder. The mule winced, and kicked him to show its love, and to assure him that its spirit was not injured by the fast.

When all was ready, Don Roberto mounted, touched his horse with the spur, and let him run across a stretch of flat ground outside the castle, and then plunged down a steep path to the river where he met the Caid's horses for the last time, as they were being led out to drink. The wounded cream-colour, now almost recovered, stood up and gave a neigh, and as Don Roberto and his party rode under the castle walls upon the stony bed of the river, the figure of the Chamberlain appeared, and waved to them in a friendly fashion.

After having followed the river's bed for about a mile, the trail led through a scrub of oleanders, then rose and entered a fantastic path worn in the limestone rock, cut here and there into pyramids and pinnacles by time, traffic and rains. Turning, they saw the Caid's castle for the last time, a monstrous, mud-built, yellowish-red pile, the mosque tower with its green metallic tiles, the cornfields, and the wild narrow valley stretching to the snow-capped hills, and the river winding in and out between its high banks. In his heart, Don Roberto thanked fortune for having kept him prisoner for twelve well-filled days in such a place. Lutaif, in spite of all his piety, muttered something which sounded like an imprecation on Mohammed and his faith, but yet confessed that even in the Lebanon there was no valley wilder and more beautiful than that of the N'fiss. Hosein felt at his beard as if to assure himself it still grew on his chin, and without stint cursed Caid and castle, tribe, place and all the dwellers in it. When every member of the small party had thus relieved his feelings, they set themselves to drive their half-starved beasts over the mountain roads.

The river was much deeper and fiercer than when they had come, owing to the recent rains, which forced them to cross repeatedly and get wet every time. The snow, which now lay thickly on the higher hills, made the wind as cold as winter, and the travellers felt great discomfort as their clothes stuck to their backs like wet paper. The sun, the winds, the want of food, the rain and dust of the road, had by this time rendered Don Roberto as dark as a Moor, and all the passers-by saluted the party with "Peace!," and never turned their heads to look at the weary travellers, taking them, evidently, for men from the Sus.

Leaving the huge wall-like Atlas towering up into the blue sky behind them, they came to the lowland; a sea-like surface of steppe across which, in the far distance, they could see

315

camel and mule trains crawling, looking like worker ants toiling towards their gigantic ant-hills in South America.

After another weary hot journey, they reached the outside of the city walls, and passing underneath the gate, emerged into the sandy lanes running between orange gardens. They passed through narrow lanes where camels jammed them almost to the wall; along the foot-path beggars sat and showed their sores; dogs, yellow, ulcerous and wild as jackals, skulked between their horses' legs. Presently they came to an open space in which a sort of market was in progress, and a ring of interested spectators sat, crouched, and stood, intent upon a story-teller's tale. The weary travellers wound their way through streets and open spaces, past mosque doors, and along narrow alleys, arched with vines which hung so low that they had to bend their heads in passing on horseback. Finally they halted at the side door of a house in which lived an old acquaintance of Don Roberto, a man of obscure origin, deeply tinged with negro blood, who called himself Abu Beckr. He had once been a camel-driver, and later became a British Agent. He was greatly feared and disliked, and yet respected, and was probably the richest man from the Atlas to the Riff and from the Sahara to Mogador.

Having stayed with Abu Beckr for some ten days, chiefly to rest the horses and mules, the little party set out once more. After four days, the Atlas dropped out of sight, and finally, coming to the last range of foothills, they saw the sea in the distance, like a blue vapoury haze. Next day, leading their jaded animals, they reached Mogador, from where, after having been paid off, Lutaif, Swani, Hosein and Ali departed in different directions, leaving Don Roberto alone, to drift into further adventures.

During his journey he had learnt a great deal about the country, but only enough to make him more curious, and to fill him with a longing to see more.

After his return to Tangier, by sea, Don Roberto set out with mules and provisions to study social problems amongst the Moors, and to prepare a statement as to work and wages, and hours of labour, which in those parts averaged something like two a day.

Whilst he was in Tangier, his friend, Sir James McLeod, who was the British Consul in Fez, invited him to a dinner that was given in honour of a number of foreign diplomats. After the meal there was a discussion about the east wind, known as the "Levanter" which has a very depressing effect on people who are not accustomed to it. Sir James said that the popular explanation of this phenomenon was that there is a microbe in the "Levanter" which causes the softening of the brain, "except," he added to amuse his listeners, "of the brains of diplomats."

Whilst merry laughter greeted this remark, Don Roberto quickly rose, raised an arm, and, when silence had been restored, said with an elegant bow: "Naturally, Sir, diplomatists come here without brains."

Together with Walter Harris—who was one of the very few Europeans who could even deceive the natives when he dressed in Moorish garb—Don Roberto made several journeys. Harris spoke various native dialects to such perfection, and had lived in Morocco so long, that he could safely go to places which no European could have visited without being killed.

Once Don Roberto met Harris in Wazan and, together, they called on the Sultan Mulai-Abd-El-Asiz who, in one of the courtyards of his castle, kept all sorts of wild animals in cages: lions, panthers, bears, zebras, etc.

In order to entertain his visitors, the Sultan ordered all these animals to be turned loose in the yard. When the ensuing battle royal ended, and the survivors had been driven back into their respective cages, some wild zebras were released, and the Sultan—who had heard about Don Roberto's fame as a horseman—turned to him and asked him to ride one.

Without thinking twice, Don Roberto asked for a long rope, and when it was brought to him, and he had quickly made it into something resembling a lasso, he went into the courtyard where, to everybody's astonishment, he soon roped a big male zebra. With the assistance of several negro slaves, the struggling animal was held, and, as soon as Don Roberto had a chance, he leapt onto its back, and then shouted to the slaves to let go the rope. Although the infuriated zebra bucked, propped and plunged furiously, and with much more speed than a horse, the rider stuck on as if he were part of the animal, and finally when it tired, he leapt off and strolled back to the Sultan who could hardly believe his eyes.

Sir John Lavery, and many others who knew Don Roberto in those days, declare that no rodeo performer they have seen could ride as he did. A certain lady told me that the first time she saw him was on the beach near Tangier. She happened to be sitting on a sand-hill when, suddenly, along the sea-front, riding like demons, a number of men came dashing toward her. One, who was racing ahead, lost his hat, and when another rider, who followed behind, approached the spot where it lay, he picked it up as he dashed past. Not satisfied with this feat, the rider stood up in the saddle, waved the hat triumphantly, jumped off, as his horse wildly careered along, and, holding the saddle with one hand leapt over the animal, from side to side.

Fascinated by this feat of daring and skill, the lady wondered who the rider could be, and in the evening, to her surprise, she saw him in the hotel, and when she went to speak to him, he introduced himself as Cunninghame Graham.

Morocco and its people fascinated Don Roberto to such an extent that, for some years, he spent a great deal of time there.

Once, during his travels, when he watched the natives "playing powder," that is, racing over a flat stretch of ground, standing on their horses, throwing rifles into the air and catching them again, shooting and yelling wildly as they dash along at break-neck speed, Don Roberto asked one of the leaders to let him join in this daring display.

Obviously amazed at the request, the native answered: "But Christians know not how to play powder."

What means of persuasion Don Roberto used I do not know, but on several occasions he was allowed to join in this difficult and dangerous display, to the wonderment and admiration of onlookers and performers alike.

Once, as in the company of his friend, Harris, he travelled through Morocco, he saw a Caid being burnt alive. This Caid was renowned as a ruthless tyrant who ill-treated and over-taxed his people. Those who were unable, or refused, to pay their taxes, he ordered to be lowered into subterranean pits where they were left to die. Finally, there was an uprising of his tribe, and Don Roberto and Harris just arrived when the tyrannical Caid paid the price for his many misdeeds.

As I have mentioned before, some of Don Roberto's wanderings through Morocco had a purpose, for when he had first decided to visit the country, he was of the opinion that to understand the Spain of the Middle Ages properly, it was necessary to see and study the Moors and Jews of North Africa.

Once, in 1898, whilst he was staying with his friend, Sir James McLeod, the British Consul in Fez, he suddenly expressed a desire to make an overland journey to the Algerian frontier, a distance of some two hundred miles. About a hundred and fifty miles of the country to be traversed was in districts over which the Sultan's authority was nominal; it was, in fact, known as *Bled Sidba* (Land of Rebellion). Certain that if his guest carried out his intention, he would be murdered, or, at least, pillaged to the shirt, Sir James turned down the project. In order to dissuade Don Roberto, the consul told him about two missionaries who, only recently, against his entreaties, had persisted in making a journey inland. Their escape was almost a miracle, for the natives caught them, threw them to the ground, and knives were at their throats when an Arab happened to pass. Having heard that the two victims were missionaries, and had passed through his village the previous night, he claimed them (according to tribal custom), as under his protection, and thanks to this friendly Arab's intervention, after a dispute among the natives, the travellers' lives were spared. Abandoning their goods and belongings, the two missionaries mounted an old one-eyed pony, lent to them by their saviour, and returned to Fez, a distance of fifty miles, attired only in their shirts.

Even this story, which he knew to be perfectly true in every detail, did not induce Don Roberto to change his mind. Fortunately, however, shortly before he intended to set out, the horse he was riding crossed his fore-legs, and, in rolling over, badly bruised one of Don Roberto's legs, obliging him to lie up and to go about on crutches for some time, after which he had to return to Scotland where urgent business awaited his attention.

Within a few months he was back in Morocco, but this time with a definite, and, what he thought, practical plan.

Before I continue, let me quote what he once wrote about European influence in Morocco, for I think this shows Don Roberto, the idealist who loved what we are so fond of calling "primitive" people, whose dragging into the European spider-net he vainly tried to fight.

In the preface to his book on Morocco, *Mogreb-El-Acksa*,* Don Roberto writes:

* Without this book, Mr. G. B. Shaw admits, his *Captain Brassbound's Conversion* would never have been written. Joseph Conrad called it a "glorrious performance" and "the book of travel of the century."

"It may be that my poor unphilosophic recollections of a failure may interest some, who, like myself, have failed, but still may like to hear that even in failure you can see strange things, meet as strange types, and be impressed as much with wild and simple folk, as any traveller who thundered through the land, Bible and gun in hand, making himself no spiced conscience, but putting into practice the best traditions of our race, confident that the one way to win a 'nigger's' heart is to 'speak English' to him, and doing so even at the rifle's mouth."

In his preface to Charles Rosher's book, *Light for John Bull on the Moroccan Question*, he wrote:

". . . How strange it is that cow-houghed, loose-put together, eyebrowless boys—who in their native Bradford, or in Leeds, have perhaps been Radicals—hie them abroad, and on returning home, after six months or so, amongst some people whose language they ignore, swell out their bellies and talk of Empire, and of course become Conservatives. . . . Neither France, Spain nor Italy, have anything to give the Moors, but gin, absinthe, *grappa*, *aguardiente* (two strong alcoholic drinks), brothels and gaming houses. . . . All it can do is to show plainly that France, Germany or Spain can but bring misery upon the Moors, and reduce them from the position of freemen (enjoying, it is true, a liberty tempered by tyranny), to the position of mere economic slaves, hewers of wood, and carriers of gin, in their own native land.

"To us (England), it brings the danger, one fine day, that some 'entente cordiale' or other may close the Straits and shut us from the East."

Towards the end of 1899, Don Roberto, accompanied by his wife, returned to Morocco City. To make a long story short, his plans, briefly, were the following: to start honest trading among the natives, supplying them only with articles and goods which are necessary for their mode of living; to employ exclusively natives; to sell without profiteering, and under no condition to meddle with Moroccan politics.

Obviously he was not so very optimistic on returning to Mogador, for in a letter he wrote from there on the 18th of January, 1899, he said:

". . . The chief came to see me in Morocco City. I made a treaty with him and got a concession to trade, but what may come out of it, no one knows, not even Allah. The chief is Bashir-El-Beirac, an independent man, of a very old family. He has written me several letters (though in Turkish), stating that he has been wishing for a long time to see some trader established in his country. At least I can stop them selling gin and guns, if I take it up; and if I refuse the concession he will take it to someone else. . . ."

As can easily be imagined, so many difficulties and complications arose, not to mention intrigues when foreign syndicates heard about this scheme, that, finally, Don Roberto gave up the idea, and returned to Scotland where, together with his wife he made valiant efforts to save his estates which, though they were well administered, failed to produce enough to pay off the huge debts his father had left.

CHAPTER XV

THE Boer War had broken out (1899–1902), and whilst it lasted, Don Roberto spent most of his time in Gartmore. His wife, though her health was far from good, still kept the books and did most of the clerical work. Against doctors' advice, she continued to smoke heavily, and although she realised the folly of it, she was unable to be without a cigarette in her mouth for more than a few moments.

Don Roberto was much too busy to take an interest in politics, but, instead, he rode about all day on his Argentine mustang "Pampa." Riding never tired him, but when he returned home in the evenings, depressed by worry, he was glad to find relaxation by reading and writing until he could no longer keep his eyes open. Had he been in Parliament he would certainly have thundered against the annexation of the Boer territories by the British Government. What the House of Commons missed—or, "escaped"—can easily be imagined.

From the year 1899 on, he took up writing seriously, that is, in his case, writing to please himself, as he put it on several occasions. Every year, until 1906, he wrote a book. Five of these were collections of short stories, but two, *A Vanished Arcadia*, and *Hernando de Soto*, dealing with Spanish and South American history, required a great deal of research work, which he did during periodical visits to Spain where he diligently read through old documents and records which he dug up in archives.

Whenever he could, he visited his mother who still lived in her house in Chester Square, in London. There he met famous writers and artists with many of whom he kept up a constant correspondence, even when he was travelling abroad.

Among his literary friends, W. H. Hudson, Joseph Conrad and Wilfred Scawen Blunt were his most intimate, for with them, in personality and interests, he had much in common. Besides these, he was on terms of friendship with William Morris, George Bernard Shaw, H. G. Wells, Frank Harris, Edward Garnett, Sir William Rothenstein, Max Beerbohm, Sir John Squire, Oscar Wilde and many others.

Once, Morris, in expressing his appreciation of Don Roberto, added: "but he's too bloody politeful."

Don Roberto, in writing to Mr. Arthur Compton Rickett, used a striking phrase about Morris, with reference to the number of "down-and-outs," and "ne'er-do-wells," who surged round him, just because he was rich and influential. Don Roberto characterised Morris as "a bull bison surrounded by a pack of wolves."

Conrad and Hudson had but few common interests, and therefore rarely met, but Hudson and Blunt were often together, and Don Roberto constantly met the three who had a great admiration and sympathy for each other.

In 1897, having read a story by Joseph Conrad in a magazine, Don Roberto was so struck by its beautiful style, that he wrote a letter to the then almost unknown author.

Conrad's answer came almost immediately, and reads:

"5th August, 1897.
"Stanford-le-Hope,
"Essex.

"R. B. Cunninghame Graham Esqr.,
"Dear Sir,—

"You've given me a few moments of real solid excitement. I scuttled about for the signature—then laid the letter down. I am a prudent man. Very soon it occurred to me that you would hardly go out of your way (in the month of August) to kick an utter stranger. So, I said to myself: 'These—no doubt—are half-pence. Let us see,' and—behold! It was real gold, a ducat for a beggar —a treasure for the very poor! You'll ruin yourself; but (I am a white man) what does that matter to me as long as the profit is mine.

"And I feel distinctly richer since this morning. I admire so much your vision and your expression that your commendation has for me a very high value—the very highest. Believe that I appreciate fully the kind impulse that prompted you to write.

"Mr. Kipling has the wisdom of the passing generation —and holds it in perfect sincerity. Some of his work is of impeccable form and because of that little thing he shall sojourn in Hell only a very short while. He squints with the rest of his excellent sort. It is a beautiful squint; it is a useful squint. And—after all—perhaps he sees round the corner? And suppose Truth is just round the corner like the elusive and useless loafer it is? I can't tell. No one can tell. It is impossible to know. It is impossible to know anything tho' it is possible to believe a thing or two.

"Pray do not regret your letter; I mean to hold to my beliefs—not that it matters in the least. If I had your eyesight, your knowledge and your pen it would matter.

325

But I haven't. Nevertheless I shall persist in my beastly attitude. Straight vision is bad form—as you know. The proper thing is to look round the corner, because, if truth is not there—there is at any rate a something that distributes shekels. And what better can you want than the noble metals?

"You did not expect such a 'tuile sur la tête' as this in answer to your letter. Well! it's only five pages at the most and life is long—and art is so short that no one sees the miserable thing. Most of my life has been spent between sky and water and now I live so alone that often I fancy myself clinging stupidly to a derelict planet abandoned by its precious crew. Your voice is not a voice in the wilderness—it seems to come through the clean emptiness of space. If—under the circumstances—I I hail back lustily I know you won't count it to me for a crime.

"I am sincerely delighted to learn that you can stand my prose. It is so hard to realise that I have any readers! —except the critics, who have been very kind and moral, and austere but excessively indulgent. To know that you could read me is good news indeed—for one writes only half the book; the other half is with the reader.

"Believe me, dear Sir,
"Very faithfully yours,
(Signed) "JOSEPH CONRAD."

The subsequent correspondence between the two is so interesting that I must also reproduce extracts of Conrad's answers to Don Roberto's second and third letters. In his second letter, Conrad says:

". . . I am both touched and frightened by what you say about being the prophet of my inarticulate and

wandering shadow. I cannot help thinking with alarm
of the day when you shall find out that there is nothing
there. How soon will you begin to regret your magnificent
imprudence?—and will you ever forgive me the triumph
of your friends when they assail you with reproaches and
a great clamour of 'I told you so!'

"You understood perfectly what I tried to say about
Mr. Kipling—but I did not succeed in saying *exactly*
what I wanted to say. I wanted to say in effect that in
the chaos of printed matter Kipling's 'ébauches' appear
by contrast finished and impeccable. I judge the man
in his time—and space. It is a small space—and as to
his time I leave it to your tender mercy. I wouldn't in
his defence spoil the small amount of steel that goes to
the making of a needle. As to posterity it won't smile.
Not it! Posterity shall be busy thieving, lying, selling its
little soul for sixpence (from the noblest motives), and
shall remember no one except perhaps one or two quite
atrocious mountebanks; and the half-dozen men lost in
that 'bagarre' are more likely to weep than to smile over
the masterpieces of our time.

"I am very unhappy just now, not being able to squeeze
three consecutive sentences out of myself. The world,
however, seems to be rolling on without a check—which
is of course very offensive to me. . . ."

The two had not yet met when, in answer to Don Roberto's
third letter, Conrad wrote:

". . . Your letter reached me just as I was preparing to
write to you. What I said in my incoherent missive of
last week was *not* for the purpose of arguing, really. I did
not seek controversy with you—for this reason: I think
that we do agree. If I've read you aright (and I have

327

been reading you for some years now), you are a most hopeless idealist—your aspirations are irrealisable. You want from men faith, honour, fidelity to truth in themselves and others. You want them to have all this, to show it every day, to make out of these words their rule of life. The respectable classes which suspect you of such pernicious longings lock you up and would just as soon have you shot—because your personality counts and you cannot deny that you are a dangerous man. What makes you dangerous is your unwarrantable belief that your desire may be realised. This is the only point of difference between us. I do not believe. And if I desire the very same things, no one cares. Consequently I am not likely to be locked up or shot. Therein is another difference —this time to your manifest advantage.

"There is a—let us say—a machine. It evolved itself (I am severely scientific), out of a chaos of scrap iron and behold!—it knits. I am horrified at the horrible work and stand appalled. I feel it ought to embroider —but it goes on knitting. You come along and say: 'This is all right; it's only a question of the right kind of oil. Let us use this—for instance—celestial oil and the machine shall embroider a most beautiful design in purple and gold.' Will it? Alas; no. You cannot by any special lubrication make embroidery with a knitting machine. And the most withering thought is that the infamous thing has made itself; made itself without thought, without conscience, without foresight, without eyes, without heart. It is a tragic accident—and it has happened. You can't interfere with it. The last drop of bitterness is in the suspicion that you can't even smash it. In virtue of that truth one and immortal which works in the force that made it spring into existence it is what it is—and it is indestructible!

"It knits us in and it knits us out. It has knitted time and space, pain, death, corruption, despair and all the illusions—and nothing matters. I'll admit however that to look at the remorseless process is sometimes amusing. . . ."

After their first meeting in London (1897), Don Roberto and Conrad became great friends. Undoubtedly, the credit of having "discovered" Conrad goes to the late Mr. Edward Garnett who died some ten days before I sat down to write this chapter. Whenever we met to have lunch together in a little Russian restaurant in South Kensington, Garnett spoke about Conrad, Hudson and Cunninghame Graham. A few days before his sudden and unexpected death, Garnett visited me in my little London flat, where we sat until late at night discussing his old friends. He told me about Conrad's early struggles as an author, and when I informed him that, unknown to anyone else, Don Roberto had assisted him through those trying days, Garnett answered that he had always suspected it.

In 1898, Conrad wrote to Don Roberto:

". . . I am making desperate efforts to write something. Why the devil did I ever begin? Qué tonteria!* I am writing *coglioneria* while I don't know how the *Teufel* I am going to live next month. . . ."

Finally Conrad decided to go back to sea. Don Roberto was in Scotland when his friend wrote from London:

". . . I saw heaps of shipowners. The fact is from novel writing to skippering *il y a trop de tirage*. This confounded literature has ruined me entirely. There is a time in the affairs of men when the tide of folly taken at the flood sweeps them to destruction. *La mer monte, cher ami; la mer monte* and the phenomenon is not worth a thought."

* What stupidity. Spanish.

Shortly after Conrad had written this, he asked Don Roberto to give him introductions to owners of shipping lines. In due time these arrived, but, unknown to Conrad, his friend had also written to the men for whom the introductions were, on no account to give Conrad a ship, for good reasons we shall see presently.

After his interview with a director of a shipping line, Conrad wrote (1898):

". . . I've seen Sir Francis Evans this morning. He was full of business with twenty people, but he received me at once and was kindness itself. The upshot of it is this: It is of course impossible to place me in the Union Line—I said I did not even dream of such a thing, but explained that I thought he might have some tramp or good collier. The Company he said owns no tramps or colliers, but he might hear of something of the kind and in such a case would let me know. He has my card but my address is not on it. Perhaps you would drop him a line *pour l'entretenir dans la bonne voie* and mention where I live. He said he would be 'extremely pleased to do anything for a friend of Mr. Cunninghame Graham.' Thereupon I salaamed myself out, and another man rushed in.

"Something may come of it. In any case many thanks. Since you have begun that trouble yourself I feel no compunction in asking you to keep it up when an opportunity offers. Now some shadow of possibility to go to sea has been presented to me I am almost frantic with the longing to get away. . . ."

Don Roberto was beginning to fear that Conrad might find a job, so he asked him to go and stay with him in Scotland, where, after a good rest, he would introduce him to shipowners on the Clyde.

Although Conrad answered as follows, he accepted the invitation, and, accordingly, travelled North.

"... Do you think the shipowners of 'Glesga' are gone mad. They will never give a ship to a 'chiel' that can write prose—or who is even suspected of such criminal practices. ... *Quelle bête de vie! Nom de nom, quelle bête de vie!* Sometimes I lose all sense of reality in a kind of nightmare effect produced by existence. Then I try to think of you—to wake myself. And it does wake me. I don't know how you feel about yourself, but to me you appear extremely real—even when I perceive you enveloped in the cloud of your irremendable illusions. I had better close before I say something that would end in bloodshed. ...."

Whilst Conrad travelled towards Scotland, his host-to-be called at different shipping offices where he told his friends, the directors, that he would soon introduce a certain Polish sea-captain to them, and he asked them on no account to give him employment, for, should they do so, he assured them that a great writer would be lost to the world.

The result was that when Conrad arrived, and was duly introduced, he was told the same thing in every shipping office: that, for the time being, there was no vacancy, that they were sorry, but that they would make a note of his name, etc., etc.

After a short stay in Scotland, Conrad returned towards the South, a much happier man, for although he had given up all hope of finding a ship, he knew that he had a real friend.

Shortly after, when Don Roberto's book *Mogreb-El-Acksa* came out, Conrad wrote to him:

"... The book is Art. Art without a trace of Art's theories in its incomparably effective execution. It isn't anybody's art—it is Cunninghame Graham's art. The

331

individuality of the work impresses itself on the reader, from the first. Then come other things, skill, pathos, humour, wit, indignation. Above all a continuous feeling of delight. . . . You haven't been careful in correcting your proofs. Are you too grand seigneur for that infect labour? Surely I, twenty others, would be only too proud to do it for you. . . ."

In two other letters, written at about the same time, Conrad said:

". . . You are the perfection of scorn—not vulgar scorn, mind, not scorn that would fit any utterance. No! Scorn that is clear in thought and lurks in the phrase. The philosophy of unutterable scorn."

"You with your ideals of sincerity, courage and truth are strangely out of place in this epoch of material pre-occupation. What does it bring? What's the profit? What do we get by it? Those questions are the root of every moral, intellectual or political movement. Into the noblest cause men manage to put something of their baseness; and sometimes when I think of you here, quietly, you seem to me tragic with your courage, with your beliefs and your hopes. . . ."

". . . What don't you know! From the outside of a sail to the inside of a prison!

"When I think of you I feel as tho' I had lived all my life in a dark hole without ever seeing or knowing anything. . . ."

". . . You have a fiendish gift of showing the futility —the ghastly, jocular futility of life. *Et c'est finement vu et c'est exprimé avec finesse—presque à mots couverts, avec de l'esprit dans chaque phrase.*"

When Don Roberto returned to England after his captivity in Morocco, Hudson sent him a letter saying:

". . . To my sick soul your life seems almost too full, your activities too many and great, your range on this planet too wide. Only yesterday I was thinking about the trouble that had overtaken you among the Mountains of the Moon, or the Atlas Mountains, I forget which, when lo! your letter came to say that you were no further than Chester Square, S.W. If it is possible to get about the world at that rate of speed, why do men trouble about flying machines and balloons, unless they want to get to the North Pole?"

In 1899, after *Mogreb-El-Acksa* and Don Roberto's next book *Ipané* had appeared, Hudson wrote:

". . . I had a delightful two hours' talk with Lady Grey about everything (politics excepted), and she said a great deal about your *Mogreb-El-Acksa* and *Ipané*—she is an enthusiastic admirer of your work, and takes a peculiar malicious delight in the way you go for everybody and everything—especially 'sacred' things. I have a colder mind, and sometimes think that the you-be-downness comes out a little too much; but the book is one that one reads and does not forget. . . ."

Many years after the publication of *Mogreb-El-Acksa* and *Ipané*, when I was staying with my friend, Don Roberto, at his estate "Ardoch," on the River Clyde, I was leafing through some of the books in his library, when I saw George Bernard Shaw's *Three Plays for Puritans*. Opening it, I read an inscription which read: "To R. B. Cunninghame Graham. The only begetter of Captain Brassbound, from G. Bernard Shaw. Jan. 1901."

Let us see what G. B. Shaw says about Don Roberto and

333 Y

Mogreb-El-Acksa which gave him the inspiration for the play, *Captain Brassbound's Conversion*. He writes:

"Cunninghame Graham is the hero of his own book; but I have not made him the hero of my play, because so incredible a personage must have destroyed its likelihood—such as it is. There are moments when I do not myself believe in his existence. And yet he must be real; for I have seen him with these eyes; and I am one of the few living men who can decipher the curious alphabet in which he writes his private letters. The man is on public record too. The battle of Trafalgar Square, in which he personally and bodily assailed civilisation as represented by the concentrated military and constabulary forces of the capital of the world, can scarcely be forgotten by the more discreet spectators, of whom I was one.

"He is a fascinating mystery to a sedentary person like myself. The horse, a dangerous animal, whom, when I cannot avoid, I propitiate with apples and sugar, he bestrides and dominates fearlessly, yet with a true republican sense of rights of the four-legged fellow-creature whose martyrdom and man's shame therein he has told most powerfully in his *Calvary*, a tale with an edge that will cut the soft cruel heart and strike fire from the hard kind ones. He handles the other lethal weapons as familiarly as the pen; medieval sword and modern Mauser are to him as umbrellas and Kodaks are to me. . . .

"He is, I understand, a Spanish hidalgo, hence the superbity of his portrait by Lavery (Velázquez being no longer available). He is, I know, a Scotch laird. How he continues to be authentically the two things at the same time is no more intelligible to me than the fact

334

that everything that has ever happened to him seems to have happened in Paraguay or Texas instead of Spain or Scotland. He is, I regret to add, an impenitent and unashamed dandy; such boots, such a hat, would have dazzled D'Orsay himself. With that hat he once saluted me in Regent Street when I was walking with my mother. Her interest was instantly kindled, and the following conversation ensued: 'Who is that?' 'Cunninghame Graham.' 'Nonsense, Cunninghame Graham is one of your Socialists. That man is a gentleman.' This is the punishment of vanity, a fault I have myself always avoided, as I find conceit less troublesome and much less expensive.

"Later on somebody told him of Tarudant, a city in Morocco in which no Christian had ever set foot. Concluding that it must be an exceptionally desirable place to live in, he took ship and horse; changed the hat for a turban; and made straight for the sacred city, via Mogador. How he fared, and how he fell into the hands of the Caid of Kintafi, who rightly held that there was more danger to Islam in one Cunninghame Graham than in a thousand Christians may be learnt from his account of it in *Mogreb-El-Acksa*, without which *Captain Brassbound's Conversion* would never have been written. . . . I have been intelligent enough to steal its scenery, its surroundings, its atmosphere, its geography, its knowledge of the east, its fascinating Caids and Krooboys and Sheikhs and mud castles from an excellent book of philosophic travel and vivid adventure entitled *Mogreb-El-Acksa*. . . ."

Wilfrid Blunt, the poet at whose estate at Crabbett Park in Sussex, Don Roberto was a frequent guest, wrote about *Mogreb-El-Acksa:*

". . . Your book on Morocco has amused and interested

me more than anything of the kind I have read for a long day. I put it next to Doughty's as a true portrait of Arab ways, and far before anything that Burton did. . . . It is a book I shall read again. . . ."

Five years later, in 1904, after Don Roberto's *Hernando de Soto* had come out, Blunt made a statement which is particularly interesting because, unlike Conrad, he paid but few compliments. Added to a letter, in which, as usual, he violently attacked British Imperialism, he wrote:

". . . I follow your literary fortunes with the greatest interest, seeing in you the only competitor to beat Kipling on his own ground. . . ."

In matters concerning Spain, Martin Hume—among Englishmen—knew most about history, Fitzmaurice-Kelly about literature, but Don Roberto was the artist.

Shortly after the publication of *Niggers*, possibly the most indignant, satiric denunciation of English Imperialism that has ever been published, Martin Hume wrote to his friend, Don Roberto—who was the author of this ironic sketch—on the supremacy and rise of the Aryans:

"Devonshire Club,
"December 13th, 1898.
". . . You are incorrigible—After all your experience you still think that the 'Great British public' can understand a joke! or appreciate irony—Not a bit of it. I can assure you 99 out of every 100 who read the paper will take quite seriously every word you say about the need for shooting down 'niggers' etc., and will gravely tell each other that R.B.C.G., is a most blood-thirsty and merciless person—'Of course,' they will say, 'in the main he is right and these inferior races *must* give way to *our* more advanced civilisation, but still, you know,

336

he need not talk about shooting them down like that, as if he wished to do it for pleasure. When you write you forget the advice of the witty Frenchman who was talking ironically to other clever persons and saw a dullard approaching them. 'Hush, let us be serious,' he said, 'here comes a fool.' For your own sake try the stupid, pompous and conventional once in a way, in order that you may be better 'understanded of the people.' Only when you do it give me notice and I shall get out of the way. Personally I prefer a flickering arc-light to a steady 'dip,' but the Great British Public don't."

Edward Garnett said about this sketch that it "gives the keynote to its author's genius, outlook and attitude to his fellows," and "would confer immortality on him, with its fellow-sketch *Success* if he had written nothing more."

In answer to an article Frank Harris had published, Don Roberto—who always defended Spain against attacks made by certain writers—wrote to his friend:

". . . I have lived many years with Spaniards, and I do not think they are more cruel than other people. True, there is the national crime of the bull-fight . . . but what of pheasant-shooting, tame deer-hunting etc.? Did you ever see a big pheasant shoot, with everyone dabbed in blood, and three thousand birds shot? . . ."

After Hudson had dedicated his book *El Ombú* to Don Roberto:

". . . To R. B. Cunninghame Graham, *singularisimo escritor inglés* who has lived and knows (even to the marrow as they themselves say), the horsemen of the Pampas, and who alone of European writers has rendered something of the vanishing colour of that remote life," he sent his friend a letter, explaining why he had made use of the word *singularisimo*. Hudson wrote:

337

". . . Certainly you are unique among English writers and your *singularity* is most evident when you write of people of other races because of the union in you of two rare qualities—or the rare union of two qualities —intense individuality, and detachment, which enables you to identify yourself even with those who are most unlike us. . . ."

About *Hernando de Soto*, he said:

"You could not have presented Soto and his companions-in-arms in a better way, for you extenuate nothing of their acts and set nothing down in malice; and better still, you are able by means of your faculty of detachment of presenting that tremendous drama from the point of view of the actors in it, and the age they lived in. It was only fit that a man who has spent so many days on horseback on lonely plains and mountain passes should be the biographer of such a one as de Soto. . . ."

Conrad was even more enthusiastic when, after having sat up half the night, reading the book, he wrote to Don Roberto (1903):

". . . *Hernando de Soto* is most exquisitely excellent. Your very mark sends spirit upon a subject that only *you* can do justice to—with your wonderful English and your sympathetic insight into the souls of the Conquistadores. The glamour, the pathos and the romance of that time and of those men are only adequately, truthfully conveyed to us by your pen; the sadness, the glory and the romance of the endeavour together with the vanity of vanities of the monstrous achievement are reflected in your unique style as though you had been writing of men with whom you had slept by the camp fire after tethering your horses on the threshold of the unknown. You have an eye for buried jewels! Pizarro

338

going about mournfully with his hat pulled down on his ears after the death of Atahualpa is new to me. He is made unforgettable at last. *'C'est énorme d'humanité,'* as the great Flaubert would have yelled to the four winds of heaven. . . . It's the most amazingly natural thing I've ever read; it gives me a furious desire to learn Spanish and bury myself in the pages of the incomparable Garcilasso—if only to forget all about our modern Conquistadores."

Once, when sick, weary and tired, Hudson sent Don Roberto a note, in which he paid a great tribute to his literary talent. Hudson said:

". . . Your writing is more refreshing and stimulating to my soul than that of any other living author."

At about this time Don Roberto wrote an article entitled: *La Vieja de Bolívar* for a Spanish magazine. About this article Hudson said:

". . . It is a new experience to read you in Spanish, and tho' you can't hit as hard in that softer tongue as in English (nobody could), you are as vivid, picturesque and racy as ever. . . ."

Although some of the critics fully appreciated Don Roberto's writings, the public remained indifferent to them, and the sales of the books were very small.

Shortly before *Hernando de Soto* was published, his affairs in Scotland reached a climax. Unable to pay off the heavy debts his father had left, Finlaystone had to be sold, and finally the inevitable happened; Gartmore, also, had to go. So great was Don Roberto's grief that when the old family property was put under the auctioneer's hammer, he stood and wept in public. After the sale came sad and busy days, taking down pictures from the walls, packing, and dismissing old servants who were more like friends. The furniture, books and even the beds had gone, and in their stead mattresses were put on the floor in the drawing-room. Finally the sad hour arrived when Gabrielle and her husband had to leave their beloved house which had been built by his ancestors.

CHAPTER XVI

GOSSIPERS, in drawing-rooms and clubs, always taking a half-sympathetic, half-malicious delight in other people's misfortunes, were wagging their tongues. "Graham is broke," "Graham is finished," and "Poor Graham will never be heard of again now," they whispered until the rumours were accepted as facts.

Only a few of Don Roberto's intimate friends knew that, after having paid off every penny of the old family debt, a considerable sum of money was over, and that, in addition to this, he was yet the owner of the valuable "Ardoch" estate in Dumbartonshire, on the River Clyde.

Having moved his books, beautiful furniture, pictures and many sentimental treasures into "Ardoch House," he and his wife, together with two or three old servants, made their new home there.

"Ardoch" comprises a neat house, built after the West Indian style of architecture, a well-tended garden with lawns, flowers and stately trees, as well as an old coach-house, a great deal of land, and several farms which are run by tenants. The garden, being surrounded by a high, moss-covered stone-wall, the place was an ideal refuge for Don Roberto and his wife, who immediately set about arranging the house to her liking, and planting many plants and ornamental shrubs. Among her hobbies was botany, and at one time she made a study of Scottish mosses, a complete collection of which she presented to the Stirling Museum.

One day, shortly after the sale of Gartmore, Don Roberto was in Glasgow where he had to transact some business. When his lawyer told him about the rumours which circulated about his supposed poverty, Don Roberto smiled and said: "Let people believe it; it gives them such pleasure."

After the sale of Gartmore—as we have already seen—his *Hernando de Soto* was published in 1903. During the years 1905 and 1906 he spent a great deal of his time in London, Spain and Tangier. Morocco had become his favourite place of retreat, for the raw English winters had never been to his liking since he had spent so much time in warmer climes.

Gabrielle's health had gradually become worse, but in spite of her frailty she was always active. During the summer of 1906, she studied history in Spain, from where she intended to return to Scotland, early in September. On her way back, on reaching the little village of Hendaye in the South of France, she was suddenly taken ill. When Don Roberto— who was in Scotland at the time—received a telegram, he immediately hurried to her bed-side which he never left until, after having lingered for a few days, his wife died peacefully, on the 8th of September, 1906. (Gabrielle was forty-five years of age when she died, and had been married for twenty-eight years.)

Taking the body with him, Don Roberto returned to Scotland where, according to Gabrielle's wish, she was to be buried in the ruined Augustinian Priory on the Island of Inchmahone, on the Lake of Menteith.

Throughout the night before the funeral was to take place, Don Roberto, assisted by an old tenant, dug the grave, a task he would let no one else perform. With only a lantern to give a flickering light, the two men worked almost ceaselessly, despite a wild wind and squalls of cold rain and sleet,

342

ARDOCH

THE WINDOW OF THE STUDY

they completed their work by lining the grave with heather.

The funeral was like a scene out of a Sir Walter Scott novel. When the coffin, borne by old servants and tenants from Gartmore, arrived on the shores of the lake, the sun was just visible through gaps in the dark, overhanging clouds, and the island, with its tall, stately trees, was barely visible through a curtain of mist. When the coffin had been placed on a strange dark-coloured boat with a high prow and stern, the few mourners (among whom were Don Roberto's brother, Charles, and Mansel, his old companion of many adventures in South America), took their seats, whereupon the strange craft slowly headed for the island. From the shore, only Don Roberto was visible now, crouching at the high stern, his long hair fluttering as he steered the boat, out of the sides of which protruded oars which moved slowly and rhythmically, bringing to mind tales of old Viking chiefs.

Suddenly the sky darkened, and a cold wild wind lashed the waters, and when the mourners entered the ruins of the priory, an icy shower made them shiver.

After a short funeral service which was read, for the most part, from the English Service Book, by the Rev. Malcolm McLean of the Free Church of Gartmore, the coffin was lowered into the grave, and in accordance with one of the last wishes expressed by Gabrielle, bunches of purple heather from Gartmore and white flowers were dropped on the lid of the coffin.

When the mourners had departed for the mainland, Don Roberto and his tenant—who had assisted him throughout the night,—stayed behind to fill in the grave over which, later, a single flat stone was laid. Into the wall of the ruined Priory was placed a bronze plaque, bearing the following inscription:

"IN MEMORY OF GABRIELA CUNNINGHAME
GRAHAM OF GARTMORE
DIED AT HENDAYE, FRANCE
8, SEPTEMBER. A.D. 1906. AGED 45
LOS MUERTOS ABREN LOS OJOS A LOS QUE VIVEN."*

After his wife's death, Don Roberto spent a great deal of his time with his mother in London where he leased a small house, No. 79A, Elizabeth Street, from where, looking out of his study window, he could see his mother's house in Chester Square. Childless and lonely, he sought solace with her and friends of whom he had many.

When the year drew to a close, his friend, Conrad, wrote to him:

". . . We have been thinking much of you this year end. It is sad to think of your feeling your loneliness at this season—though you certainly are a man round whom many affections must be centred, many admirations and even some enmities. To you life must keep its value to the last, and the words you have written the perfect expression of your rare personality shall be read in the far future with the disinterested admiration they deserve. Your magnanimous indignations will be perceived as having made their mark on their time. Words worthy of you, uncompromising and sincere shall be your descendants and the servants of your memory, more faithful than any child could be—for alas our children are but men like ourselves with short memories and but an imperfect fidelity."

That Gabrielle shared certain views with her husband may be seen from the following passage which she wrote:

* The dead open the eyes of those who live.

". . . It is not that men have grown better, that our humanity has grown wider—*one has only to survey our whole commercial system of the sweaters and sweated to give such a quibble a startling denial*—it is rather because men are no longer capable of the same depth of conviction, the same passionate energy of belief—nay, a century so emasculated as ours is scarcely capable of conceiving it —that scenes like this, not for faith but for greed, not to save our souls and those of others, but our purses at the expense of the general happiness of humanity, do not take place to-day."

In addition to her monumental and scholarly work *Santa Teresa* (mentioned in a previous chapter), she wrote in conjunction with Don Roberto, *The Christ of Toro*, a book of short stories and sketches.

Six years before her untimely death she wrote a play, *Don Juan's Last Wager*, adapted from the Spanish of José Zorilla. Sir Martin Harvey, who produced it, also took the leading part, but after a short and unsuccessful run at the Prince of Wales's Theatre in London (February 1900), the play was taken off.

In 1905, Gabrielle wrote an adaptation of *The Dark Night of the Soul*, by Father San Juan de la Cruz. In the prologue she enunciated a new theory of mystic philosophy.

Though a mystic, and by baptism a Roman Catholic, she felt unattached towards any particular Church or religious creed. Like most people who live within themselves, she was of a retiring nature.

After her death, Don Roberto published, privately, a book of her poems, *Rhymes of a World Unknown*.

Hudson, who was presented with a copy, wrote about it:

". . . These poems make me regret that she [Gabrielle], did not cultivate her genius for poetry more. A poem like 'The Legacy'—if she had done nothing else—was something to leave. It gives me that feeling one experiences on coming upon something peculiarly sterling in literature that I should have been the poorer without it, and I take that as the best test of genuine and good poetry."

THE LEGACY.

What shall I leave behind me, what?
Great fame, honour untarnished, brave renown?
No! yet these, too, lay in the lap of Time,
But Chance or Fate required them not!

Whene'r it be I lay me down
I would that some faint note of mine
May echo in another's heart and fill it with its chime.

Some note that shows I lived as well as he,
That noontide flush was sweet to me,
The swelling bosoms of the clouds at eve,
The blush of rose, the fine young grass,
The little birds' faint melody
When winter dies away to spring.

Some note to show I loved and suffered too like him,
Loved in much pain—sought God through sorrow dim,
But bright before me ever saw
The Glory of his Tainment trail o'er the darkened floor.

So shall I leave my legacy to men—
One feeble note—one only—then
Shall I die content;
And when the veil of Life is Rent,
Then shall the Darkness here turn to Light.

In the forty-seven poems Gabrielle wrote, Mr. Edward Garnett saw "a wildness, a fineness of consuming feeling" which, as he wrote: "has haunted his memory."

For the little book, printed only for a small circle of friends, Don Roberto wrote a preface in which he says: ". . . She wrote so little in verse that the metre perhaps weighed a little on her pen; but left her spirit singularly free. . . ."

One year after Gabrielle's death, her colossal work, *Santa Teresa** was republished (it had first appeared in 1894). In his preface to the second edition, Don Roberto wrote:

". . . Thirteen years ago . . . and now, sitting alone to write, with the mild thaw wind after a long frost, singing among the naked trees, just as if someone had hung an Æolian harp among the branches, but yet more sadly, for the Æolian harp I hear is in the mind, my point of view about the book is still the same as it was yesterday; for thirteen years is yesterday, though it seems a century, at least, in looking backwards; that is to say, when you look backwards without faith. . . .

"On her account the writer of the book spent all the summers of six years, wandering about the sweet thyme-scented wastes of Spain, sleeping in rough *posadas* [inns], rising at daybreak and jogging on a mule through the hot sun, to find in upland world-forgotten villages a trace of the saint's footsteps, and happy, after a long day's ride, if she came on a house where once the saint had slept. Not so her faithful servant Peregrina, a tall Galician, looking exactly like a Scotchwoman, who with the fervent faith through which a grain of scepticism ran, as often is the case with Spaniards of the lower class, at times addressed the saint in terms half of devotion and half of objurgation, promising candles for her shrine in difficulties, and telling her, the danger past, in good set terms,

* *Santa Teresa, Her Life and Times,* was later translated into Spanish.

347

of all that she had undergone on her behalf. In her devotion to the foundress and to the writer of such idiomatic
prose and strangely haunting little verses, with their
jingling quaint refrain, the author learned to read the
crabbed old court hands, of which the kind known as
la mano procesal seems a mere wavering line, whilst others
still preserve a look of Arabic.

"And as she wandered through the pine woods of
Castile, emerging now and then upon some rocky knoll
from which the hills of Piedrahita, faintly streaked with
snow, were seen far off. Landmarks on the Teresian wild
hill track, which leads from Avila, by Macotera and
Mancera de Abajo, till it emerges on the banks of the
green Tormes, close to Alba, no doubt that hunger, heat
and cold were forgotten, and she felt animated by the
thought that the saint's covered cart had jolted on the
self-same stones, three hundred years ago.

"Possibly other 'Lives' of the Castilian saint may show
more faith; but none can show more love; and love, I
take it at the day when each receives his due reward,
will outworth faith a hundredfold, in the same way that
humour outweighs wit.

"No dry recital of mere facts culled from dead books,
which in the greater part have never been alive; no
rhapsodies of mysticism can produce this kind of Life,
for no one, except perhaps some half-illuminated Spanish
friar, has ever girded up his loins to follow after the great
saint of Avila through Spain. . . . Thus, sadly, for where
the heart is, there also lives the speech, I now recommend
the book to all Teresians, knowing that it was written in
sincerity, and with a love so great toward the woman
and the saint, that it tinged all the life of her who wrote
it, up to her dying day. . . ."

Peregrina, the faithful Galician servant, returned to Spain

shortly after her mistress's death, and for many years after, until she died, Don Roberto, who gave her an allowance, kept in touch with her.

Although fifty-four years of age now, he was still as youthful and vigorous as he had been at the age of thirty, and life had yet many adventures in store for him.

His favourite Argentine horse, "Pampa," was stabled near his new London home, and as Hyde Park is close by, Don Roberto was to be seen riding in Rotten Row every day, his knightly figure overshadowing all the other riders and amblers.

During his early morning rides he held many interesting conversations with friends who wandered to the Park to have a talk with him. In those days, in order to converse quietly, he used to dismount on meeting a friend, and whilst he led "Pampa" by the bridle, slowly walked along, talking with the person by his side.

When Oscar Wilde was in sore trouble and most of his friends ignored him, he stopped Don Roberto who happened to be out riding early one morning. Wilde had been sitting alone on a bench near Rotten Row, and when he rose and the rider recognised him, he brought his horse to a standstill, and leapt off to grasp Wilde's hand.

"What am I to do?" Wilde asked after having explained his serious troubles to his sympathetic friend who had listened patiently to the tale of woe. For once Don Roberto's Spanish mannerisms led him to make a *gaffe* which he regretted to his dying day, for on several occasions he told me how, without realising it, he raised an arm, and pointing to his temple with the first finger, made a noise similising a revolver shot, by flicking the middle-finger over the thumb. Before Don Roberto was aware of what he had done, Wilde, sobbing like a child, said: "I know it's the only way out, but I haven't the courage."

What happened to Oscar Wilde after the trial is so well

known that there is no need for me to give details, but what Don Roberto wrote in a letter is interesting. He says:

". . . The judge was indeed both cowardly and cruel on the occasion of poor Oscar. Cowardly because he insisted to save himself, and cruel because he was a Bourgeois. Oscar does not seem to have shown much pluck, poor creature. But then one never expected he would. Jabez Balfour will come off with flying colours. What I want to know is if Oscar is so great a criminal, why are not the people prosecuted whose names the judges know, as they were *written* to them?"*

Hudson who, in a letter to Don Roberto wrote: "Better, I say, to live as I do, on rather less than £100 a year and be free—yes, free even of life's 'pleasures'," often strolled to the Park to see his friend riding.

A few extracts from letters written by Hudson show how he suffered, physically and mentally, and how he appreciated Don Roberto's friendship.

In different letters he writes:

". . . Indigestion, gastric troubles, rheumatism, liver and bladder troubles are my curse, and I feel inclined to give up eating altogether and die of starvation which can't be such a bad death . . . palpitations, dizziness, nervelessness and general imbecility make my life a perfect burden while it lasts . . . to me nothing is left but memories. . . . But I am a careless person and must remember that if others thought as I do, our order would be quickly reduced to chaos . . . your image, as I saw you when Pampa acted very proudly, and seemed 'proud of his pride,' tossing his mane and pawing the earth, is still vivid in my mind. . . . Fog and cloud and thick darkness over us to-day in this loathsome district, to

* Don Roberto once wrote: "If punishment does not wipe out the offence, those who punish cannot be judges, but mere torturers."

remind one of the end of this planet, the day of doom
described by the old prophets and sung by many bards
in noble numbers. Even a modern of the moderns sings
of it—

> For there shall come a mightier blast,
> And there shall be a darker day,
> And the stars from heaven downcast
> Like red leaves to be swept away—
>
> > Kyrie Eleison!
> > Christi Eleison!

"But we don't concern ourselves now about this future
event; like those busy people before the Flood we are
occupied with our own little affairs. And the result of
it all will be that when we make our cry:—'Good Lord
deliver us!' the thunder will peal back: 'Too late!' Think
of these things, oh, C.G."

Early one morning, when Don Roberto was riding in the
Park, Hudson—who felt ill and depressed at the time—came
up to speak to him. "Oh, Pampa!" Hudson exclaimed as
he patted the horse, and then he put his arms round his
neck and wept.

Wilfrid Scawen Blunt once wrote to Don Roberto:

". . . We have so many points in common, of character
and experience that it is a special satisfaction to me to
find you appreciate my way of expressing myself. In
former days, thirty and more years ago, I was much in
Spain and Spanish America and talked Spanish fluently
(I have now forgotten it), and adored all Spanish things.
Even now my sympathies have been with Spain in the
late war, in spite of the Cuban and Philippine rebellions.
It is disgusting to me to see the Anglo-Saxon race,
especially its Transatlantic variety, spreading over the

world as it does, carrying with it its Pharisaism, its Victorian architecture and its P. and O. cookery, to the destruction of more interesting races. . . ."

Blunt,* who was the champion of Eastern things, began to feel too old for active work, and so, in 1908, he wrote to Don Roberto:

". . . I wish you would take up my work in Egypt for me, as I am really past my day of being of any use there. You have done so much in the past in other directions that I think nobody could do the Egyptian and Indian propaganda better. . . ."

Having no desire to meddle with politics, Don Roberto refused to do as his friend asked him.

Blunt was twelve years older than Don Roberto. Of aristocratic lineage, having fought in the Peninsular War, wounded at Corunna, later for twelve years in the Diplomatic Service, having crossed the pampas and being a keen explorer and traveller, as well as a remarkable linguist, he had a great deal in common with Don Roberto.

Both had served a term in prison, Blunt's offence having given of too keen and active a support to the Irish Home Rule question.

Like Don Roberto, he suffered disillusionment which he clearly expressed when, in 1886, he wrote: "I look at the cause of human dealing with weaker nationalities as a lost cause in the world." Referring to the Irish Home Rule question, he wrote:

". . . Property blinds all eyes, and it is easier for a camel to pass through the eye of a needle than for an Irish landlord to enter into the kingdom of Home Rule."

---

* Blunt saved the best blood of the Arab horse. He never attempted to live long among the Bedouin. His wife, Lady Anne Isabella Noel, the only daughter of the Earl of Lovelace, and granddaughter of Lord Byron, was known among the Bedouin as "Our Beloved Lady of the Horses."

When Blunt retired to his estates, Don Roberto frequently visited him, and in later years introduced to him his friend Colonel Lawrence ("Lawrence of Arabia").

Once, when reproached for lack of patriotism, Blunt wrote:

> ". . . In answer to this I can only say that I belong to a generation of Englishmen holding an idea of Patriotism entirely different from that now accepted, and one I think saner. According to the teachings of my youth the patriotic idea was essentially connected with the land of one's birth, the passion of courage which prompted Thermopylæ and Bannockburn and the 1,001 battles where men have stood up in defence of their homes against invading strangers; also with that other moral courage which strengthened a man to oppose in speech the folly of his fellow-men whom he saw doing dishonour to that land. It had nothing whatever to do with the modern idea, now prevalent among Englishmen, of solidarity with the enterprises, often criminal, of the cosmopolitan finance of London and Liverpool and Manchester, which has usurped control over our lives and honour in its dealings with our national affairs abroad, which controls our Press, manipulates our Parliaments and uses our ancient and honourable English name for its base un-English purpose. There is no lack in patriotism in refusing to bow to this new leadership in evil, or in denouncing its ungodly doings."

Don Roberto—who was a greater patriot than any of the speechifying and flag-waving politicians and sheep-like citizens who strain their vocal chords singing "Rule Britannia" shared Blunt's idea of true patriotism, and therefore kept up his friendship until, in 1922, Blunt died and was buried, wrapped in an Arabian shawl, as was fitting for one who had waged a long fight for the Arabian cause. After Don Roberto had seen his friend laid away in the Sussex soil he had always loved, he wrote a tribute to him in which he said:

". . . Withal, as Easterns say, a great protector of the poor; not over-much concerned about their rights, but sympathising heartily with their wrongs and with their poverty. Amongst the mass of mediocrities that constitute, and will for ever constitute mankind, unless there is a new creation conceived upon a different plan, he moved among his fellow-men, somewhat aloof and unapproachable, lashing their base ambitions with a steel whip, and yet with many a foible of his own, for without weaknesses no man can be strong.

"Born out of his generation, as are the most of men who achieve anything but mere material success, he yet was a true Englishman, a very Englishman of the Elizabethan breed, with something in him of the Renaissance in his love of sport and culture, a combination rare to-day, for now the sportsman is so often nothing but a sportsman, the man of culture nothing but a prig. . . .

"He was a voice of a Cassandra prophesying in the wilderness, in the days when he warned England that Egypt would be free, that Ireland would become a nation, and that our Indian Empire was seething with revolt."

That Don Roberto was a full-blooded patriot he proved a few years later when the Great War broke out, for although he was sixty-two years of age at the time, he more than did his "bit" as we shall see in the next chapter.

During the three years following his wife's death he did little writing, but, instead, passed a great deal of his time in London with his mother, and, during the winter months, visited Spain and Morocco where he had many friends. Although he was strongly opposed to bull-fighting, he was on friendly terms with several famous *matadores* whom he always visited when he was in Spain.

In 1909 appeared his next book *Faith*, containing short stories and sketches.

His favourite horse, "Pampa," which he had ridden for nearly twenty-five years, since he rescued him out of the traces of a tram-car in Glasgow, was getting old, and so, reluctantly, he put him on a farm at Weybridge, near London, where he had everything a horse could wish for: a shed with a manger filled with hay, a field through which runs a stream, and the company of two or three other old horses Don Roberto had bought when they were about to be exported abroad, to be worked to death or slaughtered.

As it happened, a consignment of Argentine horses had arrived in London, and so Don Roberto immediately acquired a new mustang, for, without one, he would have been like a seasoned skipper without a ship.

Hearing about "Pampa's" retirement, Hudson immediately wrote to his friend:

". . . I felt grief and pleasure at the same time about Pampa. Grieved that his days of active life with you on his back are ended, and glad that you have been able to find him such a haven of rest. The fact that he is an Argentine horse made me think much of him, and I thought still more because he is a *Picaso** with a flowing tail and mane, and actually reminded me of the fiery animal I bought from an old gaucho when I was a boy —the horse I loved so much and describe in the chapter 'Horse and Man' in the *Naturalist in La Plata*. . . . I'm doing little now—perhaps, like Pampa, I've done with

* *Picaso* is a gaucho name for a horse with certain white markings on the face.

activities. . . . I'm glad you've got another Argentine horse, and hope to see you in the Park one day. . . ."

Although "Pampa" was still very fit, his end came suddenly. Due to a kick from another horse, an abscess formed on one of his knees, and despite the efforts of veterinary surgeons he finally had to be put down. He had lived thirty-one years.

Don Roberto told me that he felt the loss of the animal so much that for several days he was almost demented. In 1930, when he wrote his book, *The Horses of the Conquest*, he dedicated it as follows:

"To Pampa.
"My black Argentine—whom I rode for
twenty years without a fall.
May the earth lie on him, as lightly as he once
trod upon its face.
Vale . . . or until so long."

On the 13th of October, 1909, Francisco Ferrer, the Spanish educationist, was the victim of a judicial murder. Throughout the civilised world meetings of protest were held, and in London such a meeting was hastily called for by Don Roberto, H. M. Hyndman, the Rev. Mr. John Clifford and a number of others.

Among Don Roberto's numerous friends in London, was a Spanish gentleman who also happens to be a friend of mine, and who told me the story I am about to relate.

This Spaniard—who is well known in musical and social circles—has lived in London for many years, but, in spite of his long residence in England, he has remained Spanish to the core, and although his knowledge of the English language and literature is profound, he has never lost his strong Spanish accent. Interested, chiefly, in music and art, he is as quiet and peaceful a man as can be found anywhere.

Shortly before the meeting was due to begin, Don Roberto

hired a cab and asked the "cabbie" to drive him, as fast as possible, to the house where his Spanish friend lived. Just as the puffing and panting old nag came to a standstill in front of the house, Don Roberto's friend came out of the front door, dressed in a frock-coat, top hat and spats, and in his button-hole he wore a white carnation. Before he had time to explain that he was about to go to a wedding, he was bundled into the cab and driven to a large hall where an enormous crowd was assembled. All his protests, entreaties and supplications to let him go were in vain, and whilst he was still wondering if this was a dream, he found himself being pushed on to a platform where, after several orators had finished their speeches, Don Roberto introduced him to the audience. (Previously, in his address, Don Roberto, in referring to Ferrer, had uttered the magnificent scorn: "a dead lion is worth a thousand living dogs.")

After an agonising silence, the Spanish gentleman plucked up courage and told his sympathetic listeners that liberty and freedom were one and the same thing, that tyranny and oppression were hateful to free and intelligent men, etc., and after a few similar statements he wound up his speech by apologising for his shortcomings as an orator, and added that what he lacked in oratorical ability he hoped was fully counter-balanced by the sincerity with which he had spoken.

Having bowed and otherwise communicated his thanks to the crowd, he turned to leave, only to find that the hall was so packed with people that it was quite impossible for him to get out without doing serious damage to his precious clothes. Realising that he had missed the wedding, he waited until the meeting was over, whereupon, having thanked Don Roberto for the treat, the newly initiated public speaker returned home.

As chance would have it, this adventure was to have an amusing sequel. A few days later he was overjoyed on receiving an invitation to dine with an old friend of his, a high Spanish official who had unexpectedly arrived in London.

Whilst wining and dining to their heart's content, my friend asked his host what had brought him to London. Leaning forward and speaking in a whisper, the visitor confided that he had been sent to England in order to investigate, in collaboration with the British authorities, the activities and movements of certain dangerous Spanish anarchists who were known to be in London.

On hearing this, my friend expressed great surprise, for although he had lived in the English metropolis for a number of years, he had never heard even the faintest rumour about countrymen of his who were suspected of being anarchists; in fact, he bluntly stated that he refused to believe it. In order to convince him, his host then produced a list of names which he handed to the unbelieving Thomas. Imagine his surprise and consternation when, upon looking at the document, the first name he saw written on it, heading the list, was his own.

With visions of dungeons, handcuffs and chains whirling before his eyes, the unhappy victim of Don Roberto's practical joke felt almost sick, and he quickly handed back the document to its owner who, with typical Spanish thoroughness, carefully folded it up and replaced it in the breast-pocket of his coat, where, supposedly, it remained unread, for my Spanish friend was never molested.

In 1912, whilst Don Roberto was in Rome, a publisher sent him one of Masefield's poems to review. In answer to this request, the publisher received the following reply:

"Hotel Beau-Site,
"Rome.
"February 19-1912.

"DEAR MR. HARRISON,

"I have had a look at Masefield's poem again, and whilst admiring it very much, I am afraid it is quite out of my way to review it.

"You see, 'au fond' I am not a man of letters, and only have a mild connection with literature, so to speak, by the grace of God.

"I think it wants a regular literary man to do the poem justice. Moreover, I do not like the idea of anything that might look like a puff . . . not that Masefield wants a puff; but it might have that appearance.

"Should anyone attack him, I shall be glad to 'break a steel pen' in his defence. . . ."

CHAPTER XVII

THE GREAT WAR—DON ROBERTO BECOMES A COLONEL—
ACTIVITIES IN SOUTH AMERICA AND VARIOUS LETTERS—A
BOLTING HORSE BRINGS ABOUT A NEW FRIENDSHIP—COLOMBIA
—A LETTER TO THEODORE ROOSEVELT—NEARLY SHIPWRECKED
IN THE CARIBBEAN SEA—HUDSON, CONRAD AND DON ROBERTO'S
MOTHER DIE—A JOURNEY THROUGH THE PLAINS OF VENEZUELA

BETWEEN the years 1910 and 1914, Don Roberto wrote
four books, *Hope, Charity, A Hatchment* and *Scottish
Stories*. On the eve of the Great War, on Sunday,
August 2nd, 1914, he spoke at a mass peace demonstration
held in Trafalgar Square, his favourite old battle-ground.
George Lansbury, Keir Hardie and H. M. Hyndman were
the chairmen at this meeting during which Don Roberto
made a fiery speech. Instead of denouncing war, as everybody
expected he would, he said that England, the mother of
freedom and the home of liberty, must throw her weight in
the crisis into the scale of humanity.

The fourth of August came, followed by the invasion of
Belgium and the small British army's memorable retreat
from Mons. The situation of the allied armies was perilous
in the extreme, and in order to continue the fight which had
really only started when the armies dug themselves in, Lord
Kitchener sent out an urgent call for volunteers. One of the
first to stride into a certain recruiting office in London was
Don Roberto, who had come to offer his services as a private
in the Rough Rider Corps. The interview with the officials
was short, for when he informed them that he was sixty-two
years of age, he was curtly told that he was too old. When,

furious and indignant, Don Roberto had given vent to his
feelings, and had told the officials what he thought of them,
he left them staring at one another, and before they recovered,
he was in a taxi, and on his way to the War Office where he
had a number of friends. The outcome of his interview with
them was that he was put in charge of a section of the
Remount, with headquarters at the War Office.

On one occasion, as he was interviewing many people, a
large, truculent-looking fellow refused to wait his turn, and as
he pushed his way through the queue he raised his voice and
cursed volubly. "You'll have to wait your turn," Don Roberto
told him, "whether you like it or not; and you must wait
quietly, or you'll be put out." The truculent one surveyed
the speaker and demanded threateningly: "Oh yes? And
who'll put me out?" "I will," was the quick reply, and before
the astonished fellow realised what was happening, Don
Roberto seized him by the neck and ran him down the steps.

Horses were urgently needed, and therefore Don Roberto
was appointed president of a commission that was to travel
to South America to purchase as many suitable animals as
possible. Although he had been given the rank of colonel,
he refused to wear a uniform, much to the annoyance of some
old "fossils" in the War Office where, before sailing, he had a
great deal of work to do. In later years, whenever he
described his impressions of the War Office during those
hectic days, he said he could still smell a heavy odour of
cheap scents and face-powder, and that he could see and hear
baskets of tea-cups and saucers being dragged along the
corridors.

Towards the end of November 1914, accompanied by a
number of army officers (chiefly retired colonels), he sailed
back to the lands where he had spent his early manhood.

One or two members of the party thought this was a grand
outing, and enjoyed themselves accordingly, but when they

landed, and, instead of working, still continued to make merry, they soon found out that Don Roberto could be a strict disciplinarian, for he sent one or two home on the first convenient ship.

Already on arriving in Montevideo he must have guessed that all would not be smooth sailing, for in a letter he wrote:

"(Montevideo, Dec. 16th, 1914.)

". . . Things will not be easy here, especially as the War Office has loaded me up with a lot of men, excellent in their way, but bound to red tape and tradition."

As we have seen in the opening chapters, Buenos Aires had no port in the early 'seventies when Don Roberto landed there for the first time, and the city with its low-roofed houses, reminded the traveller of Spain.

Let us see what his impressions were when, after an absence of forty years, he returned. Upon arrival he wrote to his mother:

". . . How Buenos Aires has changed! It is a marvel—Paris with a fine climate. Motors, well-dressed women, restaurants and parks and gardens such as you can see *nowhere* else. It is the cleanest town in the world and beautiful in its own style. I was not prepared for anything like Taste, which is not what it might be; but it will come. In the parks and squares there are groups of statuary by Quiroz, Ballin and Rodin, and the wish of everyone is to beautify the place. At present intellectual life is rather starved, for all the best brains have gone into business, but not a business such as we know or as the Yanks conceive of. It reminds one after Medici . . . of course inartistic Medici . . . but still people who wish to be artistic. That is the Italian influence. The

362

Italian population is very large and important and very intelligent and public-spirited. In fact, so are all the colonies, English, Spanish and German. . . . Miles and miles of wharves and lovely harbour, but still the place is left where we landed in carts, after fifteen miles in boats from the Outer Roads. . . ."

Don Roberto was not on a pleasure trip; in fact, he was on a mission he detested, for the very idea of taking horses out of their peaceful grazing grounds, in order to send them to be slaughtered on the battle-fields in France, sickened his heart. Still, as he explained in a letter to a friend, he felt that he was doing his duty, and that, if he had not undertaken this task, perhaps a less qualified man would have been appointed in his place, and consequently the horses might easily have suffered more on the long sea journey.

In due time, he, together with the other members of the commission, arrived in a little town on the River Uruguay where they made their temporary headquarters.

For the benefit of the English visitors, the hotel-owner's son, a lad of eighteen, who "study da Eenglis," put up the following notices in every room:

The Hotel visitors are kindly notified to agree their lodgings.

On account of higienical causes, soaps, combes and brush are sell now to each guest.

The Hotel Proprietors are not responable for loss of the values, excepting ditto delivered as Manager's care.

For information, reclamations and loss of detail, reclam at the manager office.

Referring to a post-mark, Don Roberto writes: " 'R.O.' means *República Oriental* (del Uruguay), it used to be called

La Banda Oriental, but people have got too fine for that, and it is now 'R.O.' "

The following extracts from letters will be of interest, especially to readers who know something about South America.

"February, 1915.

". . . A young gaucho yesterday rode forty-eight horses for me, all bare-backed. . . . I remember the time when I could have done it myself. The gauchos are still there though rather tamer than they used to be, but still most self-respecting men, carrying a large knife. (I am eminently self-respecting). . . ."

"March, 1915.

"It is ten o'clock at night. I have ridden thirty miles on the road, possibly six or eight more, forwards and backwards, slept on the ground (the first time for some years, but with a good sheepskin under you it is as soft as ever), then I was up at four, and have been sending telegrams all day, came and had dinner and cured the backs of two horses that had got sore. So you see there is not much time for letter-writing, as I must start again by daylight. . . . Here things are changed, and yet they are not. That is, there is plenty of wild life and lots of gauchos. (I have been with them all this week, eating meat roasted on a spear and drinking *maté,* and nothing else, just as of yore.) The difference is that most of the ranches have telephones. . . . There are no roads, but, instead, fenced tracks on which motors *can* run. . . . The life has certainly lost some of its picturesqueness, but it is still very interesting. To-day, after having parted out horses, I am camped out under some paraiso trees and roasted some meat. All round me were hundreds of

364

horses, in front pampa, and to the left the great woods stretching down to the River Uruguay, and in the distance Entre Ríos.* Like in the old days, we ate the meat with our knives (I used the one I bought in Gualeguaychú in 1871), and then we lay down on our saddles and had a siesta. There was a little warm wind blowing, making pleasant music among the green tufts of Pampas grass which grew along the *arroyo* [stream], in front of us."

"March, 1915.

". . . It has been like old time, though I never worked at such high pressure in my youth. To-day a man was missing, and so I had to lazo all day, hence my writing is worse than ever, for my hands are very much cut and 'burned' for want of practice. *Quite by accident*† I got on a buck-jumper, but sat him all right. . . . Last night I and the gauchos drove some five hundred horses through the plains, in high grass. It was a wonderful sight, but sad to think it was their last happy day on earth. . . ."

Once Don Roberto had to spend a few days in the city of Montevideo where he supervised the shipping of a lot of horses. One evening, after a long and hard day's work, when he entered the hotel dining-room with his riding-boots on, a certain diplomat, who was seated at a table, protested. Don Roberto who was very tired and hungry, pretended not to hear, whereupon the carefully groomed diplomat called the waiter, and sent him to Don Roberto with the request that he take off his riding-boots.

On receiving the message, he exclaimed in a stentorian

* Entre Ríos is the Argentine province in which Don Roberto in 1871 was kidnapped by revolutionary soldiers.

† Obviously underlined to reassure his mother.

AA

voice: "Oh, I shall be delighted to oblige the gentleman, provided he takes them off for me!"

One day, Don Roberto saw a gaucho riding a pony which immediately caught his eye. When asked for how much he would sell the animal, the man replied that, although he was poor, and could very well do with some money, he would never sell his favourite to be killed in France. Don Roberto took such a fancy to the animal (a black with a white blaze down his face, a marking known as "malacara" in South America), that he offered a very good price for it, with the promise to the owner that the pony would not be sent to the war, but would be kept for his personal pleasure. When the old gaucho was convinced that the prospective buyer spoke the truth, he agreed, after much persuasion, to part with his pet.

For weeks, under Don Roberto's leadership, the English commission selected animals, for masses had to be shipped to the battle-fields in France. The gauchos were all struck dumb with sheer amazement, for it astonished them that such pains were taken in picking horses which, for the most part, would be killed in a few months.

The *domadores* (bronco-busters), sprang lightly bare-backed upon the horses, many of which bucked furiously, but the riders sat them as easily as an ordinary man rides over a low fence. To queries why they did not saddle they answered: "To ride with a saddle is but a pastime fit for boys. "

When these men spoke about the Great War they called it "barbarous," and they took a secret pleasure in the fact that it showed Europeans not a whit more civilised than they themselves. Most of the sellers, when they parted with a horse, looked at him and remarked: "Poor little chap, you will go to the Great War."

As soon as a horse had been picked and classified, Don

Roberto called to a gaucho—who was seated by a smouldering fire—to prepare the branding-irons, "Artillería!" or "Caballería!" according to the animal's size. After the branding, either on the hip for cavalry, and on the neck for the artillery, a cowboy cut their manes off, making them as ugly as mules.

Most of the sellers took payment, horse by horse, as they were bought. This took a little time, either because the gauchos could not count quickly, or, perhaps, owing to their caution in counting the rolls of mostly greasy bank-notes which they stuffed into leather pockets in their wide belts which were adorned with many silver and even gold coins.

Let me use Don Roberto's own description of how he felt when, one evening, accompanied by a number of gauchos, he drove the last troop of doomed horses towards his headquarters in Uruguay.

". . . Two hours of sunset still remained, with three long leagues to cover, for in those latitudes there is no twilight, night succeeding day, just as films follow one another in a cinematograph. . . . The horses came out of the corral like a string of wild geese, neighing and looking round. Slowly we rode towards the herd, sending on several well-mounted men upon its flanks, and with precaution—for of all living animals tame horses easily take fright upon the march and separate—we got them into motion, on a well-marked trail that led towards the gate of the *estancia* 'Bopicuá,' our headquarters.

"At first they moved a little sullenly, and as if surprised. Then the contagion of motion that spreads so rapidly amongst animals upon the march seemed to inspire them, and the whole herd broke into a light trot. That is the moment that a stampede may happen, and accordingly we pulled our horses to a walk, whilst the men riding on the flanks forged slowly to the front, ready for anything that might occur. Gradually the trot slowed down, and we saw as it were a sea of manes and tails in front of us, emerging from a cloud of dust, from which shrill neighings and loud snortings rose. . . . By this time we had reached the gates of 'Bopicuá,' and still seven miles lay between us and our camping ground, with a fast declining sun. As the horses passed the gate we counted them, an operation of some difficulty, when time presses and the count is large. Nothing is easier than to miss animals, that is to say, for Europeans, however practised, but the lynx-eyed gauchos never are at fault. . . . When the last animal had passed and the great gates swung to, a young man rode to my side, and looking at the troop said: 'The dead salute you. This is the last time they will feed in Bopicuá.'

"We turned a moment, and the falling sun lit up the undulating plain, gilding the cottony tufts of the long grasses, falling upon the dark green leaves of the low trees, glinting across the belt of wood that fringed the River Uruguay, and striking full upon a white *estancia* house on the opposite bank, making it appear quite close at hand, although four leagues away.

"Two or three hundred yards from the great gateway stood a little native hut, as unsophisticated, but for a telephone, as were the gauchos' huts in Uruguay, as I remember them nearly forty years ago. A wooden barrel on a sledge for bringing water had been left close to the door, at which the occupant sat drinking *maté*, tapping with a long knife upon his boot. Under a straw-thatched shelter stood a saddled horse, and a small boy upon a pony slowly drove a flock of sheep. A blue, fine smoke that rose from a few smouldering logs and bones, blended so completely with the air that one was not quite sure if it was really smoke or the

368

reflection of the distant river against the atmosphere.

"Not far off lay the bones of a dead horse, with bits of hide adhering to them, shrivelled into mere parchment by the sun. All this I saw in a *camera-lucida*, seated a little sideways on my horse, and thinking sadly that I too, had looked my last on 'Bopicuá.' It is not given to all men after a break of years to come back to the scenes of youth, and still find in them the same zest as of old. To return again to all the cares of life called civilised, with all its list-lessness, its newspapers all full of nothing, its sordid aims disguised under high-sounding nicknames, its hideous riches and its sordid poverty, its want of human sympathy, and, above all, its barbarous war brought on it by the folly of its rulers, was not just at that moment an alluring thought, as I felt the little 'Malacara'* that I rode twitching his bridle, striving to be off. When I touched him with the spur, he bounded forward and soon overtook the troop, and the place which for so many months had been part of my life sank out of sight, just as an island in the Tropics fades from view as the ship leaves it, as it were, hull down.

"At last we left the herd to pasture in deep lush grass. Accompanied by the gauchos I rode up some rising ground where we drew up. Looking back towards the plain on which the horses seemed to have dwindled to the size of sheep in the half-light, one of the gauchos spoke their elegy: 'Eat well,' he said, 'there is no grass like that of Bopicuá where you go across the sea. The grass in Europe all must smell of blood.' "

Shortly before Don Roberto left South America to return

* "Malacara" is the pony he bought from the old gaucho, with the promise that he would not be sent to the war. This promise was kept, for after having carried Don Roberto for nearly twenty years, the animal was pensioned off on the farm at Weybridge, near London, where finally it was buried alongside another Argentine pony.

home, he received a letter from Joseph Conrad who wrote how, at the outbreak of the war, he and his wife had been detained in Vienna, and how they had finally managed to escape to Geneva on a Dutch steamer. Among other things, Conrad wrote:

> "Orlestone,
> "February 25th, 1915.
> ". . . The first thing almost I read was a par. in some paper stating that you had gone to S. America, as president of a commission to buy horses. Well! One man, at any rate, in the right place! . . . I regretted you were gone. I could have poured my distressful tale into your ears—and it would have eased my trouble, for, I am sure, you would have understood it as nobody here can. *Enfin!* . . . When can one expect to see you? . . . It would do me good to see you. For apart from my affection (for your person), I've always felt that there are certain things which I can say to you because the range of your feelings is wider and your mind more independent than that of any man I know. . . ."

On the last day, when Don Roberto rode back to his headquarters, after having supervised the loading of the last lot of horses, a furious *pampero*—that is, a South wind—raged over the plains as if protesting against the injustice committed by man.

In the evening he wrote to his mother:

> "Fray Bentos,
> "May 24th, 1915.
> ". . . For six months I have been much worried and very hard-worked, but I have had some fine wild gallops and some nice days, seated under the trees during the hours

we allowed ourselves in the middle of the day, drinking *maté*. Now the leaf is turned down, always a saddening thing, for it makes one think of the completion of the book. The little 'Malacara' comes home with me. I came on his former owner—who looks after him—crying with his arms round his neck, so I am letting him go as far as Montevideo to-morrow to see the last of him. . . . Fray Bentos is a pretty little place, and I shall always look back to my walk after a hard day on the little pier, to watch the sunset over Gualeguaychú.* I have seen very little, but I came to work and not to see; and I have worked. . . ."

During the return journey, the ship Don Roberto and the horses travelled on, was torpedoed by a German submarine in the English Channel, but fortunately, with great presence of mind, the captain managed to run the vessel on to a sandy beach where all the passengers and horses were safely landed.

Don Roberto hurried to London by car, and at the War Office gave a full verbal report about what had happened.

The official who interviewed him was (to use Don Roberto's own words) "a typical General Fallback." "Colonel Graham!" he spluttered, striding up and down the office, "what the devil do you mean by coming here without wearing your uniform!"

"My uniform?" Don Roberto answered, amused.

"Yes, Sir, your uniform; your uniform, Sir!" shouted the official whose normally rubicund face now glowed an even darker red.

"How can I wear a uniform when I have never had one?" the Don asked politely.

---

* Gualeguaychú is the little town in Entre Ríos where Don Roberto arrived in 1870, aged 17, to ranch in partnership with the Mack brothers.

"Never had one?—Never had one?—Why the devil don't you buy one?" the official roared, to the secret amusement of Don Roberto who changed the conversation by saying that he had come to report: "All present and correct," in spite of the fact that the ship which carried the horses, had been torpedoed in the Channel.

"Oh, yes!" shouted General Fallback, getting more and more excited, "reports about the occurrence have already reached me. . . . Why the devil did you beach the ship? . . . yes . . . why the devil did you beach her?"

Now Don Roberto's blood boiled up, and he thundered back: "For fun!"

After this General Fallback calmed down at once, and, changing his tone, discussed business which really mattered.

When Theodore Roosevelt was President of the United States of America, he was an enthusiastic reader of Don Roberto's books. Among several letters he wrote to him is one in which he says:

". . . What you and Hudson have done for South America, many have done for our frontiersmen in Texas, Arizona, and New Mexico. Others have written of the Mexican frontiersmen, and written well about them. No one, as far as I know, has touched the subject of the frontiersmen of Brazil. Why don't you do it? for you have been there, know them, and speak their lingo. The field is open to you."

Don Roberto was duly flattered, and turned the question over in his mind; then forgot all about it. During his journey out to South America to buy horses for the British Government, when the ship he travelled on was entering the harbour of Bahia, on the Brazilian coast, he was gazing at the marvellous scenery when a voice beside him said:

"Friend Don Roberto, what things have happened in Bahia! And that not long ago. Scarcely two hundred miles from where we stand took place the rising of Antonio Conselheiro, the last of the Gnostics, who defied all the Brazilian forces for a year or so, and was eventually slain with all his followers. The episode took place not more than twenty-five years ago; you ought to read and then write about it, for it was made by Providence on purpose for you, and it is well fitted for your pen."

Don Roberto turned and saw an old friend from Castile standing by his side, dressed in an immaculate white Palm Beach suit.

The name of Conselheiro was known to Don Roberto but vaguely, although he knew religious movements had been continuous in Brazil since the discovery. He listened to his old friend's story, and, when they landed at the capital, bought books about it. As he read and mused upon the tale, the letter from President Roosevelt came back into his mind, and upon his return to London he found the following letter from Theodore Roosevelt waiting for him.

"Oyster Bay,
"Long Island, N.Y.,
"June 3rd, 1916.

". . . You know, I think, how much Mrs. Roosevelt and I like your writings. We feel that from you, and from some of the sketches of Hudson, we get the South American as he is given nowhere else.

"I wish someone would do for his brother, the

Portuguese-American frontiersman of the interior of
Brazil, a similar work. . . .

"Sincerely yours,

(Signed) "THEODORE ROOSEVELT."

This letter and what Don Roberto's friend from Castile
had said, made him decide to write: *A Brazilian Mystic.*
(The amazing events related in this book all happened in
the wild regions of Brazil, known as the Sertão.)

Whenever he was in London, he rarely missed his daily ride
in Hyde Park. One morning, during the war years, as he
was slowly cantering along Rotten Row, he saw a horse bolting
with a lady. Turning his mustang with great speed, he urged
him into a furious gallop and gave chase. A mounted
policeman, who was stationed near Hyde Park Corner, did
likewise, but as he had a good start, Don Roberto only caught
up with him very slowly. The runaway madly bolted through
the traffic towards Marble Arch, but fortunately the lady was
an excellent rider, and the animal did not lose its footing on
the slippery surface of the road.

Near Grosvenor Gate the mounted policeman and Don
Roberto were level, and, dashing along side by side, they soon
managed to stop the runaway. Noticing that the lady
suffered slightly from nervous shock, Don Roberto offered her
his car, an offer which was gladly accepted. Later in the day
he called at the lady's house to inquire how she was, and next
day when he again rode in the Park, he was pleased to see
her cantering along, as if nothing had happened on the
previous morning. From that day on, Don Roberto almost
daily rode in the company of this lady—whose name is
Mrs. Dummett, and who was soon to become a great friend
of his, a wonderful friend whose companionship he treasured
for the rest of his life.

Early in January 1917, the British Government again sent

Don Roberto to South America, but this time to Colombia with the mission to buy cattle. He spent several months travelling through the land, mostly on horseback. In a letter to a friend he wrote: ". . . the floods of titubating verse which, like mental dysentery, afflict all members of the Spanish-speaking race. . . . Thus, Bogotá, set in its plateau in Colombian wilds, is a kind of Athens where all men write, and poets rave through the land and only wholesome, necessary revolutions keep their numbers down. . . ."

On March 27th, 1917, Don Roberto wrote the following letter to Theodore Roosevelt:

"Cartagena de Indias,
"Colombia.

"The Honourable Colonel Theodore Roosevelt,
"DEAR COLONEL ROOSEVELT,—

"I saw by chance to-day in *Harper's Magazine* that a national monument is to be raised to my old friend Colonel Cody, that it is to take the form of a statue of himself on horseback (I hope the horse will be old Buckskin Joe), that he is to be looking out over the North Platte, and that you have kindly consented to receive subscriptions for it.

"When Cody and I were both young I remember meeting him at the Horsehead Crossing, in or about the year 1880, I think, and subsequently saw him next year with the first germs of his great show in San Antonio de Bexar, Texas. (God bless Western Texas, as we used to say in those days—it is a thirsty land.)

"Cody was a picturesque character, a good fellow (I hope the story of his game of poker on his death-bed is not apocryphal), and a delightful figure on horseback. How well I can see him on his beautiful grey horse in the show!

"Every American child should learn at school the history of the conquest of the West.

"The names of Kid Carson, of General Custer and of Colonel Cody should be as household words to them. These men truly helped to form an empire as did the Spanish *conquistadores*.

"Nor should Sitting Bull, the Short Wolf, Crazy Horses, and Rain-in-the-Face be forgotten.

"They too were Americans, and showed the same heroic qualities as did their conquerors.

"I would not have Captain Jim of the Medocs fall into oblivion either.

"All of these men, and they were men of the clearest grit, as no one knows better than yourself, were actors in a tremendous drama, set in such surroundings as the world never saw before, or will see again.

"*Anch' io son pittore*, that is to say, I too knew the buffalo, the Apaches, and the other tribes of the Rio Grande.

"May I then trouble you with my obolus, a cheque for £20 towards the national monument to Buffalo Bill?

"I envy him his burial place.

"May the statue long stand looking out over the North Platte.

"If in another world there is any riding—and God forbid that I should go to any heaven in which there are no horses—I cannot but think that there will be a soft swishing as of footsteps of some invisible horse heard occasionally on the familiar trails over which the equestrian statue is to look.

"Believe me, dear Colonel Roosevelt,
"Yours most sincerely,
"R. B. CUNNINGHAME GRAHAM.

"PS.—I congratulate you most heartily on the force which you are raising.* It is like you, and if I had been blindfolded and asked who was raising such a force, I should have answered immediately, Teddy Roosevelt.

"After eleven months in the Argentine, buying horses for the British Government, I am at present in Colombia on a mission connected with cattle, on the same account.

"R.B.C.G."

During his travels in Colombia, Don Roberto had an exciting adventure, and a narrow escape.

Even to Cartagena there came echoes of the war. An old condemned unseaworthy stern-wheeler had lain for three years in the mud. During the Great War, a company bought the old tub; and, after a summary repair, set her to run from Cartagena to Quibdó, the capital of the Chocó, up the Atrato River, and down the coast, touching at several little ports. Boats she possessed but one, hung near the stern, and used to keep potatoes, yams, or vegetables, or as a sleeping-place for deck-hands or a chance negro passenger. Her engine-room was almost open, after the fashion of old-time Mississippi river boats. Nothing could well have been imagined more unfit to cope with the rough waters of the Caribbean Sea, or round a dangerous land-point, fifteen leagues upon her way towards Chocó, for there a heavy sea gets up at the least breeze. Passengers always crowded her, sleeping in every corner, curled up on deck, or in the hammocks that the Colombians nearly always carry with them, hung on the stanchions of the awning-rail. Some few Syrian store-keepers or mining engineers going to the great platinum mines in the Chocó, secured the box-like dens called cabins. She usually was laden to within a foot of her low freeboard, and all the decks were crowded with boxes, trunks, bundles, saddles, bales, and packages of goods.

* President Wilson refused Colonel Roosevelt the necessary permission.

Her crew were negroes and nondescripts, and her engineer, of course, a Scotsman, known as "Scottie," stricken in drink and years. A young German mate, from one of the steamers interned in the bay, acted as captain. He proved himself a sailor and a man.

One day, after the usual delay of several hours, this strange craft cleared out of Cartagena in a calm afternoon. She slowly steamed through a passage between mangrove swamps, and then out into the great lagoon beyond it. There she met the gale that seems to have been blowing since the day of the *Conquistadores*. She rolled like a galleon, the heavy upper decks catching the wind like sails, seas came aboard of her and set the packages and bales upon her decks awash. The miserable passengers were soaked, and as the evening advanced the seas grew heavier, and still the feared land-point loomed a league or two in front of her as she lay labouring the sea.

The German captain dived into the engine-room and then emerged without his cap, his hair tossed in the wind, and he scanned the horizon anxiously. After a look about the deck, and a compassionate glance at the soaked passengers rendering their tribute to Neptune, he took his resolution. Advancing to Don Roberto who was sheltering behind a deckhouse, he drew his feet together, clicked his heels and said: "My name is . . . Second Lieutenant of the Reserve of the German Navy," and raised his fingers mechanically, forgetting he had lost his cap. "We are at war," he said, "but what of that?—no one cares to die without a fight. You see that headland? It is the Point of Tigua. The sea is breaking heavily upon it, and if we drift there we are lost. Only a month ago a steamer failed to weather it, and not a soul was saved. Those that were not dashed on the rocks, the sharks soon tore to pieces. Upon the other side of it we shall be in shelter; but the swine firemen are frightened and

378

refuse to work. Come down with me, and . . . ah, that's right, you have a pistol: we will help Scottie to persuade them to work on."

Don Roberto, muttering: "All right," went down below into the engine-room. The firemen, huddled in a heap, had turned that ashy-grey colour that comes into a negro's face at the approach of death, or when strongly moved by fear. A foot or two from the ship's furnaces the water lapped up dangerously. Holding their pistols in their hands, Don Roberto and the German captain distributed a kick or two and forced the negroes to fire up.

When they had passed the Point of Tigua, and the old ship had got under shelter, shaking the water off her decks, as a Newfoundland dog shakes himself on emerging from a swim, they left the engine-room and came up on deck. Don Roberto and the captain looked at one another and said nothing, and then instinctively their hands stole towards each other.

After a visit to the little-known regions near the Atrato River, Don Roberto sailed for Jamaica from whence he returned to England with a report.

The result of this journey to Colombia was the publication of two books: *Cartagena and the Banks of the Sinu* and *The Conquest of New Granada.*

At the first General Election after the war, in December 1918, friends induced Don Roberto (very much against his inclination, as letters prove) to stand as an Independent Liberal for West Stirlingshire. His blossoming out as a Liberal, together with his unconventional and racy election speeches, astonished his audiences, especially when, with irrepressible humour, he told them on no account to vote Lloyd Georgian Tory, but for the Socialists. If possible, his broad humanity was more in evidence than it had been during his election speeches thirty-two years before, and even if his listeners were puzzled by his sarcastic humour and entire disregard for party shibboleths, they were struck by the literary beauty of his addresses.

On the eve of the poll—which was unsuccessful—he wrote a letter to his friend, Neil Munro, the Scottish poet, in which he confessed that he was "sick of this infernal folly of elections."

As we have already seen, Don Roberto had been a member of the Scottish Home Rule Association ever since its foundation, in 1886. The following letter, addressed to the Secretary of the Association, needs no explanation. It is an interesting document which partly reveals the writer's attitude towards the new Ireland, and, particularly, Mr. de Valera.

> "39, Chester Square,
> "London, S.W.
> "November 23rd, 1920.

"DEAR SIR,—

"You will already have received my wire. I am not in sympathy with the object of your meeting, as I do not think for a moment that the Government is encouraging reprisals in Ireland.

"What does the word 'reprisal' signify? Truly that something has taken place for which a 'reprisal' is a return.

"Policemen and soldiers are all human, and it is, though not admirable, still not unnatural that when they see their comrades and officers basely assassinated from behind hedges and points of vantage, that they occasionally hit back. The last horrible and cold-blooded murder of fourteen young men, unarmed, in bed, and in some instances under the eyes of their wives, is enough to fill any decent man with horror and indignation. I believe these murders are instigated . . . chiefly, and certainly paid for . . . by the band of international Jews, grouped round their fellow Jew, Mr. 'de' Valera in New York, and that there will be no peace till the band of cruel assassins is tracked down and their leaders executed. I have been and shall continue to be, I hope, undisturbed by the violence of these criminals, a convinced Home Ruler. I have no objection to Dominion Home Rule, so long as the British Empire is master of its own house and controls the ports, and armed forces of the Crown. As a Scotsman I detest assassination, and despise those who resort to it, and I believe no nation was ever freed by recourse to such dastardly methods. Such were not the ways employed by Wallace and Bruce.

"I much fear I must ask you to remove my name from the Scottish Home Rule Association, as I could not be a party to any palliation, even indirectly, of the base, cruel and cowardly murders of these fourteen unfortunate young men, so foully done to death in their beds, last Tuesday morning.

"Such a meeting as you propose to hold, clearly implies that you seem to consider the slaughter of these gallant young fellows, most of whom had faced a thousand deaths on the battlefield, as of little import. At least so it appears to me .

"Believe me,
"Yours sincerely,
(Signed) "R. B. CUNNINGHAME GRAHAM.

"P S.—I have, of course, no idea of imputing complicity in murder to the Jews as a race; only to the criminal Bolshie Jews who run 'de' Valera in New York. You are aware, of course, that his father is supposed to be a Bowery Jew.

"R.B.C.G."

In 1921 Don Roberto was again asked to stand as a candidate for West Stirlingshire, but this time he flatly refused, as the following letters show. Once he said: "The dunghill of active politics is a young man's game . . . and it is a dunghill, I know, for I have been on (or in) the hill."

". . . Personally I have put away childlike things and am devoting my few remaining years to literature . . . I should in *no case* stand for West Stirlingshire again. It cost me £900 out of my pocket last time. I refused all help, for I wanted to stand for the county that my people on both sides of the house had often represented and in which my old property was situated. I did so, and do not regret the money. . . ."

"August 2nd, 1921.

". . . I shall certainly have no more to do with a Liberal Association, but *re* the Labour Party, I am not enthusiastic. They seem to me to have acquired in twenty years all the faults of the two old parties and to have added some of their own. As I see the matter, they are just as tricky and false, and as much taken up with office-seeking as the Whigs and Tories and have no ideals of any high nature; certainly the Whigs and Tories had none either. . . . I do not think I shall return to the political field. . . ."

The death of Hudson (at the age of eighty-one in August 1922) was a bitter blow to Don Roberto who, a few years later, paid a tribute to his friend, in the preface to *The Horses of the Conquest*:

"Hudson is in Trapalanda," he wrote, "the heaven to which the Indians of the great sea of grass, the Pampa,

382

imagined they would go. . . . Hell? Never! He often found hell on earth, especially when he wrote to ease his aching soul. Purgatory? No; for each man's purgatory is the earth whereon he drees his weird, seeing his errors and yet unable to avoid them, without the unerring instinct of the animals to guide his step. Therefore, looking at the matter as an old-time Gaucho would have looked at it, he must be in Trapalanda."

Two years after Hudson's death, Joseph Conrad suddenly died. Having seen his friend harboured in his grave at Canterbury, Don Roberto paid him a tribute in *Inveni Portum*, a beautiful piece of prose, the last lines of which read:

". . . The voyage was over and the great spirit rested from its toil, safe in the English earth that he had dreamed of as a child in far Ukrainia. A gleam of sun lit up the red brick houses of the town. It fell upon the tower of the cathedral, turning it into a great, glowing beacon pointing to the sky. The trees moved gently in the breeze, and in the fields the ripening corn was undulating softly, just as the waves waft in on an atoll in the Pacific, with a light swishing sound. All was well chosen for his resting place, and so we left him with his sails all duly furled, ropes flemished down, and with the anchor holding truly in the kind Kentish earth, until the Judgment Day. The gulls will bring him tidings as they fly past above his grave, with their wild voices, if he should weary for the sea and the salt smell of it."

The following letter, written to a friend, shows that Don Roberto took an interest in the theatre, and that he was very critical.

"79a, Elizabeth Street,
"London, S.W.1.
"April 27th, 1924.
". . . I went yesterday to see Shaw's *Joan*.

"My God! ! !

"I never thought to see a simple, beautiful story so vulgarised and made common. . . .

"Shaw is a clever, kind and most charitable man, who has written some exquisitely funny things, but Tragedy is not for him; all the time the jester's bells are tinkling, not in the comic passages, as Shakespeare knew so well how to make them tinkle, as a relief to the deepest tragedy; but in the serious (or would-be serious) passages.

"He is an adept at discovering the obvious. Every one who has read the life of Torquemada, Pelleo de Arfues and the other chief inquisitors, knows they were pious men, acting in good faith and generally men of blameless lives. *That* made the horror of the thing so awful. Had they been rogues, their conduct would have been natural.

"Shaw should read, or read again, more carefully, the contemporary records, especially the evidence of her trial . . . and above all what the old knight who brought her to Orleans says. He would then see that as the old knight says, she was 'modest and gracious,' that she had (and must have had to impress all those men) great feminine charm.

"Shaw makes her nothing but a 'common bitch'; there is no other word for her, as he sees her, or at least presents her. . . . Shaw does not know that men in all ages, are not impressed by women who have missions from above; but by those who have 'charm,' i.e. a mission to men. . . . Shaw, to my mind, saw (and felt) nothing, and out of the most beautiful story, has made a cultured

384

Irish Protestant farce. It is his damned suburban *culture* I kick at.

"P.S.—The sun is shining in at the window. No wonder the Aztecs and others worshipped him. We should do the same, if we saw more of him, for certainly he is a pleasanter deity than Jahve."

In March, 1925, Don Roberto's mother died in her sleep at her London residence, 39, Chester Square. Although she reached her ninety-seventh year, she remained young to the last, because she refused to grow old. Until her death she enjoyed perfect health, and her eyesight and hearing were excellent. For many years she delighted in receiving friends and hearing everything they had to tell her and retailing in return her memories extending back over nearly a century. There were few persons in the world of politics, literature, music and art whom she had not met or knew about, and, thanks to her extraordinary memory, she remembered all that there was of interest to tell about them. Until the last she attended theatres, and, above all, Shakespeare's plays, and she was able to compare with quotations the acting of the contemporary with that of the players whom she had known in her youth. She never missed an art exhibition, and there were few departments of life in which she was not interested. Brought up a Whig, she retained her Liberalism to the last, and even showed sympathy with modern Labour developments. About her it can truthfully be said that she lived with intelligence and grace. She was buried alongside her youngest son, the Rev. Malise Archibald (who had died forty years before), at the St. Giles' Hill burying ground at Winchester where he had been a curate at St. John's Church.

With his two best friends dead, and without his mother who had been his inspiration and moral support throughout life, Don Roberto felt like a lost soul. When the first frosts of late autumn began to fall, he suddenly decided (in spite of being seventy-three years of age) to undertake a journey which would even make adventurous young men hesitate before setting out. The man who, eleven years before, at the age of sixty-two, had been told that he was too old to join the Rough Riders, packed up a favourite old saddle* together with a few personal belongings, and set sail for Venezuela, and upon arrival there, steamed some 600 miles up the Orinoco River on a crude craft. Leaving the boat where the River Meta joins the Orinoco, he bought a pony, saddled up, and jogged off, alone, in a northerly direction, to explore the great *llanos*, as the plains of Venezuela are called. Seated upon a horse, and out in the wilds, Don Roberto was in his element once more.

Over these sun-scourged plains he rode, and swam across rivers and streams infested with electric eels and ravenous cannibal fish. During nights he heard the howling monkeys start their chorus, as the jaguar whetted his claws against tree-trunks; and as he journeyed on these interminable grassy flats, he observed the beauties of Nature which he later described in his masterful sketch—*The Plains of Venezuela* (see *Rodeo*, Wm. Heinemann, 1936).

Some of our modern travellers who, in writing about their "adventures," show great intrepidity, would do well to read this sketch in which the word "I" never appears, although the writer probably had more adventure on his journey than half a dozen of our modern Barons von Münchhausen put together.

As we have seen in the opening chapter, Don Roberto's mother was born in 1828, in the English flagship *Barham*, the day she made port at La Guaira in Venezuela, and his grandfather, Admiral Fleeming, had acted as adviser and

---

* Ten years later, when I rode from the South of England to Don Roberto's house on the River Clyde, he insisted on my using this saddle. (See *Bridle Paths*, published by Wm. Heinemann, London, 1936.)

DON ROBERTO AND HIS MOTHER

mediator between Bolívar and Páez, the Venezuelan heroes of the struggle for independence against Spain. No wonder, therefore, that to Don Roberto the visit to Venezuela was of special interest and that, later, he wrote his *José Antonio Páez*.

It chanced that when he arrived in a town, "Bolívar Day" was being celebrated. The houses and streets were garlanded, beflagged and festooned and, in spite of the terrific heat, a crowd was assembled in the *plaza* in front of the *palacio municipal* on the wooden balcony of which orators gave amazing displays of verbal acrobatics. Referring to this occasion, Don Roberto wrote: "Speeches, like in all Latin America, each one rose nearer to Olympus than the other, and were adorned so thickly with metaphors, classical quotations, and, above all, adjectives, that every available dictionary must have been well thumbed to furnish them."

Suddenly someone recognised Don Roberto, and although he protested, he was almost dragged up to the balcony, where, after having been introduced to the crowd below, he was asked to make a speech. The heat was so oppressive that he could hardly think, and whilst hundreds of voices clamoured to hear the *distinguido* visitor, he suddenly remembered a flowery speech he had once heard in the Spanish Club in London. Thanks to his amazing memory, he was able to repeat this speech, word for word, and, as he did so, he even imitated the grand gestures with which the Venezuelan orator in London had given extra expression and emphasis to his elaborate flow of language.

When, amid thunderous cheers, Don Roberto finished, a gentleman whom he at once recognised as an old friend, came alongside him and whispered, with a meaning wink: "I believe I've heard this speech before." "Certainly, señor," smiling Don Roberto answered, "for so have I, when I listened to you in London."

When the President of Venezuela, General Juan Vicente

Gómez heard about Don Roberto's arrival in Carácas, he invited him to dinner. However, the traveller politely refused the honour, for he had no desire to meet the man about whom he later wrote:

"Gómez, the world's bloodiest and most ruthless dictator. . . .

"He had no morals, either in the giving or taking of life. . . . He seemed to think that by increasing the population with a hundred and twenty children he could atone for the hundreds he massacred and the hundreds more he exiled. . . ."*

Having seen the land where his mother had spent the first years of her life, Don Roberto, after a short visit to Panama, returned home once more. Despite his seventy-three years, he was still young enough to mount a bronco near London, and although the animal bucked viciously the rider joyfully yelled out numbers as the infuriated animal rocketed into the air. Greatly to Don Roberto's annoyance, as he called out "sixteen!" he lost his balance, and in consequence was thrown, but what vexed him most was the fact that, instead of landing on his feet like a gaucho, he came down on all fours.†

During the following English winter (1926–27) he again returned to Venezuela, where he stayed until early in June. On this trip he spent a great deal of his time in Carácas, where he dug through archives, searching historical data. During a voyage he made into the interior he wrote the following letter to a friend in London:

"San Fernando de Apure,
"December 29th, 1926.
". . . There are not a great many more remote places

---

* Gómez died in 1935, leaving some 120 children.
† This almost incredible feat was corroborated to me by several eye-witnesses.

than this little ranche village on the Apure (it runs into the Orinoco some one hundred miles from here). I am staying with an old friend, the manager of the Vestey Brothers great ranche. There are 335,000 head of cattle, and the furthest ranche of the estate is a hundred miles off.

"You know my mother was born in La Guaira, and perhaps christened there, but although the register of the cathedral in Carácas is carefully kept, there is no entry. In the public library they showed me some verses (bad verses) addressed to my grandfather in 1828, at a banquet given him by Páez.* I knew the verses, but had never seen them printed. The other day I went on a little expedition to Ciudad Bolívar (Angostura). It took three days down the Apure and Orinoco and four days back. Such a trip here is looked on as a run over to Dieppe at home. Mean temperature 92°. The Orinoco is a magnificent river, and the sunsets on it superb. Ciudad Bolívar is a most interesting place, built on a high bluff. It was formerly a very thriving place with its trade in *balata* (rubber), *tarrapia* (Tonga bean), and egrets' feathers. Now none of these things have any price (even Angostura bitters are now made in Trinidad), and the great villas the German traders built, with their magnificent gardens, are all deserted and falling into decay. . . . An old Indian and his wife take care [*sic*] of the largest villa (a palace), and huge lizards bask on the steps. Crocodiles, large and active, some over twenty feet, boas, often over thirty feet, tigers, energetic and frequent, one killed a horse a month ago near Ciudad Bolívar and then chawed off a cowboy's arm, here, three months ago; so you see that with the mosquitoes, here known as 'La Plaga' (the plague), life is not without its little incidents. . . ."

* One of these verses is quoted in the opening chapter of this book. (See p. 18.)

CHAPTER XVIII

PERSONAL REMINISCENCES—DON ROBERTO, THE MAN, AS
I AND OTHERS KNEW HIM, AND AS HE KNEW HIMSELF

IF I attempted to give a full account of Don Roberto's
activities from this point on, two volumes would not be
sufficient to do the subject justice. Fortunately, he wrote
several other books which show better than words of mine
could, that he had lost none of his vigour, and that the fighting
spirit in him was as active and strong as ever.

In London he never missed his daily ride in the Park and,
as usual, always turned out on an Argentine mustang.
Cervantes wrote that "riding makes one man look like a
gentleman and yet another like a groom." Don Roberto
sitting erect in the saddle, eyes fixed afar—like all men who
have ridden over plains—suggested something more than a
"gentleman"; he looked what he was: a cavalier.

Every winter he made a journey abroad, to Spain, Morocco,
the South of France or to Portugal. On such occasions he
was always accompanied by his friends, Mrs. Dummett and
her sister, Miss Louise Mieville, and sometimes his niece,
Lady Brooke,* joined the party. During the summer months
Don Roberto always went to "Ardoch," his Scottish home on
the River Clyde. He often told me that every year he liked
to spend two or three months alone, for this gave him a chance
to write, read and think as he pleased.

* Lady Brooke, the daughter of Don Roberto's brother, Commander
C. E. Cunninghame Graham, and the wife of Admiral Sir Basil Brooke, who
for a number of years was Comptroller of the Duke of York's Household, a
position he retained on the Duke's accession to the throne, following King
Edward VIII's abdication in 1936.

WITH THE AUTHOR IN LONDON

W. H. Nevinson, in his book, *Essays in Freedom*, wrote about him: ". . . Too little known all his books probably are, for they move with a 'like it or leave it' air, and *noblesse* has laid their author under no obligation to please the crowd. . . . Of all living writers, probably Cunninghame Graham comes nearest one's conception of the Knight in literature. . . ."

In 1927, Nevinson and Don Roberto had a difference over the execution of Sir Roger Casement. Nevinson wrote about this in his autobiography: *Last Changes, Last Chances*. After having read the book, Don Roberto wrote the following letter to his friend:

"London, November 27,—28.

"MY DEAR NEVINSON,—

"I have just read your last book with great admiration. I have even read your strictures on myself with admiration, because they are so evidently sincere. Let us clear decks . . . but not for action.

"If ever there was a West Briton, till the last year of his life, it was Sir Roger Casement. His father was deputy grand master of the Orange Lodges of Armagh (I think). Sir Roger was a bitter, black Ulster Protestant, who, when Conrad and I knew him first, had no words, but of contempt for Irish Catholics. He passed his life away from Ireland, in the service of the country, that in the last year of his life, he called enemy. He enjoyed honours and a pension (both of which he deserved) from England. He was presumably a brave man, and did splendid work both in the Congo and on the Putumayo. The abnormality of his private life, which I hear from Conrad, from Englishmen who had known him in Paranagua and Rio de Janeiro, did not weigh with me at the least. As you say, we cannot hang all who have Casement's vice, and after all it is not a disease that is catching in the least.

"As far as I know, he never opened his mouth during his long career in the British service, to say a word in favour of Ireland. He had, in effect, lived there but very little. What he said about only being at home amongst fishermen of the west, was but mere rhetoric. He scarcely could have known them.

"Had he been made British Consul-General in New York, most probably he would have been alive to-day. Many have told me that he considered himself unjustly treated in that respect, and hence his hatred to the British Empire.

"This may or may not be true . . . who shall judge the heart, but it was common talk, long before his last adventure, i.e. when he first became a Nationalist, some fourteen months before his death.

"His speech at his trial, to me, was nauseous, for it was palpably insincere. Ireland was not at war with England, he had done nothing to entitle him to call himself an Irish Patriot. His very advent was forced upon him by the Germans, who were disgusted with his failure to engage Irish prisoners against England. He died like a brave man, and for that I respect him, as I respect the consistent courage that he showed throughout his life. I think you will allow I have been a lifelong friend of Ireland. I knew Parnell and Davitt, Dillon and all the older politicians, and was on friendly terms with Kevin O'Higgins till his lamented death. The shooting men by batches revolted me. The exploits of the two bands of scoundrels, the Gunmen and the Black and Tans (*Arcades ambo*), filled me with disgust.

"You must forgive me. . . . I know you will, for I know you are of those who love sincerity, when I say that it is an outrage (in my opinion) to Owen Roe O'Neil, Tyrconnel, Wolfe Tone, Emmst, O'Connell, Parnell and Davitt, to place such a man as Sir Roger Casement in their ranks. These men (most of them) gave their lives for Ireland, but what did Casement do? Nothing as far as I can see. Peace to his ashes. May his bravery have washed out all his short-comings and his faults.

"Of course, I shall not convince you. Whoever was convinced by facts? Let us shake hands on the one fact, that the man you thought worthy of respect and I did not, was brave.

"Yours very sincerely,
"R.B.C.G."

(*Note.*—Due to the great admiration Nevinson and Don Roberto had for one another, this difference of opinion was soon overcome, and the two remained friends.)

Don Roberto had always been a believer in Home Rule, which he once said was "the first step to internationalism, the goal which every thinking man and woman must place before their eyes."

Here are a few statements he made, in this connection:

"It is only in small States that Liberty really flourishes."

"In the dismemberment of all great empires lies the only chance of real happiness to the world at large."

"Science has no mother country, but in the realm of the Arts, Literature, Painting and Music, nationality is of the first importance."

"I fear I have no theory of empires, destiny of the Anglo-Saxon race, spread of the Christian faith, of trade extension, or of hinterlands; no nostrum, by means of which I hope to turn Arabs to Christians, reconcile

393

Allah and Jahve, remove the ancient lack of comprehension between East and West, mix oil and vinegar,
or fix the rainbow always in the sky so that the colour-
blind may scan it at their leisure through the medium
of a piece of neutral-tinted glass. . . ."

"Morality is now hung on a rusty nail, quite out of
fashion, so it seems superfluous to speak of it when
Germany, France, Spain, Italy and we ourselves, dispose
of other people's lands without a shadow of excuse,
except superior force."

"No truer Saurian ever squirmed in the primeval mud
than the Press of to-day, in every corner of the world.
Just as the Church of old concealed its tyranny, its
hangings, burnings, and its torturings, under the style
and title of the 'Love of God,' so does the Press to-day
'egg on' all Europe to war and piracy under the pretext
of 'restoring order' and 'advancing progress,' progress
of course meaning really, dumping grounds for sweated
goods."

That even the Scottish Home Rule question did not make
him lose his sense of humour he proved when he wrote:

"Scotland enjoyed Home Rule in those days (in the
time of James III), and the blessing of a national Parliament with the pleasure of knowing that the taxes were
wasted in Edinburgh instead of in London."

In March, 1928, the National Party of Scotland was
founded in Glasgow, and Don Roberto, though not present,
was named its first president.

In the autumn of the same year he was the National
Party's candidate in the Rectorial contest at Glasgow
University, but was defeated by the small majority of

SPEAKING IN SCOTLAND. SEATED, THE DUKE OF MONTROSE

sixty-six votes by Mr. Stanley Baldwin, then Prime Minister. Don Roberto received the majority of the men's votes, but the women elected Baldwin who had given them franchise. After the election several delegations, consisting of young ladies, called at "Ardoch" House to explain that although they would normally have voted for Don Roberto, they felt it was their duty to elect the Prime Minister who had supported and put through women's suffrage.*

Every year Don Roberto spoke at demonstrations held by the National Party. In 1930, although he was still suffering from a nasty fall from a horse—sustained whilst wintering in Morocco—he made a memorable speech in Stirling.

Between the years 1929 and 1930 he wrote two books: *José Antonio Páez* and *The Horses of the Conquest*.

Having seen literary papers praise *José Antonio Páez*, as one of the finest examples of English prose, a gentleman bought a copy. Being puzzled by the peculiar syntax and punctuation, he sent a criticism to Don Roberto whose reply to the (to him) unknown correspondent is both gracious and interesting. The answer came from Madrid, and reads:

"DEAR SIR,—
   "Many thanks.
"1. Praise Allah. I am not a 'writer of repute.'
"2. The matters you refer to strike me as being rather affairs of grammar than of style.
"3. *Punctuation.* I do not live by writing (or I should have starved long ago), and the punctuation I use is my own. If it were altered, my writing would lose entirely.
"4. I am in bed with a serious chill, and my head is going round with the quinine I have taken. Some of

* As we have seen, Don Roberto was one of the first supporters of women's suffrage, before Mr. Baldwin came on the political scene. Obviously the students did not realise this.

the things you refer to are simply mistakes. Others I think are Hispaniolisms as I am practically bilingual. Pray excuse this scrawl and believe me, "Yours with thanks,
    "R. B. Cunninghame Graham.

"P S.—To 'affront a journey' is an Hispaniolism. I do not dislike it. I use 'affront' in the sense of 'set face to.' R.B.C.G."

Among writers of prefaces Don Roberto stood in a class by himself. Already in 1899, Joseph Conrad recognised this, for he called him the "Prince of Preface-writers," and once he wrote to him: "Your prefaces are so good! It is quite an art by itself."

Despite the fact that for his historical studies he dug through archives in England, Spain and Venezuela, he called himself "a mere dabbler" and an "amateur." He delighted in saying that in all his life he never made a written note. "The setting down of dates," he wrote with contempt, "is, after all, an *ad captandum* appeal to the suffrages of those soft-headed creatures who are styled serious men." However, in spite of this opinion, the dates he gives are scrupulously accurate. Both in his travel books and histories his personality emanates to such an extent that they are neither travel nor history, but rather literature of a very exceptional type.

A few extracts from his writings, picked at random, will show how he felt about certain things.

Preface to *The Conquest of the River Plate*.

". . . I see a critic pricking up his ears with which nature has endowed him, grasping his pen and writing in a fury, for it has been well said that the majority of writers only write to annoy critics, that the writer has proclaimed a gospel of inaccuracy and sloth. With all due

apologies in advance for having ventured to annoy some
one or other who earns his daily bread by criticising books
on subjects with which he is imperfectly acquainted, I
submit that I am right. My object has been to present
some of the conquerors of the River Plate as human beings,
and try to show that, taking into consideration the time
in which they lived, they did not differ greatly from ourselves. We lay the flattering unction to our souls, that
our adventurers in the spacious days of Queen Elizabeth
were on a different moral plane from that on which the
adventurers of Spain and Portugal strutted their brief
hour. It has been my care to bring out the best whilst
never palliating the worst features of the *conquistadores*
of the River Plate, and specially to show the part played
by women in that conquest. . . ."

His sympathy was always with the poor and the oppressed,
and the full blast of his sarcasm was turned on the rich and
the conventional. Worldly success he looked on with
contempt, and he despised modern civilisation, with its
commerce and industrialism. His tenderness of heart was
poured out on life's failures. "For those who fail," he wrote
in his astonishing sketch, *Success*, "for those who have sunk still
battling beneath the muddy waves of life, we keep our love,
and that curiosity about their lives which makes their
memories green when the cheap gold is dusted over, which
once we gave success."

At the giant COMMERCE, he tilted again and again.
"Commerce, that vivifying force, that bond of union between
all the basest instincts of the basest of mankind. . . . Commerce, holy commerce, thrice blessed nexus which makes
the whole world kin, reducing all men to the lowest common
multiple; commerce that curses equally both him who

buys and him who sells, and, not content with catching all men in its ledgers, envies the animals their happy lives. . . ."

"Gold which has rendered dumb, priests, ministers of state, bishops and merchants, princes and peasants, and has closed the mouths of three parts of mankind, making them silent accomplices in all the villainies they see and hate, and still dare not denounce, fearing the scourge of poverty, and the smart lash which Don Dinero (Don Money) flourishes over the shoulders of all those who venture even remotely to express their thoughts."

On the development of Argentine railways, he said: "Rails can be purchased too dearly, I fear. I, for one, would rather have seen the country in the possession of the gauchos, and the Spanish provinces now depopulated inhabited by the poor creatures, who, to escape taxes and sweaters in Spain, have been made the unwilling instruments both of their own ruin and the destruction of both Indians and gauchos."

"What is important is not the actions of a man, which may be caused by circumstances, and which, rightly considered, are as immaterial as are the atoms dancing in a sunbeam, seen by the eye and not collated by the brain, but what he thinks, and more important still, that which he says and writes."

"Though matters of an ultramundane nature often leave me without enthusiasm, I have always been interested in religious enterprises pursued under disadvantageous circumstances. . . ."

"He who wishes to see Christ's kingdom upon earth, the Rule of the Saints, or the Fifth Monarchy in operation, is almost certain to be an anarchist."

"Of all the forces which move mankind, humbug is the strongest, for humbugs are always taken in by humbug, and the very men who practise on the folly of mankind fall easy victims to the manœuvres of their brothers in the art."

"All men born of women are but brief shadows, strutting their little hour on an unstable stage on which it is impossible to get a firm footing, and hence are equal—or, if a perfect democrat—each one inferior to his brother."

"I mean no disrespect to kings or beachcombers. Each of them possibly have their uses in a civilisation that to me appears to be founded on mud, cemented with blood, and sustained precariously upon the points of bayonets."

"Those who make no mistakes have attempted but few difficult things."

"Self-abnegation is the true spirituality."

Preface to *The Horses of the Conquest:*
"I who have ridden hundreds or perhaps thousands of horses have written that which I have written, out of gratitude. Over how many miles of pampa and of prairie, sabana, forest trails, and wild mountain paths they have carried me, on journeys that to them could have no meaning, and to me have been the best remembered moments of my life. Into how many herds of cattle, seas of tossing heads, fierce eyes, menacing horns, tails lashing flanks like whipsnakes, and sharp hooves ready to pound the life out of a man or horse that falls amongst them, have they borne me safely? Why, wherefore, they could not possibly have understood, they

399

who browsed peacefully amongst the fiercest herds who would have trampled the life out of anyone who ventured near them upon foot. They have swum rivers in high flood, against their instinct, I am sure, bearing me on their backs, or holding to their manes or tails, in safety to the other bank, only to be once more saddled and spurred on to a gallop, when all their nature called to them to stay about and graze. Together we have sweated, starved and shivered, rushed wildly to the front of the stampeding herd, they stretched out to their fullest speed, their rider, mad with the danger and excitement of a gallop to which the wildest gallop of the Valkyries was but a peaceful morning ride.

"Through forests, where the burning trees fell, pyramids of fire across the track, blinded with smoke and ashes over ground so hot that it must have scorched their unshod feet, they have pressed valiantly along, stifling their fear, or perhaps fearing the spur more than they feared the flames. For all their services, the fatigue they have undergone, the want of food and water, the wonder and the terror of the strange surroundings into which they have been plunged by land and water, by rifle shots and Indians' lances—for all their uncomplaining gallantry, their fiery spirit, when they were mounted, their gentle natures, and for their patience; patience, the sublimest of their virtues, patience that puts mankind to shame, I thank them. . . ."

On vivisection: ". . . the animal, upon the vivisector's bench,—calling to man who should be as his God—gives out occasionally some horrid sound, and even then knows it would be unheard. . . ."

"Death, the compensating boon which makes life tolerable."

400

"After all the years that I have wandered up and down the world, seeking for peace, I found it wherever there was grass and water for my horse."

Not without humour is the following:

"George Washington, with all his virtues, never appealed to the imaginative mind after his inhuman refusal, when a child, to tell an almost necessary lie."

In his last book, *Mirages*, published a month or two before he died, Don Roberto shows clearly that he was not in the least deceived by the savages and primitive poor peoples he has so often defended. He writes:

"Had it not been for the eruption of the Latins (2,000 years ago) against all justice and in defiance of the League of Nations of those days, Britons, who were the Abyssinians of the first century B.C., might have remained woad-painted, bathless, and in ignorance of Virgil, Horace, Ovid and Petronius Arbiter; long-haired and lousy, and content to rob upon the highway as there is no mention of a Stock Exchange in Cæsar's 'Commentaries.' But of his courtesy I pray the Empire-builder not to think that I am enamoured of the noble savage. I know quite well that he uses no poison gas or bombs, simply because he has not got them, and is constrained to do his level best with poison arrows, launched from blow-pipe or bow, and other poor devices hatched in his neolithic brain."

As I have made clear in the Introduction to this book, I will not attempt to analyse the subject of this "Life," either from a Freudian or literary point of view. In undertaking the task of giving an outline of Don Roberto's life, my ambition was to do this, and nothing else. As for his literary activities, his writings speak for themselves, and his books are available to all those who wish to read them.

From this point on I shall endeavour to show my friend as I knew him.

In the Introductory Note I have already described our first meeting in a Spanish restaurant in London. As we had a great deal in common, we soon became good friends. A year before chance brought us together, he wrote the story of my ride from Buenos Aires to Washington,* an account he compiled from information gathered from Argentine newspapers and magazines. This story was published in 1932, in his book, *Writ in Sand*, and four years later, according to my friend's wish, I included it in *Rodeo*, a collection of many of his best short stories and sketches I edited for him.

The first thing my new friend showed me after our meeting in the Spanish restaurant was the Hudson memorial in Hyde Park. Reports about this extraordinary and unconventional piece of work by Jacob Epstein had reached me long before, when I was in South America, and now I was glad to be able to see it with my own eyes. I knew that Lord Grey and Mr. Galsworthy had objected to Epstein being commissioned to execute the work, and that, when Don Roberto insisted on this choice of artist, they resigned from the Committee. Despite strong opposition on the part of several people who had a say in this matter, Epstein was chosen to make the memorial which caused a sensation and a great deal of controversy and even unpleasant incidents. When an antagonistic body suggested that "Rima" be removed from Hyde Park, Don Roberto and Mr. Muirhead Bone, the celebrated artist, sponsored a written protest which was signed by many famous people.

* My own manuscript, describing this ride, had been rejected by American and English publishers. When Don Roberto read it, he offered to write a preface. Thanks to his recommendation the manuscript was published in book-form, under the title of *Tschiffely's Ride*.

Talking to a friend, Don Roberto said that Mr. Stanley Baldwin, in unveiling "Rima" (the Hudson Memorial), "did a heroic thing," because his mother had just died and was still unburied.

It is customary at an unveiling to pull the cord, look at the monument, and bow to the artist. Actually, according to many eye-witnesses, Mr. Baldwin pulled the cord, looked at the memorial, and was so staggered at what he saw that his jaw fell and he forgot the artist entirely.

To-day, probably few people know that this monument stands almost on the exact spot where Hudson often slept when he first came to England, lonely and penniless.

Having shown me the memorial Don Roberto drove me out to Weybridge where, on a farm, he kept several old horses. Near there, in a field, close to a big shady tree, is buried his favourite mustang "Pampa." To this grave—which is marked with a cobblestone—he made many pilgrimages, and whenever friends accompanied him on his frequent visits to the old pensioners on the farm, he always showed them the spot where his favourite horse is buried.

During my first visit to Weybridge, I had an opportunity of appreciating my new friend's quick repartee and sense of humour. Just as we were about to leave, a man appeared, leading an old donkey by a rope. Doffing his cap he asked if Don Roberto could give his animal a home and put him into the field with the other old horses. Having explained that he really could not adopt another animal, Don Roberto added with a merry twinkle in his eyes: "But if you take your donkey to the House of Commons, they will receive him with open arms, and he will immediately be made a new Member."

With this he handed the man half a crown, and asked him to buy his animal a good feed, and with the rest of the money to have a drink.

In London and in Scotland, he was well known to beggars and "spongers" who constantly waylaid him, knowing that he always parted with a shilling or two. Once, when I was walking along the banks of the Clyde with him, and he had given a typical loafer a half-crown piece, I asked him if he felt sure that the man was not going to spend the money on drink.

The answer was: "If it's drink the man wants, I pity him and wish him good luck, and if he begs without needing the money I feel sorry for him, and he deserves what I have given him for sinking the last atom of self-respect. If only one out of five people who come to me, holding out their hands, needs the money, I am glad to be in a position to help him, and as for the others, well . . ." With this he shrugged his shoulders, shook his head, and we walked on.

My prolonged visits to "Ardoch" were delightful, for Don Roberto was a perfect host.

To set down all my interesting and amusing reminiscences of him, is impossible, and therefore I will only recount a few that come back to memory as I write.

One day he showed me a picture of an ancestor of his. "It's a very fine painting," he said, and then, having looked at it for a few moments, added with a naughty smile, "he must have been about to cheat somebody, for he has his hand on a Bible."

Some years before I met him, he had injured a foot in falling with a horse in Tangier. On returning home he consulted a then well-known bone-setter who attended many rich society people. Thanks to the osteopath's skill the foot mended in due time. A few years later, when Don Roberto heard that—because the bone-setter had grown too old— most of his clients left him, and that he was in financial distress, he regularly went to him for massage he was really in no need of. This he evidently did because he was too tactful to offer the man a gift of money which he knew would have hurt his feelings.

Once, accompanied by an old friend, Don Roberto visited the shrine of a well-known woman saint. When the two entered the grotto in which kneeled many pilgrims, Don Roberto took off his hat, but his companion—who was very anti-religious—refused to do the same. Knowing that this would hurt the feelings of the pilgrims, Don Roberto repeatedly asked his friend to bare his head, only to receive the answer: "I'll be damned if I will!" Finally Don Roberto said: "Now look here, if you don't want to take off your hat to a saint: you surely will not refuse to take it off to a lady." After this the hat came off, and the two men quietly wandered through the interesting grotto.

One evening, when I stayed at "Ardoch," a lady called to tell us about a conversation she had overheard on her way home. She happened to be passing a public-house when two inebriated men came out, arguing loudly. "I dinna give a damn what anyone says," one of them shouted. "Cunninghame Graham is the best bloody mon in Scotland." This story greatly delighted my friend, and when I added as an afterthought, "From the mouths of babes and drunkards ye shall have the truth," he thanked me for the compliment.

The literary editor of a well-known London newspaper sent Don Roberto a travel book to review, but as—like many such—it was written from so "sensational" an angle that it amounted to fiction, he returned it to the editor with a short note saying: "Thy servant may be a dog, but certainly not a cur."

Another time, when a friend wrote to him and, in addressing the letter, placed a hyphen between Cunninghame and Graham, Don Roberto, in pointing out this slight error to his correspondent, added to his reply: "Is thy servant a dog that thou shouldst make a collar out of his name?"

If there was one man whose very name he despised and hated, it was Gladstone's. On one occasion when I mentioned the famous statesman to him, he said: "I sometimes wish I could believe in religion, for if I did I could be sure that Gladstone is in hell."

In Edinburgh, as the two of us were lunching in the Caledonian Hotel, an elderly American tourist came up to our table, and introduced himself as Mr. X. With his usual politeness, though slightly annoyed by this unexpected intrusion of a stranger, Don Roberto said that he had not the honour of knowing him. "Why Mr. Graham, surely you remember meeting me in Tangier, some thirty years ago. You tried to sell me your horse when you were about to return home." "Oh, yes," Don Roberto answered, quickly, and visibly excited. "I remember quite well. He was a wall-eyed white, without a blemish, and quite easy to handle, provided you used a Moorish bit. You do not impress me as being nervous. Why didn't you buy him?"

When, after a few remarks about the beauties of Scotland, the American retired, Don Roberto turned to me and said: "Oh, yes, I remember this man now. He doesn't know a good horse when he sees one. How time flies!"

A few years ago my friend was in an unusual controversy which caused quite a stir—and not a little bad feeling—in artistic circles. Some time before this storm in a tea-cup broke out, he had commissioned a well-known artist to make a portrait of one of his Argentine mustangs. As a pleasant surprise the painter included Don Roberto into the picture, painting him, chiefly, from memory, standing near the horse's head with a thick tree-trunk as a background.

Don Roberto—who was rather vain in matters concerning personal appearance and pictures or photographs of himself —did not like the figure, but as he did not wish to offend the artist, he said nothing about it, and bought the picture.

However, before hanging it up in his London home, he carefully painted himself out. Several years had passed when, whilst he was in Scotland, he received a letter from the artist who desired the loan of the picture for an exhibition.

Not remembering about the painting-out, Don Roberto immediately wrote to his housekeeper in London, giving her instructions to send the picture to a certain art gallery. Unfortunately, only when the echoes of the ensuing storm of indignation reached him he remembered what he had done to the picture, years before, a "sacrilege" for which the artist never forgave him.

Occasionally Don Roberto was troubled with indigestion. Whenever he consulted his doctor about it, he always said before leaving: "Ah well! It's Providence, I suppose."

One day, when he met his doctor at a party, and he asked how his digestion behaved, Don Roberto answered: "Oh, splendidly; in fact Providence must be taking a holiday."

Once, whilst discussing some subject with a number of friends, he amazed me by exclaiming as a final remark: "Oh well, I fully realise that I am an inverted snob!"

He was very fond of anecdotes of which he had an inexhaustible repertoire. Among the favourites he had probably heard when he was in Texas were the following which he often told with rare gusto.

"One day two cowboys met in a saloon. 'Say, Elmer, goin' to the lynching?' one said, wiping his mouth with the back of his hand. When the other had spat out tobacco juice, he answered with a slow, south-western drawl: 'Hell, no; the greaser they're goin' to hang was no friend o mine!' "

The other story was about a Texan who had ridden to a distant village to be married. Very late in the evening he was seen returning to the ranch, riding alone, and when his friends asked him where the bride was, he replied: "Wal, the weddin' was grand, but just about half-way back home my mustang put a foot into a gopher hole, poor Lizzie fell off an' broke a leg, so I had to shoot her."

Among the scores of Scotch stories he would tell, one after the other, he was very fond of the following:

A Scotch farmer—who owned a property round one of the lochs—proposed to make a tour of his farms, so he told his bailiff, Donald, to take provisions in the boat. When this was done, he asked: "Well, Donald, and what have you got?" "Twelve bottles of whisky and a loaf of bread," was the reply, that made the farmer exclaim: "And what in the name of Gawd, Donald, will you be doing with all that bread?" Don Roberto was a keen observer of men, and a great mimic. Thanks to his knowledge of languages, and his perfect understanding of national characteristics, he could tell stories as a Spaniard, an Italian, a Scotsman or a Frenchman would.

His friend, the late Mr. Edward Garnett, told me that once, when Don Roberto was annoyed with a Russian sculptor (who in a mean manner tried to take advantage of his generosity), he really lost his temper, and that in giving the sculptor a piece of his mind, he spoke in broad Scottish dialect.

Often, when I was with him, and he was annoyed with something, I heard him mumble to himself in Spanish, using the kind of language gauchos resort to when a horse gives trouble.

Sometimes, at night, when the two of us sat together near the fire in his study, we chatted for hours about far-away lands, men and horses we had known. One night he told me that since Hudson's death he had not met anyone with whom he could discuss his favourite subjects, until we became friends.

One of his pet reminiscences was about a certain retired

English admiral who, every winter, went to Spain where he had bought a property. He was a great favourite with the villagers; but when, on returning one winter, he brought an English mistress with him, the Spanish peasants were most indignant and felt so hurt that they appealed to Don Roberto who happened to be there.

"Surely our señoritas are good enough for the admiral," they said indignantly, "and there's no need to import foreigners."

Driving through the beautiful Scottish country with my friend was a joy and an education, for he always pointed out famous and little known landmarks and places and gave many historical details one would not find in books.

Before we started on journeys which were to take us near, or past, the Lake of Menteith, he always went into the garden where he plucked bunches of flowers from the plants Gabrielle herself had planted. Arriving at the lake, the boatman would take us to the island of Inchmahome where, in the ruined priory, my friend laid the flowers on his wife's grave. Having done this, he sat down at the foot of the flat tombstone, lighted one of the black Brazilian cigarettes he always smoked, and in silence puffed away until it was finished. During my first two or three visits to the grave, I always left him alone, but the next time we arrived at the island, he asked me to stay with him, and, like himself, to smoke. After a while, as we walked out of the green-carpeted ruin, he told me that, shortly before his wife died, she had asked him to smoke a cigarette whenever he visited her grave.

The shortest road from Dumbarton to the lake passes through Gartmore. I noticed that, whenever we made the journey, the chauffeur drove us over one or the other of two much longer routes, and when I asked him why he did this, he answered (fortunately without my friend hearing it), that he had instructions never to take the short Gartmore road.

From the day Don Roberto had sold the old family property, he only visited Gartmore village once. This was on the occasion of the Rev. McLean's ministerial jubilee in 1914, when the old "laird" travelled especially from London to Scotland to be present at the function. On that occasion he made a happy speech, full of intimate and kindly memories of Gartmore and his old friend and minister.

Although he took no active interest in matters concerning any Church or religious creed, he liberally subscribed to charities organised by religious bodies. For thirty-four years he always attended the Annual Bazaar which the Mother Superior and the Sisters of St. Saviour's Priory, Haggerston, gave in London. If ever he was unable to attend personally, he never failed to give a cheque towards the bazaar, and when his mother died he always—in addition to his own contribution—gave the sum she had subscribed every year.

Once he wrote: "Faith, it is said, consists of the belief in something that we know to be untrue."

About death, he said: "Death, we are told on good authority, is the reward of sin, a saying that is discounted as an apophthegm, as it is also the reward of virtue, however rigorous."

On many occasions I noticed that my friend enjoyed sadness and took a mournful delight in watching the beauty of decay. He was interested in Art, and often took me to the Glasgow Gallery where, among many priceless works by old and new masters, is a full-length portrait of him, painted some forty years ago, by his friend Sir John Lavery. Whilst showing me the cathedral in the same city, we approached the choir which is partitioned off. He was just about to open the door when a verger came up to him to say that a service was being held inside. Probably due to absent-mindedness, Don Roberto did not hear what the man said, and he was just about to open the door when the verger—who had recognised the visitor—repeated: "Excuse me, Mr. Graham, there is a service on inside, but if you wish, you may go in." Stepping back a pace, quickly, and at the same time raising both his hands with a gesture of horror, Don Roberto exclaimed in a loud whisper: "God forbid, we might be saved!" In suppressing laughter the verger's now red face was a rare study. Emerging into the open, I jokingly referred to the incident but, to my surprise Don Roberto did not even know what he had said inside the cathedral. He had made that remark to the verger without realising it, but heartily laughed with me later.

Until he sold Gartmore, he was the "baron" of Buchlyvie, a small village in Stirlingshire, where he often visited farmers and old tenants whose friendship he greatly treasured.

Outside the church-hall in Buchlyvie Don Roberto made his first public speech, shortly after his return from Texas and Mexico, when he began to take an active interest in politics.

At one time the villagers had a little verse which my friend often recited to me as we drove through the little place.

> "Baron of Buchlyvie
> May the foul fiend rive ye
> For biggin' sic' a toon
> Where there's neither man's meat
> Or horse meat
> Or a stool to sit doon."

Whilst having tea in a drawing-room, a group of people were discussing Don Roberto. Most of them maintained that, in essence, his character was typically Scottish. As I did not agree, I went to the corner where he was conversing with the host, and asked him to come over to my group and to give his opinion about himself. Among other things he said: "I believe that in this case the minority of one is right, for, unless I do not know even a little about myself, I have always felt that my outlook on most things in life has been, and is, Spanish."

For many years a woman, who came from the islands in the North of Scotland, was his housekeeper at "Ardoch." Despite the fact that, with old age, she developed a very bad temper and with it an ever-increasing thirst, and was of less than no use in the household, he kept her on and continued to pay her the full salary she had earned in the past. (When, on rare occasions, she made an expedition to the upper floor of the house, two maids had to push her up the stairs.) This money she spent, chiefly, on drink. Whenever a bottle of anything alcoholic was left in the dining-room, it was always empty at night. More than once the housekeeper came tottering into the study to bid us "good-night," and when, after a great deal of almost incomprehensible conversation and tittering—to which Don Roberto listened patiently—she finally waddled out, he sadly shook his head and said, with a waving gesture of one hand: "Poor thing! it's the last pleasure left in her life. Ah well, *allá ella.*" (Spanish, meaning "That's her business.")

He treated his servants with a politeness and consideration I have never seen in any other man. His old housekeeper in London was like a confidential private secretary. She filed all his letters, kept his records, and not infrequently was consulted when he sought advice, even on private matters. He never gave servants orders; but, instead, asked them if they would be so good as to do this or that. Often, when he thought he was asking for too much in making some request, I heard him say in a kindly tone of voice: "Oh, I'm sorry. Please don't bother, I'll do it myself." A fine object lesson he could have taught all those people who complain

about the modern "servant problem," which they themselves
have created for reasons that are obvious to anyone who
knows that self-respect firstly manifests itself in the treatment
of our fellow-men who are weaker than ourselves; "weaker"
in our material world meaning "poorer."

His home in Scotland was a veritable museum. South
American horse-gear, worked in silver and raw hide, whips,
spurs and all sorts of interesting souvenirs and trophies hung
on the walls. In some of the rooms hung beautiful paintings
of ancestors and landscapes, a number of which were the
work of old masters. All this, together with exquisite old
period furniture, gave the house an atmosphere all its own.
"Ardoch," in a sense, was his fortress into which he allowed
but few people to penetrate. Even some of his most intimate
friends of many years were never asked inside the high stone
walls that surrounded the property.

A gurgling and bubbling "burn" runs through the garden,
and when, especially after a spell of rainy weather, it carries
much water, the pleasant music produced by two or three
cascades is heard in the house.

The sanctum sanctorum was the study, filled with masses
of old books, many of which were Spanish, French, Italian
or Portuguese, etc.

If ever we discussed a certain book, and we disagreed on
a point, my host would jump up from his chair, hurry to a
shelf, at once find the book, open the right page, and almost
invariably prove that he was right, even though, perhaps,
he had not read the particular book for forty years or more.

Leafing through the volumes in his library one could at
once tell that he had read all of them carefully, for whenever
he came to a passage he liked, he pencilled his old South
American horse-brand in the margin opposite.

When, after his death, he left all his most valuable books
to the London Library, the directors were puzzled by these

strange hieroglyphics, the meaning of which, however, I explained to them.

Opening his book, *The Conquest of the River Plate*, I saw the following inscription, written in Don Roberto's peculiar and almost illegible scrawl:

> "To my dear mother who read all the proofs, and corrected and advised generally to the great profit of the book.
>
> "From her affectionate son,
>
> "R. B. CUNNINGHAME GRAHAM. 1924."

There was no electric light at "Ardoch," but, instead, candles which, in their old-fashioned candlesticks with quaint shades, added greatly to the atmosphere of the house. Whenever we sat together at night, I had to rise, at regular intervals, to lower the shades. Often we only went to bed when the last remaining bits of wick began to flicker and threatened to fall into the small cups full of molten grease: all that remained of what had been candles.

He never bothered about personal comforts; in fact, he gave one the impression that he avoided them. Even when he was over eighty years of age, he could squat on a low stool, like a gaucho, and remain in this cramped position for an hour or more, without, apparently, feeling the least discomfort. The old gaucho in him showed in many ways. Although he was always immaculately dressed, he wore a wide Argentine belt, made of leather and with two or three pockets and a holster for a revolver which, not infrequently was stuck into it. However, under his coat, this favourite old belt (or *rastra*) of his was invisible, and therefore only a few of his intimate friends knew that he wore it.

Although he was probably the finest horseman in England in his day, he never hunted, and despite the fact that among the trophies in his house there were many rifles and other fire-arms, he never shot birds or animals, for he detested this form of sport. The cutting down of a tree, or even a plant, seemed to hurt him as much as if one of his fingers were being chopped off, and therefore his well-tended garden was a kind of beautiful wilderness in which everything had a history and was of sentimental value to him.

Horses, of course, were his greatest passion, but he loved all animals and never disturbed them, unless it was absolutely necessary. In London he kept no dogs, but his Scottish home was never without one. Under a tree in his garden were the graves of several terriers he had owned. The places where they were buried are marked with small plain stone blocks on which are carved the names of his old pets.

He never regretted the many vain battles he had fought; in fact, he once told me that the only real regret he had in life was that, during his imprisonment at Pentonville, he had stupidly behaved so well that he had not qualified for the tread-mill.

One of his last sorties was when, in 1935, he stood as a Scottish Nationalist for the Lord Rectorship of Glasgow University. Accepting an invitation extended to me by the students, I travelled from London to Scotland to speak in favour of my friend who, however, was defeated. Undoubtedly, in voting for another candidate, the students missed hearing what would have been the most memorable address in the history of the university. Perhaps, in years to come they will realise this, and will regret having missed their last opportunity to honour their university, as well as Don Roberto, one of Scotland's greatest sons.

About his political career he told me that it has amounted to ploughing sand, and that the only good thing he had achieved during the six years he was in the House of Commons, was, perhaps, having brought about better conditions among the miserable chain-makers of Cradley Heath.

Referring to the Socialist Party he told me that it had become semi-bourgeois, and that he strongly objected to a certain infiltration of social climbers. "I do not object to any man taking a title," he said, "but it makes the Socialist Party ridiculous. . . . The Socialist Party must, in its essence, be revolutionary. . . . There will always be Conservatives, for conservatism is an attitude of mind. . . . I see no logical halting-place between Conservatives and Communists; all other parties will be ground out between the two."

About kings and titles he told me: "I have never been opposed to good kings, but I am against all this degrading nonsense of exalting them into divinities. Titles come to most men by inheritance, after they have given themselves the trouble to be born. Dignities, titles and estates have come to many a slobbering fool, with piping eunuch's voice, weak knees and weaker mind."

In all his life, Don Roberto never wore a kilt, for he maintained that, being a low-lander, this would be ridiculous. According to him, only highlanders have a traditional right to wearing the kilt which, in modern times, has become a favourite holiday garment among certain English tourists who can trace a little Scottish blood in their veins.

In the autumn of 1935, at the unveiling of the Neil Munro Memorial near Inverary, out in the rugged country, on a bold prominence in a glen, many kilted men and numerous ladies assembled. In this picturesque setting, scholarly essays on Neil Munro's literary work were read, and speeches were delivered, but to the general disappointment the proceedings were about to close, almost without a reference to Neil Munro —the man—when one of the organisers sensed that something was lacking, and, apparently, as an afterthought, asked Don Roberto if he would speak . . . and speak he did.

Standing on that rocky knoll, with the wind blowing

through his spreading silvery hair, he made an unforgettable picture. With his gift for saying spontaneously the right thing at the right time he—in a ringing voice that was heard as none of the other speakers' had been—filled the gap that all had felt. By eloquent phrases, and freedom of gesture, he held his audience as if spell-bound and, after his inspired words, all felt that the purpose of the day's proceedings had been fulfilled.

He loved to wander through gardens and parks, admiring plants, flowers, shrubs and trees, the popular and scientific names of all of which he knew. When I asked him when and where on earth he had learned them, his laconic reply was: "Oh, I have always taken an interest in botany, and have read a number of books on this fascinating subject."

Thanks to his extraordinary memory, not only did he know the names of the plants, trees and shrubs, but, if they were of foreign origin, he knew the part of the world where they had originally come from, who had first introduced them into Great Britain, and the date when this had been done.

In his habits he was very regular. He rose at 8 a.m., and after breakfast settled down to reading through newspapers. Being an amazingly fast reader this took him about half an hour, and then he dealt with his correspondence which was very heavy. Literary men and women from all parts of the world wrote to him, and often I almost wondered if there was anybody of importance alive he did not know, or correspond with. Whenever he was tired he went in front of the house where he threw an Argentine raw-hide lasso, or practised spinning a rope in Mexican style. At 11 o'clock he never missed drinking a glass of sherry or vermouth, and then returned to his work. After the midday meal he always slept a short *siesta*, usually sitting in his favourite chair in the study near the fireplace. During afternoons, unless he went for a drive by car, he strolled round the garden or went for a brisk walk along the banks of the Clyde, or up to the hills where his farms were situated.

Although he was of slight—though wiry—build, he had powerful hands and wrists. He was very fond of demonstrating the strength in his hands and arms which was, indeed, remarkable. One of his favourite tricks was to lift a heavy chair, holding it by the top of the back, between his thumbs and first fingers, and then raising it slowly, with fully extended arms, until it was level with his chin. This I have often seen him repeat several times. Again, he took a long Moorish rifle, and placing the end of its muzzle between the first and middle fingers of either of his hands, he would raise it to a horizontal position. Many years ago, when Don Roberto met the famous Sandow—who at the time amazed everybody in London with his feats of strength—he showed him how to tear two packs of cards, a trick Sandow soon increased to three.

Conversing with one of the tenants, he told me that in shaking hands with the "laird," he felt prouder than if he were doing this with a king.

Most of Don Roberto's books were written at night. Had it not been for his housekeepers, both in London and in Scotland, he would often have worked until daybreak; but whenever they knew that he was writing they kept an eye on him, and at about 2 a.m. tapped at his door to tell him that it was high time he retired; but often they had to do this several times before he smilingly gave in.

About his own achievements he was so modest that it was difficult to make him talk about them, and when, on rare occasions, one succeeded, he invariably changed the conversation and spoke in glowing terms about some other person whom he admired.

Like all human beings, he had his weaknesses and small failings, on which narrow minds always fix, not recognising the genius and big qualities in a man. Though he dressed to perfection, and his gestures were elegant, they were always natural to him, and therefore not extravagant, excepting, sometimes, when he spoke in public. Everything he did was graceful, though not in the least degree effeminate, even when he flicked away imaginary flecks of dust from his clothes. He was often described as the last of the Elizabethans, for with his handsome patrician exterior, he suggested a courtier of the Raleigh period. Probably no man has ever been so often painted and modelled as he, for no artist could see him without longing to have him as a model. It is interesting to note that when Solomon J. Solomon was commissioned to paint Sir Walter Raleigh, to be placed in the House of Commons, he could nowhere find a suitable model. Suddenly he remembered Don Roberto who, after some persuasion, sat for the artist, and in this way it came about that the picture of Raleigh which adorns a wall in the House of Commons is, in reality, a portrait of Don Roberto, dressed in Elizabethan clothes which suit him to perfection.

People who did not know him well, often mistook his delightful and almost child-like vanity for pride. He could not pass a mirror without looking at himself. More than once I have seen him smile at his own weakness which, in reality was a kindness to his friends. He never cared an atom if people watched him pass his fingers through his abundant crop of white hair and spread it out like an aureole. His poses were so natural to him that on better acquaintance with the man they became part of him. His vanity was entirely exterior and superficial, for his inward self was simplicity, sincerity, generosity and sympathy, and, therefore, in spite of his almost coquettish mannerisms, which piqued narrow and envious minds, he loathed humbug and snobbery. His life and works bear ample testimony to this. Whatever his minor failings were, none of them hurt or injured anyone but himself, and this only in the eyes of petty narrow-minded people who judge their superior fellow-men by trivialities that really give spice to life.

When he was in London, he rarely missed his daily ride. Rotten Row again became "Route du Roi" when, slower than any other rider could, he cantered along it, usually accompanied by a friend. Whilst inspecting a stud farm, and the horses were being paraded before him, he remarked to his host that, at the age of eighty, he still preferred to mount without using the stirrup, but leaping on as the gauchos do. When the host remarked that Don Roberto surely was too old to do this, it tickled his delightful vanity, and so, without hesitating for a moment, he sprang on the animal with the agility of a cat. The horse was so startled that it reared and bucked, but Don Roberto, though he was riding bare-backed, soon calmed it in a most remarkable manner.

In a street, near his home in London, he frequently stopped to give sugar to a white shaggy-haired Iceland pony which pulled a greengrocer's cart. One day whilst on his way to visit some friends, he saw the pony being led along by its owner. Wondering where the man was going with the animal, he stopped him to inquire, and when he heard that, owing to old age, he had sold the pony for a pound, to be exported for slaughter in Belgium, Don Roberto promptly gave the greengrocer two pounds and a good "tip," and asked him to take the animal to the farm near London where he kept his old equine pensioners. As I am writing this "Billy," the Iceland pony, is still happily grazing there, together with "Rejo" and "Chajá," the two Argentine mustangs, all of which were provided for in Don Roberto's will.

Once, whilst walking in Hyde Park, he stopped to talk to a well-known circus rider who was exercising his horse. Suddenly the animal reared and threw itself over back-

"THE FENCER"
(Don Roberto, shortly after his return from Mexico and Texas.)
[*A Portrait by Sir William Rothenstein*

wards, falling on the rider who, apparently, was badly hurt. Catching the horse, Don Roberto leapt into the saddle and dashed off to advise the mounted policeman who is always on duty near Hyde Park Corner. Fortunately the circus-rider was only shaken and bruised, and his horse did not repeat the dangerous trick while Don Roberto rode him.

At the age of eighty-three, when he posed for a well-known Viennese sculptor who was working at an equestrian statuette of him, he said that he could easily ride into the studio. As the sculptor seemed to doubt this, Don Roberto immediately proceeded to prove what he had said, and when I asked him why on earth he risked breaking his neck for the sheer fun of it, he answered that it was much easier to die when old than when young.

One of the few occasions when I saw him thoroughly annoyed was when a book of reminiscences by the late Arnold Bennett was published. In this book—many parts of which had to be suppressed because they were libellous—the writer referred to an uncomplimentary remark Don Roberto was supposed to have made to him about Mr. Macdonald who, at the time when the book in question appeared, was Prime Minister.

> "You can't blame a man for being low-bred and low-born," Don Roberto thundered, "but when a man, like Bennett, had this misfortune, you can, and must, blame him for having remained low all his life!"

According to my friend, he only met Arnold Bennett twice. The first meeting took place in Hyde Park whilst Don Roberto was riding. During the ensuing conversation, which lasted but a few moments, his horse tried to bite Bennett. "When my horse attempts to bite a man, I have no use for him," was his remark about this meeting which only lasted about a minute.

The next time the two men met was in a London street during a heavy rain-storm. On that occasion, in addition to a formal greeting, Don Roberto made a remark about the weather, and then hurried on.

Wishing to apologise for what was published in Arnold Bennett's book about Mr. Macdonald, Don Roberto decided to go to No. 10, Downing Street, and as he asked me to accompany him, we went together. The Prime Minister was most charming and would not even listen to an apology which, he said, was quite unnecessary from an old friend whom he greatly admired. After a pleasant conversation which lasted over half an hour, Mr. Macdonald—although he looked worn-out and tired owing to overwork, and despite the fact that masses of documents were piled on the desk, awaiting his attention—insisted on accompanying us down the staircase, and bidding us "au revoir" at the door.

Don Roberto had, as it were, water-tight compartments, and all his friends he pigeon-holed, according to their qualities and merits, as he saw them. By "water-tight compartments" I mean that there were subjects he would never discuss with friends, or even with members of his family. If ever he was asked a question—usually of a private nature—he did not like, he cleverly evaded answering it, so definitely and with such politeness that the questioner realised that he had attempted to step on forbidden ground, and, accordingly, held his peace.

Don Roberto seemed to have an aversion to broadcasting. When, in my presence, an official of the B.B.C. asked him to broadcast, he refused to do so, even though he was offered to speak on any subject he liked, and without notes. When he spoke in public he never made use of a loud-speaker. On one occasion, at a banquet, when a microphone was placed before him, he waved it away, exclaiming in a loud voice: "Please take this ugly contraption away!" Although the acoustics were bad, every word he spoke could be heard in all parts of the banqueting hall.

About him one could not say that he merely *came into* a room. He *entered*. Looking at him one felt that the only things missing were a cloak, an Elizabethan ruff and a sword. Conversation with him was an art, and due to this, together with his exquisite manners and striking appearance, he dominated the company wherever he went.

Van Dyck's portrait of King Charles I so resembles him that one might think it was the same man. This likeness is all the more remarkable because some antiquarians maintain that he was a direct descendant of this king, as we have seen in the opening chapter.

Many people regarded him as quixotic. Rightly understood, this is a great compliment, for Don Quixote is probably the most perfect gentleman in literature. In Don Roberto were combined the finest characteristics of Don Quixote, the pictures of whom he strikingly resembled as he grew old. However, to compare him with the Knight of La Mancha is wrong, for, as we have seen, he was not a mere tilter at windmills. Like Don Quixote, his writings console us in sadness, as tobacco does hunger; they quench our thirst both of body and soul. Perhaps, like Cervantes' immortal Knight of the "triste figura," his "singular" ideas amused some people and even made them laugh, as we laughed at Don Quixote in our childhood. However, with ripening years, we often come to venerate that which, in youth, provoked our merriment, in the same way in which we come to laugh at much we venerated early in our lives. Because he owned the ruined castle of the Grahams on the island of Inchtalla in Scotland, he once referred to himself as "Hidalgo de Gotera" which, in English, means hidalgo of the dripping and leaky house.

In 1934, for the first time in his life, he visited the East when he went to Ceylon; and during the following English winter he made a journey to South Africa where he was given enthusiastic receptions wherever he went.

The fact that he was better known in South America, Spain and in other parts of the world than in England was probably due to the fact that, at home, he never sought the limelight and that those who knew him superficially thought him to be exotic, and, above all, because those who remembered him as a Member of Parliament, never forgave him for having fought for the underdogs. The "Battle of Trafalgar Square," and his subsequent imprisonment were never entirely forgotten by those who envied him for the place he could have taken in society, had he chosen the easy path that was open to him, instead of mixing with "those socialists" who, on the other hand, instinctively felt that Robert Bontine Cunninghame Graham—the aristocrat par excellence—was not one of them.

The following letter clearly shows his attitude towards public recognition.

In 1934, a committee of business men, lawyers, bankers and literary men thought of organising a public dinner, representative of Scotland, in Don Roberto's honour. On being approached about it, he wrote:

". . . It is indeed a great compliment that my friends should wish to give me a dinner. I thoroughly appreciate this kindness. However, all my life, I have avoided public recognition of anything I may (or may not), have done. Moreover, I cannot see that I deserve any recognition of the kind. Will you be so very kind as to convey to the Committee my best thanks for the honour they do me in proposing to give me a public dinner. I am as 'capable of being flattered' as any one, and certainly the proposal is most flattering, and I value it highly, as a token of the good wishes of my friends. . . ."

"Don Roberto"
(R. B. Cunninghame Graham)   With apologies to Sir John Lavery, R.A.
                                          A. F. Tschiffely. 1935.

CARICATURE BY TSCHIFFELY

CHAPTER XIX

IN the early autumn, 1935, when I spent a delightful month with my friend at "Ardoch," I noticed, for the first time, that his health was beginning to fail. Despite his doctor's frequent warnings not to strain his heart, the old warrior defied nature, and acted like a strong young man of thirty. When he went for rambles up the hills, he walked so briskly that a person had to be very fit to follow him, and whenever his heart gave trouble, he said indigestion bothered him. Occasionally, when he had attacks of giddiness, he tried to shake them off by going for walks, throwing his lasso, spinning a rope, or by performing feats of strength. One evening, on seeing the first autumn crocuses appear under a tree in his garden, he stood and looked at them for some time, and then, turning to me, said, sadly shaking his head: "There comes a time in a man's life when he does not like to see these flowers appear."

On returning to London, I noticed that he but rarely rode in Hyde Park, and when, to my surprise, he sent his horse out to the farm where his other pensioners were kept, and I asked him if he had given up riding, he answered, obviously embarrassed: "Oh, no . . . I find it is rather expensive to keep a horse in London, and, after all, he is much happier out in the open than in a stuffy stable in the city."

Although I knew only too well that these were the excuses of a man who refused to admit weakness, I pretended not to have guessed the truth, and whilst inwardly cursing myself for having asked so delicate a question, I said that he had done the right thing. Never again after this did either of us refer to riding in the Park.

Some time later, coming out of the Ritz Hotel where he had entertained Mr. H. G. Wells, Mrs. Dummett, myself and one or two other friends to lunch, he surprised me by saying that he had decided to return to South America during the winter. "This is probably my last chance to ride with the gauchos," he said, and then continued: "Ever since I first heard of your ride through the three Americas, I have had one great desire . . . to see your two horses. Well, I am going out to see them, so when the time comes, fill a little bag with oats, and I shall hand them over, personally, as a little greeting from you." However, shortly after having made this announcement, he told me that a visit to the Argentine would be too tiring at his age, and that, there-fore, he had decided only to go as far as Rio de Janeiro in Brazil. A few days before Christmas, 1935, excited like a schoolboy before a vacation, he told me that he had changed his mind, and that, positively, he was going back to the pampas.

As usual, ever since I had met him, I spent Christmas with him and Mrs. Dummett. When my wife presented him with a big silk scarf to use among the gauchos, he immediately went to a mirror to try on the gift, looking at himself with obvious delight that was fully justified, for if ever a scarf suited a rider of the plains, this man was Don Roberto.

At the time, his last book *Mirages* was in the printers' hands. I have often wondered what prompted him to write in it:

"Nothing is more like life than is a mirage, vague, fleeing, apparently stable, and yet impossible to grasp and satisfy yourself that it is your own, to use, enjoy, and to dispose of to your heirs. . . . Unlike the billowing

THE LAST EQUESTRIAN PORTRAIT TAKEN IN LONDON

mists of northern climates, the mirage had not its terrifying aspect, nor seems to harbour in its recesses something
hostile to mankind. Yet it is just as dangerous, coming
with all the graces of a serpent of old Nile. . . .

"So it may well be after all that the world of the
mirage is the real world, and that the world we live in
is a mirage. Mankind has always loved to be deceived,
to hug illusions to its heart, to fight for them and to
commit its direct follies in the name of common sense. . . .
When, therefore, the mirage spreads its lake before you,
do not allow your horse to put his foot in it or it will
vanish from your sight. Behind the mantling vapour rise
castles, towers, cathedrals. . . . All these exist in the
mind's eye, the only field of vision where there is no
astigmatism. Rein up your horse, before his feet destroy
and bring them back again to earth. . . . Why peer
behind the veil to see life's desert all befouled? . . . At
any cost preserve your mirage intact and beautiful. If
riding in the desert you behold it slowly taking shape,
turn sideways in your saddle, pouring a libation of tobacco
smoke towards your Mecca and muttering a prayer."

For some weeks I had been working at an omnibus collection of Don Roberto's most representative short stories and
sketches. Unknown to me, my friend wrote a preface to this
book (published under the title of *Rodeo*, early in 1936),
and on the day before he sailed for South America, he called
at the offices of the publishers and placed his preface on
Mr. Charles Evans's desk. Contrary to the belief of some
critics, the selection of the stories and sketches was entirely
made by myself, with the exception of *Tschiffely's Ride*,
which Don Roberto insisted on having in the book. *Rodeo*
is curious and unconventional for several reasons. Firstly,
because a story about myself is included, secondly, because it

is dedicated to me, although I wrote the introduction, and, thirdly, because Don Roberto, in writing the preface, seemed to sense that his end was near, for in addressing the "incurious reader," he wrote:

"Just as a drowning man is said—though I do not believe it—in one brief moment to review his whole past life, I have perforce to write an introduction, to crimes against the English language, errors in taste, and faults in grammar committed over a period of forty years.

"Better, far better, to find oneself swept down a flooded river, striving to keep clear of one's horse's whirling feet, half choked, and clutching to his mane, than to take pen in hand to speak of things that any man left with a shred of self-respect would like to bury in oblivion.

"Because, you see, incurious reader, and give thanks to Allah that you are incurious, what I have written, I have written, and whether it is true or not, about the drowning man, it is the case, without a doubt, when one surveys an Omnium Gatherum, Hotch-Potch, Sea-Pie or Salmagundi—call it what you will—of one's writings. *Madonna Mia!* How could I have written that! My excuse I hope was youth, the period of omniscience. But still, I might have finished all those sentences; not broken off to moralise right in the middle of the tale; split less infinitives; and remembered those rules of grammar that I have disregarded, as freely as a democratic leader tramps on the rights of the poor taxables who put him in power. . . . When, wrapped in fragrant contemplation of my travels, I mean through life, not merely of the Marco Poloesque peregrinations through foreign lands, I look at the great pile of proofs before me with a feeling of amazement, for they rise up and seem to say, was this really your handiwork? . . . Then turning once more to

my proofs, I seem to wander in a cemetery full of tomb-
stones that Time raises for dead souls.

"I recognise friends that once were alive in the way
that one recognises names of friends upon the headstones
in an old-world country churchyard, half buried in lush
grass. . . . All is well with the souls who sleep so soundly,
lulled by the whispering trees. It may be that they are
all as dead as are their bodies that once sheltered them,
enabling them to live. That I leave to greater and more
learned clerks to comment on, and leave the question
still unanswered, after their use and wont. . . ."

On the 18th of January, 1936, I went to see Don Roberto
depart at Paddington Station. As usual when he went
abroad, Mrs. Dummett and her sister, Miss Louisa Miéville,
were with him. I found my friend in great spirits, though
somewhat excited, and when I handed to him a tiny bag of
oats, to be given to my two horses in the Argentine, he put
it into his handbag as if it were a priceless gem. His niece,
Lady Brooke, and Captain A. Gyde, representing Messrs.
William Heinemann, the publishers, had come to bid Don
Roberto *bon voyage*, but as they had to hurry away before the
train started, I was left alone on the platform, chatting with
my friend and his two travelling companions. When, at
last, all the passengers were on board the train, and the
guard blew his whistle and waved a green flag, giving the
engine-driver the signal to start, I shook hands with Don
Roberto.

Somehow I sensed that this would be the last time that
I would see his flowing shock of silvery-white hair, and that
I would never again shake his strong and friendly hand; the
hand which was equally dextrous with the reins, the *lazo*,
the revolver and the sword as it had been with the pen, the
hand that had helped the fallen to rise and had done many

noble deeds which, owing to Don Roberto's modesty, I am unable to record in this book.

For a few moments I walked beside the slowly moving train, and when it picked up speed and I could no longer follow it, my friend—who was leaning out of the window of his compartment—shouted a last *"A Dios!"* to me. Then, until the train was out of the station and disappeared round a curve, I saw him at the window, one hand raised like an Indian chief of old bidding his last farewell.

In the meantime the sun had hidden behind dark clouds, and shortly after I left the station it began to rain in torrents. In the afternoon a thick fog descended upon London, and towards evening this was followed by a heavy snowfall. Thus, on the 16th of January, 1936, Don Roberto departed, cheerfully, though obviously aware that the end was near. The closing chapter of his life was to be as miraculous as his existence in this world had been, for, like a comet, he was destined to set, bright and luminous as ever, far beyond the horizon.

On the journey to Rio de Janeiro, he began to lose weight at an alarming rate, but although this worried his companions, they pretended not to notice it. His plans were to stay in Petropolis (Brazil), for a few days, and then to proceed south, to Buenos Aires. From Petropolis he wrote several letters to me. In one he said that he had again changed his mind, and that he was definitely not going to Buenos Aires, fearing that he would not be able to stand the strain of the many receptions that had been planned for him by his host of admirers in the Argentine.

On the 14th February he sent me a cable saying: "Starting half hour Rio to catch boat for Buenos Aires. *Palmaditas pingos.*"*

Shortly before his final decision to proceed to the Argentine,

* Caresses horses.

430

he startled Mrs. Dummett by asking her to promise to take his body to Scotland, should anything happen to him.

Towards the end of February he arrived in Buenos Aires where he was given a wonderful reception. Although he was only a shadow of his former self, and getting very weak, he refused to admit it, and only supreme will-power kept him alive.

On leaving the docks, the car, he and an Argentine friend were travelling in, stopped near a marine policeman. When he saw Don Roberto's face and flowing hair, he asked a bystander: "Is this *caballero* a poet?" "A poet and a gaucho," answered the man who had recognised the visitor in the car; but hardly had these words left his lips than Don Roberto —who had overheard the conversation—broke in, laughing merrily: "Oh, more gaucho than poet."

In the same fashion as instinct calls migratory birds north or south, something had stirred Don Roberto to return to the Pampa, for in his youth he had heard and comprehended the mysterious noises that rise from this desert of grass, and when he sensed that the end was near, he again heard, and obeyed, their call.

When he saw the modern city of Buenos Aires with its sky-scrapers, miles of docks, traffic and noise, he must have been sad, and probably had visions of the past.

Arriving at the hotel, reporters bombarded him with questions, all of which he answered patiently and politely, though he badly needed a rest. When asked what he was writing, he replied that he was just finishing a preface to Hudson's works, and when the reporter inquired: "And then?" Don Roberto looked out of the window for a few moments, and shrugging his shoulders, said: "Just the preface to my death."

At a reception given in his honour, everybody praised him, and when a friend asked him what he thought, his answer was:

"Although I know that I do not deserve all this flattery I like to hear it, and I feel like an ugly señorita in Seville, with her face hidden under a mantilla when a young man, on passing her, says: '*Adiós*, precious darling, blessed be your mother.' "

A servant who was sent to his hotel with a message returned home and told her mistress that she had seen the "caballero." "The caballero?" the lady asked, mystified. "Yes, the caballero," the servant said enthusiastically, "it could not have been anybody else, for he opened the door of the lift for me, and said: 'After you, please.' "

Whenever he had time, he wrote to me, and I could not help noticing that his strange hieroglyphics were becoming more and more shaky, though he wrote as cheerfully and interestingly as ever. A few days before he intended to go out into the pampas to visit my horses "Mancha" and "Gato" and to ride with the gauchos, he visited "Los Veintecinco Ombues,"* the house near Buenos Aires where his old friend W. H. Hudson was born in 1841. From a room in the modest abode, he wrote the following letter to Mr. Morley Roberts, who for many years had been one of Hudson's most intimate friends, and who later became his biographer:

"The House of the Twenty-Five Ombus.

"February 28.

"MY DEAR M——

"I have made many pilgrimages in my life, to Rome, to Santiago de Compostela and other places well known to the whole world.

"I have never been more impressed at any of these places than I am in this humble *rancho* with its wooden

* The Twenty-five Ombú Trees.

432

IN BUENOS AIRES, 1936

roof, its brick floors, its primitive doors and its air of aloofness from everything modern (*gracias á Dios*).

"It can have altered little since our great and beloved friend passed his boyhood here. The same tall thistles grow in the plain that flows all about the house, just as the sea flows about an atoll in the Pacific, almost as it were lapping at the foundations of the house.

"The same flocks of birds, *tijeretas*, *viuditas*, *bien-te-veos*, and *horneros* still haunt the trees which have grown up in the deserted *chacra*.

"The same stream, the same rivulet of which he writes in 'El Ombu' still runs between the house and the Monastery of Santo Domingo.

"Little I think has altered. Nature of course is resuming her sway; but three remain of the twenty-five ombus.

"All the plants that Hudson loved, fennel, evening primrose and the rest are here to mourn him.

"There is a chestnut horse, unfortunately a *mestizo*,* tied to a post in front of the house. It is, I think, waiting for Hudson to throw a sheepskin on its back and ride down to the *arroyo* to water it. You will understand; you are of the few who will understand in the way that the villagers in Cornwall understood when they cut upon the stone 'W. H. Hudson used to sit here.'

"We knew, appreciated and loved him and I have breathed your salutations to his spirit silently.

"Yours affect.,

"R. B. CUNNINGHAME GRAHAM.

"PS.—The man who brought me here is Dr. Fernando Pozzo, of Quilmes, the greatest lover and prophet of Hudson in the New World. By his kindness and that of his wife I have been able to make the pilgrimage."

---

* Mestizo: mustang crossed with thoroughbred.

On the 14th of March, he felt so unwell that a doctor had to be sent for. After an examination the diagnosis was: "bronchitis," and the patient was ordered to stay in bed and rest for a few days.

On the 16th of March, Don Roberto wrote his last letter to me. Too weak to write himself, he dictated the following which reached me three weeks after his death was announced in the London newspapers:

"MI QUERIDO AMIGO,

"Many thanks for your interesting letter. It finds me in bed with bronchitis. Unluckily I shall not be well enough to go to 'El Cardal,'* but Mancha and Gato are coming here to see me. I have just got *Mirages*. It makes a very nice little book, and the reproduction of my bust on the cover is excellent.

"The weather has been frightful here. I never remember such heat anywhere. It has now broken after two days of rain.

"We sail on the 26th on the *Almeda Star*.

"With best love,

"suyo aff*mo*.

"R. B. CUNNINGHAME GRAHAM."

Obviously he was very weak, for when, in signing the letter, he tried to place his characteristic rubric—or flourish, under the name, he could not finish it, and the nib stuck into the paper, blotching the page with ink.

Whilst lying in bed he received a copy of his last book, *Mirages*, in which he relates the story of "Charlie the Gaucho," an Englishman of good family who, after a stormy life in the pampas, spent some years at home, finally to return to South America to die with his boots on. I often wonder if

* "El Cardal," the ranch where my two horses are spending their old age.

WRITING TO MORLEY ROBERTS IN HUDSON'S BIRTHPLACE

HANDWRITING 1936.

435

the story about "Charlie the Gaucho" (whom he had known as a youth), made him decide that this was the right way to die with boots on, and on the old trails.

Sixteen years before, his friend, Joseph Conrad, had written to Don Roberto: ". . . May you ride, firm as ever in the saddle, to the very last moment, *et la lance toujours en arrêt*, against the Enemy you have defied all your life!"

And so it happened.

On the 19th of March, the invalid, feeling slightly better, insisted on motoring some twenty miles out of Buenos Aires to help a friend who was translating some of Hudson's works into Spanish. For three hours he worked incessantly, and when his friend—who happened to be a doctor—looked at him, he at once saw that he ran a high temperature. Immediately he was rushed back to the city. On the way he calmly said: "I feel the end has come, I am a dying man."

Arriving at the hotel he was so weak that he had to be undressed and lifted into his bed. When a specialist who had been hastily summoned, arrived, he stated that the case was a serious one and that two nurses would be required immediately. However, a difficulty arose, for Don Roberto's friends knew that he would object to this. After a short debate it was decided to send for the nurses, but to ask them to come dressed in ordinary clothes, and to pose as two of the specialist's friends.

When the first nurse entered the room, Don Roberto put his head back on his pillow and, laughing weakly, exclaimed: "Good God, imagine me with a nurse!" However, he did not protest, but when the night-nurse arrived and gave him an order in a tone of voice he considered to be impolite, he was so indignant that he sent for the specialist to whom he said that the nurse must go at once, for even though he was a dying man, he would take orders from no one, and much less would he tolerate incivility.

Accordingly, the offender was requested to leave, and her place was taken by an amusing Irish nurse with whom the invalid got on splendidly.

When an Argentine doctor came to the bedside, Don Roberto asked him a question which shows his incomparable gentlemanliness. Afraid that, in making certain remarks, he might shock the caller, he asked: "Sir, are you a church-goer?" "No," answered the doctor, and then, thinking the patient might be shocked at this, he added as an afterthought, "But I preserve the beliefs my mother taught me."

"Well, I do not," Don Roberto replied, "for long ago I have even discarded these. Some people need religion like a wall to lean against, but I have never needed it."

He spent a comfortable night, but next day, towards noon, suddenly took a turn for the worse. Still, he remained calm and chatted with his friends who had been called to the bedside. Having thanked them for all they had done for him, his speech gradually became incoherent, and within a few minutes he passed away peacefully. Thus, on the 20th day of March in the year 1936, Don Roberto died in Buenos Aires, aged nearly eighty-four years. Surely his memory will live amongst men, for he was a great patriot and cosmo-politan, a man in whose veins ran the blood of martyrs and heroes, a true aristocrat who had fearlessly done his duty for freedom and truth, a man who fought for the underdogs without the least hope of reward. With his passing on, the world lost one who was born to be an inheritor of unfulfilled renown, a man who—according to his own choice—never became a vulgar idol of the millions, a noble-minded warrior who will remain a living memory when most of our modern and, in many cases, almost indecently over-boosted popular heroes will have passed into oblivion.

An Argentine doctor who was with Don Roberto during the last days of his life said of him:

"I only saw greatness in him, never fear; not even in the most difficult moment . . . the moment of death."

In describing how Argentina said: "Good-bye" to Don Roberto, I can do no better than to reproduce parts of a long account published in the *Buenos Aires Herald*.

"For nearly twenty-four hours the body lay in state in the Casa del Teatro (formerly, the Cervantes Theatre), during which time a continual stream of persons filed reverently by, as a mark of homage to the great lover of Argentina. Among the distinguished visitors to pass the catafalque was the President of the Republic, the Minister of the Interior and the President of the Argentine Academy of Letters.

"In the early afternoon the British Consular authorities arrived and placed the official seal on the casket. While the metal casket contained in the polished coffin was being sealed, an Argentine gentleman approached the bier, and with his penknife scratched the following words on the metal surface:

'DON ROBERTO—CARIÑO Y ADMIRACIÓN DE LOS ARGENTINOS, BUENOS AIRES, MARZO 25, 1936.'

"Floral tributes, large and small, continued to pour in, and more and more persons entered the hall until no further room could be found inside, and then a crowd started to grow in the street.

"When Sir Nevile Meyrick Henderson, the British Ambassador, arrived, he stood in silent homage by the bier for a few minutes.

"The coffin was then carried by the Ambassador, a colonel representing the President of the Republic, and delegates of various literary organisations, to the entrance of the building where it was placed on a stand during the orations.

"In addressing the huge crowd which stretched to the other side of the street, the President of the Argentine Academy of Letters described Don Roberto as a 'great spirit of the past.' 'To-day,' he concluded his very remarkable oration, 'we bid farewell to his body, but his great spirit will ever remain within these shores.'

"The British Ambassador then addressed the gathering in English. Dwelling on Don Roberto's history he referred to his works with which English literature has been enriched, and he concluded his speech by saying: 'The world is the poorer for the death of Cunninghame Graham, the lover of freedom, the friend of the common people, the champion of reform—at times when reform was not always popular—the defender of the cause of small nations and of backward peoples. He was, let us admit it, a lover of the past rather than of the present. His sympathies were with the gaucho rather than with the modern farmer, with the covered wagon and the bullock-cart rather than with the train and the Pullman. . . . But with it all, as is so often the case with the true lover of the people, he was himself the authentic aristocrat or, if you will, Hidalgo. . . . Aristocrat and Hidalgo, by birth as well as by nature . . . was ever a man more industrious than Cunninghame Graham, who in his youth wandered throughout South and North America . . . giving at that time no suggestion of his ancestral past, or his brilliant literary future? . . . Somewhere beyond our ken there lies indeed a 'Land of the Leal' and in that land, in which there will surely also be horses, there will be a place for one who was 'aye leal and true' to his friends, to the causes in which he

439

believed and for which he was ever ready to fight; a place where he will be welcomed by those animals as well as human beings whom he loved on earth. Don Roberto, Ave Atque Vale."

Later, as the long procession slowly wended its way through the streets of Buenos Aires, the hearse was followed by my two faithful old horses, Mancha and Gato, led by two gauchos, and so, like the prairie riders of old, when they set out on a long journey, Don Roberto was followed by two spare horses which, during my travels with them, must often have crossed his tracks which have long ago been covered over with sand and dust.

Finally the casket was carried up the gangway on board the *Almeda Star* where British and Argentine flags were draped with black crêpe.

Thus Argentina bade farewell to one of the greatest friends she ever had, an ambassador of the heart.

"I sail on the 26th on the *Almeda Star*," my friend had written to me before he died; and he kept his promise, but . . . Shortly after his death was announced in England, Mr. Ramsay Macdonald wrote about him:

"I find it difficult to express fully my feelings for such a great man. His Socialism was curiously like that of William Morris's, although the roots of Morris's Socialism were in craftsmanship. Graham's Socialism was based on romantic ideas of freedom and his profound feeling for the bottom dog. He was a very typical Scot. His temperament was that of a soldier of fortune—you will find many a Scot belonging to this group. That was Graham. I always think of him as a finely caparisoned medieval charger, fighting towards some great ideal. . . ."

MANCHA AND GATO FOLLOWING THE HEARSE

Among the masses of letters of condolence Don Roberto's
heir, Captain Angus Bontine Cunninghame Graham, R.N.,*
received, from people in all stations of life, was one written
by taxi-drivers who have a rank near Elizabeth Street. In
expressing their deepest sympathy, they added that with the
death of Don Roberto, they lost the finest gentleman they
have ever driven, one who never left their cabs without
making some pleasant remark or telling them a joke.

On Saturday, April 18th, 1936, Scotland bade farewell to
her most distinguished son of modern times. "Ardoch"
looked dismal and forlorn when I arrived to pay a last tribute
to my departed friend. Early in the morning it snowed
heavily, but by ten o'clock the sky had cleared and the sun
shone as if to wish him joy on the journey to his last resting-
place. The trees and bushes and even the early spring flowers
in the garden appeared to be thoughtful and sad, and the
burn which flows down in cascades through a small glen near
the house, seemed to be murmuring mysteriously as I walked
along the gravel path which leads towards the front door.
As I approached the house, memories flashed through my
head in quick succession. Now I imagined myself to be
walking with my departed friend, joking and talking about
far-away lands and people, and then, suddenly, I saw Don
Roberto on the lawn, throwing an Argentine lasso or spinning
a rope. The sight of people clad in black brought me back
to reality with a start, and when I thought that all these
pleasant dreams belonged to a past which would never
return, I was overcome by a feeling of depression.

In the middle of the drawing-room where I had often sat,
was a magnificent mahogany coffin with elaborately adorned

---

* Don Roberto's second brother, Commander C. E. Cunninghame Graham,
had two children, Capt. Angus Bontine Cunninghame Graham and Olave,
now Lady Brooke. Capt. Angus Bontine Cunninghame Graham, who has
two children, a boy and a girl, became Don Roberto's sole heir, excepting
grants to a few friends, institutions and servants. In addition to the valuable
"Ardoch" estate, Don Roberto left a considerable fortune.

silver handles, a gift from the Argentine Government. The room was filled with beautiful flowers that had been sent by friends, rich and poor, as tokens of respect and esteem.

One of those present, an elderly, round-faced old man who was dressed in an exceedingly long and roomy frock-coat and who wore a peculiar black velvet skull-cap, brought a note of humour into the sad proceedings, for a few moments before the service was about to begin, this wily Scot came to the corner where Captain Cunninghame Graham, a lawyer and I were conversing in low tones, and said with a broad Scottish accent, pointing at the coffin: "What guarantee hae we that Meester Graham's body is in there?"

Obviously the good man wanted to be quite sure that Scotland had not been deprived of a treasured possession. For a moment I almost expected to hear the sound of a familiar merry laugh come from inside the coffin, for unconscious jokes of this kind always greatly delighted Don Roberto.

During the short and simple service which was held before the cortège slowly moved out of the gate, "Tim," a wire-haired fox-terrier, incessantly howled behind the house, as if realising that he had lost his master. (Strange to relate this dog disappeared shortly after the funeral, and has not been seen since.)

Later, as we sped towards the Lake of Menteith in cars, I admired the beauty of the hills and the blue waters of Loch Lomond in the distance. Cattle and sheep were peacefully grazing in the fields, and as the motor hearse passed, farmers respectfully bared their heads. Finally, after having followed a road that winds through woods, I had a glimpse of the lake which appeared like a glittering mirror in which the white clouds and surrounding hills were reflected. Ben Lomond, capped in white, looked at his very best, completing a scene which the cleverest master of the palette and brush could not have improved on.

Mourners from all parts of the country, from as far apart as Shetland and London, gathered at the lakeside to attend the funeral service in the little church which is built in the Gothic style of architecture, simple and suitable for its surroundings.

Villagers and farmers mingled with representatives of literature, art and politics, without regard to rank or wealth. The Duke of Montrose, Chief of the Clan Graham, was among the mourners, and so was Mr. John Fergusson, the old village blacksmith from Gartmore with whom Don Roberto never lost touch.

After a short and very simple service, a number of old tenants of Gartmore and estate workers from Ardoch bore the coffin toward a little jetty on the lake.* As the cortège filed along the road a pipe-major in full uniform played: "Scots Wha Hae," and when the launch moved off over the sparkling sunlit waters, the people who could not get to the island remained standing on the shore, bare-headed, and listening to a funeral oration, delivered by the President of the Scottish P.E.N.

There could have been no finer setting for a crusader to be taken towards his last resting-place than in the ruins of the old Augustinian Priory where, beside his wife, Don Roberto was soon to be laid to rest.

On the grassy carpet that covers the island, hosts of golden daffodils nodded as the pipe-major once more led the procession to the strains of "The Flowers of the Forest." The larch trees, stately Spanish chestnuts, sequoias, silver firs and birches appeared to be bowing their heads.

Just as the eight chief-mourners—which included the Duke of Montrose and the old village blacksmith of Gartmore—

---

* At about the same time a Memorial Service was held at St. Michael's Church, Chester Square, in London. It is of interest to note that at neither Service was the name of Don Roberto mentioned by the officiating clergy.

slowly lowered the coffin into the grave, the sky suddenly darkened and a wild, cold wind swept down from the hills, carrying with it flakes of snow which were whirled through the broken arches of the ruin. But almost immediately there was sunshine again, and the great bank of wreaths beside the grave was aglow with colour.

My own last tribute to Don Roberto consisted of three strands of hair (white, blue-black and golden red), I had cut from his favourite horses' tails. These I placed on the coffin before it was lowered.

At the end of a simple committal service, the wild plaintive notes of the lament "Lochaber No More" rose from the nave of the ruined priory, and after the piper, who stood at the foot of the grave, had given a smart military salute, the mourners sadly turned away to return to the mainland.

Don Roberto's epitaph was pronounced by an old crofter who had come down from the highlands. Unashamed of the tears which dimmed his eyes, he said with a sigh: "Aye, he was a bonny fighter, an' a grand gentleman."

And so we left our friend, resting alongside his wife and among some of his ancestors.

The silvery moon will bring him greetings from the Southern Cross, the bright constellation that often guided him during rides over the infinite pampas. Perhaps, some day, during a warm summer night, whilst the chanting of the Augustinian monks will be heard in the priory, Mary Queen of Scots (again a child), will laugh and chatter with her playmates in the garden and bower of boxwood, where she spent her only happy days. King Robert the Bruce and the Earls of Menteith and other spirits of the Past will assemble in the banqueting hall of the now ruined castle of the Grahams on the island of Inchtalla. When the mists will rise from the lake, to shift over the heather-covered hills, assuming the appearance of Arabian dancers' veils, and the lapping of

THE FUNERAL IN SCOTLAND

THE TOMB

Note: According to Don Roberto's wish his old Argentine cattle brand
was carved into the tombstone.

waves and the murmur of wind in the trees and bulrushes will gradually change into the soft twanging of guitars, the whinnying of a horse will be heard, and Don Roberto, seated on his fiery mustang, Pampa, will ride on. . . .

DON ROBERTO'S LAST SIGNATURE.

BIBLIOGRAPHY

1895	*Notes on the District of Menteith*	A. & C. Black
1898	*Father Archangel of Scotland*	,, ,,
1898	*Mogreb-El-Acksa*	Heinemann
1899	*The Ipané*	Fisher Unwin
1900	*Thirteen Stories*	Heinemann
1901	*A Vanished Arcadia*	,,
1902	*Success*	Duckworth
1903	*Hernando de Soto*	Heinemann
1905	*Progress*	Duckworth
1906	*His People*	,,
1909	*Faith*	,,
1910	*Hope*	,,
1912	*Charity*	,,
1913	*A Hatchment*	,,
1914	*Scottish Stories*	,,
1915	*Bernal Diaz del Castillo*	Eveleigh Nash
1916	*Brought Forward*	Duckworth
1920	*A Brazilian Mystic*	Heinemann
1921	*Cartagena and the Banks of the Sinu*	,,
1922	*The Conquest of New Granada*	,,
1924	*The Conquest of the River Plate*	,,
1925	*Doughty Deeds*	,,
1926	*Pedro de Valdivia*	,,
1927	*Redeemed*	,,
1929	*José Antonio Páez*	,,

1930	*Thirty Stories and Sketches* Selected by Edward Garnett	Heinemann
1930	*The Horses of the Conquest*	,,
1932	*Writ in Sand*	,,
1933	*Portrait of a Dictator*	,,
1936	*Mirages*	,,
1936.	*Rodeo.* Selected by A. F. Tschiffely	,,

PAMPHLETS AND TRANSLATIONS

1898	*Aurora La Cujini*	Leonard Smithers
1914	*El Río de la Plata* (in Spanish)	Establecimiento Tipográfico de Wertheimer
1923	*The Dream of the Magi* Limited to 250 copies for sale	Heinemann
1924	*Maripunga* Translation from Gustave Barroso Limited to 350 copies for sale	,,
1929	*Bibi.* Limited to 250 copies for sale *La Vieja de Bolívar*	,,

A bibliography of the first editions of R. B. Cunninghame Graham's works, by Leslie Chaundy, was published by Dulan & Co., Ltd., London, 1924. The edition was limited to 500 copies.

ACKNOWLEDGMENTS

THANKS to the generous assistance of numerous friends—known and unknown to me—who supplied me with much valuable material for this book, I have been able, more or less, to reconstruct the whole life of its subject.

First of all, I must thank my late friend, Don Roberto himself, for the weary hours he patiently endured whilst I "pumped" out of him stories of the Past. I shall for ever remember with gratitude his guidance whilst I compiled the masses of notes I have woven into this story.

I owe thanks to Captain Angus Bontine Cunninghame Graham, R.N., Don Roberto's nephew and worthy heir, for having put at my disposal old manuscripts, notes and letters written by his late uncle, and for the encouraging interest he took in my work.

Unfortunately, lack of space makes it impossible to mention all the names of those—some in far-away lands—who kindly sent me many letters written by Don Roberto, and I regret being unable individually to thank the many others who generously supplied me with much interesting information. Therefore, due to the reason already mentioned, I regret that I must express my gratitude *en masse* to all those willing helpers.

I offer my sincere thanks to Gerald Duckworth & Co., Ltd., for permission to quote from *Faith, Hope, Success, Progress, Charity, His People* and *A Hatchment;* and to A. & C. Black, Ltd., for allowing me to use and quote passages from *Notes on the District of Menteith* and *Father Archangel of Scotland;* and I wish to thank Messrs. Ernest Benn, Ltd., for permission to reproduce certain passages from *The Ipané.*

I wish to acknowledge the kindness of the Controller of H.M. Stationery Office in granting me permission to reproduce extracts from the Official Reports of Parliamentary Debates; and I owe thanks to the British Foreign Office for putting at my disposal documents concerning Don Roberto.

The Librarians of the British Museum have my sincere thanks and everlasting gratitude for all the trouble they have taken in helping me with my researches, and for the kind and patient manner in which they have assisted me.

I am indebted to Mr. George Bernard Shaw for his permission to quote some of his printed remarks concerning the subject of this book, and I thank my friend, the late Mr. Edward Garnett, the Duke of Montrose, the Rt. Hon. John Burns, Mr. J. Middleton, Secretary for the Labour Party, Prof. Frank Dobie of the University of Texas, Dr. Fernando Pozzo, of Quilmes, Buenos Aires, Prof. Antonio Pastor of the University of London, the Authorities of the Museo Histórico Argentino, Lord Monteagle, Lady Olave Brooke, Mr. H. W. Nevinson, Sir William Rothenstein, Sir John Lavery, Mr. James Bone, Mr. Jacob Epstein, Sir James McLeod, and the many others who generously came to my assistance with advice, documents, reminiscences, letters, photographs, reproductions of works of art for illustrations, etc.

I also acknowledge the kindness of Joseph Conrad's and W. H. Hudson's literary executors for their kindness in permitting me to use some—and quote from others—of the many letters written to Don Roberto by his friends, Conrad and Hudson.

Last, but by no means least, I wish to express my gratitude to Prof. Herbert Faulkner West, of Dartmouth College, Hanover, New Hampshire, for having allowed me to use any part or parts from his excellent *Cunninghame Graham*, published in 1932, by Cranley & Dey, Ltd. London. With such a foundation to build on, my work was made much easier than otherwise it would have been.

A. F. TSCHIFFELY.

INDEX